"*The Score* is a uniquely rewarding, ear-opening visit with some of Hollywood's most exciting weavers of musical magic. Michael Schelle, himself an accomplished composer with a seemingly encyclopedic knowledge of films and film scores, poses insightful questions that result in fascinating and often delightfully unexpected discussions of specific scores and cues, Hollywood politics, behind-the-scenes details, etc. His easy rapport with these composers and his intimate awareness of their works result in candid, you-are-there dialogues that allow readers to feel that they know these major talents personally."
— Tom Null, president, Citadel Records

"*The Score* is a fascinating look into the techniques, problems, and pitfalls of providing music for movies. It is an interesting read for the layman as well as the professional."
— Thomas Pasatieri

"Schelle's thoughtful questions elicit surprisingly candid responses and unusual insights from some of the most dynamic composers in the field."
— Jon Burlingame, film-music writer, *Variety*

the SCORE

the SCORE

interviews with FILM COMPOSERS

by MICHAEL SCHELLE

SILMAN-JAMES PRESS   LOS ANGELES

First Edition

10 9 8 7 6 5 4 3 2 1

Library of Congress Cataloging-in-Publication Data

Schelle, Michael.
The score : interviews with film composers / by Michael Schelle
p. cm.
1. Motion picture music History and criticism.   2. Composers.
Interviews.   I. Title.
ML2075.S34   1999   781.5'42'0922--dc21   99-26610
[B}

ISBN 1-879505-40-1

Printed in the United States of America.

SILMAN-JAMES PRESS
1181 Angelo Drive
Beverly Hills, CA 90210

CONTENTS

PREFACE

As I conducted the interviews for this book, I found that many of the composers with whom I spoke had experienced critical artistic crossroads in their lives as they opted for film music or returned to film music or juggled a variety of musical lives. My personal artistic crossroads occurred in 1980: Just after completing my Ph.D. at the University of Minnesota, I found myself torn between an unpredictable future in concert music and the exciting lure of Hollywood. Opting for the former, combined with university teaching, I have no regrets whatsoever—I love working with young composers, opening their eyes to that big world out there, and my composition career of orchestral commissions and performances has been successful beyond my wildest dreams. However, my interest in film music has never really left me.

I have always had a great respect, admiration, and appreciation for film music and those composers who write it. I've especially enjoyed the Golden Age masters—Korngold, Steiner, Alfred Newman, Tiomkin, Waxman, Rózsa, and Herrmann. I've gotten a great kick from the work of many 1950s sci-fi and horror composers, Ennio Morricone's Italian thrillers and spaghetti Westerns, and many Japanese monster-movie scores. I've also deeply enjoyed those film scores that have interpolated source classical music (*Brute Force*, *The Blue Gardenia*, *The Brain Eaters*) or manipulated modern jazz or avant-garde orchestral styles. However, the demands of a family, a full-time concert-music career (composing, traveling, and staying current with new musical trends), and university teaching left me little time to explore film music beyond its surface.

This all changed seven years ago when, in the matter of about three weeks, I was struck by three bolts of musical lightening that changed my perspective forever: First, my composition student Richard Pressley handed me a cassette of Chris Young's *Hellbound: Hellraiser II* and said with great enthusiasm, "Hey, Dr. Schelle, check this out!" (To which I probably responded, "Yeah, sure, whatever.") A few days later, my composer friend Dr. Jack Gallagher sent a cassette of Bruce Broughton's *Young Sherlock Holmes* and said, "Hey, Mike, check this out!" ("Hmmm, pretty cool.") The next day, I picked up recordings of Jerry Goldsmith's *Alien* and *Poltergeist*, John Williams' *Close Encounters of the Third Kind*, and Chris Young's *The Vagrant*. Well, that was it—Boulez, Berio, Stockhausen, Penderecki, Husa, Nono, Reich, you're all terrific, but what have I been missing? Since that pivotal month, my film-music appetite has grown insatiable, and with each new discovery (be it Raoul Kraushaar, Paul Glass, Akira Ifukube, Loek Dikker, or Krzysztof Komeda), I am reminded of how completely professional, artistic, innovative, dramatic, and entertaining film music can be.

During the past six years, my ongoing film-music research has led to the establishment of a History of Film Music program at Butler University, which opened that career option for the student composers. If they are interesting in pursing Hollywood, they can now at least get some basic training and a most sympathetic teacher. My film research has recently evolved beyond film music to other aspects of filmmaking and film history—cinematography, screenwriting, Japanese film history, and film noir. Finally, I would be seriously remiss if I failed to mention that my study of film and film music has been a powerful influence on my own compositional work, my teaching, and my outlook on life.

ACKNOWLEDGMENTS

My first thank-you must go to Jim Fox of Silman-James Press for the opportunity to write this book. I will be eternally grateful to Jim for his friendship, invaluable advice, intelligent observations, film-music industry insight, creative suggestions, encouragement, painstaking editing and diligent research, and for his never-ending assistance with so many practical, literary, and aesthetic concerns. I also thank Jim for helping with what turned out to be the extremely complicated task of scheduling many of the Los Angeles-area interviews and for providing the dependable Fox taxi service to many of my all-over-the-map appointments. Finally, thanks to Jim for so many times providing a place to crash during my visits to Los Angeles—bed, breakfast, beer, wine, pretzels, and an ashtray, Hoosier homecookin', cats, and long, long talks. I also wish to thank Jim's Silman-James colleague, Gwen Feldman, for her enthusiastic support of the project.

I owe a great debt of gratitude to my "technical support group" from Butler University in Indianapolis: especially to Jan Diggins for helping with so many of the interview-tape transcriptions and Maren Urness for her extremely patient computer and technology assistance. My sincere thanks to Dr. Michael Sells, Dean of Butler University's Jordan College of Fine Arts, and to Dr. Daniel Bolin, Chair of the School of Music, for their encouragement, support, and flexibility; thanks also to Stanley DeRusha, Music Director of the University Symphony, and to his executive secretary, Vonna Knapp, for collaborating with me on the 1997 Christopher Young Halloween Concert and for establishing interview windows with John Corigliano during his visit to the campus in 1998. Thanks to my remarkable university colleagues and good friends Dr. Robert Grechesky and Dr. Frank Felice for their enthusiastic and flattering moral support and for providing endless round-trip airport transportation for interviews scheduled in Los Angeles and New York; special thanks to Dara Grechesky and John and Neely Blair for their compassionate, sympathetic, and dependable cat-sitting with George, Ariella, and Rimsky (R.I.P.) during my many travels; and thanks to Aimee Mell, for reasons above and for her objective, critical eyes and strong shoulders.

A most sincere thank-you to my university composition students Derrick Lefebvre, Joel Matthys, John Blair, Gregg Medley, Rex Martin, Chad Gard, Luke Benton, Frank Echeverry, Dainis Michel, Gao Ping, Bill Wolf, Kim Kramer, Frances Bell, Josh Jones, Chris Barton, John Richard, Patrick Dwyer, and many others for so graciously understanding, accepting, and patiently accommodating those endlessly rescheduled composition lessons and JCFA Composers Orchestra new-music ensemble rehearsals during the past two years of research, travel, and writing—Yes, guys, the book is done! Stop asking!

Thanks to my long-time composer friends for their advice, suggestions, and observations during this project: Rocky Reuter (Capital University, OH), Jack Gallagher (Wooster College, OH), Elliott Schwartz (Bowdoin College, ME), Dan Godfrey (Syracuse University, NY), Phillip Schroeder (Sam Houston State University), and John Jeter (Music Director, Fort Smith Symphony Orchestra). Thanks also—in ways they'll never know—to Barbara Petersen (BMI), composer Jamie Aikman and his family (University of Michigan), Rick Cox (L.A. film composer/studio musician), Eileen Scott (Butler University), Mark Spraggins (USC), Reverend Jim Coyle, Claude Desmeules (Tronics 2000), Tom Null, George Budd, composer Richard Pressley, Katy and Milt Mondor, and Tyrone.

Special thanks to Laurie Barry; my new friend P.J. Robowski (KUAF-FM Public Radio, Fayetteville, AR) for providing the contact lead to Elmer Bernstein's management's e-mail; to Lisa Edmondson, who set up the Bernstein interview; to Angela Gilliam for helping to arrange the Terence Blanchard interview; and to Kazuko Tanosaki and E. Michael Richards (co-directors, Music of Japan Today III: Tradition and Innovation, 1997, Hamilton College, NY) for so graciously making interview time available with guest composer Toshiro Mayuzumi. I also thank Vasi Vangelos of Vangelos Management, Carol Sue Baker of Ocean Park Music, the Kraft-Benjamin Agency, Jamie Richardson of Gorfain-Schwartz, Robert Townson of Varèse Sarabande, and Michael McGehee for helping me contact many of the composers.

To the fifteen composers who speak in this book—and for whom I have the greatest respect and admiration—I express my deepest appreciation for their sharing their time and their lives and for their open, honest, and sincere reactions to my many, many questions. I also thank my own composition teachers—especially Arnold Franchetti and Aaron Copland—for creating in me the love of and respect for all genres of good music.

My deepest gratitude to my wonderful family, who has been so completely and unconditionally supportive and encouraging of my work—not only this project, but of my entire professional composition career, even when they didn't necessarily like the music. To these fantastic people, I dedicate this book: my eternally youthful, magical, and visionary parents, George and Claire Schelle; my *Star Wars*-music-loving surgeon brother Patrick and his family; my talented and compassionate R.N. sisters Meg and Beth and their families; my rambunctious yet totally lovable and perfect kids, Katie and Paddy, and their dedicated mother, Joyce; to the Cape Cod Schelles and the Stryke/Mieger/Boorn West Coast wing; and, finally, to my late Aunt Peggy, the musical and philosophical Margaret Mann Stryke, who once said to me many years ago, "Frank Zappa's bad enough, but George Crumb? Now *there's* a composer whose name sounds like his music!" I couldn't disagree more, Auntie Pegs, but I love you for the challenge.

INTRODUCTION

For many, many years, classical musicians and the musically "educated" public in the United States have drawn an inappropriate and unfair distinction between the so-called "real" composers and their film-music brethren. This distinction has led to the erection of hastily cobbled walls that are meant to separate the misunderstood, unappreciated, visionary, starve-for-your-art "serious" composers from what many ill-informed "music lovers" perceive to be the "artistically limited prostitutes" who cater to the public as they ply their trade in Hollywood for the big bucks.

While Americans have long respected the film-music experiments of such composers as George Antheil, Aaron Copland, Virgil Thomson, Leonard Bernstein, John Corigliano, and Philip Glass, they have done so only because they embraced them as "real" composers first. Such distinctions, however, are not so readily the case in England, Europe, and Asia, where the worlds of concert and commercial composing often cross over very smoothly, and good music—in any category—is accepted and appreciated simply for its own sake (good examples might be the work of composers Michael Nyman, Alfred Schnittke, Wojciech Kilar, and Toru Takemitsu).

As we glide into the twenty-first century, the critical, artistic, and commercial successes of such composers as Elmer Bernstein, Danny Elfman, Elliot Goldenthal, Jerry Goldsmith, James Horner, and John Williams are altering this situation for the better—the American public is becoming more musically aware and respectful of the artistry of its film composers. At this same time, a new generation of both film and concert composers is beginning to emerge—devil-may-care younger composers bred not only on Bach, Beethoven, Bartók, Stravinsky, Cage, Glass, and Zorn but also on John Coltrane, Miles Davis, Cecil Taylor, and Anthony Braxton; The Beatles, Jimi Hendrix, David Byrne, Soundgarden, and Pearl Jam; six decades of film music; and all types of music from around the world. In many ways, these younger composers stand at the forefront of a natural evolution in our country's struggle for a musical self-perspective.

Today, as has been the case during much of the past seventy years, Hollywood's composers display much more artistic integrity and versatility than closed-minded music critics and concert musicians give them credit for, especially when one considers the often-restrictive environment in which they work (where conflicting musical edicts from directors and producers abound) and the incredible time limitations under which they toil (having less than five weeks to complete a sixty-minute orchestral score is not uncommon).

The versatility and creativity evidenced by many film composers is remarkable. Many times, even within the most oppressive situations, these composers' scores speak with imaginative and uniquely inspirational voices. Some of the most original, effective, influential, and communicative new music in the past fifty years has come from Hollywood. And I hope that the interviews in this book will help garner more respect for the complex artistic talents of all good film composers.

That said, one must also acknowledge that not all film music is great, as film composers themselves readily admit. However, for each insignificant or inconsequential film composer or film score, there exists an equally insignificant or inconsequential parallel composer or piece in the concert-music or academic world.

For *The Score*, my intention was to procure revealing interviews with a cross-section of film composers who represent a broad sampling of diverse approaches, attitudes, and aesthetic concerns and a diversity of age, experience, genre, tradition, style, and background—from long-established masters to relative newcomers; from jazz- and pop-oriented musicians to concert composers who occasionally work in film; from "A"-list composers to those eager to get there.

The questions I posed to each composer were usually very specific to that composer's work, and rarely of a generic nature. I designed my questions to generate dialogues that would offer the reader specific insights into each composer's personality, historical perspective on film music, and life in the film industry, while also allowing for unique "stories behind the stories," interesting observations, and practical advice to composers who might be entertaining the idea of working in the field.

While conversations about each composer's signature mega-hits are included, I have also included numerous questions about each composer's lesser-known, unusual, and offbeat films that are rarely, if ever, discussed in magazine interviews or textbooks. Time and again, these questions stirred delightful, long-dormant memories that resulted in animated detours full of insight and information.

Many of the questions I posed dealt with specific musical cues—knowing how so-and-so got started in the business or which composers are his or her heroes is nice, but the real insight into a composer's creative heart, mind, and soul can only surface when we learn why he or she wrote a retrograde double-fugue exposition for the bloody decapitation scene or why spatial notation and serial procedures were unleashed for the white-tie-and-tails ballroom sequence.

Most of the composers on my original want list were interviewed, and I thank Jim Fox and Silman-James Press for being so agreeable to my preferences. But, unfortunately, interviews with a few composers on that list never materialized. Among those was Toshiro Mayuzumi: I had arranged to interview Mayuzumi at the 1997 Music of Japan III conference in New York, where he was to attend as the featured guest composer and I had been invited to give a seminar on the history of *Godzilla* movie music. However, he was forced to cancel his American trip at the last minute and, sadly, passed away a few days later.

Once all the interviews for this book were transcribed and edited, I faced a most daunting task—how best to present them. After investigating numerous chapter arrangements (based on mood, length, age, name, rank, and serial number), I chose a simple alphabetical ordering. And, by just good old Jungian synchronicity, this arrangement seemed to offer the most engaging variety and contrast.

The interviews that follow were conducted between the summer of 1997 and the summer of 1998.

Barry, John Barry. The name instantly evokes a world of secret agents and soaring themes and bold harmonies—an expressive music of passion and integrity. Through the scores he has composed for more than a hundred films during the past forty years, British-born Barry has created one of the most recognizable musical voices in the film world.

Not a composer to be hemmed in by any one musical style or tied to any one genre of film, Barry has contributed effective and varied scores, all of which bear his musical signature, to an extremely broad body of movies: his action-packed music of intrigue that propelled a dozen James Bond movies; his sensual, atmospheric jazz of *Body Heat* (1981); his darker jazz references of the suspense-filled *Jagged Edge* (1985) and *Masquerade* (1988); the emotional orchestral statements of *Raise the Titanic* (1980) and his Oscar-winning scores for *Born Free* (1966), *The Lion in Winter* (1968), *Out of Africa* (1985), and *Dances With Wolves* (1990); and his "three-handkerchief" tearjerker *Somewhere in Time* (1980), all of which exemplify the Barry sound of expansive themes and lush orchestrations. His avant-garde explorations have surfaced in *The Day of the Locust* (1975) and *The White Buffalo* (1977), while his adventuresome music for *Zulu* (1964), *King Kong* (1976), *The Deep* (1977), *The Black Hole* (1979), and *High Road to China* (1983) contrast with the fragile intimacy of *The Whisperers* (1967) and *Chaplin* (1992).

With such more recent scores as *Cry, The Beloved Country* (1995), *The Scarlet Letter* (1995), his nostalgic *Across the Sea of Time* (1995), and his suspenseful *Mercury Rising* (1998) and his powerful concert piece *The Beyondness of Things* (1998), it's clear that John Barry continues to write as passionately and directly as ever.

We met for this interview at his home in Oyster Bay, Long Island, where we chatted for nearly four hours.

john BARRY

Would you talk a bit about your musical upbringing?

I studied piano from the age of eight. When I was fifteen I started studying trumpet, classical harmony, and counterpoint. I also studied the Joseph Schillinger composition system with Roy Williams, a Schillinger-licensed teacher in Manchester. I thought it was a terrific course, very enlightening. But at that time, no one ever thought that being a musician was a serious career choice. We're talking about the 1940s in the north of England. My school had no real music facilities—you were pulled out of a geography lesson or a French lesson to take your piano lesson on an old upright in some back room. It was a terrible way of doing it.

Your education was interrupted by service in the army?

I went into the army when I was nineteen. This was the last year of conscription—I had to go, I didn't volunteer. One good thing about the situation was that, if you went in for more than two years, or a minimum of three, you could choose your area of service. So I selected the military band for three years, instead of two years of God knows what.

As a trumpet player?

Yes. I auditioned and was awarded a position in the Yorkshire Green Howards regiment. I thought that I was going to be staying in

Yorkshire, but I was wrong. I finished a ten-week basic training and was then sent out. I had a year in Egypt, playing in the military band and with the regimental bandsmen.

I subscribed to *Downbeat* magazine through all this. When I returned to England for a month's leave, I noticed an advertisement in *Downbeat*: Bill Russo, who was living in Chicago, was taking on a few pupils in composition and orchestration for jazz orchestra. But in the early 1950s, there were incredible restrictions on currency—dollars were impossible to trade—so I knew that the Chicago course would be only a dream.

I was soon shipped back to Egypt for about a week, then quickly on to Cyprus. On my first day in Cyprus, I wandered into this little shop, and the Armenian shopkeeper asked me, and I don't know why, "Do you want to buy any dollars?" The Armenians will sell you anything. [Laughter] I said, "What do you mean?" and he said, "I'll sell you dollars for Armenian money." It didn't make any sense, but I thought, why not? So, every week, I'd go down to the shop and buy dollars, stick them in an envelope, and send them on to Chicago, to Bill Russo. I took Russo's whole course while I was stationed in Cyprus.

Was this the same Bill Russo who, in the 1970s, recorded a number of original fusion works for jazz band and orchestra?

Yes, with the Chicago Symphony Orchestra. He had maybe twelve students in all, and he was interested in me because I was an Englishman. When I finally came out of the army, I wanted to arrange for the big bands of the day—Jack Parnell, Johnny Dankworth—but it was very slow going, doing the arrangements, writing out all the parts, preparing for the broadcasts. Plus, the big bands were all suffering through a social change. They were all breaking up because the whole rock-and-roll thing had started. So I formed my own seven-piece group—three guys I had been in the army with, three local musicians, and John Barry—all essentially jazz guys. It was a strange group, but it worked. And we got work—we were a functioning band at clubs and various functions. We were very successful. We had the first bass guitar in England, a German Hofner. I soon contracted with EMI Records as a recording artist, but I also wanted to produce. In those days, there weren't such things as producers—they were A&R men who took care of the artists. George Martin was one.

The fifth Beatle?

Yeah. Actually, George Martin used to produce comedy records, if you can believe it. Anyhow, four or five guys were on the EMI staff, and they would select the artists and the material for records. I would do arrangements, but usually not get credit for them.

Later, I produced a singer, Adam Faith, who was totally against the grain of what they were purchasing at EMI. He had that raw, raunchy Gene Vincent sound—dirty rock-and-roll, kind of heavy metal for its day. I took this guy who had a very live voice, used a lot of percussion and four violins playing very hard pizzicato—taking on an almost metallic sound, which wasn't pretty, it was percussive. It worked. After the A&R man heard it, he said, "You will never be allowed to work in this studio again. [Laughter] This is against everything that is on the market." Of course, the record went to number one in about four weeks. We went on to have a string of hits—seven number ones in row.

How did you move from EMI to film music?

The singer, who was like the poor man's James Dean, got a movie offer. He had none of Dean's charm or depth, but he had this face that was marketable and absolutely lit up on screen. All the kids went crazy for him. His movie was released in the states under the title of *Beat Girl* [a.k.a. *Wild for Kicks*]. That was my intro to film music, to actually doing it.

But film and film-music awareness must have been already deeply inside you because of your family.

My father had eight theaters, so I was brought up around all of this. My first experience in cinema was my father taking me into this big building—going through the foyer, going through huge swinging doors into this big black area, and being lifted up over a barrier at the back of the hall to see this big black-and-white mouse on the screen, with jazzy music, that Mickey Mouse stuff. That was in the mid-1930s.

It was the family business. In a family business, you don't just do one thing, you help with everything that is part of the business. I ran movies. I sold ice cream. I sold orange juice. I passed out programs. I swept the floor. When I was fifteen years old, I could go up into the projection booth and run the whole thing. Those were the days when you had to rewind a film after each showing, and repair little broken frames and so forth.

And after all this?

Then school, then the army. And when I came out of the army, I started up as a professional musician. I must say that I had always wanted to write music, but I grew up in York, two hundred miles from London. At that time, London was the only real musical center in England. But, with the Beatles in Liverpool and the orchestras, things started opening up and spreading to areas outside of London. Prior to that, the rest of England was very isolated. If you wanted any kind of professional life in music, you had to go to London.

It almost sounds as if all this was a means to an end, to film music.

Yes, it was. From when I was ten or twelve years old, I would listen to Max Steiner, Korngold, and Waxman in my father's cinemas. I used to sit and watch movies, often the same movie, over and over.

I think I know every line in *The Treasure of Sierra Madre*. My wife was impressed the other night when I spoke along with it on television, but I've probably seen that movie twenty times, and maybe in *one week*. But I also heard the music over and over again. It was a hell of a training ground. When I think back, I wasn't all that intellectual or studious about it.

You just soaked it in?

Right. It was fascinating—I was learning what worked and what didn't work, and why. I didn't necessarily always concentrate, but it all—what was good, what was bad, what was boring—became part of me. I *particularly* noticed what was boring. It was an instinct.

Looking over your long list of film scores, virtually every genre is represented—drama, action, suspense, comedy, romance, Western, jungle, romantic-thriller, historical, war, science-fiction. What genre haven't you worked in, and what genres would you like to work in again?

The only thing I haven't done is a horror movie. I'd love to do a classic horror movie like the original *Frankenstein*. There are so many dimensions to those old Universal horror movies.

Those films were also very romantic, sensual.

There you go. They were very touching—you sympathized with the characters. When I was a kid, I was totally crazy about Boris Karloff. I still am.

But I've done every other kind of movie. *The Legend of the Lone Ranger* was not the greatest Western ever made, and I never interpreted *Dances With Wolves* as a Western. I did *Alice's Adventures in Wonderland*, but it would be fun to do a full-fledged musical. I'm so impressed with Johnny Green—he's forgotten more about musicals and arranging than most people learn in a lifetime. Nobody knows film music—technique, arrangements, craftsmanship—better than this guy.

The Legend of the Lone Ranger **was written the same year as** *Body Heat*—**two completely disparate styles back to back.** *Body Heat* **is considered to be** *the* **quintessential torrid score.**

Body Heat is a terrific example of the lack of promotion of a soundtrack. Bootlegs are around, but the real album will come out eventually.

The music in *Body Heat* **is evolutionary: Sweaty, humid music becomes more suspenseful and less erotic as the film moves along. Was it difficult to write around the busy, crackling Bogart/Bacall-style film noir dialogue?**

No. I love writing behind dialogue. I did a lot of it in the early movies, like *Seance on a Wet Afternoon* and *The Whisperers*. Those were both very dialogue-oriented.

Writing for dialogue is a terrific challenge. You have to take into account the personalities of the characters and the actors who play them. A good example would be Gregory Peck: He has a wonderful deep voice and a very slow delivery with marvelous cadences. When working with dialogue, you isolate the tone of the character's voice: Is he a tenor or a baritone? We're not talking about exact notes, obviously, but there's always a range. And then you write the music to that central voice—under it, over it.

Gregory Peck's voice becomes a musical line?

Exactly. Absolutely. It has its own niche; it has its own timbre. Now, if you wrote a cello line along with Greg's voice, it would take his ground, eat up his resonance. Another interesting voice would be Bogart, who had this twangy monotone voice, but was always very enticing. That Bogart delivery would be wonderful to write around—above it, below it. Another interesting voice would be Jack Lemmon, whose delivery is very fast, very harsh, a kind of rat-a-tat-tat delivery. Sometimes the tempo of the voice can help to move the music, and you don't want to get in the way of that. Greg Peck's voice would be like a beautiful, slow baritone melody, whereas, with Jack Lemmon, you would write more sustained sonorities because his voice is so active. You take the tempo of the voice, the timbre, the range, and where it fits in terms of the orchestra and you leave that area open and write around it.

How did you specifically apply this compositional technique to the *Body Heat* stars?

William Hurt has a very interesting voice. I think he's one of the few actors around today who does have an interesting voice. That kind of pausey delivery he does is very distinctive. Kathleen Turner also has a very unusual voice. It's slow and sexy, but capable of explosive emotions. The sax seemed to work the best for the mood, or the tone, of the picture, as well as being complimentary to the actors' voices.

How the dialogue is recorded is also critical to where the music fits in: Is the dialogue what I call "front screen"—right in your face, right in front—or is it off to the left or the right? If the dialogue is "front screen," the sax needs to sound as if it were coming from off stage, otherwise you're in trouble. The instruments can move the actors—push them back or move them forward. By being aware of dialogue duration and distance, you can create a cushion behind the whole thing.

I always like to use a large orchestra behind dialogue scenes. With a large orchestra playing softly, you get weight and depth on the screen. A small group dwindles down to nothing by the time you take it back against dialogue. And, believe me, they're going to do that.

Two rare Barry scores: *Hammett*, which was Wim Wenders' first American film, and *They Might Be Giants*. What are your memories of these unusual projects?

Francis Ford Coppola produced *Hammett*, and they virtually made that movie twice. Francis's *Hammett* is a highly stylized version. Wim had different ideas. It turned out to be a very interesting experience. Going in, Francis wanted some things that Wim didn't want, and vice versa, including ideas about the music. The first two or three meetings and viewings were problematic. Wim, a tall Germanic figure who wears all black all the time, looks like a Mormon, and he's pale. I don't think he's seen a ray of sun all his life, so you have this daunting, ghostly image already.

How did you reconcile the differing attitudes and opinions about the *Hammett* score?

Wim went to Germany for a couple of weeks. And while he was there, I had this idea for a solo clarinet and a small string section. I did this very light, bluesy, kind of funky, whiskey-smelling, smoke-filled-room type of score. I went into New York and recorded it as a demo with a rhythm section and synthesizers, sent it over to Wim's apartment in Germany, and waited for his return. A few days later, about 3:00 A.M., the phone rings. I pick up the phone and it's Wim, who'd just returned from Germany. He said, "I've been playing your demo tape for three or four hours. I think it's just fantastic, it's wonderful, it's great. It's just exactly everything I want."

After Wenders' approval, was everything smooth sailing for *Hammett*?

Absolutely smooth sailing. But, after it was all done, I had the most peculiar compliment from Francis: "Dear John, I'm so glad I thought of you for doing this movie," signed, "Francis."

They Might Be Giants was another peculiar situation in that I had started to work with Alan Jay Lerner on the stage musical, and I'd promised him that I would not do the movie while I was going through this process. Then, Tony Harvey, who had done *The Lion in Winter*, called me to do the movie. I said I just couldn't do it. And he said, "Oh, John, you have to do it." I said, "I could write three or four themes and supervise the recording, but get someone else to do the other stuff, I just cannot take on the whole project." He said okay, so I wrote several themes and Ken Thorne did the rest of the movie and I supervised the recording. That, to me, was very unsatisfactory in the long run. I never want to do it that way again—I never want to divide the music responsibilities. Ken is a fantastic musician, and his work was fine for the movie, but I have trouble trying to blend multiple musical minds for one score. I know many composers do that today, but I believe you should do the whole thing yourself—write your own music, orchestrate, conduct your own music. It's the only way to go.

Coming from the concert world, I find it impossible to imagine other musicians making decisions about my orchestrations or motivic developments. I understand the problem of time restrictions in film music, but you are one of the few film composers left who finds ways to, as you said, do the whole thing.

Those composing teams do some very good work, but it's not the same as an individual personality stamp on the music. Because of the nature of the team process, you can't start saying, "Well, *you* do it," because the other fellow will say, "No, you do it." In the recording session, there's trouble unless all egos are checked at the door, and, with composers, that's difficult to achieve. Then you get bad feelings or confrontations. In my case, Ken Thorne's instinct is to write very busy music, and many times I was frustrated because I felt it slow, or I'd want to change his orchestrations.

King Rat **is an unusual World War II film score. It's introspective, reflective, and personally tortured—not the militaristic,**

combat-heavy action music of most war films. Would you offer your thoughts on this score? And why did you use the cimbalom?

I had worked with Bryan [Forbes] in England and he wanted to bring me to Hollywood for this picture. That's not always a good idea, taking a limey to Hollywood! Anyway, Bryan brought me in on the movie. I read the script, I saw some footage, and I really wanted the music to play off of the emotions of war and the effects it had on all the characters.

Around that time I had become interested in the cimbalom, a Hungarian instrument. I loved the sound of it. I did a demo in England with a terrific player named John Leach. John had an incredible collection of ethnic instruments. Every year he would take off to foreign countries for three months and buy all these weird things and learn how to play them. That's how he earned his living. I recorded a demo with John playing beautifully, then I phoned the Los Angeles orchestra contractor and asked if they had a cimbalom player for the score. They said, "Oh, yes, and he's a terrific player. Don't worry." But when I got to L. A., I learned a lesson: Never take anybody's word on this kind of stuff, never. When you're going to use an unusual instrument, make sure you hear the player yourself. I guess the cimbalom player they hired was the best they had, but what wound up in the movie was some of the demo work that had been recorded with John Leach and the orchestra recording from L.A., but none of the stuff the L. A. cimbalom guy had done. We brought in a fantastic guitarist who could virtually simulate the cimbalom sound. He was way ahead of his time in terms of experimental guitar sounds. He used an acoustic guitar, which we processed through all kinds of electronic gear. We had to do it that way because there was no time to bring in John or find another cimbalom player.

The Knack is a period jazz score that explores surprising harmonic twists and turns. It has some Jimmy Smith/Shirley Scott-style

Hammond B-3 organ material, and you sound completely at home with it.

Yeah, I love that. A terrific player named Alan Haven, an English guy who came from Manchester, played it. He was just terrific. He couldn't read a note of music, but he could play just about anything. He had the most extraordinary technique. I wrote out bar numbers and chord charts and gave him some general explanations. He had a terrific ear and could instantly grasp what I wanted.

***Lion in Winter* is a significant, award-winning score that's filled with classic compositional techniques—imitation, counterpoint, thematic growth, extended harmonic development. It also has a number of extremely effective unaccompanied choral pieces. What was behind your inclusion of the choral music?**

At the time, everybody said choral music was a new thing for me. And, in terms of what I'd done up to that point, it was. But I had studied with Dr. Francis Jackson, the organist and choirmaster at York Minster. I had studied tons of choral music during those three years before the army. This was just my first opportunity to use choral music professionally, in a film, but I'd done plenty of choral writing before. I was actually going back to my roots in a sense. Also, at the time of *Lion in Winter*, I was madly in love with the Kodály Hungarian Girls Choir. They had just released a new recording of choral music by Bartók, Benjamin Britten, Kodály, and some rare early-twentieth-century Hungarian composers. It was just a wonderful sound, a wonderful choir, so I told the producer I wanted to record the score with this choir.

At that time, was it difficult to engage an ensemble from a Communist country?

Right. But this guy who used to handle Herbert von Karajan and many other classical artists in England arranged to bring over the director of the choir and their management secretary, who was a big Communist woman, and the two of them followed us everywhere. It was very interesting, and it was a little bit scary. I thought there was some hanky-panky going on between them, but she was a true Red. Anyhow, we made all the arrangements for them to come over prior to seeing the movie—I was only going by the script. Immediately after seeing the movie, I decided we needed a complete, full mixed choir—women *and* tenors and basses—to meet the drama. There was really only one scene they could have done by themselves, the herb-garden scene. The limited dramatic range of the choir wouldn't have fit the wide scope of the movie. I was disappointed because I was envisioning sixty young, nubile Hungarians [Laughter] for a week.

By the time we get to the 1970s, producers and directors and audiences are realizing that there is an incredible versatility to John Barry—orchestra, wordless choir, James Bond, pop bands, cimbalom. But I think *The Day of the Locust* is your first "soft-shoe" music, complete with waa-waa trombones.

Right. [Laughter] That was great, I loved doing that movie. That's what I love about film music, you get these things, these images, coming at you—areas that you'd never think of writing music for in that vein, areas that would never occur to you in an abstract sense. That was a very interesting score because of all the period variety— the soft-shoe, the dance-hall music.

But it also displays a strong presence of the avant-garde—tone clusters, dissonant harmonies . . .

Yes, very much that Penderecki thing with the quarter-tones, clusters, all that bizarre string writing. And it was strange getting those guys to do that stuff. I had the Glendale Symphony Orchestra, and they had never seen this kind of notation—lines, dots, smudges, instructions. The first recording session was a teaching session.

Graphic/spatial/proportional notation is very confusing for traditional musicians, not to mention their traditionally conservative bias against such things.

Right! Symphony musicians' whole goal in life is to play together, in tune. And here I am saying, "No, don't play together, I don't want that," which was totally against all their training. But they are an intelligent lot, and they figured it out. It was a very effective technique to use for that movie. And when they saw the effect of it on the movie, they came around to my way of thinking.

Penderecki, when he worked with the Los Angeles Philharmonic, doing some of his works at the Hollywood Bowl, had to cancel the concert because he needed too much rehearsal time. He knew they weren't "getting it," and when they *did* "get it," they weren't giving of their souls, they weren't entering into the spirit of it—the playing was insincere. So he canceled and left for Warsaw.

So film composers sometimes face the same aesthetic confrontations with orchestras that concert composers face?

Absolutely, especially with music like this. It's difficult to get the players to do these strange things, and as you know with your music, sometimes they get silly about it, like children mocking you behind your back, which becomes even more frustrating and more irritating. You ask them to do these unusual things and they look at each other like, "Oh, this guy's strange."

And here we are, twenty years later, and not much has changed—most American orchestras are still very stuffy and very "safe" and very traditional when it comes to programming.

I know. It's too bad. It's a real big problem because they're ignoring an awful lot of important music from our own time, and music the audiences would actually enjoy.

There do seem to be exceptions, especially among the Los Angeles studio players, who must eat contemporary music for breakfast. The experimental/contemporary demands of music by Goldenthal, Goldsmith, and Christopher Young seem to bring out the psychotic best in these players.

That's true. And you do see contemporary pieces pop up on programs across the country from time to time, but I think that's probably the result of politically correct lip service or some big grant from some organization, some funding, so they *have* to play this new piece, not that they really *want* to.

In the mid-1970s, many of your scores, *King Kong* and *The White Buffalo* to name just two, used extensive contemporary compositional techniques—orchestral improvisation, graphic notation, etc. We all know and love John Barry for James Bond music and such gorgeous, sprawling themes as *Somewhere in Time*, but your *The White Buffalo* score is a remarkable musical analysis of a neurotic, paranoid, obsessed Charles Bronson.

Thank you. That character had a lot of emotional problems. He was tortured.

The 1970s was also the disco era. How did you reconcile the producers' demands for the inclusion of disco—in *King Kong* and *The Deep*—with the more serious, dramatic musical statements you needed to make?

That was so bizarre in *King Kong*. That's when they display him in New York for the first time, when they open him up to the public for the first time, isn't it? It was like a 1970s American circus—there was disco, there was "Ave Maria." I had two or three shots at that scene, not because they would reject my ideas but because it was a scene that the director kept re-cutting.

That was such a strange movie to work on. When we started,

Universal was planning a *King Kong* remake and Dino [De Laurentiis] was planning his own *King Kong*, the one I did. They were both going to start production at the same time, and I wondered, "What's going to happen? Are there going to be two *King Kong*s out at the same time?" But it didn't seem to worry them.

Dino said he was going to shoot the entire movie in sequence. In such a complex movie, that would be nearly impossible: Imagine the problems! Then he said, "And we're going to score in sequence—you're going to score and we're going to dub alongside, in sequence." I thought, "Oh, my God! I don't know what the end of the movie is; I don't know how he'll change things along the way!" I knew the script, but it's always entirely different on screen. How do I develop the themes? How do I incorporate earlier themes later on, and vice versa?

Were you limited to working with dailies?

I was working with cut film. The editor was terrific, he's won Academy Awards, but it was extremely difficult to score reel by reel—and that's how we progressed through the entire movie.

Anyway, we were talking about the first public display of Kong: They kept changing that scene, so the final piece you actually hear in the movie is a mixture of three previous edits, previous versions, the whole ball of wax. But I loved it, it was so bizarre. I said it was like the American circus because there's so much going on at the same time—center ring and the high wire and the clowns all happening at the same time. And those awful Sunday morning religious television shows! "Ave Maria" to disco—just a huge pot that everything went into.

How were the disco decisions made?

They wanted Donna Summer, the rage at the time. I had heard her do some other things, not disco, and I thought she had a terrific voice, a most extraordinary voice. I was surprised at how well it worked.

In *The Deep*, the movie was getting into that pop thing. They recorded it on Casablanca records, a label associated with pop music.

Pressed on transparent aqua-blue vinyl—transparent, like Jacqueline Bisset's T-shirt!

[Laughter] That's right. The business was going through *that* whole thing, and the guy who ran Casablanca records was promoting things like crazy. He was incredibly energetic, he was all over the place. Aside from the Bond things, these were, I guess, my first explorations of the pop world in movies.

But the James Bond pop music always feels as if it's a necessary part of the complete texture of the movie, whereas these disco examples almost feel like afterthoughts—they seem to embrace popular culture as an additional source of potential revenue.

Yeah, they did.

In preparation for *your King Kong*, or just out of curiosity and nostalgia, did you watch Max Steiner's 1933 *King Kong*?

I didn't have to go back and watch it, I had seen it a million times. It was made the same year I was born, 1933, so maybe there was some cosmic ray that brought me on as the composer for the remake. I didn't watch it, but I noticed that some reviews said I had paid homage to the Steiner score. If so, it was very subconscious.

Aside from some jungle drumming, which is a requisite for the genre—be it *King Kong*, *Congo*, or *Jurassic Park*—I detect very few, if any, similarities to the Steiner score.

Exactly. I think a couple of reviewers picked out two notes or something and said I was rehashing Steiner. They didn't know what else to say. I suppose it's a natural response in a case like that.

The main titles in your *King Kong* are very fragile—never resolving—in B♭ minor: B♭ to A, B♭ to A. Maybe those are the two notes that critics were referring to, because Steiner's *King Kong* motive descends in three half-steps, C-B-A♯.

Let me tell you a little aside about that. I played the main theme for Federico, Dino's son who was later killed in a helicopter crash. I said, "Your dad's going to like it. It's going to remind him of all those nasty weekends he used to spend in Naples." Dino didn't attend the recording sessions, he was busy producing. So, when we did the main titles, maybe the director would be there or maybe nobody would be there, because everyone was still doing what they were doing out on their own. When I did the main title, knowing Dino, I thought it would be fun to slip in a little trick. So, when his name comes up in the titles, there's this big ugly splat! I sat next to him at the viewing, keeping a totally straight face, and his reaction was just terrific! [Barry makes a tortured grimace.]

White Buffalo, Dino De Laurentiis, producer. I've heard that this was a Christmas present.

Actually, *I* was the Christmas present—the first time in my life I had ever been a Christmas present. *White Buffalo* was finished just before Christmas, and somebody had already done a score prior to that, but it wasn't working out. Dino was frantic, he called me and said, "John, this score's not working. You have to do *The White Buffalo* for me!" He also said that the guy who kept asking for me was the writer. Dino said, "I want to call the writer up on Christmas day and say, 'Your Christmas present is John Barry, the composer, all right already?!'" I said, "Sure." Dino gave the happy writer my phone number, and we talked a long time on Christmas day.

Let's talk about two of your science-fiction movies, *The Black Hole* and *Star Crash.*

I'd rather not talk about *Star Crash* [Laughter], and I'll tell you why. It was one of the few things that I've done that I wasn't very interested in. I always try to take on only those projects that I really enjoy. When I saw some rough cuts of *Star Crash*, it looked like it might turn out all right, so I said I'd do it. But when I saw the final cut, I cried, "Oh, my God! What have I gotten myself into?" I did the best I could with what it was.

What I find interesting about it is that it contains the germs of some future classic Barryisms—compositional devices or techniques that you develop over the next twenty years' worth of movies.

All right, I see what you mean.

For example, third relations—the magical melodic pattern E-F-A-C repeats, without alteration, in the upper voices while the harmonic motion moves in thirds: F to D♭ to B♭ to G.

Yeah, I love those things. Maybe when you get a film that bad [Laughter], you don't give any consideration for the story, you just kind of go off and say, "I don't know what the hell to do here, so I'll try this," and just do whatever you like, whatever you want to try. You really open up—it's called writing over what's on the screen! [Laughter] Seriously!

Star Crash was an Italian film, wasn't it?

I don't know what the hell it was! I think it was made out of a suitcase.

Another Barryism in *Star Crash* is the irregular subdivision of 4/4 into 3+3+2. It's also the rhythmic push that's in *The Legend of the Lone Ranger* and numerous later Barry scores of the 1980s.

Right. That rhythmic pattern is perfect for moving things.

The overture for *The Black Hole* has an Elgarish pride and optimism. Many British composers are fiercely proud of their English composers of the past—Elgar, Britten, Holst, Vaughan Williams, and even Purcell. How about you?

It was heroic, and my idea of heroism is English. I do love many of the English composers—not Britten, he never got to me, but most certainly Vaughan Williams, most certainly Gustav Holst, and definitely Edward Elgar. I feel particularly connected to Elgar. Elgar was English Catholic and I'm English Catholic, and there's a certain spiritual emotion in that music—English music of a Catholic nature—that isn't found in Britten or Holst. That's a part of me and my education and my background that naturally comes through in my music.

Let's talk a bit about *Raise the Titanic*. Was your score ever released as a recording?

I wrote *Raise the Titanic* in Los Angeles, where I lived before moving to New York. The last score I did in L. A. was *Somewhere in Time*, which became a best-selling record. No *Titanic* recording was released because, in those days, the late 1970s, soundtrack albums were not big moneymakers for the record companies. A lot of terrific scores never saw the light of day beyond the movies—except for scores by guys like Johnny Williams, who stimulated an interest in movie music because of the *Star Wars* trilogy.

I'm not a huge fan of *Raise the Titanic, except* for the five-minute scene of the actual raising of the ship from the bottom of the sea. It's a powerful scene, and your music is perfect for the mystery and the majesty and the incredibly awe-inspiring reality of the situation.

Raise the Titanic had so many inconsistencies, like all the underwater stuff. How are those people supposed to see underwater, that deep below the surface? It's a license you take. *Reap the Wild Wind,* which was a great underwater movie from way back, seems more believable because they shot through clear water. In *Raise the Titanic*, the water is so murky you think, "No wonder it sank!" One spot I really liked was the Victorian waltz scene, trying to conjure up what we might have heard in the dining room that night before she sank. I agree, the raising of the ship is *the* great moment in the movie, and I think they knew it. That *was* the movie. I felt the music just seemed a natural commentary on the event.

As the ship is being dislodged from the bottom of the sea, the sound is all effects—scraping metal, bending, creaking iron—no music. Only when the bow of the Titanic finally breaks through the ocean surface does the music begin to break through. Was this critical, dramatic placement of music your decision or the director's?

It was all mine, absolutely. The choices about where the music goes in a movie are the most important decisions you can make. You often get a director who says things like, "Oh, I wanted it earlier" or "I need some help here," and I say, "No." If he insists on something, I might put in some little things—almost subliminal—like musical sound effects. But waiting for that special moment that really counts, where you can lift it over the top, is the most important and the most rewarding for a film composer. Choosing where you put the music or where you lay out are the big discussions with the director. I absolutely believe that those choices will make the difference between a good score and a bad score, not to mention help make a good movie or ruin it. The relevance that you attach to your music and how you explain yourself to the director will make or break it.

Sometimes the director can get foggy because he is seeing the scene in an uncut version, and probably carrying some emotional baggage about musical thoughts he's had long before the composer arrived on the movie. So it's up to the composer to say, "I think you're wrong. I think this scene is working beautifully up to this point, and the music needs to wait until here." The good directors will be very responsive. But, sometimes, you need to cover yourself. Sometimes, I will write what they want, but I will make it clear to them that this is only if they realize that it's probably temporary, before cuts. And I will write it in such a way that the music editor can make a very clean cut, so that it won't sound like a cut.

Your *High Road to China* score embraces broad, soaring themes to accompany the soaring airplane and the sprawling scenery. But the airplane is *so* loud it drowns out your score. What kinds of problems need to be worked out in balancing sound effects and music in the final mix?

This is the big fight, always. The prime examples I can give actually refer to the James Bond movies. At the time we did *Goldfinger*, certain movies had exaggerated sound effects. But with *Goldfinger*, they really, really did it—with the hits and the screeching car sounds and the runaway trains and the fist fights—everything was just way over the top, very noisy. I was frustrated, so I asked if we could have the senior sound editor involved with the music score. For one car-chase scene, as an example, I suggested that the sound effects could be at high volume for the first part, but then we would find a given point where something changes in the action—another element of danger or an imminent escape—where the effects would then dissolve into my music for the second part. The music would lift the emotions and the effects would be subliminal, except maybe for the last five seconds, where everything—effects and music—would crescendo to a fevered pitch.

So, on a lot of the Bond movies, I would work side by side with the sound guys. And the formula worked very well. If you ask people why the Bond chase scenes worked, they don't really know. But I believe it's because of this careful blending of effects and music. When I get a movie nowadays, and we enter into that "action" area, I use the same approach: find out what the sounds are, and fade the music in and out of the effects. In the five-minute buffalo hunt in *Dances With Wolves*, for example, they initially had laid a very loud temp track over the entire scene, but I pushed for beginning it with *only* the sounds of the buffalo, which were such terrific sounds by themselves, without music. Let's give the audience the feeling of what that must have been like if they were there—let's give that to them first, and then I'll come in when some element changes and the effects can fade into the background.

Many recent action movies mix high-volume effects and loud music simultaneously.

And that makes me scream. It's just a jumbled mess—incredibly loud effects and loud music at the same time. You can't tell the difference between the two sound sources.

When the effects are *that* loud, there's no way you can work around them. Seriously, you can't. Range extremes—adding high piccolos, xylophones, bass trombones, tubas, contrabass clarinets, that kind of thing—is really the only way to try to find a register that's not being eaten up by the effects. But it's still too much sound. A lot of composers will write a loud, full-orchestra tutti against the effects, and then nobody wins. Even worse, now they throw synthesizers into the mix—synthesized effects, synthesized music—all with the orchestra and the natural sound effects, which produces just a huge fusion of way too much sound information. You can't tell who's doing what. It totally loses its dramatic impact. It's supposed to be very exciting, but it becomes boring. It becomes too "Johnny One-Note" or, actually, too "Johnny Million-Notes!" [Laughter]

You've composed the scores for the majority of the Bond pictures. Were you asked to do the recent *GoldenEye*?

I was asked to do that picture, but I was committed. I had too many things to do already, which was maybe too bad. Because of the nostalgia element, it might have been fun to return to the series. But I actually thought that I'd done enough of that—that was the past, just too many years had gone by and the theme wasn't right anymore. Also, I didn't think the movie was going anywhere at all. So they asked me who I would recommend. I'd recently heard an Eric Serra score, a synthesized score, but a very attractive score, and I suggested that maybe this might be a new way to go for the contemporary Bond image. When I finally saw the movie, nothing worked. I was confused. I truly don't know what happened. It should have worked, I believed that the idea was a good new direction for Bond. But he didn't do anything close to what I had heard in his earlier score, the score that prompted me to make my recommendation in the first place. He just went off on another tangent.

Critics seized the opportunity to reminisce about the good old days—the John Barry/James Bond tradition.

That's true. And I received one of the best reviews of my life for *not* doing it! *The New York Times* review, in the first paragraph, said something like, "The real James Bond audiences are going through epileptic fits because there's no Bond music in the movie," or something to that effect. And I thought, "Great, you don't do a movie, and you're praised." If I *had* done the score, the critics would have said, "Oh, John Barry's doing his same old Bond shtick." [Laughter]

You Only Live Twice and On Her Majesty's Secret Service are two very aggressive Bond scores—more tension and suspense music than in many of the other movies—but not quite the good-natured, "wink-of-the-eye," matinee-hero action implications of the others. Were the changes in your Bond scores inspired by the scripts, the directors, the changing 007 actors?

You Only Live Twice was an Oriental thing. [Barry whines an augmented second-heavy motive.] So that was obviously a huge directive. It was also one of the first times in a Bond movie, if not the first, that a character that you liked died. Usually, when they kill somebody, it's like "Ah ha!" which can almost be a musical invitation to a laugh line. But this time, the emotions were more dramatic. There was a lot of sympathy in that movie. The composer can't play that lightly. And Sean Connery's playing of it was straight, too. This was very serious.

You can do two or three cues in a movie that have a slightly different tone and everybody says, "Oh, the score is so different," when it actually isn't. If you hit two or three areas where dramatic impact is different, it gives the impression of different music, something radical. But that's the nature of the beast. The music I write adapts to the situation, based on the intensity level of a scene.

On Her Majesty's Secret Service?

That was another "first time" problem—a new face! To help the audience through the change, the entire opening sequence is very tradition-heavy. It establishes everything that had gone before, everything that was very "Bondian." The movies before it were always moving away or moving ahead, but this was a giant step back, as if to say, "Listen folks, it's okay, this *is* James Bond, James Bond, James Bond."

There were first-class action sequences in that movie, technically. Also the song was a new idea that I liked. That movie didn't move you as it should have done when she dies at the end. The chemistry just didn't work. I wrote what I thought was one of nicest songs I've ever written, "We Have All the Time in the World." I wanted it to work like "September Song." I wanted the irony of an old man singing around this young girl's death—and that's why I wanted Louis Armstrong. I could think of no one else but Louis Armstrong from the start.

That breaks with tradition as well. Previous Bond songs were recorded by such popular, sexy young artists of the time as Tom Jones and Nancy Sinatra.

Right. When I went to them and asked, "How about Louis Armstrong?" they were surprised, they weren't sure what to say and asked why. I explained my reasoning, and they said, "Great." If that same theme had been for Sean Connery and a really great Bond broad, for want of a better term, it would been an entirely different picture!

I hate to use the words, but it's like "shoveling shit against the tide" when you feel a strong chemistry by reading the script, but on screen it's just not working. You can play just about anything against it—you can play Rachmaninoff, you can play a Bartók piano concerto—but you're still not going to get anywhere emotionally because it just does not work. When directors say, "This isn't really working here, but once the music is over it . . ." I say, "Wait! No, no. It actually makes it worse." And, in a strange way, it actually *does* make it worse because the audience subconsciously senses a cover-up. They know it's not working, they know you're attempting to cover up for what's missing between the actors. It almost makes it laughable, it almost becomes a parody or a send-up.

Many of your movie themes are in F major.

Absolutely. I love that key. It just sings so beautifully. There's an openness and a romantic richness and fullness of depth with the string orchestra in that key. The chord progressions rarely stay in the same key—they usually detour off into some other area, but then often return home.

As you're composing your themes, are you just naturally drawn to improvise on the piano in F major? And are your themes eventually transposed for the orchestral score, or do they often remain in the original keys of their conception?

If it's working beautifully in a certain key, I'll feel it and keep it there. I'll change the orchestration a little bit or alter certain harmonic, non-chord tones. It actually depends on the situation, what instruments I'm going to use.

Strings sound better in sharp keys, winds sound better in flat keys?

It's partially that, but it's also the dramatic impact of the colors. I love the inter-relationships of keys, not only key changes and modulations, but inter-relationships within a single key—creating progressions that make sense and feel dramatic but might not be standard moves. When you listen to the entire album from *Dances With Wolves*, the key relationships between the different cues sound connected.

Many of your themes move in harmonically parallel modes—C major to C minor, with no pivot or modulation. You also favor the minor dominant, for example, a G-minor dominant in the key of C major.

Right. That's all part of it. I love those changes.

In *Until September*, you alternate between the pitches B♭ and E in the melody, and the harmony rocks back and forth between C⁷ and F♯⁷.

The tritone was actually Mozart's favorite interval. It has an extraordinary life and power to it.

We often associate the tritone with horror and suspense and fear—*tonus diabolus* and all that. But you take this historically sinister interval and transform it into an erotic love theme!

Right. Well, there are common tones between them—F♯⁷ and C⁷ both have B♭s, or spelled A♯ in the F♯ key, and both have Es, and these two entirely different people have something in common between them. It's like lifting the theme to a new level, moving it up over the mountain.

One of my favorite songs is *I Love Paris*, by Cole Porter, who was a brilliant composer. He admitted writing that whole intro in a

Jewish mode, with the augmented seconds and all that Eastern European inflection. [Barry sings the intro to *I Love Paris*.] And then he breaks into a much more diatonic, bright version of the same theme. Think of the song, you'll see what I mean. Well, that's the kind of harmonic change I love. If Cole Porter had written the whole thing in a Parisian way, it would have been a trite little song. But, with that introduction, moving to the body of the song, we're transported to another world. It's just terrific.

Was *I Love Paris* in your mind when writing the *Until September* score?

That *trick* was in my mind, which I suppose means the song, by extension, was somewhere there, too.

In *The Cotton Club*, I discovered John Barry the great jazz composer. You seem very much at home in jazz and blues, solo clarinet and snarling trombones.

Those are my roots. People forget that side of me. I loved doing that movie, at least the musical parts. But it did have its production problems: We already had the source music—the Cab Calloway stuff and all that—selected, but I think Francis [Coppola] did it backwards. Normally, you get that material recorded, and then shoot the picture. But Francis first shot the picture, and then we had to record around it, which was a technical nightmare. I understood his thinking, but it wasn't practical.

I said I'd like to use strings, horns—this classically oriented score—for contrast against all the jazz, so it's not all so monochromatic. He thought that was a good idea, and I wrote the underscore that way. He liked most of it but, well, games get played, and they needed more time to re-cut the movie. And, believe me, the composer's a great guy to turn to when you're looking for a time extension. [Laughter] You think I'm kidding? Believe me, I could give you devastating information on that subject. In the long run, that was not such a happy movie. The ins and out, the arguments among the people, that guy who got murdered—there was a lot going on.

John Barry on *The Cotton Club*: The Real Story!

Absolutely. It was more of a saga. So, Francis and I had this meeting on the phone, and he asked, "How did we get all this string-orchestra stuff throughout?" Apparently this was coming from the music editor and everyone else. I said, "We discussed it at length, Francis. That's how it came about." But he said maybe we should try for a little more of the Ellington sound. So, what I did was hire five terrific sax players to cover the low string lines—they literally played the low string-orchestra parts. I had to make very few changes to the harmony or the ranges, and it gave Francis the sound he wanted.

***The Jagged Edge* is one your most synthesizer-oriented scores, but it sounds very orchestral.**

It was entirely synthesizer, except for solo flute and solo piano. I'm not good at all that programming, so I spent some time with a very good composer named Jonathan Elias, who knows that technology inside and out. He helped me learn some basic techniques about certain textural things, timespan things. I made my own list of points of reference about certain sounds and effects and just came away with a shopping list, for want of a better term, of what I thought would work well—things that would be appropriate for the movie. The rest of it was written pretty much like an orchestral score—low string sounds, brass sounds, and a smattering of synthesizer effects, like clusters and shock chords. I enjoyed that movie, I enjoyed learning more about electronics.

***Masquerade* has a very suspenseful Herrmannesque score.**

Right. That was Bob Swaim's idea. I liked that movie, and it was fairly successful. I think it went to number one the first week out but couldn't sustain its audience.

Perhaps because of the leading man?

That might have had something to do with it, because it was a well-made movie. How many times do you sit down and see a movie and ask yourself, "Could you imagine if so-and-so was in this role?" And it usually has to do with dead people: "Can you imagine what this might have been like with Bogart? Oh, my God!" Casting is such an important decision. It's an awareness.

The leading man was popular at the time.

Well, he was a name. I loved what Marlon Brando said to Val Kilmer about this recent *Island of Dr. Moreau* movie. Brando said, "Sonny, you're confusing your acting ability with your fee for this movie."

The love theme in *The Jagged Edge* is quintessential Barry, with the exception of the unexpected flatted blues-third, suggesting a suspicious nature to this romance.

Exactly. I especially love the very end of the movie, after the funeral, the end credits. Everything's kind of finally resolved, but my music has become totally black and grim. The audience reaction was, "Is there going to be a sequel?" because there's nothing dramatic at all happening on the screen.

The love theme and the suspense music merge as the film moves on. The love theme gradually dissolves, taking on more and more characteristics of the suspense music.

Absolutely. You set up certain parameters. You deal with what's on the screen. It all starts off with this love thing and then the intrigue and then it all begins to disintegrate, so the music begins to disintegrate.

When Rob Lowe and Meg Tilly first make love, what one would expect to be an erotic scene of passion and romance is surrounded by music of anxiety and evil.

And that's a lovely thing, when you can write against the story. Another love scene that I think was very interesting was with Robert Redford and Meryl Streep in *Out of Africa*. The romantic thing was never played over them. When I wrote it, I wasn't sure what was needed. I liked what I was writing, but I thought that it had absolutely nothing to do with a love scene. It was one of those instinctive things. When I played it against the movie, it worked like a bitch. I'm still not exactly sure why it worked—I was writing it out of running away from something rather than going to something. I was writing against what everyone was going to expect. It just worked beautifully.

Did director Sidney Pollack like the idea?

He thought it was wonderful, but he was already going after a certain strangeness in the movie, if you think of the dialogue. The music fit right into his scheme of things. I love writing against the movie, but the opposite has to be very real for you, it has to be very specific and have a good reason for being there, otherwise you hit something called "confusion!"

When Puccini would come across complicated dramatic scenes, he would write instinctively, and it would work. It was as if he was *meant* to be an opera composer in this life. You must say, "I know why I'm a film composer" at moments like the *Out of Africa* love scene.

Yes. And you have to have courage when you take a shot like that.

You have to trust your instincts. The only thing I'm really concerned about is, "Is the director going to go along with this?" It's a funny thing, it's very simple—when things work, they work.

Speaking of when it works, your *Chaplin* music is incredibly personal for Chaplin the man. It's nostalgic and introspective, but it has humor and it has heartbreak. The opening titles tell it all.

I think the whole key to that entire score, and to the entire movie, is that opening sequence: You see Chaplin enter the dressing room with his hat and his cane—all that "Little Tramp" business. And as the opening credits unfold, he slowly strips away all that this is— his fame. He takes off his hat, puts his cane over the back of the chair, removes his mustache with spirit gum and cold cream. He's stripping down to the real man. I thought Robert [Downey, Jr.] was just wonderful. That last shot, as he gazes into the mirror and wipes off the last bits of makeup—as the man Chaplin emerges from beyond the famous star—it's almost like a Leonardo Renaissance painting or a Francis Bacon poem.

I think that, even by today's standards, perhaps Chaplin is the most famous Hollywood person of all time. His films were silent, but known throughout Europe and Asia. We have big movie stars today, but nobody knows them in China or India. Chaplin was huge, but it was his *image* that was huge. If you saw the real Chaplin walking down the street, you wouldn't recognize him. I remember, when I was a little kid, seeing a photograph of Chaplin sitting in a nightclub. As a little boy, I expected him to be sitting there with his hat on, with his cane and his funny shoes, because that was his image, you rarely saw him in any other way. When you actually saw him, he was gray-haired, he was a totally other person. I thought it was a printing error or a mis-identification of the photograph, seriously.

I was brought up on Chaplin movies. What it must have been like, at that time in history, to take all that off and look at yourself as no one really knows you! It must have been quite a staggering emotional revelation, day after day after day. This is me! Not what I just put on the chair, not this hat, not this cane, not what everybody knows as me, but this face looking into the mirror. Or is it? It's staggering when you think about it. That was my inspiration for the opening theme. I never told Richard [Attenborough] anything about it, but when I eventually played a demo for him against the movie, a little demo that had been done on piano and synthesizer, he started to cry. He said, very quietly, "Jesus, I never expected this." I asked if he hadn't seen it this way, and he said he thought it would be "against" it, but in another way, in a brighter, more optimistic way. But he said, "This is terrific, just terrific. It's a total surprise." Then he played it for the other people, and everyone loved it. That sadness was the key.

When my father came to Liverpool from Ireland, he worked at the little repertory theater in Liverpool when Chaplin was sometimes there, and Stan Laurel was there. My dad used to tell me Chaplin stories, so I already knew a lot about Chaplin's personal life. I brought a lot of that into the score. It really helped.

Tell me about *The Specialist*, a Bond-style action film.

I enjoyed doing that movie. I hadn't done one of those in a long time. The thing that I really liked was the idea of a guy falling in love with an image and a voice—the challenge of creating a love theme for two people who never meet. I thought that score went very well.

Your score uses a wordless chorus.

Yeah, the scene where they go to the funeral for the identification of the body of the old woman. I love treating scenes with that religioso business. I guess it's my Catholic chapel upbringing. I love that whole thing of the big cathedral, that big spiritual sound of God and angels and music playing against Sylvester Stallone and

Sharon Stone with an automatic firearm stuck in her stocking top. It's so bizarre to go against all of this with the big God music—it's almost surreal! Those are the kinds of shots that I really like. They're such a creative pleasure to work on. It's so much fun to have a setting that allows experimenting with bizarre combinations of different influences and impressions.

Many of your Bond movies have that same kind of "over-the-top" approach.

Absolutely. Sometimes you just have to go with it.

In your earlier period/costume extravaganzas, such as *Mary, Queen of Scots*, you often use chorus. In the 1960s, of course, there was no alternative to contracting a real chorus. In the 1990s, many composers simulate the choral sound with synthesizers.

I know they do. That's too bad. There's nothing like a real chorus. In *The Specialist*, that's a real chorus. Synthesizers can do a lot of things, but they can't do saxophones, they can't do strings, they can't do voices. They can imitate an altered voice, but if you want the real thing, there's really no substitute for the real thing.

Tell me about *The Scarlet Letter*.

Does everybody know the history of that movie? I don't know all the details, but Morricone was Roland's [Joffe] first choice because he had done that wonderful movie with De Niro, *The Mission*. I don't know what went wrong, but suddenly Elmer Bernstein came on it. I don't think Morricone had written a complete score; he may have written certain things. But Elmer did do a full score. I had lunch with Elmer in London when he was doing it. Then, when I got back here, I got a call from the producer, saying that, for whatever reasons, they had to change the score, and asking if I was available to do it in only five weeks, including recording time.

What kind of arrangements and/or concessions were they willing to make to accommodate the time crunch?

First of all, I said, "Send me a cassette," because I had never read the original book—it's an American classic, not an English classic. Then I said, "And I'm not going anywhere if I only have a few weeks. You come here! And there are certain things we need to do if we're going to finish it on time." I had just heard a wonderful new recording of Samuel Barber's *Adagio for Strings* arranged for unaccompanied voices. It was just gorgeous. I thought that would be so wonderful over the long sermon and a few other places, so I said, "If you can buy that, it would be a big help." There was also a Dvořák piece, *Serenade for Strings*, that I liked, but it didn't end up in the movie. Altogether, there was about an hour's worth of music in the movie. Anyhow, I said that if the producers and directors could fly to New York, we could contract a studio in the city to spot it, and I could just drive a few hours back and forth from Long Island. If I had to fly back and forth to Los Angeles, it would be so time-consuming and I would be tired. So, they came to New York and the recording sessions worked out fine. I don't mind working fast once I have all my basic material. Once I have a damn good idea of what it's all about, I can finish a score in four weeks. But to work a four-week period from a standing position, from scratch, I will never, ever do that again.

Were you ultimately pleased with the score?

Under the circumstance, I think it was pretty damned miraculous. The movie, however, was ripped apart by the critics. Believe me, going in, the word out on the street was very strong about *The Scarlet Letter*. But I knew the ending had been changed. I had worked before where the big question was, "Should he die or should he not die at the end?" Usually, when they die, audiences keep away in droves. So, to keep him alive, they had to rewrite it with almost a little kid's matinee-type battle with swords. I think the writers could have eased into it in a smoother way, but they were probably pressed for time as well.

It was a very adult movie until the fabricated happy ending.

Yes. I went along with the idea of the contemporary casting of the two leads and the new-age overtone to go with the contemporary behavior of two young people. I thought it was an interesting concept—more American. That approach would never have taken place in England, it would have been much more classical.

In spite of the time constraints, your score has a great deal of musical variety—wonderful rhythmic material, sweeping tunes, Algonquin Indian source music . . .

That was thanks to Peter Buffett, a terrific musician who specializes in simulating ethnic sounds on the synthesizer. Without him, we probably just would have used a lot of tom-toms and Indian sounds. We hired Peter and rushed and spotted-out all the Indian areas, and Peter did the music for all of them. He had an amazing instinct and a knack for finding very interesting overtones and colors while still sticking with the basic Indian sounds they wanted. So, with Peter and the Barber *Adagio for Strings*, at least my job became a little less impossible, and we could guarantee getting everything finished on time.

When Hester first secretly watches the good reverend bathing naked in the lake, she is, in a sense, meeting him for the first time. The music for this scene is quite dramatic. It presents an atmosphere of innocence and purity. Was there ever a thought that the scene should be played more vixenish or more sensually?

No, never, not from me. And I don't think from Roland, who wanted to maintain that innocence.

How were decisions made about the inclusion of Barber's *Adagio for Strings*?

The Barber *Adagio* is first used when he's giving a sermon, which I thought worked beautifully. But the other place where I wanted to incorporate the Barber was in the Demi Moore bathing scene, when she's getting in and out of the tub. I spotted the scene that way, but they didn't like it; they didn't think it worked as well as it did over the preacher scene. I said, "I think you're wrong. I think it really brings her thoughts of the preacher to the front line, and it also gives a nude scene a touch of class, keeping it on a higher level." They didn't go for it, so they repeated my main love theme in the bath scene, which I thought was totally wrong. Even if I had had the time to write a new theme there, it wouldn't have sounded anything like that. It's just one of those areas where you disagree and, in retrospect, I still think I was absolutely right. It was a scene that the critics took a real stab at, but I believe the Barber would have helped.

Although *The Scarlet Letter* was criticized for its eroticism, it really had only one truly erotic love scene, and you played it the way Miklós Rózsa did in *The Eye of the Needle*—when Lucy (Kate Nelligan) reaches orgasm, the chord changes, the key changes!

[Laughing] Subtle it's not! I learned that in the Bond movies. Sometimes you try other things, but then sometimes you realize you've just gotta go full throttle for the scene. Many times, I'll go with that traditional style when I've tried two or three other things and they're just not working. That says to me, we've got to go with the classic approach; it just has to be.

In *The Scarlet Letter* and in *Masquerade* and *Jagged Edge* and many of your other scores, a character might stand alone, deep in private thought, and be accompanied by a solo violin or a solo cello.

Sometimes those things are just necessary. The whole scan of orchestration is very important, too. A lot of people out there write a few lines and a few chord progressions and then hand it over to orchestrators. I have orchestrators who copy into full score, but my sketches are extremely detailed and totally complete—voicings, all the harmonic coloring—with extensive indications about solo this or solo that. It's a twelve-stave score and it's all there. When you hear a brass chord, it's my arrangement and distribution of the brass colors. Orchestration is so much a part of the score, the scale of the music. Transitions, pushing you into scenes, pulling you out of scenes—that's all to do with the orchestration. The themes are important, but it's how they're colored and harmonized that counts.

Orchestrations also convey the personality of the composer—such and such sounds like Stravinsky or like Bartók. John Barry music can often be identified by its orchestrations alone.

That's true. I love the thing in *Body Heat* when he returns to the office and realizes they're going to kill the husband. The whole thing begins very quietly and at a distance. As the camera pulls up, the orchestra increases and climaxes with a full-face shot and tutti orchestra. You seize those moments, and the refinement of the orchestral colors you choose is so important. That's why I always work with a Moviola. I have the video and all that playback gear to look at the overall thing, but I always use the Moviola for particular scenes, which I mark off with a pencil. After orchestration, the next most important thing is the conductor.

Do you always conduct your own scores?

The only thing I didn't conduct was *The Legend of the Lone Ranger*. At the time, the musicians union in the States was on strike, so we went to Paris, but I couldn't conduct for union reasons—I would have been breaking the lines. But we had a very good conductor and it turned out fine. The advantage of conducting your own scores is the ability to move things around a little bit—all those things you do on the recording floor—begin something a few seconds earlier, hold a sustained chord an extra second or two. It also saves a great deal of time when there are questions and suggested changes from the booth, because the composer knows his own score better than anyone else.

Especially if the composer has orchestrated the score.

Absolutely. When you've written everything yourself, you just have much more control. Nowadays, an entourage of nameless composers work on a score. That's why nothing sounds individual. They are excellent musicians, but the orchestrations are spread too thin between too many imaginations. There's no personality. All the musical subtleties, the nuances, come out of the orchestration. I need to make all my own decisions about those. I did the love theme from *Dances With Wolves* with strings, woodwinds, and horns. The first time it appears it's almost sotto voce—I didn't want the big sound, but I wanted all the players for expression.

Do you get many opportunities to guest-conduct concert orchestras?

I've done concerts in London with the Royal Philharmonic in Royal Albert Hall, concerts at the Hollywood Bowl with the Los Angeles Philharmonic. I was going to do the Seville Festival with the Royal Philharmonic Orchestra, but about three days before we went down there, the stage of the new opera house collapsed and killed a couple of people. So that was obviously canceled. But I love the studio environment. With concerts, you just don't get enough rehearsal time. When I went to L.A., my plane was delayed and I ended up with only one morning rehearsal, so the concert was virtually a read-through. Can you imagine what a nervous wreck I was—going out on that stage in front of thousands of people, knowing the orchestra really doesn't have a clue? When it was over, I was a wreck, and I decided this is not the life I want.

As you know, this is typical for concert orchestras—a composer may get a one-hour rehearsal for a brand-new twenty-minute piece.

Right. There's no refinement, no shading, and really no interpretation. They're just reading down lots of notes. It's a murderous thing.

Across the Sea of Time is an IMAX film with a nostalgic score dedicated to your son. Your score looks back at New York City at the turn of the century.

A little immigrant boy stows away on a Russian trawler and comes to New York, jumps overboard at the docks, and wanders into the city. All he has is a collection of letters and old photographs from past generations of his family in a crumpled bag. The story is his journey from house to house, trying to track down certain people.

The set pieces are so charming—the waltz in Central Park, the NYC hustle and bustle.

And when he goes on the Coney Island rollercoaster and the night flight over New York. It's the feeling of America at that time in history. You walk out of the theater believing you've been there. It's a very touching movie—all the people in the photographs are dead. They found all this stuff in some vault in San Francisco.

Since your full recovery from a life-threatening situation a few years back, your scores have been especially emotional—*The Scarlet Letter, Cry, the Beloved Country, Across the Sea of Time* . . .

Well, I have a new outlook on life.

In 1999, composer Elmer Bernstein continues to write stunningly beautiful film music at the same hectic and productive pace that established his career nearly fifty years ago. When he first began writing for movies, Bernstein's was one of but a few truly American voices in competition with the many European-born and European-trained film composers working in Hollywood. During the 1950s, Bernstein, along with a handful of likewise visionary composers (including Leonard Rosenman and Alex North), brought forth a new music for film that featured decidedly original and American sounds—a music that is, today, still extremely influential and often imitated.

The list of Bernstein's well-known film scores is obviously extensive. It includes, just for starters, such classic Westerns as *The Magnificent Seven* (1960), *The Comancheros* (1961), *The Sons of Katie Elder* (1965), *True Grit* (1969), and *The Shootist* (1976). Other significant Bernstein contributions to the evolution of the art can be found in a wide variety of film genres—from the haunting evocation of innocence and Americana of his Oscar-nominated *To Kill a Mockingbird* (1962), the action-packed scores of *The Buccaneer* (1959) and *Zulu Dawn* (1979), the introspection of *Birdman of Alcatraz* (1962), the martial strains of *The Great Escape* (1963), the delicate emotions of *My Left Foot* (1989) and his Oscar-nominated *The Age of Innocence* (1993), the relaxed wickedness of *The Grifters* (1990) to the driving Bartókian rhythms of *Kings*

Go Forth (1958) and *Some Came Running* (1959). The groundbreaking jazz-influenced scores of his Oscar-nominated *The Man With the Golden Arm* (1955), *Sweet Smell of Success* (1957), his Oscar-nominated *Summer and Smoke* (1961), *Walk on the Wild Side* (1962), and *The Caretakers* (1963), a style which he has kept alive in such more recent films as *A Rage in Harlem* (1991), *Hoodlum* (1997), and *John Grisham's The Rainmaker* (1997) have inspired composers around the world.

Bernstein's scores display a wide range of extremes—a natural sense of comedic timing erupts in his "straight" dramatic scores for *Animal House* (1978), *Airplane!* (1980), *Stripes* (1981), *Ghostbusters* (1984), and *Spies Like Us* (1985), while a dark and sinister musical imagination maintains an evil presence in such films as *Sudden Fear* (1952) and the psychotic musical impressions in *See No Evil* (1971), *Cape Fear* (1991), and *The Good Son* (1993). His consistently memorable and effective scores are stylistically all over the map, but what else would we expect from a composer who's first few jobs in Hollywood included music for *Robot Monster* (1953), *Cat Women of the Moon* (1953)—in 3-D!—and Cecil B. DeMille's legendary *The Ten Commandments* (1956).

When we met for this interview at his Santa Monica studio, Elmer Bernstein proved that he, like his music, is full of charm and wit and drama.

elmer BERNSTEIN

Martin Scorsese wrote, "It's the rush of emotional immediacy that is the true soul and deepest bounty of Elmer's music."

I think that the whole charm of music and film is that it is an emotional art, and I'm not shy about expressing it.

Do you find that there are times when the need for hustle-bustle background music gets in the way of *your* need for emotional underscore?

First of all, your mindset as a composer of a film has to be to do what's best for the film. Sometimes what's best for the film is to be out there emotionally, and sometimes what's best for the film is to be subtle, to be quiet, to kill time in an interesting way. I think that, certainly as far as the craft is concerned, the ability to do that kind of thing is part of the job. It isn't as much fun as doing something emotional or something splashy, like *The Magnificent Seven*, but there are things that you have to do simply because the film needs them.

Have you found there to be times when you're trying to be emotional but the director may say, "Elmer, back off a little. Let the actors do the emotion."?

Only all the time! Well, that's sort of a facetious answer. Generally speaking—and this is a terrible generality—younger directors are afraid of emotion. Older directors are not. Younger directors are shy, and somehow a little embarrassed by real emotion. I think it's somehow or other a sign of the times, of what values are today, that younger directors do not tend to be lovers. Older directors are lovers.

Do you think it's part of the social climate?

Yeah. I think it's part of the climate. I think that the times are fairly emotionally brittle and cautious. The tremendous move in filmmaking toward sensation, sensationalism, and special effects is part of an assault on the sensibilities that has nothing to do with real emotion. And I think that we now have a whole generation growing up with that.

You've worked in so many genres—Western, science-fiction, action-adventure, animation, comedy, relationship movies. For projects down the road, what genre would you hope to work in again—perhaps a genre that you haven't worked in enough or that you'd like to try again?

My career consists of doing many different kinds of things. I generally do that on purpose. I don't want to do two pictures in a row that are similar. That's just me. I got stuck in comedies for two ten-year periods. I had to get out. Finally, I said I'm not going to do another comedy. And I haven't done another comedy. The last comedy I did was in, I think, 1988. But I'm doing one now. See, once again, I'm coming back. When I do *that* comedy it will be twelve years since I've written a comedy. It'll be fun. It's a big, splashy, nutty comedy called *Wild Wild West*, from the old television program. I recently did a film called *Twilight*, and one of the things that attracted me about that film was that it gave me the chance to write in a manner very unlike myself, very unlike other things that I've written before, and I was very anxious to do it just for that very reason. So, I think that the answer to the question that you posed is, if it's something different than what I've done the last time, or recently, I'll be interested.

In your early film career, in such big-budget, important movies as *Sudden Fear*, with Joan Crawford and Jack Palance, we heard a new sound in movie music—solo instruments; transparent, jagged piano figures; small, intimate chamber ensembles; and so on. And then, around 1952 or 1953, something happened politically or business-wise that kept you from moving ahead.

That was all political. That was part of the McCarthy era. I was, you know, Red, so I was persona non grata here for a while. And that's when I did, in a row, *Robot Monster*—in 3-D!—*Cat Women of the Moon* . . .

With your name spelled "Bernstien" in the opening credits!

Yeah. I was gray-listed for strictly political reasons.

Guilt by association?

No, I had been very active in left-wing causes.

Your student days were spent with Aaron Copland, Stefan Wolpe, and Roger Sessions. I so often hear not only hints but strong acknowledgments of that "contemporary" sound.

Well, I learned a lot from those guys. Aaron Copland is the musical father for all American composers. I also learned a lot from Wolpe. He, of course, was a serial composer, but a lot of the rhythmic energy that you hear in my music came from my studies with Wolpe. He was very wonderful teaching rhythmic energy.

Was there any particular Sessions contribution to your development?

Sessions was very solid. He was the most conservative of my teachers. From Sessions, I learned a lot of nuts-and-bolts kinds of things in terms of harmony and counterpoint and all of those things—the nuts and bolts out of which the structure is built. With Wolpe, we did a lot of analysis of other composers' works. We once spent a whole summer in Maine just analyzing. You learn a lot from that.

As you became successful with *The Ten Commandments* and such, did you keep in touch with your teachers? How did they respond to your Hollywood film music?

Wolpe, of course, was perfectly cool with what I was doing. But he felt that I ought to write one concert piece a year. That was his advice. I pretty much lost sight of Copland during that period. Oh, I'd see him every couple of years. I guess my greatest problem with Aaron was when they did a television series called *The Chisholms*. They wanted to base it on Aaron's music. They didn't mean to use it literally, note for note, but to adapt it to the programs. At first, Aaron was kind of cautious—not very anxious for this to happen. Then, he decided it was okay as long as I was the person who did the adaptations. And I thought that was as good as it gets. So, we actually did it.

Let's stay in television for a moment. *Johnny Staccato* had a tough, urban main theme in 5/4. They just don't write 'em like that for TV anymore.

I'll tell you, there were a lot of reasons that *Johnny Staccato* sounded the way it did. At about the same time, Hank Mancini was doing *Peter Gunn* with the same players, actually. But a lot of *Staccato* had to do with John Cassavetes, who had a very strong hand in the show. He was very into the music. And he really, really got involved on many levels. He was a lot of fun to work with.

I saw *Riverboat* as a little kid. I don't remember much about the

program, but I do recall that your *Riverboat* music presaged your Western style or, more specifically, your *Magnificent Seven* style.

It certainly did. It was a rehearsal for *The Magnificent Seven.* And every once in a while some astute person will discover that. It was the first time that I had a chance to sort of splash out with that kind of music. It was a lot of fun to do. It was also a fun show because it was the first show that was ever shown in color on television, and we were all pretty excited about that development.

The television miniseries *Captains and the Kings* begins to explore your fascination with Irish musical culture, which resurfaces later in your scores for *Da, My Left Foot,* and *The Field.*

Captains and the Kings was great fun. I really, really enjoyed exploring that music. And I'm very fond of that score. The people on that show were very supportive and very into the music. There was one episode a week for a very long period of time. They were well produced, beautifully done.

Tell me about the powerful, disturbing *Guyana Tragedy: The Story of Jim Jones.* The film was produced just a few years after the actual horrific event. What kind of research went into your work with that particular film?

The people who made the film had real tapes of what went on there. We heard all those tapes of the real tragedy. There are some projects that are really, really emotionally difficult, and so you sort of blank out on them. At this point, I can't remember a thing I wrote for that. You just wanted to go away from the subject as soon as you could. It was very exciting at the time we did it, but I thought the whole thing was terribly depressing.

At around this same time, you did *Genocide*, which must have been very emotional for you. You incorporate an often-mutated "Dies

Irae" motive fused with a distorted, fat, and ugly "Deutschland über Alles."

Yeah. *Genocide* was easier to do simply because the musical atmosphere was something with which I was more familiar. And with that kind of subject matter, it's hard to miss.

Let's talk for a bit about animation, and two pictures in particular, *The Black Cauldron* and *Heavy Metal*. What was your *Heavy Metal* experience like?

Heavy Metal was a sort of bastardized concept. The *original* concept was very, very interesting. Originally, Joe Walsh, when he was with The Eagles, and I were going to do it together. Joe was going to take care of the rock thing and I was going to take care of the orchestral scoring. In the long run, as you know, they got a lot of different groups together, so the music is not in any way integrated—you have rock songs and a symphonic score that have nothing to do with each other. I had fun doing the score, just letting loose. We had a huge orchestra, and I thought that the music was very satisfying to do. I saw the film recently and thought that it could have been such a wonderful film, but it just never really jelled.

The Black Cauldron?

I found that really, really difficult. The animation world is a very different world. Psychologically, it's funny. When you're used to looking at real people all the time, you learn to identify with real people. Plus, I'm a *real* person, so there's a built-in association. I found it very difficult to identify with the drawings. But, it was enjoyable. I was thrilled, I remember, when I got the assignment to do it. It was a terrific ride for me.

It was another situation where the project was different, so you took it?

That's right, exactly. Very different. That's why I was so thrilled when I got it.

You've used the Ondes Martenot, an electronic keyboard instrument, in dozens of your scores. How did this start?

It's a long story; I'll make it as quick as I can. In 1981, I was invited to do a series of lectures at a film-music weekend in England. Sharing the program with me was Christopher Palmer, who was my orchestrator at the time, and another composer, Richard Rodney Bennett. During the course of the lectures, Richard Rodney Bennett and Christopher talked about the Ondes Martenot the whole time. I didn't know the instrument. When the conference was over, I asked Chris, "What was that you were talking about?" He said, "Well, it's an instrument," and he described it to me. And he said, "As a matter of fact, there's a really good place for it in *Heavy Metal*." I asked where, and he gave me his suggestions. So I said, "Fine, let's use it if you think it's the thing to do." So we got Jeanne Loriod, who's the great "Queen of Ondes" in France, to come over and play it. I'll never forget it: The Ondes Martenot was set up behind me. And when I started to conduct and she started to play that thing, my hair stood up! I was just absolutely blown away by the sound of that instrument. After that, I realized I had to learn more about it. I said to Chris, "We've got to get somebody who'd be willing to learn this instrument and tell me about it, how it works." Well, a very bright young lady, Cynthia Millar, had played the piano on some pieces of mine. So, Christopher said, "How about the pianist, that bright young lady?" I said, "Cool!" I asked her if she'd be willing to be paid to learn the instrument well enough that she could teach it to me and teach it to somebody else. She said she'd do that. So she went to study with Jeanne Loriod, and she also studied with a man in England. She fell in love with the instrument and said to me, "I want to play it." To make a long story short, she's now one of the world's foremost experts on the Ondes.

She's just terrific. She just did Messiaen's *Turangalila* with us here in L.A., and she's done it with Previn and a lot of orchestras. She's all over the world.

And she does a few film scores.

Yes. She became a composer. She's working on a film as we speak.

In *My Left Foot*, and in many of your other intimate, transparent chamber scores, you use the Ondes as a melodic instrument. But then, occasionally, as in *The Black Cauldron*, you use it as a spooky sound effect, a kind of a post-1950s-Universal Studios sci-fi theremin.

Its use in a film like *Twilight* was very subtle indeed. You would hardly notice it as itself.

Allow me to make a big jump: from the Ondes Martenot to Danny Kaye, Sylvia Fine, and your *The Court Jester* experience. There's no credit for Elmer Bernstein, but you worked on the score?

Not exactly. Basically, I worked with Sylvia, who is a songwriter, but not a trained musician. I transcribed the songs for her and helped with some of the arrangements and that kind of thing. I was sort of a music secretary. I really didn't deserve the credit. What I did in *Oklahoma* would have more deserved a credit. I was the rehearsal pianist and did the ballets for the film. But I didn't get a credit on that, either.

Did Cecil B. DeMille come to you for *The Buccaneer* and say he wanted the same kind of effect you gave him for *The Ten Commandments*?

No. He didn't say anything. DeMille, first of all, tended to be very loyal to his people. I had just done the music for *The Ten Commandments*, which he liked a lot, and he didn't tell me much at all about the music for *Buccaneer*. But, since I knew him, I knew what he would expect.

Tell me a bit about the jazz influences in *The Man With the Golden Arm*, *Some Came Running*, etc. How did you come to utilize that genre in such uncharted waters?

My father was a great jazz aficionado. In the house, we always had records playing—Louis Armstrong records, Kid Ory, and all those great old jazz people. I was brought up with that. It was part of my musical heritage. I was never a jazz pianist or anything like that—my training was classical—but jazz was sort of in my head. When I did *The Man With the Golden Arm*, I had no idea of the impact the music was going to have. It seemed to me just the right thing to do at the time. Here was a film about a tough guy who wanted to be a jazz drummer, and that was his whole life, that was his musical environment. So, it came to me very naturally, not realizing that it had never been done in quite that way before. Jazz used that way appeals to me very much. And I enjoy the direct, driving force that it has. It's a tremendous force. In *The Man With the Golden Arm* and *The Sweet Smell of Success*, it sort of bangs right on.

In *The Man With the Golden Arm*, in the scene where Frankie Machine is trying to quit drugs, to go cold turkey, your score goes totally bonkers with almost Don Cherry-style action jazz, free-jazz improvisation.

Yeah. The withdrawal sequence was one of the rare times, probably the only time, I had one of these experiences where I didn't know what the hell to do. But I just got up in the middle of the night one night and knew exactly what to do. I went to the piano and wrote it down.

In *Sweet Smell of Success*, the audience sees Chico Hamilton, Fred

Katz, and Paul Horn, who were all major figures in their time, playing in a combo. Was this a collaboration that included you?

Well, let's put it this way, there was a lot of contact. I listened to what they were doing, and we talked about it.

Hoodlum and *The Rainmaker* recall your *The Man With the Golden Arm, Sweet Smell of Success,* and *Some Came Running* approach to scoring. Do current directors often call you because they want that particular kind of score?

No, I don't think so. In the case of *Hoodlum*, I'd done two pictures with Bill Duke previously. It was just working together. In the case of Francis Ford Coppola and *The Rainmaker*, Francis was one of the executive producers of *Buddy*, and it was from *Buddy* that the connection was made. Originally, Francis wasn't going to have an original score in *The Rainmaker*. He was going to do it all with source music, Memphis stuff. And then he decided that he needed a score. Actually, the score evolved through a great deal of discussion with Coppola. We retained a lot of that Memphis flavor in the score—the Hammond B-3 organ, which is something we don't hear a lot these days, the muted trumpet, the guitar, and all that sort of thing.

In *The Rainmaker,* in the big attack on Kelly's husband, all the elements of the score come together, thrown into a musical blender and poured out over this ultra-violent scene.

That's right! I composed the basic structure for it, and the solo instruments improvised wildly over that structure. I didn't care what they played, it just had to be wild and uncontrolled, bloodcurdling.

Film scholars often discuss the direct correlation between *The Magnificent Seven* and Kurosawa's *Seven Samurai.*

Well, believe it or not, I never saw *The Seven Samurai* until many years after I did *The Magnificent Seven*. At the time of *The Magnificent Seven*, I didn't know that Kurosawa's film even existed. So that was never an issue for me. If it *had* been an issue, it would still be a non-issue because the films have very little to do with each other, really. I treated *The Magnificent Seven* for what it was in itself. I always wanted to do a Western, so that was one of the films I fought very hard to get. And I really enjoyed it. But, ultimately, it led to too many Westerns for me. I think I did John Wayne's last seven films.

Your score for *The Shootist* is transparent and detached, and it gradually disintegrates along the way. Was that a psychological choice because John Wayne's character is dying through the course of the picture?

No, not so much. Well, let me put it this way: Emotionally, it was bare because he was dying. I don't mean dying as a person, but as the character in the film, although he was also dying as a person at that point. In the film, there was really no room to open up for beauty, because it was not about beauty—it was not about the big country, which you normally play in Westerns. It was about death. It was about a dying man. It was pretty grim.

The Comancheros, **which you worked on a year after *The Magnificent Seven*, is another film that turned out to be its director's last effort.**

[Laughter] Yeah, look out for me! I've worked on everybody's last film. *Boots Malone* was William Dieterle's last film, or his next-to-his-last film; *The Comancheros* was Michael Curtiz's last film; *Seven Women* was John Ford's last film. There are others.

Was working with Michael Curtiz, the highly respected European-born director of the Errol Flynn classics, a daunting experience for you as a young composer?

What was much more daunting was meeting John Wayne! John Wayne was like a monument! He was a great figure of a man. In those days, directors had relatively little input into the scoring. I don't remember, offhand, ever discussing the score for *The Comancheros* with anybody but the Newmans.

In your Western scores are numerous mixed-meter jazz rhythms— fives, sevens, 3+3+2s, and so on—that emerge with a Western atmosphere, a Western aesthetic. Is your inspiration a mix of jazz and Copland?

Probably so. I've always been interested in keeping rhythm alive. If you fall into a four pattern for a very, very long time, you don't necessarily lose interest, but it can become numbing. You can certainly heighten interest by doing something unexpected, rhythmically.

Your comedies, *Animal House*, *Airplane!* . . .

At first, I really enjoyed all that. It all started when John Landis called me to do *Animal House*. I've known John since he was a young man; he and my son were best friends in high school. When he described what *Animal House* was, I said, "Why me? What's this all about?" And he said, "Come look at the film, and we'll have a chat." I looked at the film, and it was very funny. John said that the idea was not to score it as a comedy, but as a dramatic film. So that's what I did. And I think the effect is very funny. In *Airplane!*, I took it a step further and made up a role for the composer—here's this young, inexperienced composer composing this score; here's somebody who's worked on minor, low-budget films all his life and, finally, this is his big chance to do a big score for a big film!

In *Spies Like Us*, you have a sweeping, expansive theme that is used many times. It is especially effective as they're crawling across the desert. Very *Lawrence of Arabia*ish. Is that a specific reference?

No, but it was intentionally almost *Lawrence of Arabia.*

Zulu Dawn is one of your more propulsively aggressive percussion-oriented scores. Did you research the indigenous music?

Oh, no, no, no, because there were some tracks of that kind of stuff—the real thing—already in there. There's one particular sequence in *Zulu Dawn* that I really liked a lot—the sequence where the army moves off. It's a big movement early on in the film. And I enjoyed the association with director Douglas Hickox, it was lovely.

For *Hawaii*, did you research Hawaiian music?

Yes, very much. I actually went over to Hawaii on several occasions and spoke to historians and listened to local folk musicians. One historian I spoke to was a lady who took care of the tombs of the kings. Fascinating. We did a lot of research on *Hawaii.*

In the *Cape Fear* remake, you reworked Bernard Herrmann's score for the original *Cape Fear.*

That was a job I went after. I'd met Martin Scorsese because he had produced *The Grifters.* When I heard he was redoing *Cape Fear*, I called him and said I'd love to do it. And he said there was really nothing in it for me to do—he was going to use Herrmann's original score. I said, "Well, Herrmann was an idol of mine. I'd really like to be involved somehow. It would be a big thrill for me." In the long run, we were pretty faithful to the original. We didn't mess with his music, but it was not always in the same place that it had been in the original film. I contributed, as a composer, relatively little. I wrote half of the main title and some connective things, but it's mostly all original Herrmann. Some of it had to be re-orchestrated from his sketches because we didn't have access to all of the original scores. I also incorporated some music from the rejected Herrmann score for Hitchcock's *Torn Curtain* into the *Cape Fear* score. It was a great experience working with Herrmann's music and Scorsese. It was a tough film to live with, though, a really scary film.

Mad Dog and Glory interpolates rap music into your orchestral score.

Actually, I've done several scores with a lot of interpolated music. If you take a film like, let's say, *The Devil in the Blue Dress*, which has a lot source music and very little score, somehow or other they work quite well together, surprisingly. But that's because Carl Franklin is a director of tremendous taste. In the case of *Mad Dog and Glory*, there are a few things interpolated, but they really don't particularly impact on the score.

The Good Son is an intense, versatile score. You have the gift of musically conjuring up the magic of children—whether they're good children, bad children, cartoon children, adult children, or To Kill a Mockingbird children dealing with racism.

I like kids. Now, before *The Good Son*, I had just finished *The Age of Innocence*, and this was about as different as you could get! That was the great attraction of doing *The Good Son*. I remember, in particular, I liked some things I did early on in that score. There's a sort of interesting, sad feeling in that score.

For both kids—the good kid and the evil kid. And there is a detached, icy coldness to your score that envelopes the evil kid's actions. That score, along with such more recent scores as Buddy and Hoodlum, shows that you're often involved with making a strong emotional connection. There seem to be many times when you definitely have one foot in the Korngold/Steiner corner. Do you feel it's important to keep such traditions alive? Many younger film composers seem to ignore those opportunities.

Well, it's strictly horses for courses. It's the shoe fitting. I'm prepared to do whatever the film needs. The film talks to me. I don't talk to the film. I'll get hold of a film and look at it twenty times. I'll spend one week just looking at the film—once in the morning, once in the afternoon—until the film tells me what to do. I'm not married to any particular type of procedure. I'm not a disciple of any particular style. But I believe there are times when it's good for the music to be very specific to a scene, sometimes even very specific to an action.

Has your approach to composing for film—your actual working habits and procedures—changed much over the years? Have you always let the film sort of wash over you for a week?

What has stayed the same is that the film *always* talks to me. The film is the thing, and if you want to talk about letting the film wash over me, yes, always. Generally, my working procedure is to learn the film by myself before I have to talk to a lot of people about it. I'm much better off if I have a chance to develop some of my own ideas about what should be done before I begin to hear what other people have to say.

In recent years, I'm a little bit less devoted to the necessity of starting with, so to speak, a particular theme. Possibly because the films today are not as demanding of such a thing. A film like *Twilight*, for instance, is an atmosphere. The film I just finished, *The Deep End of the Ocean*, is a film that had to be treated very delicately. There was really no place in it for a big theme. I'm more willing now to approach a film in terms of its atmosphere rather than what the big theme should be.

What are your thoughts about the state of film music today?

I think that the state of film music is a reflection of the state of commercial motion pictures, which is a reflection of the state of the times. I think it's unfortunate that composers have a very difficult time getting a chance to write real film music, good film music. It's not for lack of talent—talent is tremendous out here. There are all sorts of gifted people, but they don't get much of a chance to really write good stuff because of the nature of the films. I ask everybody this question: "When was the last time you came out of a theater and could really remember something—sing me something, tell me something about the music, tell me about what you've heard?" [Laughter] But that's not necessarily the fault of the composers. The talent is out there. I teach at USC and, I'll tell you, any one of those people I teach at USC could do a film right now.

terence BLANCHARD

Jazz of one style or another is not uncommon in movies, and jazz musicians, among them Quincy Jones, Duke Ellington, and Oliver Nelson, have long been composing original film scores. With jazz-influenced scores, as with every style of score, what distinguishes successful, innovative work from hackneyed pastiche is the composer's ability to capture the dramatic essence of a scene by any means necessary. Today, no jazz-based composer does this better than internationally acclaimed trumpeter, composer, and arranger Terence Blanchard, whose film music extends and expands on the legacy of those artists mentioned above while, at the same time, creating a highly charged, personal musical language.

Closely associated with the films of director Spike Lee, Blanchard's scores for *Jungle Fever* (1991), *Malcolm X* (1992), *Crooklyn* (1994), *Clockers* (1995), and *Get on the Bus* (1996) showcase a versatile composer of reflective, emotional music that speaks directly to the human condition. Such other Blanchard scores as *Assault at West Point* (1994), *Trial by Jury* (1994), *Eve's Bayou* (1997), and *Summer of Sam* (1999) display his fine ability to capture mood, time, and place.

Blanchard remains extremely busy on both the jazz concert circuit and in the film-music world. We met on a Friday afternoon at his Embassy Suites Hotel room in New York City, where he was relaxing before his evening performance at the Blue Note.

terence BLANCHARD

You are one of the few Hollywood film composers who has a complete, full-time other life in jazz. You've been doing jazz much longer than you've been doing film music. What attracted you to film?

It was *School Daze*. I was just a side man on the session. Spike [Lee] wanted an orchestra, and his father, who's a jazz musician, hired a guy by the name of Harold Vick to do the contracting. By him being a jazz guy, he hired nothing but jazz musicians. And they called me to play on the session. I met Spike through them. Spike is the kind of guy who is all business. When I met him it was like, "Hey, how're you doin', man," and then he was gone. Then I came back and played on *Do the Right Thing* and *Mo' Better Blues*. During the prerecords for *Mo' Better Blues*, I sat down at the piano and started playing one of my compositions that I was getting ready to do for my first solo project for Columbia. Spike heard it and said, "Man, what is that?" I said, "Well, this is something that I'm working on." Later, he said, "That song, can I use that?" And I said, "Sure."

In which film?

We used it in *Mo' Better Blues*, and Spike liked it a great deal. We had recorded it as a solo trumpet piece for when Denzel [Washington] was on the bridge. This is right when he kind of got it that Wesley [Snipes] was sleeping with his girl. So, he was depressed.

He walked on the bridge and pulled out his horn. When Spike saw the scene, he thought that it was kind of empty. So he said, "Can you do a string arrangement for it?" I said, "Yeah." I'd never done one before, but I thought, shit, what does that matter? So, I called my composition teacher in New Orleans and said, "Look, man, I got this thing I need to do."

Who was your teacher?

Roger Nixon. He's composed a lot of great pieces. So, Roger says, "You know what to do. Just rely on your instincts." That was that kind of prophetic thing that teachers do. When I did the arrangement, Spike loved it and said, "You have a future in writing for film." I'll never forget that. I'm like, "Yeah, right, man. Okay." And then the film came out and everything was cool. Afterwards he called me to write the score to *Jungle Fever*. I was like, "Yeah, okay, cool." When I got off the phone, I thought, "Damn, I got a whole film to do now."

You'd struck a nerve and started up another classic collaboration, like Herrmann and Hitchcock.

Yeah. But what was funny was that he was so stuck on that melody from *Mo' Better Blues*, that that's what we used as the main theme for *Jungle Fever*. I kept writing all these other things, and he'd say, "No, that ain't it." And I'd say, "Well, what about this?" And he'd say, "No, that ain't it." Then, finally, I guess he just got tired and said, "You know that thing for *Mo' Better Blues*? Why don't we just use that? We only heard it once in *Mo' Better Blues*. People are not really going to recognize it." I said, "Okay, fine."

You recently released an album honoring the Jazz Messengers. What was your connection with that group?

People always call that band the finishing school for jazz composers. Art Blakey was the kind of guy who really nurtured young talent.

And he did it in such an interesting way for me. He just let us go, basically. It was almost like the grandparent syndrome: The parents are the ones who say, "No, don't do this; no, don't do that." But the grandparents are the ones who kind of let the children run wild. They just make sure the children don't fall or burn themselves. They basically let the children do what they need to do to figure out things. That's how Art was. He let us run the band. We had to write all the compositions. Everybody in that band had a talent for writing.

When were you with the band?

I was in the band from 1982 through 1986. I was the musical director. I called all the shows, called all the rehearsals. It was a great experience for me. Here's a guy, Art, a great legend, who just gave me this safety net to work in. He kept telling us, "Look, you're in the band. You need to take advantage of this situation. Why don't you just write the craziest shit you ever dreamed of and, if it doesn't work, we'll try to figure out a way to make it work." That was a good thing for me. Before that, I was in Lionel Hampton's band, which was a totally different situation. With Art, I learned a lot about life. I learned a lot about music. I learned a lot about the history of music. I learned how to pace myself with the shows. And I learned how to just deal with people. I always tell people I felt like I aged forty years in four years. Art Blakey was the kind of guy, very much like a Miles Goodman, who'd never talk down to anybody, and never talk above them. You've got to talk right straight to your audience. That's what they want, and that's what they deserve.

He sounds almost like a spiritual musical mentor.

He did a lot for me. When I got into jazz, man, I wanted to be Miles Davis—I wanted to be the cutting edge, just out there, a free-wheeling, crazy jazz musician. I thought, what better gig than Art Blakey? He was like *the* "jazz messenger" himself. He was a pioneer in music. When I got in his band, the first thing he made me realize was there's still a show—it's still entertainment, people pay money to hear us play. It threw me for a loop because this was a guy who I thought was true to his art. Fuck everybody else, he needed to express himself. You know what I mean? The thing that I learned was he had all of those qualities, but he knew how to bring them together to make it entertaining for other people. That's when I started appreciating people like Louis Armstrong. You start to see that Duke Ellington, Louis Armstrong, and all of those people had great stage presence, but they were still great musicians and you could never deny that. When I was a kid, we used to talk about how Louis Armstrong was an Uncle Tom. But when you get older, you start to realize how ignorant a statement that really is, because of what he brought to the music. It's like Sammy Davis. Sammy Davis brought a lot to the entertainment industry. And we can't look at these musicians without looking at the times in which they were working.

And the limitations they were working under.

Exactly. And when you look at that, it even makes them greater.

Mark Twain said, "The older I get, the smarter my father gets."

That's true. You want to hear a story about that? That's how I felt about my father. When I was a kid, I grew up with a cousin in the house. His name was Eric Ray. Eric got a set of drums, a red, metallic set. Man, I'll never forget it. Eric was so excited when he got it, he set it up in the living room and started playing this James Brown soul beat. He played it for like two hours straight. I guess my dad got frustrated, so he said, "Get up, let me show you something." My dad had studied opera and wanted to be an opera singer, but he also hung out with the jazz musicians. He is like eighty-three now, so he hung out with some of the famous guys. So, my dad said, "Look, you don't know how to play the drums, boy, let me show you how to play them." He sat down on the drums and played

4/4 on the bass drum and 2/4 on the high hat. Man, we thought that was some of the corniest shit we had ever heard. We fell out laughing. We were like on the floor. He got upset. He said, "Man, you all don't want to learn nothing," and he went in the back.

You remember this so clearly—it has stuck with you a long time.

Yeah. I went through all of my growing up, through all my music schooling and all of that shit, and I got to this Miles Davis phase I was talking about—you know, being on the cutting edge. I go through all that shit, play with Lionel Hampton and all those cats, and I finally get to Art Blakey, the man who I figured was like my new jazz savior. Well, we do this first gig and he plays 4/4 on the bass drum and 2/4 on the high hat! Can you imagine my surprise? I looked at that shit and I called my dad and apologized. He didn't understand what I was talking about because he had forgotten all about it. But I said, "Man, he's doing exactly what you did." That blew me away. So, that's really true: The older you get, the smarter your father gets.

In *Jungle Fever*, a number of strategic scenes have no music or have the music abruptly stop. How strong is the Spike Lee influence on those dramatic moments?

Very, very strong. Even today, he's that way. Spike'll say, "I want music to start here; and I want music to be out there." But he'll give me a little leeway—like a few seconds. The interesting thing about *Jungle Fever* was I didn't see the video for it. I didn't have video or film or nothing. But that was part of Spike's growth process back then. He was a young filmmaker, and like most young filmmakers, he had this kind of paranoia about his film getting out to the public, which is a valid thing. I would go to dailies and see it there. I just had time sheets, starting and ending times. I can't watch that film because there were some things that I tried to do that didn't work.

Could you give an example?

The last part of the film, when Wesley goes back to talk to his wife and sees his daughter was a real tender moment. He's leaning over the bed, and the fucking orchestra is huge! It's just wailing away. And I sit there and go, "Oh, man, turn it down! It's just too damn big!" That's part of the problem with trying to sit down to write a score without being able say, "Look, this is what's happening here."

After that experience, did you say you needed to see a little more film footage?

Oh, yeah. When we did *Malcolm X*, I said, "There's no way that I can do this film like *Jungle Fever*." Spike understood. He's an interesting guy because he's very determined and very opinionated about certain things. But when he sees the benefit of something, he reacts. He's not stubborn in that way. So, when he saw the benefits of what that did for the music, he was fine. And, as a matter of fact, on the last film that I did with him, *Get on the Bus*, I got three sets of tapes—I got ∫inch, I got °-inch, I got 8mm.

In one scene in *Jungle Fever*, Angie's brothers pick on her little Italian boyfriend. The three of them sit on the front steps, and the brothers ask him, "You fuckin' our sister?" It's a humorous moment, and the music is almost a little variation of "New York, New York" in a light, contrapuntal texture. The three characters are in a dialogue with vibraphone, then trumpet, then flute. When Angie comes out, as the fourth character, it's an entirely new tune, and then they all interact.

Yeah. When I got my very first film, I was really excited and started studying scores. I studied Stravinsky's *Rite of Spring*, Debussy's *Nocturnes*. But once I got to see the picture, I realized, "None of this shit's going to work!" So I had to sit down and think about the characters. And when I did that, I started to realize that Spike was really doing "dramodies," for lack of a better term. I started to understand that some of the shit was comedic. My jazz background took over, I saw where I needed to play up the personal side of the characters. That whole macho thing of "You fuckin' my sister?" was kind of a put-on—they were just messing around. And that's the thing I really wanted to show, because I know some guys take that shit seriously. When she came out, I kept feeling this frustration for her, like "I live in this situation; I'm surrounded by this shit. This really ain't me, but I gotta deal with it, so let me just go on out of here and deal with it and go about my business." That scene was one of the ones that was real easy to score. What's going on is in your face.

Spike's certainly right—you *do* have a future in film, because I don't believe that scene would be so in-your-face to a lot of other composers. I brought up that particular scene because it showed such a natural playing out of subtle comedic elements.

Well, maybe it's because I lived in New York, too, that I understood it. Maybe I had some sort of instinct. You know, only do films that you know the social issues of.

You don't want to score any cowboy pictures?

No! Well, you know what I have a fear of doing? Comedy.

But in *Jungle Fever*, with Ossie Davis as the crazy, off-the-edge Baptist minister, you played off that kind of thing so naturally with the gospel choirs, the tongue-in-cheek orchestra . . .

This is where I started to realize how music can add and how music can get in the way. Spike and I had a disagreement about this one particular scene where he used a source cue at the end of the movie where the good reverend shoots his son. I saw that scene with no music—to draw right into the mother's pain. Right in. I cried because this mother is anguishing over her son. And the reverend's completely out of it—he's like in a zone, he's somewhere else. You hear this woman screaming for her son and, man, it just drew me right to it. I told Spike, "That shit is powerful without music." But he wanted to put a hymn there. So we put the hymn there. It works, but it's a little distracting for me because it kind of takes you out of it.

Using the hymn, you become more of an observer, rather than being right there with her. Do you think Spike chose to include the hymn in that scene to add more power to the fact that the good reverend was becoming "non-reverendly"?

No, I think he chose it because the reverend always used to listen to those hymns on the record player. And, see, that's the interesting thing about film—everybody looks at one scene and sees different stuff. To me, that's the most amazing thing about this shit. In *Crooklyn*, I fucked up a scene like that, and we had to go back and correct it. It was a scene where this little girl goes on vacation and her mother writes her a letter. The girl gets the letter, and as she starts to read it, you can hear the mother narrating it. Then the letter goes into real time, where you actually see the action of the letter. The action of the letter's kind of funny. I played up the emotional thing of the girl missing her family, the emotional thing of her sitting down reading this letter, and then it gets to the comedic shit, where I played the comedy. We recorded it like that, and then Spike went back, looked at it again, and said, "You know what? I think we missed it on that. I think we should go back and just play the emotion of the letter because this is the little girl's moment." So that's what we did. I had to rewrite the whole thing and just do the little girl. It makes the comedy different. But it was cool. That's the way it goes. And that's why you have directors.

There's a lot of source music in *Crooklyn*—salsa, Motown, *Soul Train* kind of music. Do you have a lot of input on which tunes are selected for the film?

Spike does everything. The only thing he really calls me to do is to write the score. But he's got to tell me what the source music is going to be. I've got to know what's up front of me and what's behind me at all times. And he's pretty good about that.

In *Crooklyn*, the dad is an aspiring jazz composer/performer. When he finally gets his big break, his big concert, is it Terence Blanchard music that he plays?

Yeah. That's my thing, but it's Roland Hanna playing it. At one point, they shot a scene with one of his kids playing. They didn't use it in the final film, which is kind of strange because it was a lot of fun. Spike was cracking up. He had a good time watching us record this. So, here you have Roland Hanna sitting at the piano, and I'm sitting next to him. Roland is playing my song, and I have to act like I'm his little kid. I'm just like wacking out, man. We had a great time doing that.

In the *Crooklyn* scene where time gets compressed, the music is humorous, almost cartoonish. This is after they get to the relatives' house, but before the dog dies and they have the funeral for the dog. It's all really fun, and your music plays along with it in a kind of squished way, too.

We really wanted to play up the notion of this out-to-lunch aunt, because we all had relatives like that. We could have gone a number of ways with that: We could have played up the kids' reaction to the shit, but we didn't want to deal with that, we wanted to stay more with the crazy aunt. When I saw that scene, it told me exactly what to do. I said, "Okay, I know what's going on."

That's the great thing about Spike and our relationship. Spike is very detailed in terms of where he wants the music. He's very detailed in terms of the melodic material for the music. Once all of that is done, he lets me go. He doesn't even want to talk to me until we get to the session. I feel good that he has that much confidence in me.

So it has pretty much evolved into a Spike Lee/Terence Blanchard collaboration?

It's at the point where he doesn't have to tell me much. He'll give me general information of what he wants for a scene—he'll say, "Look, man, I want a small score—maybe your band and some synths." Well, that was a big revelation for Spike, because he was not at all into synthesizers. I used them on *Clockers* and he really liked the sound. I said that maybe we could use some strings in some select spots. He said, "Fine," and that was it. Simple. I sent him some tapes and asked, "What do you think of this theme? That theme?"

Since he trusts me so much, he likes to get in the studio. And although he doesn't tell me, he tells everybody else, "Let's see what he came up with for this scene." He really likes that. And then he tweaks here and there—just minor stuff, not major. He never cuts my music. Out of all the films I've done with him, I think only one scene has been cut.

That's something to treasure. I haven't heard that story from anybody else.

I know. When I started working with other directors, oh boy. I worked with one director who was just laying cues on top of cues. I got to the screening and I said, "Oh, shit! This is what this is really like? Spike, Help!"

I have a few specific questions about *Clockers*. When Strike's in his room, playing with his trains, the camera cuts back and forth

from Strike's escapist environment to the heavy drug deals going down on the corner. Every time we get back to Strike, the camera's a little more distant, and your two contrasting styles of music begin to fuse. The scene seems pregnant with so many possibilities that it could be either wonderfully inspirational or confusing for the composer.

It was all of that. When I first looked at that scene, my initial reaction was to write something very cold and solitary for the drug dealers and something light and busy for Strike. When he's in that train room, he's a little kid! He's no drug dealer, he's another guy, you know? But I decided *not* to take that approach. I decided Strike should have the solitary music, almost as if he's playing with his trains and praying, "Man, I gotta get out of this fucking shit. Why am I doing this? This is crazy!" You know what I mean? Like he's reflecting back on what's going on with these pregnant girls out there buying drugs. That shit was the dramatic part—how ludicrous this shit really is. Here you have this guy who realizes the woman is pregnant and he still sells her the drugs. For me, that was a very heartfelt, very powerful situation.

Composing against the action, you enhance the tragedy for the audience?

Yeah. I wanted the shock of it to register with people. That's one of those scenes that could be used in a film school as an exercise for the kids to score in a number of different ways. There are many ways to view it, and everybody has their own opinions. Oddly enough, for me, that was one of the scenes that was screaming for a lot of music. When I watched it without the music, it just didn't register. With film scoring, we get a chance to express the intangible. I wanted to make a commentary on that scene and say, "Here's this drug dealer, sitting all alone. This is a drug dealer who loves being by himself." That's something you don't normally equate with the drug culture. You think of all these guys being in this gang together, always hanging together. But this guy, when he finished doing his job, he'd go home and relax and play with his trains. By taking this whole solitary approach with him, musically, it forced me to go in another direction for the girls.

It's an incredibly powerful scene, and I feel that your musical choices have contributed a lot to its success. Equally powerful is the scene at the end of the film when Rodney's jumping on Strike's car and trashing it with a baseball bat. Many composers would simply have written baseball-bat-smashing-the-car violence music, but you surprise us with this cold, quiet, detached, atonal string orchestra—you composed against the action. For me, it intensified the tragedy of their lives.

That's a real surreal fucking moment. It's one of those moments where the shit is so dramatic that it's unreal. So, I wanted it to be surreal. I wanted it to be one of these almost operatic moments. Actually, I wish we could've used a choir for that one scene. Rodney's so fucking pissed off. He treated this boy like a son, like a little brother. His world is about to crumble. For me, the other side of Rodney's frustration is that Strike's actually turning out to be a decent guy, which is what Rodney really wanted to be. That's what I saw as his frustration. He was smashing the car because he was pissed off at Strike and pissed off at himself, and he's just losing it.

Trashing everything, and the car is the symbol of his ruined life?

Exactly. The symbol of what's going on with him. If you've ever been *that* angry, it's like reality goes out the fucking window. And when you come back, you're like, "Damn. What did I do?"

The Inkwell has very little underscore. It's there mostly for long shots of the ocean or the mountains. There are a lot of pop tunes.

Was that a frustrating score? Did you wish you had more opportunity?

I wish I had more direction. That was an interesting film to score because that was my first lesson in dealing with scripts. It was a great script. I can't emphasize that enough. That's what attracted me to the movie. The thing I loved about it, being black in America, was that we finally had diversity within one family—different opinions. One guy was a Republican, the other guy was a Black Panther. You can't get any broader spectrum than that! This whole thing about them having discussions about class and culture and all that shit really intrigued me. This script could be about anybody. It's not a script for a black family—it's colorless.

But when I saw the film, I was disappointed. It was a lot lighter than what I had expected. The issues weren't handled in the same way that I thought they would have been handled. It was a totally different film, and I had to reorganize in my thinking. When I talked to the director, he didn't have much input at all, which was very frustrating for me. There are some hard scenes in that film—hard scenes in terms of the script and in terms of the acting. And that was one of the first movies where my music got cut. We did a jazz thing for a locale and another jazz thing for the opening credits—a simple melodic thing, a simple swing thing, not a lot of rhythms, very easygoing. Everybody loved it. Everybody loved it, right?

This is where my jazz career gets me in trouble sometimes. Scheduling problems for jazz-concert engagements didn't allow me to go to the film mix. That's where all of this got turned around. The music editor was a friend of mine, so he called me up and said, "Look, man, I'm just warning you: There are a lot of changes being made here, stuff's getting turned around." When he told me about the opening credits, I said, "Wait, that song for the opening credits was a source cue. There's a lot of talk, it's a party scene—I basically stayed out of the way. I didn't want to distract the dialogue, so I just wrote the musical glue. I wrote some horn parts, and I did the 1970s Earth, Wind & Fire thing." He told me they used that for the opening credits and I said, "Oh, no!" So, I had a long discussion with the director. That was a rough one. Now I could see what these guys were talking about—I started to learn. It's tough when you put all of your efforts into something you really believe in, and somebody just says, "I don't like that."

The director was using your score, but not where you'd originally intended?

Yeah. Take something else that you were using for some*place* else and put that over there.

As you indicated a few moments ago, sometimes you work so hard and you pour your heart and soul into a project, but the director simply says, "No, I don't like that." I suppose that artists who face this sort of thing either become numb to this kind of rejection or collapse under the pressure. As you go on in your film career, will this problem become easier or more difficult to deal with?

I'm not sure. I think it becomes easier because you just get tough-skinned. But there are a lot of guys who retire, who don't want to deal with it anymore. I think it's easier for me because I have another career: I have something else to go to. I play whatever I want to play on my own show. But it is frustrating, and that's the thing you can't get around. One guy told me that the reason we get paid a lot of money is because ten percent is for actually writing the music, the other ninety percent is for the frustration and aggravation.

The aggravation of having to deal with all the other people making decisions about the music?

Yeah. I'll probably get no more work because of that line.

Two big courtroom dramas: *Assault at West Point* and *Trial by Jury*. One is an all-black trial movie, one is an all-white trial movie. Both scores demonstrate a very similar compositional approach, and the tunes are very similar. I transcribed them and found that the *Trial by Jury* motive is almost an exact inversion of the *Assault at West Point* motive. Which came first?

Assault at West Point, I think, came first.

In the opening credits of *Trial by Jury*, the score floats around an extended C pedal, then the title of the movie suddenly comes up and, wham, a big harmonic change—good, old-fashioned, dramatic mickey-mousing.

Yeah, yeah yeah. That's a definite film thing. And the director wanted that. I just wish I could have had a big orchestra. The orchestra doesn't sound as big as it should have sounded. It's like, "Okay, man, I did it," but it was really screaming for one of those big, hundred-piece orchestras. I've been at big sessions like that. I hung out at the *Sommersby* session. Danny Elfman had written the opening credits. That shit was *bad*—it was big, it was huge—and that orchestra was enveloping. While they were playing, I was thinking, "Man, this is it!" Then the director said, "That's too much." So they had to pare it all down.

Trial by Jury seems more chromatic and harmonically advanced than *Assault at West Point*. But, in both films, every time we return to the court, there's a big curtain-raiser shock chord, and then no music at all during the trial scenes.

That's a director's thing. Directors have this reverence for the courtroom. This was especially the case in *Assault at West Point*. If you notice, when they pan across the court—the American flag and all that shit—it's like, "Man, this is it!"
   Trial by Jury was the first film that I had done with a director who

didn't want any melody. But he didn't know how to say it. He kept saying that my music was making too much of a statement on the scene. I kept saying, "I thought that was my job." I was confused as to what he really wanted. Then, at some point, it just clicked. I took the melody out and I played some other stuff for him, and he said, "Yeah, that's it." He wanted a lot of underscore—colors.

For me, the most important thing about this business is the communication between the director and the composer. It's a serious issue. You've got two people who basically grew up and developed in two totally different areas: Directors are dealing with color, lighting, and all that stuff; musicians are dealing with music. All of a sudden, directors come to the music and now they have to try to figure out how to communicate what it is that they want. That's why a lot of composers like working with the same directors over and over. You establish a cool relationship and a pattern where you can communicate and understand each other. I talk to a lot of guys about this. They all have the same problem. When I work with a new director, I try to get a lot of information. I probably piss them off.

Because you're always hanging around, asking questions?

Yeah. Because I really want to know. Because I really want to get it right. I don't want to take anything for granted because—especially in my situation—I'm labeled with the term "jazz," and that means a ton of things to a lot of people. When people tell me they want it to be "jazzy," I need to know exactly what it is that they're talking about, because that means one thing to me, but it could mean something totally different to them, and I've had that experience.

I was up for this film, so I flew out to L.A. to meet with the director. I told him, "Look, I just don't hear jazz for your film, I hear a small chamber ensemble or maybe even a small orchestra, with some quirky kind of music." But the director was a jazz fan. He said, "What about something like Thelonious Monk?" I said, "Well, I *could* do that," but I kept reiterating that I didn't hear jazz for this film. And he kept saying, "I'm right with you, man. I'm right on the mark. You're going in the right direction." So, I go through all of that and then the director calls my agent and says, "Well, Terence is great, but I don't want a jazz score." That's one of the big frustrations for me in this business. People just want to categorize me as a jazz musician, which I am, and I'm proud of that. I'm not trying to run away from that label. But that's a big problem for me, a big problem. People hear my name and say, "Oh, he's the jazz musician."

Clockers is perhaps your most "traditional" film score. And people hearing _Clockers_ might say, "He _is_ a jazz guy, but he's something else, too."

Clockers was the first film where I really got a chance to do that. The other side of this is that I've had to learn how to deal with the limitations: _Trial by Jury_ was a thirty-piece orchestra, but the director wanted a big, massive sound. At the time, I wasn't into synthesizers, and I wasn't that knowledgeable about how to use them with the orchestra. Had I known then what I know _now_, I could have beefed up the sound a number of ways. That's all a part of my growth process in this business. When I got the chance to do _Clockers_, I realized immediately, here's a chance for me to do a big orchestral score and use some synthetic instruments with the orchestra. I was very happy with that film. I really like writing for large orchestra. It's a blast.

Although _Clockers_ has your largest traditional score, you also used some very traditional film-scoring techniques in _Trial by Jury_. When they throw her in the trunk and slam it shut, you give us this big, dissonant zonk in the brass. I notice that you're smiling now. Do you smile when you write things like that, even though they're deadly serious and full of suspense? Is your inner voice saying, "Yeah, we really need a chord like that here"?

Exactly. Sometimes the scene cries out for something like that. What was rough about *Trial by Jury* was not only the fact that I had a thirty-piece orchestra, but also that there wasn't much action in the scene. And the director wanted me to fix that.

He wanted you to provide the action?

Right. And I tried it, but it becomes like a cartoon when you do that. You have all that stuff going on, but the guys are just standing around. It doesn't work. I wish I'd had a larger ensemble to work with on that score, because I was stretching my orchestration chops. And I felt sorry for the brass players, who had to play double roles. I'd have to use them for these low things and then I'd have to use them for these high things. They never got a break. But they were professionals and they handled it in a great way.

In a suspense film, sometimes you need those bold, brassy diminished chords under the big discovery, no matter how corny it might sound. It's almost expected by the audience.

And that's exactly what that film deserved. It's kind of like acting: Sometimes guys will do a scene where they cry. Then, they look back on it and they cry for laughing. But that's exactly what that story needed to give you the whole picture. It was a lot of fun for me. I learned a great deal from it, too. But Spike doesn't like that sort of thing at all. Spike doesn't really like action music. He doesn't like stuff to be pinpointed musically in a scene. He likes general mood music. So, with *Trial by Jury*, I got a chance to kind of flex my muscles with that kind of thing. I'd love to have another opportunity to do a film like that. Hopefully, I will.

Trial by Jury concerns the Mafia in New York City, but your score doesn't contain one bit of Carmine Coppola-style *Godfather* music, which we've come to associate with Mafia pictures.

It's just too cliché. It's kind of like the whole thing with love scenes: If it's a jazz score, you hear a solo saxophone. I'm so tired of that. I didn't want to go that route. It was bad enough that I was doing the traditional kind of action thing. So, I really didn't want to go over the top and do *Godfather* or do an opera or some shit like that. *Sugar Hill* was the same thing.

You mentioned earlier that Spike Lee's not a big fan of mickey-mousing, that he prefers more abstract, reflective, psychological or philosophical uses of music. In *Clockers*, your score is reserved for the intimate, emotional moments, while the action scenes are accompanied by source cues.

That's true. See, again, we're talking about clichés. And that's why I shied away from it in the score. For me, it would've been very easy to do urban jive with that film. I could have reiterated or done some things that were taken from the source cues.

I have this thing about African-Americans being pigeonholed into this stereotype of what we are. I know the diversity of the culture, so my whole plan was to not give in to that easy stereotype and, instead, to try to build up the characters in other, unusual ways: To say that they're just like anybody else. They have the same issues of family, loyalty, responsibility, and all that shit. That was rough because there was a lot of source music in the film. I would try to break the momentum—start a cue a little late and start it with just maybe a simple string pairing, so the viewer can get a little break from all this. But, you're right, it is like two distinctive things. For me, the urban stuff was the real shit. You know what I mean? And that's the way I looked at it.

Your music, as you say, sometimes grows *out of* or grows *into* source cues. Is this difficult to achieve—to have something already there, such as a rap source cue, and out of this pull a foreign, dissonant string-orchestra chord, which now leads us in another direction?

And sometimes you don't even know what the source cue is going to be—sometimes they're buying songs at the last minute. For a lot of it, I knew what was going to happen, but there were a couple of scenes where I didn't really know. I kept saying, "I need to know because I want the pitches to relate. They don't have to be the same, but they should relate in some way." Then, at one point, I said, "Well, fuck it! If I can't do that, I'll just try to think of my score." That was the first time I really organized my entire score. Miles [Goodman] showed me how to organize the score in my mind before actually writing it. He was a methodical kind of guy. So, I sat down with the film and checked where specific points in the film happen and where the film takes a turn, which I expect all great composers do. How many cues do I have for this guy? How many cues do I need for this kind of situation? In this way, you know if this one situation is building and you have some kind of thematic material or orchestration or sound for that situation, which you can develop and have relate to many other things. For me, it meant making a lot of notes to myself.

You mean prose notes, as opposed to musical pitch notes?

Yeah. Prose notes about what I needed to do—which scenes were in what situation and then how to cross-reference them. I'm excited about doing more films because I learn a lot with each film. Maybe one of the reasons I'm having all of these experiences is because I need to learn all this stuff about orchestras and about using synths with orchestra and about how to bring all the aspects of these different types and styles of music together to create this one type of sound with an orchestra or a small ensemble in order to write a piece for an album or a large orchestral work just for me, aside from a film. So, I look at all of this as being a great learning experience and opportunity for me. And I'm getting paid, which makes it greater.

Your attitude is so refreshing. You combine a gentle modesty with the sort of youthful, wide-eyed innocence and idealism that's often crushed by the system in guys our age.

Yeah, I know. Miles [Goodman] used to say that. Miles used to get upset with me because I'd say, "Man, I need to learn." Miles would say, "You know how to do it. Just relax." But that's the way I really look at it. I try not to take anything for granted. People say, "You're a film composer." And I'm like, "Yeah, up until my last film. Yeah, I *was* a film composer. That doesn't mean that I'm still gonna be one." You never know, so I try not to take it for granted. And when I do get a film, I try to do whatever it is I can do to support the film. I like challenges. I like people stretching me outside of my normal stuff—like with this next film, which Miles and I were doing together. Hopefully, I'll finish the film. I've been talking to the directors about it, and they want me to finish it. The film is a little different way of scoring for me. But I'm up to the challenge, and working a great deal with Miles before he died gave me a lot of insight. We basically went through the whole score and knew what we wanted to do, we just hadn't written anything down yet. One of the great things about this business is it gives me a chance to write some of the craziest shit for the most outrageous orchestrations and ensembles—music I wouldn't get a chance to write just being a jazz musician.

True. Sometimes I hear people complain about the dissonant, experimental style of some of my orchestral music. Then you watch *Clockers* or *Planet of the Apes* or *Alien* and you hear the same stuff, but everybody loves it because it's got this other thing that goes with it—the movie. It doesn't just sit alone in a stuffy concert hall with all those dangerous ghosts of Beethoven and Mozart and Tchaikovsky floating around it.

Exactly. There's some wild shit that I've written for film. When I wrote *Trial by Jury*, man, I got my rocks off. It's great because you realize that if you did that in a concert piece, people would completely hate it.

Oliver Nelson wrote film scores, maintained a major jazz career, and composed concert pieces. Are you thinking about writing some concert pieces someday soon?

Oh, yeah. There's actually a project that I've been working on bit by bit. It's like my hotrod: You know, some guys have a hotrod in the garage and they go work on it a couple of hours a week. That's kind of like what it is for me. I have these things in the back of my mind, and I know exactly what I want to do.

I'm always asking questions about why I'm getting these cool opportunities. I feel blessed to have a dual career. I know a lot of guys in film who want to play. They're very appreciative for what it is they have and for what the industry has done for them and their families and all that stuff, but they really want to play. I feel blessed that I have that.

In my film career, I'm one of the new guys. I have to take advantage of that, and one of the ways of doing that is giving back. So, if I'm learning all this stuff, if I'm getting all this experience, then I should give back to the community, as opposed to just saying I'll only write for orchestra when I do. Bullshit. I'll let you in on a little secret. I did an album called *The Billie Holiday Song Book*. Miles Goodman did all the string arrangements. One of the reasons I hired him was because I knew Miles was a very modest, very humble guy. I knew that if I asked him for lessons, he wouldn't give them to me. So, I asked him to do the string arrangements so I could see how he would approach them. And he was excited about it because it gave him a chance to step outside of the film world. I learned a lot about writing for strings from that. I never told him. I don't know why.

I understand that you were with your close friend Miles Goodman when he died recently?

Man, it was about twelve minutes until the paramedics got there. But the doctor said that whatever it is I saw him go through, once that started, there was no saving him. That makes me feel better only in that I know I tried to do all I could do, three times. I really think the paramedics went to the wrong address. I heard the sirens coming, then, all of a sudden, the sirens went off. But they weren't in front of the house. Then a couple of minutes later they pulled up.

When something like that happens, something so close and so personal, you're always going to second-guess yourself: "Did I do everything I could have done?"

Yeah. Well, everybody's going through that now. His girlfriend is going through that because she went jogging two minutes before. She keeps going through, "What would have happened if I would have stayed at home?" And I'm going, "Maybe I pumped his heart too hard." I was conscious of trying not to hurt him, but I was trying to get him to come back. It's weird because you go through two sides of it—your intellect says you couldn't have done anything else, but your heart tells you something totally different.

He was a really loved cat. You could see this at the ceremony. We had it at a theater. About 900 people showed up—every seat was packed. Miles Goodman was unique. This guy was really not competitive. If he was, he didn't show it—I never saw any signs of it. I met him on *Housesitter*, after I'd just done one film, *Jungle Fever*, and he was talking about trying to get me an agent. He was saying, "I know these guys and I'll get their number for you if you want." He's saying this to me and I'm just a side guy on the recording session. He's saying, "If you want, I'll give them a call and talk to them before you call. That will give you some kind of entrée into talking to these people." I thought, "Damn! Who is this guy?"

After that, our lives kind of paralleled each other's. He introduced me to a bunch of people. He knew I was a fan of Thomas Newman, so the day before he died, he called Thomas Newman to see if we could have lunch, so he could introduce me. He had been talking about me meeting Johnny Mandel. Johnny Mandel was his cousin, who he worked with for a long time. That's how he got his start. I met Johnny at the service, and he said, "Miles always talked about us meeting." Miles was a guy who gave and gave of himself, whatever he had to offer. And that shit's rare, man, because most people in Hollywood hoard all of their information. Miles was totally the opposite. And I did the same thing for him in terms of the jazz industry, because he was getting into that, making records and producing and a lot of things. But still, the stuff that he had done for me. We were working on a film together.

When he died?

Yeah. We were co-writing the score to a film called *'Til There Was You*. Co-writing a score was something he had always talked about. I'll give you an example: Miles and I were up against each other for a film that never happened, a Betty Boop remake. I felt really weird, because here's a really good friend of mine and it's the first time I've ever been in direct competition like this for a job. But Miles was cool. He said, "Hey, man, don't stress out about it. Either you get it or I get it. It doesn't matter. But what would be really cool is if we both did it." So, after that, he kept talking about doing a film together. Then this thing came along. We had been working on the music. We had made some breakthroughs in terms of the direction of the score, and he was really happy about that. And then he dies. It's weird, man. Maybe since he was that way, he had already earned his place.

bruce BROUGHTON

Bruce Broughton is a composer whose immense musical talents steadily drew him from television series to major feature films. Following his studies at USC, he worked for CBS as music supervisor on many television programs, including *Gunsmoke, The Wild, Wild West,* and *Hawaii Five-O.* After ten years of "paying dues" and learning the ropes—all the while composing effective scores for such high-quality made-for-TV movies as *The Master of Ballantrae* (1984) and such miniseries as *The Blue and the Gray* (1982) and scoring endless weekly episodes of *Dallas* and *Quincy*—Broughton hit his stride in the mid-1980s with his rousing, rambunctious, Oscar-nominated score for *Silverado.* Arresting, highly original, and technically stunning orchestral scores for *Young Sherlock Holmes* (1985), *The Boy Who Could Fly* (1986), Steven Spielberg's *Amazing Stories* television series, *The Monster Squad* (1987), and *Harry and the Hendersons* (1987) soon followed.

While *The Rescuers Down Under* (1990), the genre-jumping *Stay Tuned* (1992), *Honey, I Blew Up the Kid* (1992), *Homeward Bound: The Incredible Journey* (1993), *Baby's Day Out* (1994), and *Homeward Bound II: Lost in San Francisco* (1996) show off Broughton as a versatile, clever, and magical musical chameleon and a kid at heart, his dramatic, aggressive, and sometimes unnerving scores for *The Presidio* (1988), *Last Rites* (1988), *Tombstone* (1993), *One Tough Cop* (1997), and *The Shadow Conspiracy* (1997) take us on a tour of his musical dark side. His facility with sensitive, long melodies comes to the fore in *Carried Away* (1996) and *Infinity* (1996). Recent IMAX projects, such major motion pictures as *Lost in Space* (1998), and a steady flow of concert works balance with his ongoing activities as conductor for numerous critically acclaimed re-recordings of classic film scores.

We met for this interview at his home in the hills overlooking western Los Angeles.

bruce BROUGHTON

I'd like to start off by talking about your early career in television and a few of your lesser-known film scores.

You can talk about anything, because *I* will talk about anything.

For *Ice Pirates*, 1983, you wrote a campy blend of many styles, not unlike your eclectic homage approach to *Stay Tuned* a decade later.

The thing that I remember most about *Ice Pirates* is that it was under-budgeted for music. I had worked on just one feature film before then, which was a movie for Billy Graham, the evangelist, not the rock star. The music director on *Ice Pirates* wanted someone who would be happy to work within the budget, i.e., a newcomer who would be happy to have the opportunity to do a decent score. He called me and, of course, I was willing do it.

The movie was, frankly, a mess. It had been put together in a chaotic way, and the studio didn't like it. I thought that it was too bad that the studio didn't get behind it as a *Star Wars* send-up, because some scenes were actually very funny. The producer was John Foreman, and I had more to do with him than the director, because the director—Stewart somebody, who obviously I have not seen since—was so busy on postproduction and trying to fight off the studio that he didn't have much time to think about the music.

Did the director eventually become involved during the recording sessions?

I recorded most of the score with John in attendance. Stewart didn't see it until the dub, which was a disaster. It wasn't that Stewart hated it so much, but more that he just had no investment in it. Then the studio saw the film, hated it, and forced the director into massive re-cuts, giving him only a few days to do it. At that point, scenes started to get transposed and scores started to get thrown everywhere. It was such a huge hack job at the end, I really couldn't tell you anymore what cue was written for what. I haven't seen the film since it was made. I do remember that John thought the recording of it was wonderful. That was the last good comment that I got. It was a scoring-stage hit!

Tell me about *Monster Squad*. It's one of your more frightening scores, yet you have the ability to make scary music seem family-oriented.

Monster Squad seemed to be a monster movie for kids, made by an overgrown kid, Fred Dekker. I remember that the opening was done in the old-fashioned style of Lugosi's *Dracula* and all that stuff. I don't know that the movie was scary, but it was silly. The music actually made me laugh because it was so over-the-top. I guess the music reflects whatever the movie is about.

One thing that I do remember about writing the score is that there was enough presence of the Dracula character in the movie to bring me down while I was writing it. I get infected by the quality of the film when I am working on it. It was supposed to be a comedy, and I guess you could call it a comedy, so I wrote kind of frothy. But when it was grim, I tended to get fairly grim.

I know this might sound weird, but I had this pervasive sadness as I was writing the score. I couldn't figure it out until I realized that the character of the undead is basically sadness—they don't have a place to go, they can't get to where they are supposed to go, wherever that is. I thought that perhaps that spoke well of the film, because there must be some real quality, an intelligent thinking level, in it. If you think it's scary, that's great.

One thing that *Monster Squad* did do was introduce me to the producer Peter Hyams. Peter actually stood back pretty far and let Fred do what he wanted to do. But, if it was necessary, he would lead Fred or guide Fred. Fred adored him.

What other films have you worked on with Peter Hyams?

I think we did three of them. After *Monster Squad*, I worked with Peter on *The Presidio*—Peter was the director—and on *Narrow Margin*. Then we did *Stay Tuned*.

In *Monster Squad*, there is a lot of effective classic mickey-mousing. *Stay Tuned*, by the nature of the beast, is also packed with mickey-mousing. Would you consider yourself as having roots in traditional Golden Age film techniques?

Well, there are three ways of doing it: You pay attention to the action and follow the film, which is mickey-mousing, which is really extreme. Or you don't pay attention to the action, you just play the mood, which is what most of us do. Or you don't refer to anything in particular, which is what some guys do—maybe because of their own limitations, maybe because of the style of the film.

The style these days tends to be non-referential to the action. I think there are probably a lot of reasons for that. Music is more, at the moment, alternative sound effects—sort of a pad and a Band-Aid for pictures that shouldn't have nearly as much music or nearly as much film.

Mickey-mousing? I did it in *Silverado* and, in fact, I did it in *Young Sherlock Holmes*, too. In *Silverado*, it was an intentional thing. I asked Larry Kasdan if he wanted me to follow the action. He said,

"What do you mean?" And I said, "If a bad guy falls on the ground, do you want there to be a timpani hit?" He said, "Oh, yeah, I want that." It was a particular style we were going for.

Young Sherlock Holmes is almost non-stop synchronization.

Young Sherlock Holmes was almost like an animated action-cartoon. The scenes were all made so that one scene would just rush into the next scene. And that style seems to lend itself best to the mickey-mouse scoring approach, rather than the standing-back-in-the-shadows approach.

    Monster Squad seemed to be somewhat like a cartoon, too. And frankly, the picture was so flat that I tried to do something with the music that would give the film some defining points. If you see these scenes by themselves, they don't start anywhere and they don't go anywhere—someone just put the camera up and they shot. I'm not saying that _Monster Squad_ was entirely like that, but, in terms of staging, it wasn't the richest film I have ever seen. That probably contributed to my musical choices, but not as much as the fact that it was a cartoon-like comedy. Since then, I probably mickey-mouse too much, but I try to pull back wherever I possibly can. It's just a style, and you use it or you don't use it.

Amadeus was released one year before _Harry and the Hendersons_. Was the immense popularity of _Amadeus_ an influence on the Mozartian drive in the opening scenes of _Harry and the Hendersons_?

No. That Mozartian drive was actually used for a goofy reason. It was right around the time of _Harry_ that the temp track started to become a really big deal, and _Harry_ was pretty much completely temp-tracked. It was a big, expensive movie, everyone was nervous, and there was a big problem with what to do about the main titles.

The temp track usually would be music by another composer?

The temp track is just music that comes from anywhere. It can be from other movies, from classical pieces, from the producer's record collection, from your synthesizer—from anything. It doesn't matter where it comes from because it's not going to go into the final film, and there is no licensing, it doesn't cost anything.

The problem is that once the temp track is there, everyone gets used to it. And, very often, the director and producer don't want you to vary too much from the feel of the temp track. If the film performs well with the temp track, they don't want you to screw it up and take the chance of a bait-'n'-switch reaction from the studio. So the temp track is an important element in deciding what the composer is going to do. The composer can ignore it at his own peril or follow along its lines. For this reason, you will find many movies that sound very similar.

So what happened to *Harry*'s main titles?

Before I was on it, they had to figure out what to temp for the main title. The music editor came up with, and I don't know how, a Mozart piece called *Ascanio in Alba*, an overture, a little piece that I didn't know. It seemed to have the light, jaunty feeling of what they were looking for.

When I got to *Harry*, I knew they were committed to that piece, and they liked the style. So we kicked it around and thought that maybe one of the gags in the movie would be that the Henderson family was always listening to Mozart. They would have the radio on in the house or in the car, and during all the things that they did, they would be listening to Mozart. So we recorded a Mozart piano concerto, we recorded a little bit of a Mozart symphony, we recorded all sorts of things.

The main title starts off as my music and then, at one point, dissolves into Mozart, and then back to me. And you can't find the seams! I took the score to *Ascanio in Alba* and just copied the style, incorporating my themes. The goofy thing was that, by the time we got to the completed film, the Henderson family's Mozart obsession had pretty much disappeared and we were left with this arcane main title, which has never made much sense and I am sure has caused a lot of confusion. But I like the music. I think it was a good rip-off.

Not so much a rip-off—more a consolidation or a reconciliation of Mozart and Broughton?

I guess. I remember that the former concertmaster of the L. A. Philharmonic was in the orchestra when we recorded the main title, and he thought I had written the whole thing. He didn't know where it was Mozart and where it was me. So I took that as a big compliment.

The rest of the score was difficult because, basically, I got fooled by the size of the film. It looked like a very rich film when, in fact, it is not. It is really a simple film.

I came up with this tune that was very simple, which the director, Bill Dear, liked a lot. But producer Steven Spielberg did not like it. And, frankly, Spielberg wasn't really much in attendance throughout that movie; he was waiting for his son Max to be born. They would record cues and send them to him, not in synch but as close as they could on a cam with the picture, and he would make his decisive pronouncements.

Bill was difficult to work with. He really isn't too knowledgeable about music. He is a nice guy, and he is very funny, but he was telling jokes in the booth as I was recording. I don't think that he was really paying attention to the score until we would come into the booth and ask, "How was that?" And he'd say, "Let's listen to it."

I would end up rewriting everything—literally, every cue in that movie was rewritten once or twice, sometimes three times, or it was changed on the spot. There isn't anything in the movie that is the way it was originally written. I remember being so distraught at one point that when I saw Lionel Newman, who was then the head of the music department at Fox, I said, "Lionel, I don't know what to do." And he said, "Hey, kid, you've got no one supporting you. Just do it as well as you can and get out."

Now in the middle of all of that, my wife and I separated. We were recording for a week, separation came, I was rewriting, and then we recorded for another week. It was not a happy time for me, emotionally. I find the picture very difficult to watch. Since then, I have worked amicably with Bill and Steven many times, but that picture is not a happy memory. So the fact that you liked it or anybody likes it is nice to hear. There *is* a lot of pretty music in it.

It's a wonderful score—the opening zip, the more aggressive, atonal confrontational sections. And that perfect main theme moves with Mozartian style and grace, but it also bubbles, moves gently, moves nervously. And, when Harry finally shows his big heart, it transforms itself into teary-eyed, delicate simplicity. The tune is a classic Hollywood chameleon.

Yeah, it is. And it pays off at the end. It was a very simple tune, and I realized, after the picture, that Harry himself is a very simple character. All the passions and the hyper-craziness of the family were overshadowed by Harry's simplicity and directness, which, in a strange way, is how the score turned out. It has this very, very simple tune that I actually wanted to throw away when it came up, but I couldn't get rid of it—it was stuck in my brain, it seemed to be *the* tune. But *Harry* was also maybe a little overdone with a lot of music that was probably too big. I don't know. I have kicked that one around for years. It is not a film that I have a lot of straightforward feelings about. A lot was going on during that time.

Let's try to find happier memories. How about *Rescuers Down Under*? Was this your first shot at feature animation?

Yeah. When I was boy I wanted to be an animator—Walt Disney was my hero. Composing came later. I never had the same passion for composing as I did for animation when I was a boy. So, when I got the opportunity to do *Rescuers*, I really jumped at it. It was basically, "Yes! I want to have your baby!"

They liked *Silverado* and they wanted this animated adventure film to have a *Silverado* feel. They thought I wouldn't be interested because it was just animation. They didn't realize that I had wanted to do animation for a long time and, up to this point, hadn't done any.

Rescuers was painful, too, in that . . . God, I sound like a cry-baby composer! . . . we did four cues and then had a scoring session just to see how it was going to go. I played the music for Jeffrey Katzenberg, and he didn't like it at all—didn't like the theme, didn't like the action music. I'd have to say that he wasn't completely wrong. I had worked on the film for so long, but it still wasn't happening. So I reworked the material, rewrote some cues, and had another meeting with him. I played the new stuff and it turned out fine.

The main title music is very ethnic-sounding, and more suspenseful and dramatic than the typical cartoon jungle-drumming.

Jeffrey wanted a very ethnic-sounding score, which was difficult because there just isn't very much musical material to work with in Australia—boomerangs, didjeridoos, and that's about it. In fact, when I did a television interview in Sydney, I mentioned this to the host—I said, "You know, they were looking for indigenous, ethnic sounds." He said, "What is that? The sound of beer cans popping?" Anyway, we found something, but that original opening cue was one of the less successful cues. It just didn't have the power, didn't have the drive, so I reworked it and added some extra drum pounding and that little theme that goes over and over again, and it turned out great. I think we used six percussion players overdubbed a couple of times.

Did you use indigenous drums?

Yeah, relatively speaking. We have animal bones, we have all sorts of high and low native drums and bass drums. And there are some whistles. It is all music that is indigenous somewhere, but not necessarily to Australia. I don't think there is any actual Australian music in it. We explored didjeridoos, we explored all kinds of whistles and pipes and scratchers and all this other stuff. There is a didjeridoo sound that was used for the kangaroo calling the boy.

When the rescuers first take off for Australia, they depart in a blinding blizzard to the 1960s surf-guitar sounds of Dick Dale and the Deltones. It is wonderful, a complete surprise. It cracked me up, but I don't get it.

[Laughter] I don't remember exactly how that came about. The character, whose voice was done by John Candy, was like a big beach bum. Somehow the idea surfaced, and we just all thought it would be a very funny idea. We talked about it a lot, and just ended up doing it.

Rescuers **has some hilarious moments of mickey-mousing, and other times it is very dramatic, suggesting something beyond an animated movie.**

I would say that if Jeffrey had had his way, there wouldn't have been any mickey-mousing at all. But many of the scenes were so active, like the scene with all the animals trying to escape, that there was just no way you could let them sit there—the musical commentary was screaming to me.

I think that when Horner does animation, he basically places action music in an action situation, which is certainly one way to do it, and I think Jerry Goldsmith also plays them as action pieces. I don't think there is anything wrong with playing the action, particularly in a cartoon. The music gives the characters weight. I know that they have sound effects now, and everything is effects-driven, but cartoons have always been over the top with sound effects. But, when you see these things with just the music, the horns, the xylophones, the wah-wah trombones, the bass drum give the characters weight and the movie more energy.

One of the things about *Rescuers* that I noticed right away was that the animation was spectacular, as all Disney animation is. It looks as though it is almost human. But a cartoon actor gets from the left of the screen to the right of the screen much faster than a human actor would. And one of the things music can do is make a time-reference change. Music can modify time-references. You actually can increase the energy content in an animated cartoon by the properties of music. And when you are trying to get very excited, very energetic, very heightened, there is nothing wrong with pushing the music. *Lion King* isn't like that—Alan Menken doesn't do it that way—but I am not ashamed of it at all. For one thing, I think I do it really well. I know that on the scoring stage, before it gets laden with sound effects, everybody enjoys it. It makes the picture look so cool, especially when the animation is so terrific.

Rescuers Down Under became your first of many projects in the animated feature-film world.

Serendipity. Pure serendipity. Since *Rescuers*, I have done a lot of work with Disney, and I have done a lot with animation—I have done two Roger Rabbit shorts, that big cartoon sequence in *Stay Tuned*, and another short called *Off His Rockers*.

I like working with Disney because they are a very efficient company. They're great. I have done movies for them, and I have worked a lot with their theme parks.

Theme parks, IMAX movies—these seems to be new options for composers.

Yeah. Lots of guys have done them. They are really interesting projects. They are entirely anonymous, but they are seen—and heard—by millions of people.

The one that I am finishing now is the new energy show at Epcot. Another one I did at Epcot was "Honey, I Shrunk the Audience," which is, basically, great entertainment. It's a big 3-D screen that looks and sounds like a live show, but, of course, the whole thing is film. And I have one show that has two different scores—a circle-vision show that runs in Paris that is basically the same show that runs in Florida. Actually, it *is* the same show, except one is in French and one is in English and they have different scores. I wrote one in France that accompanies the French-dialogue version, but over here they thought that it was too tame, that it wasn't energetic enough for the American version with Robin Williams and Rhea Perlman. So I wrote a completely different score for the American one. You can have a lot of fun doing these things, and you get free trips out to the parks, where you get to ride the rides.

Are these projects full orchestral scores?

Yeah. They are big scores. And, as with the animation studios, they take you on as a creative partner.

In most films, that doesn't happen—often, you are the guy who comes in at the end. They are very suspicious of you because they have already had the marketing blitz—they have their numbers, and they don't want you to screw it up. You know, "We need music, just don't do too much. We've got this fifty-million-dollar investment, don't blow it. . . . don't do this, don't do that . . . don't be too emotionally big, don't change the emotions here, don't say too much there, don't be too overt, don't be too mys-terious, don't be too energetic . . ." It's not like it was even a few years ago.

In the "good ol' days," were there fewer restrictions? Was there an easier relationship between the director and the composer?

Not always. If you read the stories of Rózsa and Tiomkin and all those guys, they all complain. Waxman complained about the way it was. There's nothing more common among composers than stupid-director and stupid-producer stories, which are often unfair, because, frankly, I wouldn't change shoes with the director for any amount of money. Talk about real problems. Directors have the real problems. If there is anyone who should cry about their lot in life, it should be a director and not a composer. And, after directors, writers have it a lot worse than composers, too. At least we get our music on the picture; writers aren't ever assured of getting their words on a screen because directors won't use them or actors decide they want to use different lines.

I have a writer friend who went to see a film he wrote a few years ago. He hardly recognized anything. His name was on the screen, it said that he wrote it, but he sat there with his wife and said, "I don't know what this is. It sure isn't mine." Composers don't go through that, don't have too many big shocks. There are a few—Alex North's *2001* and some Carmine Coppola stuff—but, mostly, composers are asked to change things ahead of time.

Composers like to think that what came out of their brains is perfect, but sometimes it's just not right for the picture, even though the music might be great. Composers make mistakes. We've all heard bad scores, and I have contributed to them as well as everyone else. Everyone has written bad scores, or written good scores that are inappropriate for the picture. That's just part of the process. Also, scores that may be well-received at the time are later found to be not so hot. Or vice versa—scores that were at first ignored became part of classic film-music history later on. It's the same thing with all music, I guess.

Do you do your own orchestrations?

Yes. I devised a short-score-paper format a couple of years ago that the copyist could copy off of because I have everything there, all the information. I name all the notes, all the instruments, every-thing. I'll show it to you. [Broughton pulls out a score.] I use the top three lines for winds; I use the next three lines for brass; then there are keyboard, harp, percussion lines; and five for strings. I get everything on there. You can see that it is clearly marked as to who is playing what all the time. Also, I write little information notes to the copyist. If I have to resort to colored pencils, I'll do that, too. That leaves no question. The score is in C; the copyists do the transposing for the parts. And, frankly, as I do this more and more, I've simplified my writing a little because the more complicated it is, the more useless it is in the film.

It's pretty impressive—you even have the pedal markings for the harp. Aside from your work with acoustic instruments, do you work much with electronics?

I do use some electronics, but mostly for sounds integrated with the full orchestra. I don't have the patience to sit and search for weird sounds. I should probably do it more, and probably will do it more as I get more equipment.

When I write, I write mainly with the piano, and then I transfer it into the synths so the director can hear it, and so I can see it. I haven't figured out how to do that really well. If I am writing real orchestral music, it doesn't transfer well into the synths, especially when it begins to get emotional. When it begins to get truly emotional, the synths are flatter than a pancake. I have had a lot of problems with directors not being able to feel the emotion because they can't feel the synths, so there is still a lot of anxiety until you get to the scoring stage. But, usually, the gestures are right, and there are a lot of corrections I can make with the director. I have found it to be a useful device as much as I hate it.

I need to, at least, be able to do some sort of temporary orchestral mock-up with the synths. But to do a whole synth score? I might do it, eventually, maybe, if anyone ever calls me. But why would anyone call me? A lot of guys do it a lot better than I do. I have friends who do it really well—guys who do small-budget films with a lot of terrific synth stuff and use a little bit of acoustical music in front of it. So, call them.

But if you want the ninety-piece orchestra score, call Bruce!

Call me, yeah. [Laughter] And small orchestras, too. I love the intimacy and experimental sound possibilities of chamber orchestra.

Basically, I learned how to orchestrate doing television—doing all those episodes of *Dallas* and *Quincy* and *Hawaii Five-O*, where we usually had orchestras of eighteen to twenty-four players. And on a show like *Dallas*, which, every week, was basically the same show, in order not to write the same music, I would change the orchestra personnel. I tried to find the overlying emotional quality of the show and then find an orchestration that would match. So, one week, it might be all strings and a harp. One time, I had an oboe, English horn, trombone, strings, and harp, or something like that, so it was a very specific color. *Then* you start writing specific music for the orchestra, which is an approach not unlike what Bernard Herrmann did.

I learned a lot. Some weeks I made terrible mistakes, which I didn't make again, or I would keep exploring certain sounds trying to figure out how to do something, and let them pay for it. And the producers liked it because they knew that I was actually paying attention to their show—every week I would give them something different. Once, I did a *Quincy* that was all strings. They hated it, which I never really understood because I thought it was kind of a cool score. I was apologetic, but they said, "No sweat. We just figured you had a bad week and next week will be something else." They didn't really care. They just figured it wasn't one of my better ones, you know? They get to trust you in a series.

Some of the *Quincy* scores are impressive—I'd always sensed that there was a very strong, individualistic composer at work on that show. Were you doing any film scores at the time of *Quincy* and *Dallas*?

No, I started working for CBS television right out of college. I was in the music department as a music supervisor for ten years.

Where was college?

College was USC. I just got a bachelor's degree in composition. I didn't want more than that.

I was fortunate to get a job right out of school, but, basically, my job was to track TV shows, to select music and keep selecting music. I worked *Gunsmoke* and *Wild, Wild West* and, eventually, *Hawaii Five-O* and a lot of shows that Jerry Fielding was composing for. We had various composers come in and score episodes, and we, just three or four guys, were just tracking everything. And as we would find cues lacking, we would rewrite or add new cues ourselves, and eventually do entire episodes.

My first full episode was *Hawaii Five-O*, but I was still working as a music supervisor at CBS. I left there after ten years to become a composer, doing what I knew best, which was television, because I knew the people and I knew the style.

Have you done any recent television scoring?

Yeah, I did. In fact, I even got an Emmy nomination for the theme to the TV show *JAG*. I think the last one before that was *O Pioneers!*, which was more like a movie. I don't do a lot of TV anymore, but I do it from time to time for whatever reason.

***Stay Tuned* is a frantic film that gave you an opportunity to write in so many styles—heroic neo-Korngold, game show, silly sitcom, 1940s film noir/gangster, manic neo-Stalling, expansive wilderness music, neo-Morricone spaghetti-Western stuff. There must be a dozen different kinds of music.**

That was the most interesting thing about the movie—it had so many different styles. It had this 1940s detective style with all the black and white scenes; we had all the bizarre commercials; we did this *Leave It to Beaver* kind of thing; the Clint Eastwood Western bit, which was actually pretty funny after having done the big, serious Western *Silverado*. I hadn't done *Tombstone* yet, which was yet another Western style, a darker style.

The goofy thing about *Stay Tuned* was that Peter Hyams had temped it with *Young Sherlock Holmes*. He wanted the energy of *Young Sherlock Holmes*, a score that he liked a lot, but whenever I would do it that way, he wouldn't like it. It was kind of confusing. But, in the long run, I think I wrote a lot of neat music. I haven't heard it in a while, but I enjoyed it.

The cartoon sequence in *Stay Tuned* is nonstop, wall-to-wall madness—seven minutes of frenetic mickey-mousing.

Yeah, it was great. It was just old-fashioned Looney Tunes style. But it was mean and aggressive because the cartoon was so mean and aggressive. I really liked that section.

In the "Thirtysomething to Life" segment, the music is directly styled after *Thirtysomething*. In the wild "Northern Overexposure" segment, you recreate that distinctive *Northern Exposure* sound. Were acknowledgments made to the original composers, or is the music generic enough that you can just ape the style?

Actually, I don't know. But I do know that the typical movie composer's contract says that what you are writing is original and not based upon anyone else's music. And if it is, you are held responsible for it. For this picture, I made them take that clause out because there was going to be so much music that was based upon other music.

"Driving Over Miss Daisy" was another great clone.

Yeah. I didn't use the original *Driving Miss Daisy* themes, and I don't remember using the same exact chords, but I used the same kinds of instruments, the same feel. That in itself is interesting: What are people hearing that would give them the idea that it was the same music? Even though my "Northern Overexposure" music was different, most people think that they're hearing the original *Northern Exposure*.

It's somehow psychological.

Yeah. Years ago, one of the guys I worked for at CBS was Morty Stevens, who had written the *Hawaii Five-O* theme. Mort said that, every once in a while, someone would call him up and say, "Hey, Mort they're using your theme in a commercial." He would watch the commercial, but it was never really his theme—it was something else done in the style of it. I started to pay attention to this and realized that people can't, for the most part, remember specific melodies—they don't actually remember much of anything except instrumental color. And if you do a certain musical gesture, which in *Hawaii Five-O* was "chuckabump," that rock-and-roll drum and trumpet style based on those old Herb Alpert records, people will hear it as being the same music when, in fact, it is not. A musician like you or me would be able to tell the difference immediately, but to a non-musician, it's all the same music. Different ears.

A few months ago, I had a director scream at me that I had cribbed the theme of a movie that we had worked on together from another theme of mine. So I said, "What are you talking about?" He said, "The other day, my wife and I saw another movie that you had done, and you'd ripped off the theme from that movie and used it in the picture that we did together!" I said, "You are out of your mind! I've never done that in my life!" But there was something that he heard—a gesture or a phrase—that reminded him of something else. I know that I have never stolen another theme of mine, at least not intentionally. But, to him, it was the same music. He said, "Note for note, it is the same music!" And I said, "No it's not. It's impossible!"

Let's talk a bit about *Honey, I Blew Up the Kid*.

That's probably my favorite score—I love it. It was a wall-to-wall score, just tons of music. It was the sequel to *Honey, I Shrunk the Kids*, and we couldn't use the James Horner music from the original film. Horner had referred a little too closely to a famous Raymond Scott tune called "Powerhouse," and Disney got sued. It was such a big deal that, for the sequel, Disney didn't want to have anything to do with anything that sounded like it at all, which was great for me, because I didn't want to use it anyway. So I was able to come up with something completely different. I was able to do whatever I wanted. There was a temp, but it wasn't a big temp. It was, I remember, pretty non-specific, with a little bit of this and a little bit of that.

The *Honey, I Blew Up the Kid* score was written at a bad time, but I enjoyed it a lot, and I still enjoy listening to it now. And the playing on it—the way the orchestra performed—was spectacular. There was one piece that we did with just one rehearsal. I knew that if I rehearsed it more, it would get polished, but the spirit of it would suffer. So we just took it immediately, with all that energy, everyone just flying for notes. There is one piece in the score that is almost impossible to play, but you get so much energy from all this hysteria from the musicians. It is some of the greatest playing in all of Hollywood in terms of sheer energy, massive amount of notes, and style and time and rhythm. Just terrific.

It *is* a manic score. There are moments when it's just scurrying all over the place. For such a demanding score, with rapid-fire passages, complicated counterpoint, surprise harmonic and rhythmic shifts, can you have extra rehearsal time with the orchestra?

Sometimes. But they are just ferociously good readers here. They play everything as if they've played it for years. Of course, the downside of everything being sight-read is that no one really gets a chance to absorb the music. If you want a real performance, like what you would get with a symphony orchestra, a performance that is passionate, you don't get that. It is, basically, a sight-read performance, but it is awfully good. I mean, I wouldn't put a score like *Honey, I Blew Up the Kid* in front of any contract orchestra in the world, and certainly no symphony in the world, and expect it to sound the way it did on that sight-read recording. It is a very American score, played by an American contract orchestra located here in Hollywood. I can't imagine anybody *but* Hollywood musicians being able to nail that score.

In *Homeward Bound* and *Homeward Bound II*, some material from the original carries over into the sequel—the themes are similar. But, in the sequel, there were more opportunities for aggressive music as the threesome is lost in San Francisco.

They are different in that the first one is all outdoors, all in the country. It has the kind of grandeur and sweep that you find in those pseudo-documentaries where the animals walk through the forest encountering bears and all sorts of other stuff. The focus in the first one is a little less direct than in the second one.

In the second one, they really knew what they were about. The story was about dogs getting lost in San Francisco, and one of the dogs has a little love affair with another dog. There was a little love interest, so there's a new love theme in the second one. You meet up with street dogs instead of grizzly bears, and there are the good street dogs and the bad street dogs. But there was no countryside.

One problem we had was that the young dog, Chance, had a little bit of that country orientation. I could do that with acoustic guitars and all that, but in the city it wouldn't come off as well. I had his theme very well set up from the first one, and I thought about writing him another theme, but it just didn't seem to work. Nothing I came up with seemed to work as well as the bouncy theme from the first film. So there is a lot of music in the second one that may seem to be a little inappropriate for the location, but it plays the dog.

It plays the dog rather than the environment.

Yes and no. If you compare the two films, the first one relies much more on that very grand, wide-open-spaces *Homeward Bound* theme. That theme, which I liked a lot, was obviously very difficult to use in the city. The city is just not grand like the Canadian Rockies or wherever it was that they shot the first one. In that way, the score reflects as much of where the show is taking place as anything else. But the themes are the same. It was lot of fun to get to work with the themes all over again, to find different ways of variation, of harmonizing, or just to use earlier material straight.

There is one extended variation of the theme that I used in the first one that I was able to use again in the sequel. I could reorchestrate it and rewrite it—it was like real composition, instead of just one-shot writing for the movies. It was like a real, through-composed piece.

Did they instantly go to you for the sequel or were other composers considered?

Joel McNeely was supposed to do it, but Joel fell out because he had a scheduling conflict. I had mixed feelings about whether I wanted to do the second one, but I thought, well, geez, I did the first one, so why not?

And as it turned out, I'm glad that I did, because I liked the people. Duwayne Dunham, who did the first movie, was a very nice guy, and David Ellis, who did the second movie, was a very nice guy. I made friends with the producers: Don Ernst, who I have worked with a couple of times in animation, was the producer on the first one, and Jim Pentecost on the second. From the standpoint of making friends and having a good time and being around nice people, the films were pleasant. And kids like 'em, mothers like 'em, fathers like 'em—there is just no downside to doing a film like that.

I've done a lot of family films. I don't know why, I just have. I sometimes might grouse about the kind of film I am getting, like anyone does, but when I look back at the films I have done, whether or not they have been commercially successful, a lot of them have been very successful with families and with kids. They have lasted for a long time, and a lot of people see this stuff on video. So I really can't complain.

These aren't just fluffy, happy-family films—there are many opportunities for you to take out your aggressive, atonal, *Young Sherlock Holmes* chops.

That's true. And they aren't drippy films. Every film is different, no matter if you think that you've been there before, you really haven't been there before, musically.

This afternoon, for instance, I am going up to master a second of two albums. The first one is called *Infinity*, which is a low-budget project that Matthew Broderick directed—his first film—based on the life of Richard Feynman, the physicist. There is no money in it, the orchestra is tiny, the music is very specific, it doesn't have huge sweeping cues because there are no huge, sweeping scenes. There are some big relationship scenes, but the scale is very small. The next movie is called *Shadow Conspiracy*. It's a political thriller, and has a lot more money in the budget, and a lot more action music. There is a lot of sound, a lot of mass, and the music is often very dark and frightening. Well, you couldn't have two more different kinds of music. That's one of the great things about movie music, aside from the fact that people listen to it and find some kind of emotional attachment and involvement.

Baby's Day Out is a crazed and manic family movie.

I love *Baby's Day Out*!

The opening tune is wholesome, optimistic, and innocent, yet there is this evil, stubborn, ominous recurring tritone figure—the bad guys are waiting around the corner.

Yeah, the bad guys have the tritone—that little three-note figure. The little jaunty tune is the baby's tune.

There is a ton of music in that movie. I'm glad they did it, but I was afraid it was stomping on all the gags—to me it was a very funny movie all by itself. You know, music can take a gag's timing and move it south, but this one worked out really well.

I looked at those scenes over and over again. I never worked so hard in my life. But as I'd look at those scenes, I'd laugh myself silly. Some people did not find the movie to be funny at all, just appalling. I have heard both sides of it. I happen to be one of the guys who thinks it is a very funny movie. I really enjoyed working on it. I enjoyed meeting [writer/producer] John Hughes. I enjoyed [director] Patrick Johnson.

In the scene where the bad guy's crotch is on fire and the other bad guy is stomping out the crotch fire with his boots, the loud music is pulsing to the stomping rhythm and, immediately after the fire is out, you give us five big bass drum hits still in the rhythm of the boots. And this is a family film?!

That was one scene that I didn't want to play because I thought music would stomp on the gag. But they were very adamant that they wanted music there. It was an afterthought—I had basically written the whole score, and then they said, "We've gotta have music there." And I'm glad I did it because that is a totally crazy scene.

You just can't believe that anybody is going to have any problems with it. But somebody said to me, "That's a sadistic scene." I just thought it was really funny. Little boys think it's funny.

The entire picture is loaded with classic mickey-mousing.

I did that because of the kind of movie it was. Actually, there was some confusion in the movie—the director and the producer didn't agree about the way the movie should go.

I think that if John had entirely had his way, it would have been a flat-out slapstick comedy. Patrick didn't see it that way. He saw it as a typical family film. He thought it had much more to do with the baby and family values than the slapstick thing.

When I first started working on the film, Patrick wasn't around. I had to rework the film when he came back because, for whatever reason, they decided to go Patrick's way. I thought it was just a hysterically funny film, but Patrick said that we didn't want the audience to think of it as a funny film, we wanted them to think of it as a warm film. I said, "Say what?" He said, "We want them to feel as though the family has been reunited." The focus of the film— whether it was comedy or warmth—was very confusing to me. But I just couldn't ignore the fact that it was a very funny movie; I was drawn to play it the way I did.

Did the original score, or first draft, play even more of the slap-stick?

Yes. As I said, I thought we were going to have an off-the-wall slap-stick film with strong comedic situations. Actually, we ended up having that anyway, but there is a lot more warmth and tenderness than would have been there had not Patrick told me of his direction.

I am not unhappy with the way it turned out. I think it turned out fine. But there were very different choices being made as a result of all that, which is a part of the process that is very important.

If you can't talk to the director, if you can't figure out what the director wants, if the director won't be clear with you for some reason, you are going to write a score that's *not* the score everybody is looking for. It can be very difficult because, sometimes, the director doesn't know exactly how to verbalize what he or she wants—

you have to translate and hope that you are sensitive enough to what they are speaking about that you can get the right idea.

Is it common to find directors who are musically confused?

Not really. There are times when the director tells you exactly what he or she wants and you have to hope that you are *not* translating. I have been in situations where I have stepped into it up to my chin, and the director suddenly says, "No, not that. I wanted such and such," which was exactly what he wanted all along, but I had translated wrong—I had thought he wanted something else. So, I had to rewrite it.

This brings up an interesting consideration: This is all commercial music, music-for-hire, music that is written for very specific reasons. Part of what we do is write music that solves specific problems. There are always subjective situations, but they are usually solved in an objective way. Somebody says, "It's too romantic," so you have to rewrite to a point where they can say, "Fine, that's better."

In concert music, that never happens. In concert music, no one ever questions me as to what note this is or if I should hold the note a little longer. No one is going to say, "that's too long" or "that's too short" or "that's too romantic" or "that's too dissonant." In movies, they do that all the time. They say, "I don't like that note" or "I don't like that instrument" or "I don't like that sound" or "the music is too fast" or "it's too slow" or "it's not big enough" or "it's too big." In film music, all these things are coming at you all the time. It is a very different kind of music, given the fact that it is very specific to begin with—you are dealing with very specific emotions.

You've touched upon concert music. Let's take that detour for a few moments. At the university where I teach, your name shows up on programs from time to time—a tuba piece, a wind ensemble piece, etc. Actually, the director of bands there, Bob Grechesky, who first turned me on to *Silverado*, is a fan of your concert works.

How do you juggle concert music with the demanding full-time film scoring career?

I don't kid myself that I will ever become famous as a concert composer. I don't think Stravinsky's reputation has anything to fear because I'm hot on his heels. But I do feel that it is important to write concert music for myself—to write foreground music and not just always background music.

Most film music is background music; it is accompanying. Sometimes, I just get tired of writing the Schubert piano accompaniment parts and not ever hearing anybody sing. So, when I do concert works, I don't try to set the world on fire in terms of form or style or inventiveness, but, as a composer, I work on my technique, I work on interesting formal problems, I work on music that *I* want to hear and pieces that people will ask for. I have a tuba piece that is very popular. Last year I did a piece for horn and strings. I have a piccolo concerto. I'm reworking a violin piece. These are all pieces that have been performed, and will be performed again. People enjoy them, and I get really good comments about them. I have a piece called *The Magic Horn* that is used a lot in family concerts with a mime group—I had something like twenty performances of it last year.

Concert music just provides you another opportunity, another outlet, to write music. I love working on movies, but I like doing cartoons, too. I also like working on the theme-park projects. If I had the chance to do a straight record, I would probably do concert music. I enjoy having lots of variety, even in one specific outlet: In movies, I love comedy but I also love tragedy. In concert works, I like to write a violin concerto, then write a crazy piece for a family concert. I like to write anything and everything, because they all have different interesting problems to solve, they all keep me from being bored, and they all go out to the people.

Music from *Silverado*, *Tombstone*, and *Young Sherlock Holmes* could easily be reworked into concert pieces. Is it ever frustrating to leave

things in a film that you know, were these ideas to be more fully developed and/or extended, could have successful lives as concert pieces?

Silverado and *Tombstone* do get played as concert pieces—they are basically self-contained suites. I have never thought about reworking those two; I have heard them for so long that I am used to their form and structure. I liked the way they were originally. Revisions don't seem to be necessary.

How much crossover of technique, style, or aesthetic interpretation exists between your concert work and your film work?

I find that the concert works help my technique as a film composer, and vice versa. Because you write so much as a film composer, you develop this incredible technique—you develop a lot of orchestral technique and a lot of just note-to-note technique that you can then apply to your concert music. Concert music forces you to focus on longer forms and structures, which helps in film music for extended scenes with no dialogue. Concert music also helps motivic development for film. But writing for a live concert audience is obviously not the same as writing for a mixed film audience, you have to do many different things.

It is interesting to wear different hats, even though the differences may seem very subtle. I've noticed that, in the world of classical music, composers very often will do things slightly different, even though their overall style sounds as though they are doing the same thing. Take Ravel: If you compare three or four of his major orchestral works, they are all orchestrated differently. They're all very unique, sometimes in subtle ways, and they keep their own personalities. Yet, because of his style, or whatever you want to call it, they all sound like Ravel. So we just put them a in big bag marked "Ravel," even though they are all very different.

Great composers eventually develop a recognizable style, even though each piece is quite different. Some people can identify Broughton or Webern in an instant. Stravinsky still sounded like Stravinsky, even after he turned to serialism in the 1950s.

Absolutely. Stravinsky did the same thing. Rachmaninoff did the same thing. You find a lot of guys attacking different problems in different ways, but their overall style and musical preferences make them sound as though they are always doing the same thing. It's a subtle delineation.

I probably do the same thing. If I had feature dramatic film or an animated movie or a live-action picture or a theme park or a concert piece, large or small, it might all sound like Bruce Broughton. But to me, it all sounds different—I am doing something different for each project, and I am struggling with different ideas. I had a huge advance in my compositional technique when I did *Young Sherlock Holmes*. I took another huge advance in my technique when I started working on *Tiny Toons*, because there were just a million very specific problems that I was trying to solve. I think that, in some respects, even *Shadow Conspiracy* moved me along. Every once in a while you find that big step forward.

The problems to solve in concert music are self-inflicted, but also immune from the obvious direct influence of the visual stimulant in films or cartoons.

I learned a lot about concert-music form when I was working on the big horn piece. I had no picture to follow, I didn't know where the double bar was supposed to be. I couldn't just say, "Okay, that's enough of that. Twenty-nine seconds and I can go home." Everything was fair game. It wasn't over until it was right to be over, until it made sense on its own. And, at the performance, I learned even more things about it, because it wasn't done on a click-track and it wasn't done to specific timings—I could change phrasing, I could hold something a little longer, we could play something faster, louder . . . whatever *I* wanted to do. It was also a very different experience to hear it from within a live audience environment, rather than hear it from a sound booth, with the director, the producers, and the hysterical executives breathing down your neck.

It sounds like you are one of those composers who will keep exploring, with wide-eyed wonder and curiosity, until you go to your grave. So many composers—both concert and film composers—hit on something and stay put, keep rewriting the same piece. On your bookshelf, I notice a lot of Stravinsky scores and books. Is he a hero?

I don't know that he is a big hero, but I focus on him a lot now because he had such a huge range. I have the published original sketches of *The Rite of Spring*. Now that is really interesting—to see something written by the guy in his twenties and then to hear *The Flood*, which is a serial piece from much later. It is interesting to think that it is the same guy, but you can hear that it is.

The other day I was listening to one of Strauss's early tone poems, which was written when he was about eighteen. Compare that to the oboe concerto written in 1946, when he was an old man. To hear that range and yet still see where the personalities of these guys are is fascinating. I love that.

I admire Stravinsky for the way he articulated his material and how, sometimes, when his material wasn't that wonderful, he could set it in a great way. We all know that problem—when we just can't come up with great ideas but still have to write them through. We find that problem in Bach, we find it in Britten, we find it in a lot of guys. The thing about Stravinsky is that he seems to be the most conscious composer, the most purposeful composer. It went down because he figured that was what he wanted, not only because it felt good.

Is your concert music always commissioned by universities and professional groups, or do you sometimes just write because you want to write?

Both. The pieces are commissioned or requested. The horn piece was actually written for a specific concert in England. The piccolo concerto was written for a convention of the National Flute Association. The tuba piece was written for a friend of mine—Tommy Johnson. I used to accompany Tommy and I wanted to write a piece for both of us to play. The violin piece was written more or less as a request, being revised for a specific purpose. So, yeah, I try to write music that is going to get performed; I don't like writing music that's going to sit on the shelf.

I tell young composers all the time, if you want to learn about orchestration, learn by writing. You just have to write a lot. You can't spend all your time studying. You have to spend your time writing and listening to as much stuff as you possibly can. You want to make your own corrections and see what sounds good to you. You have to find out where the good notes are for you—you are the only one who knows what the good notes are. You want to find things that work best and speak best for you.

When you set music orchestrally, you are setting your individual ideas. It is an interesting thing to orchestrate somebody else's music, like Ravel did with Mussorgsky's *Pictures at an Exhibition*. But, in fact, to set your own music properly is a big enough deal. And, frankly, *Pictures at an Exhibition* doesn't sound anything like Ravel's *Daphnis et Chloé*. The two pieces sound like they were written by two different guys because they *were* written by two different guys.

If I keep writing the same music all the time, I am going to get bored, and the music is going to get boring. I might still make plenty of money as a film composer, and I might still continue to work, but those aren't the reasons why I want to write music. But those are the reasons why *some* guys write music.

You have a strong aesthetic commitment, and it shows in your works.

Maybe it's a neurotic commitment, I don't know. I do have a strong commitment to it, but there are a lot of people who live only to write or live only for the next music. I try to have a life, too. I spend time not writing. I like to have a good time. I like to travel. I do listen to a lot of music and I know a lot of musicians, but I like to read poetry, and there are a lot of books up there on those shelves. I like to meet people and see things. I like to eat well, and all that stuff. But I think it is all part of the same process. All these things help make me a better composer. I find that writing music is really hard if you do it right. But I do it, and I really enjoy it. And when it comes out great, it is really exciting and incredibly rewarding.

To keep a private life, to avoid compositional burn-out, to keep original or whatever, do you limit yourself to a certain number of films and/or projects each year?

I would say three or four films a year, I guess. This year they are all getting released at the same time—when it rains, it pours. I don't like to do more than four—that's a lot of work. I can fill it in with other stuff, but I seem always to be busy doing something or worrying about something or fixing something.

Carried Away **is in the Broughtonesque,** *O Pioneers!* **Americana style and offers an absolutely beautiful principal theme. I transcribed the complete tune to decipher your enigmatic chord progressions. Lo and behold, there's a big tritone progression, which feels as natural as can be when we get there. Was there a dramatic reason for the tritone progression, or did it just feel good as you were messing around at the keyboard?**

The answer always is that it felt good. I saw a film the other day that a young composer had scored, and he had done a very nice

job on it. When I complimented him, he said, "Hey, did you realize at the end how I transposed and super-imposed 'Jingle Bells'
with the augmented inversion of the theme of such-and-such a
song?" And I thought, who cares? It just sounded good. The hell
with the intellectualizing. He'd found the right notes for that scene,
whether it was "Jingle Bells" or "The Hallelujah Chorus" or "I Am
The Walrus." Who cares?

**I think that many people are curious about that heart/head dis-
tinction. Franz Waxman loved complex contrapuntal writing,
fugues and canons, and found appropriate scenes to inject such
intellectual adventures, as in *Taras Bulba*. Do the practical limitations of film prevent too much musical analyzing and intellectualizing from occurring?**

There are some composers, I think Alex North is one, who could
solve a lot of their musical problems intellectually. Bernard
Herrmann, too. John Williams, sometimes. And I think that, to
some extent, Jerry Goldsmith has done it. Jerry will often sit down
and "figure it out." Maybe Horner used to do it, also. Listening to
their music, it certainly sounds as though some serious thought has
been given to development and variation. It's not just background
thunder.

I always think about my music, but I can spend weeks thinking
about it and still not have a clue as to what I *need* to do in a particular film. With *Carried Away*, a score that I really wanted to do
because I liked the movie a lot, the director, Bruno Barreto, wanted
a very, very, very simple score—I mean, *really* simple. When I would
play things for him, he would just kind of smile, shake his head,
and say, "Take out some notes." He wanted silences, he wanted big
pauses. There are a lot of solo instruments; there is no counterpoint.

**There are a few imitative musical moments, especially in the clos-
ing scenes.**

Well, as the character gradually develops this emotional life, the music becomes richer. In that way, it was sort of an intellectual decision. But it was Bruno who called it as much as anybody. At the beginning of the film, these characters are so emotionally empty, so emotionally repressed and tied down, away from their own lives, that you don't want much warmth or complexity for the music. Bruno didn't want warmth. Whatever lyrical quality there was had to be restrained. As they go through their things, emotionally, you get these little musical hints that things are beginning to happen, little emotional jabs here and there. But most of the music is very restrained until you get to the end, when the guy finally gets to the ocean, which is a big deal. Then the music becomes much more passionate.

Even the action scenes in the film are scored delicately or against the action.

There is a barn fire in the movie, and, normally, in a Hollywood barn-fire score, everyone in the orchestra is just blowing and hitting and sawing away like crazy. But not in this one—this one is a very dispassionate barn fire, because it wasn't about the fire, it was about the people and their emotional situations. They are still repressed! It is the most repressed barn fire, I think, ever in a movie. They still don't know what has happened to them, even when they have had that huge emotional/sexual thing. So, in that way, the music was well-thought-out dramatically, but mostly the decisions made were emotional decisions, not so much what's the inversion of this retrograde and all that stuff. The director usually straightened me out afterward. "You screwed that up, you know." Once, in fact, one director looked at me and said, "Oh, you're so smart, too." And I looked at the screen and thought, no, it just felt good. That was what it was. Period.

Well, your dramatic instinct is on the money.

I hope so. You know, I never liked working on *Quincy*. The people involved with the show were great, but I just didn't like the show. We would look at it on Friday, we would score it on Monday, and it would go on the air on Wednesday. There was never any chance to sit on it or think about it or intellectualize about it. I had no clue as to what the shows were really about, because they were just thrown together. And I really like to understand what a picture is all about, or at least what they're trying to say. I would sit there and try to figure out why such-and-such a character had said this or that, but, after a while, I just realized that life is too short—don't think about it, just write it.

I would get a show, and I would literally start at the top and write my way to the end. Then friends would say to me, "Boy, you have such a great dramatic instinct, because in these *Quincy*s . . ." I thought, no, I just had no clue! I look at them now and I think, well, I guess that works okay.

I saw *Independence Day* the other night, and, if I had to do that job, I would have been stopped dead in my tracks by thinking about it, because that movie just makes no sense at all. I almost walked out about ten times—it is just a waste of film. But they made a lot of money off it.

Let's talk about the contrast in sound between your two big, sprawling Westerns: *Silverado* and *Tombstone*. *Silverado* is Coplandesque Americana—lively, but aggressive and cautiously optimistic. Your score sets the mood and plays the action, with some of the greatest American brass writing of all time. *Tombstone* is darker, meaner, more dissonant and more detached, with more irregular rhythms. Was *Silverado* something of a tribute to the Republic serials of the 1930s?

With *Silverado*, [writer/director] Larry Kasdan was trying to make the original Western, trying to make a Western for people who had never seen a Western. But when you look at the film without music, it actually isn't such a big movie. At the time, I thought that it could have been done with much simpler forces, but that isn't the way he saw it. He saw it as the return of the big Western. And he wanted a big score, a big traditional score, which was fine with me, because I love that stuff.

Another thing about *Silverado* was that it had two main elements: a lot of family friendliness, a lot of warmth, a lot of friendship, but also a lot of very strong machismo—these guys are big guys and they are doing big things. So the music was like that. It had very little real counterpoint. It was basically structured vertically and made for power, *always* made for power. Larry said he liked a lot of cellos and horns because you could get that kind of emotional warmth that he wanted.

Tombstone had a different message—more Sergio Leone, less John Wayne.

That's right, *Tombstone* wasn't at all like *Silverado*. *Tombstone* was dark and nasty. These were bad people. They were a completely grim lot. Even the hero wasn't a good guy—he had his nasty side. His nastiness was relieved only by what he felt for the girl. And whatever sweetness and whatever light she could bring to it was all there was for *Tombstone*.

When they go down to the OK Corral, it is stark, dark misery. The score is tuned about a fifth lower and includes a lot of unusual low-end instruments, like a contrabass sousaphone, and a contrabass trombone. The score is weighted down again for power, but not for passion. There is a grim determination in *Tombstone*.

One of the things that I liked about *Tombstone* was that [director] George [Cosmatos] likes old American movies, likes a lot of feeling. And he, himself, has a lot of feeling, which sometimes works okay and sometimes doesn't in his movies. His movies have a lot of emotional mass to them. And no matter what music you put to *Tombstone*, you can never fill it up enough—there is so much emotional stuff in it.

In *Tombstone*, I finally felt unrestrained—I could put all this big emotional stuff in the film. I think that is what people liked about the score, that is was so big and so emotional. You won't find that in *Carried Away* or even *Harry and the Hendersons* and scores like that, because the people didn't want it—they hadn't made movies that had big emotional statements. But *Silverado* had it, *Young Sherlock Holmes*, in a sense, had it, *Honey, I Blew Up the Kid* had it, in a way—at least it had the energy. But *Tombstone* really had it. *Tombstone* is a very emotional film, and I think that colored the score more than anything else.

In *Young Sherlock Holmes*, as in *Tombstone*, you use a less traditional, or more avant-garde, approach to composition and orchestration.

At the time of *Young Sherlock Holmes*, I was working with a young orchestrator named Mark McKenzie. I was still doing essentially my own orchestrations, but we would talk about the problems in *Young Sherlock Holmes* a lot. Mark is very well-schooled and very well-trained and very gifted.

The film, itself, had so much variety, and there is all that weird hallucination business in the cemetery. We were trying to figure out how to do that—how to write it and how to notate it. We would go through scores of Henze and Penderecki—anything we could find that was similar to my ideas. We would both bring in things we knew about and study them, struggling with just how to do it.

The writing itself was somewhat like that, too. There was an awful lot of music—eighty-five minutes—and I had something like four weeks. I thought I was going to die. I was writing more music in a day than I could now. I put all this extra filigree and fine-tuning into *Young Sherlock Holmes*. I could have put it into *Silverado*, but I wasn't permitted to. The truth of the matter was that I was a new movie writer, and this was my first chance to really get out there and write some great stuff.

I liked *Young Sherlock Holmes* a lot. It held together very well dramatically and held together emotionally. It's unfortunate that the film didn't do better than it did, because it was really well-made. And it was a great thing for me to have accomplished, particularly after *Silverado*, where I'd felt so restrained to write this vertical music with all these power chords.

Let's make a sharp turn here and discuss your family's long-standing involvement with the Salvation Army Band.

My family was very involved with the Salvation Army, which has a huge music program for its evangelical stuff—street-corner musicians and all that. And, as a kid, anyone who grew up with the Salvation Army learned how to play the horn. So even though I was primarily a pianist, I did learn how to play the trumpet when I was a little kid, and ended up playing baritone and horn when I was in the Salvation Army Band. When I was in the real army, the U.S. Army, I played French horn, so I know all the brass. My brother is a terrific trombonist—a studio trombonist for years who still plays the movies when I do one.

Here is a great photograph of my grandfather with all these film composers. It was taken in 1946, when I was one year old. [Broughton takes a photograph from one of his bookshelves.] Here's Franz Waxman, Dimitri Tiomkin, Meredith Willson, William Grant Still, John Green, Miklós Rózsa, Victor Young, and Wilbur Hatch, who did the *I Love Lucy* shows. And that is my grandfather, wearing a Salvation Army uniform. This guy, who is sitting next to Meredith Willson, was the head of the international Salvation Army Music Department. Meredith Willson was a big admirer of the Salvation Army and their music and had scheduled a fancy lunch for all these film composers to come and meet him. And my grandfather, who was in charge of music that year, was invited to attend. Here is Miklós Rózsa in 1946, and, fifty years later, this guy's grandson is conducting recordings of this other guy's music.

You have a strong link to a distinctive musical style. Was this influential on your personal compositional style?

What that gave me, and you often find this with singers like Aretha Franklin and Little Richard—singers who grew up with the church as the center of everything and sang in their church choirs—was a feel for a certain kind of music. The certain kind of music that I grew up with was a lot of British brass-band music, which I have actually been trying to get away from for years and years. But anybody who knows me from that time recognizes that a lot of things in my film work are from that style of music.

Whatever I first learned about melody and harmony had its roots right there. The Salvation Army had these music camps for kids every summer, which is where I learned basic harmony when I was eight years old. When I went to college, it was redundant because I'd really learned most of it as a child. I learned to play piano when I was about five or six. So I had a fairly good, solid musical education. If being raised in a musical environment has anything that contributes to it, then mine was about as solid as it could possibly be. My dad's father was a composer who wrote a lot of brass-band music, and all four grandparents were musical. My dad is a pianist. My mother could read well. I have an uncle who is a songwriter and an aunt who is a pianist. It is a very big musical family.

When I was a younger guy, in my twenties, I wrote a lot of Salvation Army music, and, now that I am in my fifties, it is all getting played. Unbelievable, horrible—they proudly send me CDs, and I think, oh, no, don't play this! I don't have any involvement in the Salvation Army any longer, but I do get the CDs.

Paul Chihara's influential orchestral and chamber works were receiving international attention in the 1970s when, out of the blue, he seemed to disappear from the classical music landscape, only to reappear "at a theater near you." Considering that his first venture into the world of film was his score for Roger Corman's infamous *Death Race 2000* (1975), why Chihara all but abandoned an extremely successful and well-respected concert-music career for Hollywood may have more to do with the unsettled social climate of the time than anything else.

During the late 1970s, Chihara's film-music career progressed steadily as he scored a number of feature films, the haunting documentary *Farewell to Manzanar* (1976), and more than a dozen network television movies, including *Night Cries* (1978), *Mind Over Murder* (1979), and *The Darker Side of Terror* (1979). However, in 1981, he received widespread national recognition as the composer of an impressive, unsettling score for director Sidney Lumet's critically acclaimed motion picture *Prince of the City*. Throughout the 1980s, while by choice remaining active in television, for which his many scores include the 1985 remake of *The Bad Seed*, *A Bunny's Tale* (1985), *When the Bough Breaks* (1986), *Killer Instinct* (1988), and numerous episodes of the *China Beach* television series, Chihara also composed highly original and eclectic scores for such feature films as *The Survivors* (1983), *Impulse* (1984), *The Morning After*

(1986), *Crossing Delancey* (1988), *James Clavell's Noble House* (1988), and *Penn and Teller Get Killed* (1989).

One of the most animated and optimistic composers I've ever met, Chihara has, in the 1990s, found a way to balance his re-ignited concert-music activities with his teaching at UCLA and his active film-music career. During the course of our lengthy interview at Dolores' Restaurant in Los Angeles, he spoke about how his classical roots have influenced his film work and vice versa.

paul CHIHARA

In the 1970s, when I heard your piece *Tree Music*, I thought that you were one of the great unsung composers of our time.

I'm still unsung.

And then, all of a sudden, your name seemed to disappear from the concert world. Why the move to Hollywood and film music at a time when your concert career was becoming very successful?

During the late 1960s, I started to go through a change. California in the late '60s was the love-child generation—the Mamas and the Papas, Jimi Hendrix, and all that. It was a terrific time. It really was free love, by the way. But it was also the time of the Vietnam War, which lives in all our movies and mythologies. For those of us who lived through that time, and we were very young, it was a terrible reality because we all had friends who literally were with us one day and dead the next. It was not just a chic political stance that we took—we were really concerned about many, many serious things.

At the time I made the move, I was a tenured professor at UCLA, which was my first and, basically, my only full-time job in academia. And I was strongly pressured to stay there because they needed prominent, ivy-league-trained Ph.D. professionals who were minorities. At the time, I was quite unique, especially on the UCLA campus. The University of California is a very different scene now.

I knew that if I had stayed in academia, I would have a good career. My concert music was taking off, I was Composer-in-Residence with Neville Marriner and the Los Angeles Chamber Orchestra, and I was one of the program annotators for Zubin Mehta and the Los Angeles Philharmonic. I was also one of the music directors for the Monday Evening Concerts series. So, in terms of being academically and professionally respectable, it was a very good time for me. But all of these things added up to my feeling terribly trapped and compromised. I felt that I had painted myself into a corner where I had become Mr. Famous Minority Contemporary-Music Composer.

I actually didn't want to become an academic—I always wanted to work in the movies! I grew up in Seattle, in a Japanese relocation camp. I'm the generation that did not have opera or symphony—we had radio. For me, romance and adventure was the movies. Going to the movies every Saturday was a great religious experience! As I became more successful, I realized that I wasn't being fulfilled, I was just being successful. So, the decision that I made was a very important one.

I had no Hollywood credentials whatever—I did not study film music, there were no real courses in that sort of thing, and I knew nobody in the business. I was a Cornell-trained minority from Seattle, meaning that I had no real connections whatsoever.

So I was giving up a known and established world for one that was completely unknown, which, to be honest, combined with a late-sixties mentality, was part of the appeal. Looking back, I think it took either a lot of courage or a kind of stupidity and naiveté—probably equal measures of all those things. I resigned my UCLA position without anything whatsoever to fall back on. Hollywood wasn't calling me. It wasn't as if I had been given a movie. For about six months, I was quite insecure—I had no job—I even started to teach composition privately, which I think is the worst possible job in the world.

When did you resign from UCLA?

1973, but I had been considering it for some time. In 1969-70, after only two years at UCLA, I took a sabbatical and spent a year in New York. Then I came back for two years, and, in the third year of my return, I resigned.

Why?

First of all, I don't like to talk too much about music, especially my music. And I don't really have an interest in teaching counterpoint and things like that.

So, how did you survive?

I somehow struggled along. I had no family and nothing to fall back on, but I had saved a little money in my last years at UCLA.

It's very strange—when you do the right thing, the right thing happens. I got two phone calls almost immediately: one was from the San Francisco Ballet, which had heard about me from Akira Endo, who was, at that time, the conductor of the American Ballet Theater. They commissioned me to write a ballet on a Japanese Romeo and Juliet theme called *Shinju*, a classic Japanese tale. At the same time, Neville Marriner asked me to be the first Composer-in-Residence with the newly formed Los Angeles Chamber Orchestra. That was a very good move for me because it eventually led to work with the London Symphony, writing little arrangements and working on commissions.

But when was your break into Hollywood?

Around the time that all this stuff was happening, I got a strange phone call from Roger Corman's secretary. I was officially still on the faculty at UCLA, where I had been in charge of the electronic studio, and she said, "We would like to have one of your electronic

composition students do some cues for a new science-fiction movie."
So, I said, "Sure, I'll send my best student." Of course, I went myself
and, since I looked very young then, the ruse actually worked.

I said to Roger, "Why don't you let me do the entire score?"
He's no fool—he could see talent and hunger, but he could also
see a quick buck. So he said, "If you do the score, I'll give you a
thousand dollars," which, to me, at the time, seemed like an enormous annuity. I did not realize that this was not my fee—it was the
entire music budget. It was a package deal. The picture was *Death
Race 2000*.

**This thousand-dollar budget was to finance your time, the con-
tract players, union fees, recording space . . .**

Everything. I can't tell you all the ways that I used to do it, but I
did it, of course, losing money. I had no experience whatsoever in
writing film music, and there were a lot of other neophytes on that
project, many of whom have become very famous—Robert Towne,
who later wrote *Chinatown*; David Carradine, before his *Kung Fu*
series; John Landis; Paul Bartel; and Sylvester Stallone.

For me, it was a crash seminar on how to write for films. I knew
nothing about a click track, I had no music editor, I had to do it all
myself with a Moviola, which I promptly broke. I had no experience, but I had a lot of enthusiasm and I was a good composer and
I loved movies. You *have* to love movies.

Notice I didn't say "film." When you say "film," you're talking
about Kurosawa or Truffaut or Bergman. When I say movies, I mean
Steve Martin or John Wayne or Alan Ladd, you know? To me, these
were works of art. I suspect that the Italians in the nineteenth century went to the opera in the same way. I don't think they went to
Wagner or Mozart, they went to see the latest gut-busting, heartbreaking Puccini—the top of the line for them—and a lot of other
stuff that we don't read about in the music history books.

Critics agree that *Death Race 2000* was the principal inspiration for the *Mad Max* movies.

Absolutely. It's very clear.

Paul Bartel still refers to *Death Race* lovingly. All of us who worked on it refer to it lovingly. We were a collection of total amateurs, all learning together. It was great.

After resigning from UCLA and, for all intents and purposes, leaving the concert world, where you had become a recognizable new-music success, what sort of reactions did you receive from the concert-music community?

There were two rejections: The first rejection came from academia itself, at least at UCLA. As a matter of fact, I was surprised and delighted when I met you, even though that was many years later, to know that you still had some respect for me as a serious composer, or didn't think that it had been a compromise to quit academia. But I know many of my colleagues said, "Oh, he never would have gotten full professor anyway," or they felt I was becoming too shallow.

Were your former colleagues a little jealous? Envious of your courage?

I don't think it was jealousy over my career move, but it might have been a jealousy of my move, period. The comment that I heard, straight to my face, was, "Oh, he's gone Hollywood," which shows you how the world has changed. At that time, a comment like that was a vicious insult, but I really don't think that it would be considered so anymore. From my perspective, we've changed for the better. Corigliano, John Adams, Phil Glass—people who are extremely established and respectable in the concert world—haven't lost respectability because they've done real Hollywood pictures.

Do your early concert pieces survive through performances by major orchestras?

The ballets have a very good shelf life. *The Tempest*, for example, is performed quite a lot. Live, on the radio, on television. I've heard it in New York, Pittsburgh, a lot of places. It was written in 1979 and, at the time, critics complained that it was just another cheap Hollywood score from a once well-respected composer. But they don't say that anymore because of a wonderful term—*post-modernism!* Suddenly, my score has become respectable.

The score to *Death Race 2000* is an extremely eclectic blend of compositional styles—complex baroque-style writing, 1970s disco/ dance music, light neo-classical chamber music, and avant-garde Chihara.

First of all, I did not record that score to picture. I was given the print and a Moviola, but I stripped the print almost immediately, and I didn't have the courage to tell them because I thought they would fire me. So I was composing wild, so to speak.

Luckily, Paul Bartel had a very unusual way of working—if he'd hear something that he liked, he'd say, "I can use that!" and then he'd put it wherever he wanted to. For example, Paul used my Bach fugue over all of the final chase, the climactic chase of the movie. I didn't intend that—I don't know what I wrote the fugue for, but he stuck it over that chase and it was brilliant. I wrote what I thought was appropriate, but Paul Bartel, in his lunatic genius way, put the music wherever he wanted to. I learned so much from that—it was like a great seminar in film composing.

Did you compose both the acoustic and electronic elements of the score?

I wrote a lot of analog electronic music for the chases—you know, fast chase equals lots of sound effects and fast electronic rock-and-roll music. Now, remember, back in those days, electronic rock scores were very unusual, almost unheard of. Vangelis hadn't come out yet with *Chariots of Fire*, there was no *Miami Vice*, there was no Harold Faltermeyer. The big record on the scene was *Switched-On Bach*, and the great arbiter of electronic music in Los Angeles was Paul Beaver, who did some of the electronic effects—mostly ring modulation and very simple analog effects—in Kubrick's *2001*. Those were very effective sounds, by the way. I'm not sure that we can come up with those stunning sounds with all our sampling and ProTools and all the rest of the stuff that we have today. In fact, it's interesting for me to see contemporary editors using digital equipment to approximate or recreate analog sounds.

Were any specific sections of your score composed to specific scenes?

I would always put fast music on chase scenes, love music on love scenes, and so forth. What did I know? I just gave Paul so many fast cues and so many soft cues, and he assembled them like so many Lincoln Logs.

There's one chase scene where the car is running out of control, but it's actually a love scene. Well, I played the scene on the nose, but Paul took the saxophone theme that I had written for the earlier bedroom love scenes and just stuck it over the car chase. It worked extremely well. I used a lot of that approach for my Sidney Lumet movies.

Are many elements of the movies that you've worked on assembled in the cutting room?

They say that films are assembled in the cutting room. We see examples of that time and again, where great directors assemble things from footage that may have been designed to come in some sort of linear sequence but which the director disrupts for some other vision. This is the first time I realized that you do that in music, too.

During these early Hollywood experiences, I still had my concert career—I was still receiving commissions from the Cleveland Orchestra, the Chicago Symphony, and the Boston Symphony. But I was never the same composer after that experience of assembling a piece, so to speak, from the cutting-room floor. As long as I was writing good music, good footage, so to speak, I felt that I could assemble it in almost any way. And, in a way, that's a good definition of post-modernism. In a way, I was lead to what is now considered a post-modern stance by my work in film music.

Assembling music of different styles, combining eclectic approaches?

Yes, but I'm talking about my concert music now. Back in the 1970s, when critics would hear pieces like *The Tempest*, they could only use the word that was very popular at the time—"eclectic." People would say things like, "It sounds like it was composed by a committee." But, as I said earlier, no one really says that anymore about me or other composers, like you, who, in effect, assemble pieces.

***Death Race 2000*'s closing credits use "America," but it crumbles into a densely chromatic, almost dissonant arrangement. Did you specifically write that for the closing scene?**

I didn't write it for the end credit. It was written for the scene where Mr. President turns out to be a fraud.

All the grotesquery was planned by me. I wanted to write an American version of "Deutschland über Alles" from the Haydn Kaiser string quartet. But, of course, I couldn't use "Deutschland über Alles," so I chose "America," and wrote it in a classical, Haydnesque style. But, if you listen between the lines, you'll hear references to Wagner's "Siegfried's Death." I was mixing styles in an Ivesian way, but not as stream-of-consciousness, more like Haydn motives become Wagnerian.

The Survivors is a black comedy/social satire with Robin Willams and Walter Matthau. Your score bears similarities to *Death Race 2000*—sarcastic pseudo-patriotism, baroque-style writing, Wagner references . . .

Yeah, and I had a real budget for that one, and a real orchestra.

The first half of the movie has virtually no music, and the final half has almost wall-to-wall music. The music first appears when Robin Williams brings home his newly purchased arsenal of weapons, and we hear a beautiful, innocent love theme as he caresses his new assault rifle.

In many ways, this Michael Ritchie movie was prophetic—way ahead of its time in dealing with the whole idea of survivalists, militia groups like we heard about with Tim McVeigh. Militias have become much more of an issue now than they were then. It seemed to many people who saw the movie at the time that we were exaggerating or taking cheap shots at one or two well-known people. Now it seems, if anything, understated.

Michael Ritchie, who was known at that time for the *Bad News Bears* movies, one of which I did, also directed a very well-respected picture called *Smile*, a biting satire on beauty pageants in California, which was later turned into a Broadway show with a score by Marvin Hamlisch. Ritchie is primarily a satirist—Harvard-educated, very bright, very articulate—and his films tend to be very talky and script-oriented. *The Survivors* was one of those.

That explains the absence of music in the first half of the movie, whereas the second half is much more action-oriented, with less dialogue.

Yes. You can't get in the way of the dialogue. The music can be another voice in a the dialogue, but you don't want it to become an argument with everyone talking at once.

Michael Ritchie had a very clear idea of how he wanted the music to operate. He always does. At that time, he heavily temp-tracked his pictures before the composer was hired, which, of course, is like a private message to the composer. Ritchie specifically wanted the Huey Long song "Every Man a King," because he was drawing a parallel between the economic conditions of the 1970s and the Depression—both economically depressed situations created a sort of desperation that let to vigilantism, rebellion, and exaggerated patriotism. He got the rights to Randy Newman's arrangement of that song, which, when I came on the picture, was already pre-determined by the studio and Michael Ritchie to be the main title.

Were your expected to interpolate "Every Man a King" into your score?

At first, I thought I should use it somehow, but Michael did not want me to make the score a set of variations on the theme song. He wanted me to compose it by going into the fantasies of the characters in the movie.

By the way, the big movie of that year was *Yanks*, with a score by Richard Rodney Bennett. And the big song in it was "I'll Be Seeing You." *Yanks* had a lot of love music—sincere music, romantic music—for a movie about a war that was *just*. Michael loved that. There were no war protesters for that war, nor should there have been. He wanted to have that same sense of cause, that same sense of belief and naive acceptance of warfare as the only way to survive. That's the emotion I was trying to get in the gun cue, but you're quite right, it plays against the military implication of the weapons as Robin falls in love with his guns. It's sarcastic, but it's also frightening and grim and funny at the same time. It *is* the first time the music was allowed to make a commentary on the action. Up until that scene, the movie is primarily exposition about the bank robbery, setting up the characters, all that stuff.

That scene is a striking first appearance of music. Not only does it comment on the relationship between the Robin Williams character and his guns, but it also clearly establishes the satirical direction of the movie.

I really feel that's the beginning of the movie.

But it takes a while to get there.

That's right. And that confused us, because getting up to that scene, Jerry Reed, the bank robber, became a more and more important character in postproduction. His character, because of the strong appearance he made at the beginning, began to take over and Robin's role actually began to diminish a little bit.

During the first training session at the militia camp—super-macho guys in aggressive physical activity—the score is a campy vocal arrangement of "Life Is Just a Bowl of Cherries." And the rhythm of the song synchronizes with the action—it slows down to a crawl as they struggle to scale the wall, then it accelerates as they slide down the other side. This *has* to be your own arrangement.

[Laughter] You're right, the arrangement is mine, the recording is mine, the production is mine. I worked it to the scene. I had a couple of the Hi-Los singing with me on that, and I made the arrangement by listening to their original chart. I took some liberties with it, which I thought were appropriate, but I was *shocked* when, at the recording session, one of them stopped me and said, "That's not an A-major chord, that's an A minor 7!" I was like, "All right, all right! What's the big deal?" I thought it was a clever touch. I didn't think it was the wrong chord, just a different chord.

In the suspenseful music that accompanies the highway scenes, driving to and from the militia camp, are you having fun with

Hitchcock and Herrmann, like John Morris played off that style in *High Anxiety*?

Are you talking about the driving scene from *Psycho*? [Chihara sings the *Psycho* driving theme.] Sure. But, to be honest, there's a very strong Jerry Goldsmith influence. Jerry has always been, and he still is, a role model for me. He is *the* great film composer. Look at all those great scores—*Planet of the Apes*, *Poltergeist*, something like 300 scores—and a lot of them are just terrific. His big movie at that time was *Patton* and, I must admit, I have *Patton*-like military references in my score, diluted and wacked-out to fit the nature of *The Survivors*. *Patton* was real epic, our movie was mock-epic.

The wholesome fife-and-drum-corps music that accompanies the wacko militia . . .

I had four field drums and four piccolos. And that is very much Jerry Goldsmith-influenced. When I quote, or when I'm referential, I want people to know what I'm quoting. I want people to know this is *Patton*, but only *Patton* as seen in the imagination of Robin Williams.

Why three different references to Wagner's *Ride of the Valkyries*? At one point, Robin Williams even sings the tune as he's escaping on the dogsled, after his satirical line "Oh, God, I love the smell of malamute in the morning."

Well, I had to do that. If a character, a visual source, sings something on screen, it's as good as a command to me to pick it up. When I got the cut of the picture, Wagner was already in there.

In the final showdown between Robin Williams and Jerry Reed, as they chase each other through the forest, military music dissolves into Carl Stalling-style cartoon music fused with Chihara *Tree Music*.

That's right! And the stalking around in the snow was mostly doublebass that was specifically from my concert piece *Logs*. Michael had heard a recording of *Logs* and liked it a lot. He actually cut it into the picture at one point and liked the way it worked. What I wrote is self-referential—it's not the same piece, but it's the same texture.

You've scored two Sidney Lumet pictures, *Prince of the City* and *The Morning After*. I read that some of the music you composed for *Prince of the City* didn't make it into the final version of the film, and that you rearranged the music and created a concert suite for the Varèse Sarabande recording.

That's true. Sidney Lumet himself talks about that in his book, which is probably where you read it. The reason why some of my music did not get into the picture was that the scenes for those cues were cut.

It was very interesting how this picture developed. There was much more action in the rough cut—there were scenes that had a more melodramatic style and therefore prompted a more melodramatic score. On subsequent screenings, as the picture began to evolve in Sidney's mind, he began to see it as a classical tragedy, where all the violence and action takes place off stage, or off screen in this case. For that reason, much of the more extroverted, tormented music that I had written was no longer appropriate for the picture—the scenes that the music had accompanied were simply not there anymore.

Director Arthur Lubin said, "Most film scores duplicate the action or emotion already being played on the screen or are so neutral that they simply fill silences like Muzak in an elevator. The key to a good score is finding a function for the score that is not being filled by any other element in the picture." Did that sort of thinking inform your work on *Prince of the City*?

There's a lot of sex in the movie, but Lumet did not want any romantic music, except when the cop buddies were together. He specifically said he wanted a love theme for the buddies, which, by the way, is very much like Michael Ritchie saying he wanted a love theme for the gun in *The Survivors*. This is what I would call a musical point-of-view. Just as the camera has a POV, I think music should, too.

There are a number of prominent alto saxophone solos in your score. How did you decide on instrumentation?

I felt that any movie that has to do with New York City detective life, modern film noir, if you will, has to have alto saxophone. For me, film noir of the Raymond Chandler type *is* alto saxophone, so I decided to use it. But I didn't think that it would be playing over Detective Ciello and his cop buddies, I thought it was going to play over Ciello and his wife, because there are many tender scenes between them. But Sidney took the recording and played it over a scene where the guys were just sitting around discussing something, and it worked so touchingly. With that, it became clear that the only real love, the only real loyalty for these guys was for their buddies, their partners. It's a very macho world out there, and they wouldn't be caught dead talking to each other affectionately, but we can *hear* that's where the true love is. In fact, Ciello says, "I sleep with my wife, but I live with my partner."

Sidney Lumet seems to have a strong dramatic instinct when it comes to music.

I've never had a director be so specific. He didn't try to write the music for me—he didn't say, "I want it in D minor here," or something like that. But what I liked about him was that he knew how he wanted the music to operate musically. By this, I mean that he wanted a theme to deteriorate as a character deteriorates—things like that. He asked specifically, "Can you write a theme that begins to crack up?"

I've talked with other composers who have worked with him, and they all say the same thing—he's an artistic director who has very clear ideas about how the music must operate dramatically, which is extremely helpful.

Do many directors have trouble trying to communicate their ideas about the music?

Some. Lumet's telling me that he wanted the theme to crack up was a very direct way to talk. I knew exactly what he meant, and it made sense. He might not know the big fancy academic words like diminution or retrograde or whatever, but his directions were crystal clear. He also said he wanted another theme to be very high in register, as if it's in the person's imagination, haunting him.

On the recording, there is a sprawling contemporary orchestral fugue, "The Set-Up," which I couldn't find in the movie.

That was a scene that we agonized over, and the music lost out. It's a very important scene—the first time that Ciello allows himself to act as a snitch. It's a very quiet scene filled with innuendo. Sidney specifically said, at the spotting session, that he wanted us to feel that the character is being drawn into quicksand. I suggested a fugue because, to me, the idea of growing complexity suggests counterpoint.

Lumet says that themes need to weave a path throughout a film— "they join, they part, they touch, they explode, they mix." Isn't he actually thinking contrapuntally?

Yes. He never used that term but, you know, directors and filmmakers think contrapuntally all the time. They'll use a phrase like "simultaneous story" or something.

I have a question about large-scale harmonic relationships in long, through-composed movies. A falling, half-step, sighing motive—

B♭-A, B♭-A, B♭-A—opens *Prince of the City*. At the big climax, in
the middle of the picture, the sigh returns more fully orchestrated,
but transposed up a tritone to E-D♯, E-D♯, E-D♯. Does this follow
the Bartók philosophy of tritones being equal?

Well, partly, yes. But the main reason I chose those pitches is because I'm a violinist. I knew that when the climax arrived, I wanted
that sighing motive, but I had to have it as intense as possible. On
the violin, if you have an E♮ natural, played as a harmonic, with a
D♯ against it, you get a scream. When the climax comes on that motive, it is extremely intense. The harmonic E on the E-string is like
a file going through teeth, a very harsh sound.

    Also, with the B♭-A opening that you mentioned, the harmonic
A is a soft sound, which, when you put the B♭ against it, has a lyric
color that is warmer than the climactic E-D♯ combination. The fact
that they're a tritone apart was perfect for the storyline. Classical
composers would plan entire pieces around that, right?

In your film music, are you in total control of your orchestrations?

Always. I even did all my own orchestrations for *China Beach*, unless I was really in a time crunch, which occasionally happened.

    I orchestrated every note of *Prince of the City* myself. For com-
posers, orchestration should be a fun part of the creative process.
And for those of us who come through the university, how often
do we get a first-class orchestra—sixty to eighty pieces? I'm not
going to pass up that great opportunity. No way!

**Bernard Herrmann felt that orchestration was a completely per-
sonal part of the creative process. To emphasize that idea, he once
said that if he gave the first fifty measures of *Das Rheingold*, in
sketch, with clearly defined orchestrational indications and markings, to twenty different composers, none of them would even be
close to the original Wagner.**

I agree. Orchestration, when you have the luxury of time, becomes the actual sounds we hear. Far beyond the cute little themes and perky little melodies, it's part of a score's final success or failure. It's like another level of motivic development. The simplistic motive of Beethoven's Fifth would never be successful in the hands of an amateur. With Beethoven, it's not only powerful, it's also menacing, it's also carefree. It's all these things because of motivic development *and* orchestration.

What are your feelings about ghost-writing and scores that are the work of multiple hands/minds—scores where the credited composer will get the job, but farm out much of the work to a stable of other composers, usually struggling young composers who are trying to get a foot in the door?

Well, I'm not against that; it's a different world now—it's a different sensibility, it's a different audience. But *I* could never do it. Certain of today's movie scores are produced like records. The product is a group product, so the important thing is no longer the writer or the arranger, but the producer.

The producer, which is basically the role assumed by the guys that you're talking about, has the primacy of artistic direction. They compose some, but they primarily manage everyone else and keep control over the group product. I do admire a good producer of that kind of collaborative effort, because it's very complicated.

But don't we lose the individual voice of the composer?

Yeah, but . . . By the way, I think *Prince of the City* sounds like me, doesn't it? I mean it sounds like my concert music.

It's definitely the Chihara sound.

Thank you, but you also know where that sound comes from. You're familiar with the international contemporary music that came from

Eastern Europe in the 1960s and 1970s. It was a sound that we all heard, and many of us learned to apply it or incorporate it into our own works. I was among the first, I think, to apply that international Penderecki school in a controlled environment in film. But now, sounds like that are simply being sampled and placed within a rhythmic context that suggests contemporary pop music. The sampling process has totally changed how music is being composed or, I should say, how music is being produced for movies today.

I tend to use the word "produced" a lot more these days because of my role in my latest Disney animation project, in which I'm actually more of a music supervisor than a composer.

Because you're a good composer, you'll be a good supervisor?

I think so. The producer brings together all the collaborative elements. He is actually creating all the time. Good producers have done that all along, even though they've used somebody else's tune or idea.

I do think, however, that if this method of composing by committee is extended to the *traditional underscore*, it's regrettable. Scores that are orchestrated by many different people and composed by many different people are sometimes quite weak and often mediocre and disappointing, usually because they're referential—they're trying to sound like Bernard Herrmann if it's a suspense movie or trying to sound like Tiomkin or Elmer Bernstein or Ennio Morricone if it's a Western. They lose focus. A referential score works only if you have a strong composer who knows when he's being referential, when he's paying homage.

John Morris?

John Morris is an excellent example. You can almost hear and see the scene that he's referring to. But you're supposed to because Mel Brooks is doing the same thing—you're supposed to see *The Bride of Frankenstein*, you're supposed to see *Vertigo*.

Sidney Lumet has an eclectic awareness for music in his films: Mikis Theodorakis' ethnic music in *Serpico*, the scoreless *Fail-Safe*, Quincy Jones' urban jazz score for *The Pawnbroker* . . .

That's right. Did you know that Sidney wanted John Cage for *The Pawnbroker?*

I think he also went after Gil Evans and then John Lewis and the Modern Jazz Quartet.

Yes. Sidney's book, *Making Movies*, has a wonderful chapter on scoring for pictures.

The Morning After, your second score for Sidney Lumet, has a great deal of orchestral music. You have three primary musical ideas in that score: the suspense music, which is basically the classic Chihara *Tree Music* style—atonal, cluster-filled, contrapuntal; the soprano sax theme, which is sort of *Body Heat*-style, but in a more complicated harmonic world; and a funky mid-1980s urban groove. As in *Prince of the City*, you find many ways to develop these three ideas, separately and fused in various combinations.

This conversation is making it clear to me that Sidney has actually influenced my concert thinking. You use the word "fuse," and he would say that, too. But now we use a different word for that same thing, we use a term borrowed from the computer world— "morph." Visually, we see that all the time—one face dissolves into another face. It's not a jump, it's a morph. Musically, most good composers have been doing that all along—for centuries.

Movies like *Prince of the City* are not action-packed, but they are emotionally active.

Right. *The Morning After* deals with the same sort of spiritual growth. *Prince of the City* is actually spiritual destruction, spiritual fragmentation. *The Morning After* is the reverse—two people who are considered losers find each other and recover. Sidney's always very clear about character development; he would have been a fantastic director for Broadway plays.

In both movies, we had long discussions as to where the big change occurs. In *Prince of the City*, where does Ciello finally go off the deep end? In *The Morning After*, where is that point when Jane Fonda stops being in denial and begins to accept love and admit her alcoholism? For Jane Fonda, we decided that the point comes in the scene where she's reflecting on those old Nancy Drew novels.

The music for that scene is so subtle. It's tender, sentimental, healthy, reflective, and innocent—a complete contrast to the manic, dissonant score that has supported her frantic life up to that point in the movie. It's a terrific spot.

Yes. Thank you. That actually started out as counterpoint.

Sidney thought that the theme for Jane Fonda should be with the oboe. I suggested that, since she has an alcoholic, split personality, there's this very dark side to her—she really exists in the dark world of film noir, which, of course, for me, means my favorite film-noir instrument, saxophone, right? [Laughter] But I didn't say alto saxophone in this case, because the soprano saxophone and the oboe are so much closer in range and timbre and agility and so forth. The soprano sax is like the sexy, smoky, sleazy side of her split personality. The theme is introduced as a saxophone theme but, as she starts to get healthier, it changes to oboe. At the end, it's all oboe, which sounds much healthier.

When the soprano sax is playing, I may have a rhythm section with it, and always a cocktail piano under it. I asked the piano player to play it like he was playing a smoke-filled room where everybody's drinking scotch and martinis. Later on, when the same tune comes with an oboe, there's no cocktail piano at all—now there's harp and strings. It's as if the development of her theme parallels her emotional development. I kept the theme in the same key throughout the picture because she's always basically the same person, we're just gradually stripping away all the extraneous crap from her life, and from the music.

The Jane Fonda music gradually relaxes throughout the picture—the harmonic motion becomes more simplistic; the theme begins to focus; the material becomes less complicated, less chromatic, less non-functional. Like Jane's character, the theme becomes a more secure entity.

Yes, it does. It's always the same tune, and often with the same basic harmonization, but the dissonant, "wrong" notes, if you will—the added tones in the accompaniment, the blues notes—gradually disappear throughout the picture.

In the telephone scene, which reminded me of Franz Waxman's opening credits for _Sorry, Wrong Number_, the phone is knocked off the hook, and that annoying beep - beep - beep - beep lasts for nearly two minutes while your atonal string figures sort of float in-time with the telephone pulse. I assume that you worked your score off that pulse.

Absolutely. The telephone plays a very important part in this movie. In the very first scene, she's on the telephone while, unknown to her, there's this dead body lying in bed next to her. When she hangs up the phone, "click" comes on the downbeat of that cue. I put a streamer to that click.

I know Sidney and, as much as he likes music, he's not going to let it drown out something important, like a phone click or ring or buzz. Also, a phone buzzing like that is, as you said, a very annoying, tension-filled sound. Clearly, it was an expository element that I knew I could capitalize on.

Earlier on in the film, when the Fonda character is frantically clean-ing blood off of the sink and the mirrors and the toilet . . .

That's very Bernard Herrmann.

It's nonstop suspense music, except for the moment when she extracts the bloody knife from the dead body, which is played against silence. As she resumes her mad cleaning spree around the bedroom, the suspense music resumes. It's chilling, but it's also almost a moment of comic relief.

Yeah, that's Sidney. The *sound* of extracting the knife was the mu-sic for that moment.

There's another theme that you may have missed—a very brief twelve-tone-like theme played by the bass flute in the lowest pos-sible register. That's for the cat! You see, in every murder mystery, there's always a witness—in this movie, it's the cat, which I played with this little atonal bass flute motive. The presence of this motive tells us that she's not alone. The cat knows the killer, right?

Anyhow, I know Sidney, and I knew he would want to play the sound of the creaking floor, so, when I wrote this section, I didn't use any rhythm track—the floor creaks were my rhythm track. I think it worked very well. That was the reason he mixed the music so loud there—it wasn't in any way fighting the dialogue or the sound effects.

In the exciting grand finale, all thematic materials pull together, explode, and eventually generate a happy ending. In a picture that is so emotionally complicated and, in some respects, virtually sur-realistic, do you feel that the good old happy ending might be a bit of a sell-out? I was disappointed that everything worked out just fine.

You've got your finger on a problem, but I think your discontent has a different source. I liked the happy ending—the fact that she recovers and that Jeff Bridges was her savior, so to speak. It's unusual for Sidney to have a movie with such a happy ending. I liked having the opportunity to finally play her theme straight.

The problem has to do with the denouement or the clarification of the plot right before that point. The original version of the picture was different—it did not have the fight scene where the killer tries to drown her. The original ending was much more complex, but had less action. For me, personally, it was more satisfying. It had to do with Jeff Bridges and Jane Fonda setting a trap for the killer. They have to get him to admit, in front of witnesses, that his girlfriend was the killer and that he's covering for her. It's a little bit talky, more consistent with the rest of the picture, and the cat, again, plays a very important part. Well, for some reason, when we screened this, some of the "suits" said, "We don't have a clue what's happening." One of the realities of filmmaking is that it's not a committee of three, it's a committee of three thousand!

Was the entire scene reshot to satisfy the producers and the audience?

Yes. The last scene was actually reshot after everybody had gone home. And, to be honest, it was filmed without Jane Fonda and Jeff Bridges being there at the same time. If you look at the scene, knowing that, you'll be impressed with how cleverly it was put together. As an isolated scene, I think it really works, but it's not like the rest of the movie. In the original version, when the denouement came, with Jane Fonda visiting Jeff Bridges in the hospital, I felt that the temperature, the pacing, was correct. But now, coming out of that intense action scene, it does feel a little bit like a tacked-on, gratuitous happy ending, but it's not the happy ending that was tacked on, it's the fight scene before it.

I wrote a very complex, contrapuntal action sequence for that scene—Sidney said, "Pull out all the stops here. We really want to give them a big ending and make what's happening clear to everybody."

Crossing Delancey has very little underscore, but uses a lot of source. Were your decisions as composer, music director, and music supervisor a reaction to a temp track?

She [Joan Micklin Silver] did not temp the picture, but she had very specific ideas about how the music should work. She wanted me, from the very start, to work with The Roches, and she wanted the song "Come Softly to Me." When The Roches sing "Come Softly to Me," they sing it a cappella. They were a terrific a cappella group. They were a lot of fun to work with.

How did you work within and around these prescribed musical decisions?

Being given an assignment that is very specific about music, I had a number of problems to deal with. For example, if we wanted to begin with "Come Softly to Me," that's the wrong period, unless we're going to say it's a source cue. So I had to rearrange it—what you hear is not the Roches record, it's my arrangement, my production. If you listen to it carefully, you'll hear this disco background, because we're saying this is the 1970s, yuppie upper-West Side—a very time-specific environment. Right away, we're setting the time and the place through the music. That's a classic use of film music.

Other choices included using Prokofiev's *Lieutenant Kije.* [Chihara sings *Kije* theme] That was because I felt that this yenta, marching off to get people married, reminded me of someone going into battle. It's mock-heroic.

What about your work on the miniseries *King of the Olympics*?

That was a Turner Productions miniseries about Avery Brundage. The score was done almost entirely on Synclavier. I had a string quartet and a few winds and percussion, but we're moving into the 1980s now, and sampling is becoming more frequent. It was a fun picture for me because it was a fifty-year retrospective of a man's life.

For any picture that carries a long time span, the music, like costumes, is one of the principal ways to establish the period. So, that was fun for me—I got a chance to write in a lot of different styles, which I enjoy and have been doing since *The Tempest*.

You scored a remake of *The Bad Seed*. The original film was an intelligent but shocking Freud vs. Jung classic that had an extremely effective and disarming Alex North score—a score which also incorporated bizarre, polytonal distortions of that cute little French folk song for psycho Rhoda's piano practicing. Did you look at the original when you got the new *Bad Seed*?

No, I definitely did not. I already had my own idea for it. You're going to laugh, but I was actually influenced by Verdi's *Aida*. [Laughter] Seriously, the opening theme of *Aida*—that high violin line, that celestial stuff, not the triumphal march and all that pyramid stuff—always seemed so spooky to me, and yet so engaging and alluring. I played Rhoda like an angel, not like a bad seed—I played against picture. Actually, if we believe all that genetic-code stuff they're talking about in the movie, none of this is really her fault. I mean, it's just bad luck, right? It's a bad seed inside of an otherwise perfectly darling little girl. So my score wasn't actually against picture.

Your approach might generate a little more sympathy for Rhoda.

Maybe. I hope so.

In the past few years you've been traveling a lot. You've been Composer-in-Residence at Princeton University, Duquesne University, professor of film studies at UCLA. Now, from one extreme to another, you're working as composer/music supervisor on Japanese-animated Disney films for theatrical release in the United States.

I'm only a visiting professor at UCLA. I have a few composition students and teach a course on film music.

About the Disney projects: It's a brave new world. It's a world that I have never seen before. I am working in a studio in which, in postproduction, there is no film anywhere. I, in my analog mind, still say, "advance this fifteen frames" or whatever. And I'm good at it, I'm very accurate after all these years, and I can conduct to picture without streamers and all that stuff. But it's no longer necessary. We can get orchestral sounds without a live person anywhere. I'm still composing, I'm still coming up with the melodic material and the ideas, but the realization is either in my hands or in the hands of my engineer or a combination of both.

You work with placing ideas in specific context to the picture?

Yes. Ideas are everything. I know that sounds very philosophical. You know, Toru Takemitsu and I were very good friends, and, when he first came to the Marlboro Music Festival, I was the composer-in-residence along with him. I'll never forget one of the things Takemitsu said to me when I was criticizing a performance of one of his works. He said, "Oh, no, don't worry about that, that's unimportant. The idea was good; the idea was important. The idea is everything."

I believe that's true—the idea that you have *is* everything—like Sidney Lumet's idea that he wants a theme to crack up and deteriorate. The realization of it, he left in the hands of his trusted composer. Working in this brave new world of Japanese-animated Disney movies, the ideas are what I have to sell them.

john CORIGLIANO

Internationally esteemed composer John Corigliano writes wildly eclectic, complex, intensely emotional, and brilliantly orchestrated music that players, academics, and the public genuinely enjoy. Among his many important concert works are Concerto for Piano and Orchestra (1968), the innovative Concerto for Clarinet and Orchestra (1977), *Pied Piper Fantasy* (1982), and the searing and impassioned Symphony No. 1 (1989), for which he received the Pulitzer Prize. A commission for the 100th Anniversary of the Metropolitan Opera in New York City generated his critically acclaimed grand opera buffa *The Ghosts of Versailles* (1990-91). Although Corigliano has but three film-music credits to his name, he is considered to be a significant contributor to the art form—like composer Alban Berg, it's quality, not quantity, that counts.

Corigliano's film scores are extensions of his identifiable concert-music language, employing the same compositional techniques and gestures and a fusion of tonal and non-tonal materials within the contexts of dramatic function and artistic integrity. His modernistic score for *Revolution* (1985) followed an extremely aggressive, innovative, and influential Oscar-nominated score for Ken Russell's *Altered States* (1980), music that has since enjoyed a successful concert life as *Three Hallucinations for Orchestra*. His score for *The Red Violin* (1999) explores musical ideas of broad historical and international implications. The inherent drama and theatrical flair of his music make him a "natural" film composer who many Hollywood composers recognize as a powerful influ-ence on their own work.

During his visit to Butler University, as guest composer with the university's symphony orchestra, we found a few hours to discuss his film music.

john CORIGLIANO

Are you aware of any of your concert-music scores being used for film temp tracks?

Oh, yes, there's quite a bit used in temp tracks. *Altered States* is used a lot. For example, there was a rather grade-Z movie called *The Hand*—one of Oliver Stone's first directing jobs, I believe— with this little severed hand that went around killing people. They asked me to come to Hollywood to look at the movie. They had put a lot of *Altered States* music in it as temp, which was why they wanted me to compose its score. Because it was a genre horror film, I quite seriously suggested to them that they get some of Bernard Herrmann's scores, adapt them to the film, and rerecord them in Dolby stereo. I said, "It's wonderful music that would fit this kind of movie—it was really made for the kind of world you're recreating." Well, they didn't like that suggestion at all. They just shipped me back to New York. But they used *Altered States* as a temp track, and I know that a lot of other films have used it and my concert music as temp tracks, including the new *Red Violin* movie, which used things from my Symphony and other pieces as temp tracks.

Has any of your concert music been used in the final cuts of films, in the way that *The Shining*, *Fearless*, and *2001*, for example, used existing contemporary concert music?

It's been used on television, which I found out about afterwards. But, no, I've not had any specific things used in films, at least that I am aware of. Many film composers have used my techniques in their scores. My scores are at Warner Bros., and a lot of composers have written to me that they went there and studied them after hearing *Altered States*. They found my scores very appropriate for film work, especially some of the harmonies and the notation—the duration technique of time cues rather than beating meters. My student Elliot Goldenthal, of course, has some of that in his music, too. He's a very rich and versatile composer in terms of what he does.

What are the legal ramifications regarding use of your concert music in film and television?

I suppose the rights are provided through my publisher, because they own the copyright. I know that Samuel Barber, who was ill with cancer at the time, got a phone call from the *Platoon* people, asking about using his *Adagio for Strings*. Barber was delighted with that. They negotiated a very favorable contract because the movie was already out.

After your artistic and critical successes with *Altered States*, were you offered more films?

Tons and tons of films. But there's a real problem for a concert composer if he starts doing a lot of films. If you do a lot of films, you start to lose your artistic credibility, unfortunately. But that may be changing now, slowly.

Changing for the better in some ways—positive critical recognition of Goldenthal, Christopher Young, Howard Shore, et al. in the concert-music community.

Right. But, remember, even Korngold and Rózsa lost a lot of the prestige they had in the concert world by going into films, which is ironic and a real shame. *My* particular world of music is what I want to write. *Altered States* was a film that allowed me to do the kind of music I wanted to do. Most films do not. In a film, the director basically says, "Well, now I want a kind of Beach Boys thing here and I want this other kind of thing here and I want that kind of thing there." Unless you're willing to do that, you really shouldn't write for films.

Is your criteria for accepting a film based on how much musical and dramatic freedom you will have?

It's a combination of freedom and whether I think the film will suit me as a composer.

Suit you as an additional vehicle of expression for your music?

Right. And that is not what most film composers do. A film composer usually adapts himself to the film at hand, which is why I am not, basically, a film composer. I look at a movie and ask whether it's a movie in which what I do can be of use, rather than saying, "Whatever they want, I can do it." This is a conscious decision I've made. I *could* do other things. I did *Naked Carmen*, which is rock, so it's not that I couldn't do it, it's that I've *chosen* not to do it anymore. I do the films that I think can benefit most from me. Because there are such astoundingly good composers in Hollywood—composers of such incredible technique and quality—there's no real reason for me to go there unless I do something a little bit different.

Music that's specifically Corigliano?

Yeah. And one of those things that I do that is not very appropriate for most films is developmental architecture—designing the whole piece. Film writing usually means start-and-stop writing—short little cues—but I'm interested in the large architecture. In film, it's the film itself that controls that, and the music comes in now and then to support it, to comment on it. So, for me, film music is less interesting as an art form because what I like and what fascinates me is the big structure, and how to plan that.

Did *The Red Violin* allow you to realize a large structural plan?

In *The Red Violin*, I planned a big structure of seven chords, which literally formed the basis for the entire movie. Everything that happened in the movie came out of those seven chords. Because the movie was involved with the tarot, involved with classical music and a violin, and involved with many different ages of music, I felt that one had to tie everything together. If you just wrote baroque, classical, romantic, and so forth, they would all be detached, since the only thing that threaded through the 300 years was this violin. One needed a musical thread that had to be thematic and harmonic. Therefore, these chords became the basis of everything. That was an intellectual decision that I made. I told the director about it and got his approval. At first, he wanted to use traditional music for the live playing and have me write just the underscoring. But I said, "No. The movie will not have a center because we have five different casts, five different countries, five different languages, five different plots. Unless you tie it together with some common thread, you will not feel the organic quality of the movie."

With *The Red Violin*, did you sense up front that the opportunity to be an architect was going to be there for you?

Yes, I felt the opportunity would be there. But, more importantly, the director, who did *32 Short Films About Glenn Gould*, is really interested in the musical side of it. And the production company is basically a television and film company that deals with music—they work a lot with Yo-Yo Ma and people like that. So I felt that the producers and the director would understand and let me go with what I felt was right. And that's what has happened.

The entire score is only strings. Well, there are a few percussion knocks on a bass drum, but, basically, it's a large string orchestra. No winds, no brass. Strings can do so many things. But Herrmann's *Psycho* is one of the only other film scores that uses only strings.

Is it an enlarged string orchestra?

It's enlarged. It's about sixty pieces, and it got up to eighty at one point. We divided the orchestra into two parts for some wave-sequence things. So, we had twelve double basses, because I needed six on either side. We recorded in Abbey Road Studios, which has a wonderful resonance for strings. The Philharmonia Orchestra produces a very rich sound, so it doesn't sound like a constricted score that's limited because of the size of the string orchestra. But when I wrote the concert piece with materials from the movie, I used full orchestra so they'd become different pieces.

***The Red Violin* CD includes the film score and the concert piece?**

Right. Peter Gelb at Sony wanted me to write a concert piece, much as Michael Nyman did for *The Piano*. I was reluctant to do it because I wasn't sure that the thematic material would fit a concert piece. But, before I knew it, he had already scheduled the piece for a San Francisco Symphony premiere and a tour with the Boston Symphony and violinist Joshua Bell.

The order in which the film and the concert piece progressed was unusual. I precomposed "Anna's Theme" for the film, since that material in the film had to be shot to the fingerings of the pieces. Then, while I waited for the film to be completed, I wrote the concert piece for violin and orchestra. After that was premiered in San Francisco, the director came to me with the final cut. And, as I composed the film, I was able to extract stuff from the concert piece. So, in a sense, it's a cross-pollination, which I found very, very effective.

Wasn't there a similar cross-pollination between *Altered States* and *The Pied Piper Fantasy?*

Yes. I had to stop the composing of *Pied Piper Fantasy* right at the end of the cadenza, which is about halfway through the piece, to do *Altered States*. Right after that cadenza, there's this huge, very wild battle scene between the Piper and the rats. Well, coming back to *Pied Piper* after *Altered States*, where I was inventing many techniques for my own notation and for ways of playing, I was able to use the motivic material of the *Pied Piper* and the sonic material of *Altered States* and put them together for the battle with the rats.

How about *Revolution?*

A sort of similar situation occurred with *Revolution* and Symphony No. 1. The film has a seven- or eight-minute piece that accompanies a battle between the British and the American revolutionary soldiers, which I wrote as a huge, very slow lament. I was able to incorporate some of that into the first movement of the Symphony when I again wanted that feeling of great loss—the sorrow for the dead of AIDS. In a sense, it was the same kind of massacre, so the music had the same tone. I think cross-pollination happens all the time if you're a concert composer. It happens from piece to piece.

Tell me a bit more about your work on *Revolution.*

I did *Revolution* with a little trepidation. It wasn't exactly what I thought I should be doing, but I used James Galway in it and thought the score turned out fine. But the mix in the dubbing room did not, because of the sound effects. So I said to myself, if we don't put out a CD, if no one's ever going to hear the final recorded version of what I really did on this movie, it isn't really worth it. The CD was in test pressings, ready to come out, but the film was so disastrous that they yanked the CD release. The CD is still sitting in the vault at BMG—just sitting there, beautifully mixed and ready to release, but not released.

Are you surprised that BMG hasn't jumped on your successes in the last decade with a commercial release of this music?

They might still do it. Jimmy Galway wants it released. He's mentioned it to them. It's very complicated because Goldcrest has been sold and there are so many things that have happened with that company and the publishing side of it.

Other than Elliot Goldenthal, do you have any former students working in the film-scoring field?

I have a few. Jorge Calandrelli works in film a lot. He worked on *The Color Purple*. I have a young composer out there now, Peter Boyer, who's starting to do films. But, Elliot is the one who really has jumped in and done a lot of it. By the way, I'm a member of the Academy because I was nominated for *Altered States*.

Fame **won that year.**

And then they changed the categories. Until then, they had put things that basically are musicals in with dramatic scores. The minute someone is singing, it has nothing to do with the kind of score that is an underscore. After that year, they made two categories because they felt there was an inequity there—those two types of scores don't have anything to do with each other and really shouldn't be judged together. The one with the words and someone singing is going to win.

Do you keep up with what's going on in film scoring?

I watch a lot of the new movies. I have a beautiful home-movie system with an eight-foot screen and a projector and seven surround speakers. I love being at home, watching the new movies and listening to their scores.

How do you react to what you hear?

A lot of the composers are wonderful. The quality of film scoring is enormously high these days. I have great respect for film composers. And I think people are trying to cross-pollinate a lot more now. The Los Angeles Philharmonic's conductor, Esa-Pekka Salonen, is having film composers write for the Philharmonic, and even score short films that are shown with the Philharmonic playing. He conducted *The Red Violin*, which is probably the first time a conductor of the Los Angeles Philharmonic has ever done a film score. He's very film-friendly, and I think it's very important for the community that the conductor of the Los Angeles Philharmonic has done a film. And there's this festival that I'm going to attend that David Raksin is doing with Bill Kraft, where concert music by film composers is going to be played. But there's still a very difficult problem with the critics, who tend to pigeon-hole people. If you're a film composer, it's very easy for them to hear everything in terms of your being a film composer.

Damned if you do, damned if you don't?

Right. Anytime you do something theatrical in a piece—something that any other concert composer would do—you're damned for it because you're a film composer. Elliot has told me horror stories of reviews. And he's said to me, "My God, if you or Charles Wuorinen did this, you or he wouldn't be accused! But, just because I've written films, they won't let me live it down." This is so true. Critics are usually the last people to know and to change, because they usually come from the academy to the critics' world. And there are no standards for hiring critics. The people who hire them don't know anything about them; they hire them simply if they can write prose well. There are no required degrees, no required standards. And if a critic says something wrong, they're never called to task for it. Someone can write a letter, but that's not going to do any good. It usually doesn't get printed, and, if it is printed, the critic writes a huge critical response to it! Any occupation that has no standards and no accountability has great problems. So these critics have very narrow minds about things, and film composing is certainly one of them. And the composers suffer a great deal for it. I've heard some extremely exotic pieces by John Williams, for example. His Flute Concerto is an attractive non-Western piece, but it will be accused of sounding just like another John Williams movie score if it gets played anyplace.

Bruce Broughton is another one, and Thomas Newman and John Barry have been doing some concert music recently.

And Leonard Rosenman, who did one of my favorite film scores, *Rebel Without a Cause*. When I first heard that score, I thought that Rosenman was such a great composer because not only can he write the dissonance and chromaticism and anguish of these complex situations, but he can, when he wants to, create an Americana innocence that is as beautiful as anything Aaron Copland ever wrote. I thought the principal theme in that film was just the highest level of pure American simplicity and beauty. And I know he composes lots of concert music.

From what I understand, he feels that he has those scarlet letters FC—film composer—on his chest.

He's right. He does. You can't get past it. It's a crime. I've spoken about this with Jerry Goldsmith, who's very bitter. And I don't blame him. I really blame the critics for this, not the audiences. The critics like to type you, because then they don't have to listen, they can just simply assign you a role and never, never let you change. But art is about change and about exploring many things. I wonder how Picasso got away with changing the way that he did. And

Stravinsky, too. But, if you're a film composer, you're commercial—you're a panderer, you're selling out. It's really ironic that the best performers and orchestras in the world are the film orchestras. There is no horn player in the world like the horn player who played in *Altered States*, who could play the same patterns over and over again for three hours and never miss a note—and play them with complete tonal beauty. These people are the best. And yet you would never hear that from the critics. It's a shame, but we deal with that. I deal with that as a concert composer if an audience is appreciative of my work. Bernard Holland once said to me, face to face, that if an audience likes my work, that means that I'm pandering and selling out. I asked him if he had the same view of Mozart, because Mozart not only pleased audiences, but was very concerned with reaching them. And, of course, he didn't. There's very little explanation for that, excepting the horrors of Romanticism when it strikes into the critical mind. You really have to fight that. And since films reach the large public, and since they are the only thing in classical music that does, they're going to be the ones most suspect and most given to negative criticism.

Some film-music critics and many fans believe that your score for *Altered States* ranks with *King Kong* in changing the direction of film scoring. Did you do a lot of preparation for your first score? Did it in any way frighten you? Here's an industry that's loaded with excellent, experienced, professional film composers, and here you are, walking into their world. Did you study a lot of film scores in preparation?

No, and I'll tell you the reason. First of all, I am theatrical. That's one of the things I have confidence in—my theatricality. And I knew that Ken Russell specifically wanted me because I was not in the film-music loop. It's like when [James] Levine commissioned me to write the opera for the Met, one of the things he said was, "I want a composer who's never written an opera, who's got to make his own solutions. I want to see a new view, a completely fresh view." I think that Ken Russell wanted me to do this as a symphonic composer, to really use the techniques of the twentieth century that were not used in films. So, in a sense, if I studied film music, I would be not doing what he wanted. He said, "I want you to go as far out as you want," which is not the usual thing that's said to film composers. That is why I took it, along with the fact that there were huge ten- and twelve-minute sections where there were no words. The idea of being able to construct larger shapes of music, not just short cues, and being allowed to experiment and to go further than I have, intrigued me. I isolated myself from the film-music world and wrote the score.

There have been many film scores that have used modern-music techniques and music from the repertoire—I think *The Omen* came before *Altered States*, and I know directors have used Ligeti and Penderecki and such. But I don't think there had ever before been a composer who actually designed music for film using those techniques. This was probably the first time that happened. And that is important, because now they often do it.

That one score sent word to the profession, "Here's something new."

Well, it's a vocabulary that actually is very useful to the film composer. For primitivism, they had been using the vocabulary of *The Rite of Spring*, which is what Ken put in the temp tracks, and Bartók's *Miraculous Mandarin*. Both are fabulous pieces, but they had come to symbolize the horror-movie vocabulary. The idea of contemporary science-fiction and horror movies having a primitivism of the teens and the twenties, I felt was wrong. I felt we had evolved into a whole other world of sound that could be much more effective for the movies.

What are some of the techniques you employed to get beyond that *Rite of Spring* primitivism?

First of all, the instruments in those pieces always sounded like the instruments. I often make them play in manners where they *don't* sound like themselves—they sound like something else. Most people don't realize that *Altered States* is ninety-five percent natural, acoustic sound and only five percent electronic music. Only the ending of it has electronics with orchestra. The entire first four-fifths of it is purely orchestral—all the techniques used are orchestral techniques. That's why the concert suite, *Three Hallucinations*, sounds like that in the concert hall. You can play this stuff live and have it actually sound. That was a challenge to me. For film composers, I think it was interesting because they had been using electronics to solve a lot of these problems of new sounds. Now they could go back to the orchestra and see that it could provide them with even richer new sounds.

How were you selected for *Altered States*? I've heard that Ken Russell had heard your Clarinet Concerto in a live concert.

Simply that. The next morning, he called me. Incidentally, John Williams, whom I'd never met, walked backstage, introduced himself to me, and said, "I love your Clarinet Concerto, I love your music." He commissioned me to write *Promenade Overture* as his first act on becoming Music Director of the Boston Pops. I said, "Oh, I just love *Jaws*," which had been a recent movie then. And he said, "Yes, it was my sixtieth film." Can you imagine? Really amazing. He paid his dues. People don't realize that.

***Altered States* was successful as film music and as concert music, *Three Hallucinations for Orchestra*. The film score has a natural dramatic flare, but knows when to use traditional film-scoring techniques in the tradition of Max Steiner, Hans Salter, Tiomkin, et al.—the door opens to very low strings, the baboon man jumps out to a big shock chord, and so on.**

Well, there are times when you want to do that, or just *have* to do that, and times when you want more of a fabric, a texture, an atmosphere.

Were those decisions yours or a combination of yours and Ken Russell's?

Mostly mine. He would tell me the mood he wanted for the general thing, but specific decisions like that would be mine. I think there are times when you want specifically to echo emotion and times when you want to create a panorama. And there are times when you want to play against it, like in *Revolution*, where the battle scene was frenetic and the music was slow, which we talked about earlier. Those are artistic decisions. And, hopefully, the director will let you make them. But, sometimes directors don't like something, and they'll say that they want it to be something else or faster. Then you have to rewrite it or they're going to fire you and stick in somebody else's music. As a composer for a film, you are an employee. It's like Mozart writing for specific people or Haydn with Prince Esterházy—you have a job to do, and you have to please someone. On the other hand, you also have to please yourself. And that's the balance you try to maintain as a film composer—to please yourself and still satisfy the director and the producers.

That's a tough one.

It *is* a tough one. But it's the one that great composers have survived. Beethoven was very concerned with satisfying and pleasing and exciting his audience as well as saying things that were deep and profound that they would never get the first time through. I think the job of any real composer is to grab the attention of the listener or the director or the producers and say something that will excite them and make them realize that his way is the right way. And then have layers of music underneath for them to find. Those layers are what make the music rich. The first layer is what makes it immediately accessible. And any composer who really cares about music in a deep way tries to have lots of layers, not just the first layer. Those esoteric composers who only compose the fifteenth layer on never attract anyone because they never speak in a visceral, human way. I think any great composer, whether he's a film composer or a symphony composer, realizes that *all* of these layers must be present.

In *Altered States*, when the baboon man first stumbles into the little toy shop, the music is eerily innocent yet surreal, edgy, and nervous—quarter-tone pianos, etc. The same music is also associated with Dr. Jessup's child.

Right. And, if you listen to the low, low sounds of the contrabassoons and the strings, you'll hear that the sounds of the animal are the same sounds that get played by the quarter-tone pianos. The pianos play simple melodies, repeating the same notes a quarter tone apart, so you can actually hear the shift, which surrealistically takes it out of this world. Quarter tones don't really work if you try to do them in other instruments, like strings or voices, because they just sound out of tune. But when you do them with fixed-tuning instruments, they're really quite wonderful. Last spring, I wrote a piece for two quarter-tone pianos.

What are some of the other unusual sound and/or compositional elements used in *Altered States*?

Do you remember the whirlpool scene, when the pipes in the ceiling were bending? Very surreal. Well, I had a great thing there, but Ken cut it out and, I must say, I really regretted it. I went down to Trinity Church in New York City, which has a great, old, beautiful organ, and we recorded the soprano voice, then the alto, then the tenor, then the bass of the traditional hymn "Rock of Ages." Then, in the studio, we took a harmonizer, which is a thing that can change pitch without changing tempo, and attached it to each one of the voices and started, as they were playing, to bend the alto voice up, then the tenor, then the soprano, then the bass. So we had this "Rock of Ages," this hymn, the symbol of all that solidity, but the organ sound would bend, which is an impossibility. The whole organ didn't shift up and down, just one interior voice, then another one, then another one, until the explosion. I thought it sounded great, but Ken didn't want it. I really felt discouraged because it was an unusual, mighty sound, and it was symbolic of the film— the idea of "Rock of Ages," of the very title of the hymn, tearing apart, suddenly being shattered.

I thought, symbolically, the bending pipes were like the organ pipes. It was perfect. But that's what happens. You're not the master. You're not in control. If only I had been in the dubbing room with him, I know I could have played that at the right moment and he would have seen it. But composers don't get into the dubbing room. The only people in the dubbing room are the man who's dubbing it and the sound-effects people. So you get all these sound-effects people refining their sound effects, and the composer's not able to say anything like ". . . but if you played it this way . . . started it later . . . changed the volume here . . . it would work." We don't get that chance. It's very frustrating.

Did you know that there were going to be lots of loud sound effects in the finished film?

No! And there were huge sound effects! I was really upset when I first heard it. And it wasn't just in that scene that the sound effects bothered me—the sound effects in the "Mushroom Dance" covered the great, wild stuff I did there. And I found a great frustration in the fact that I didn't have to write, for example, the busy music I did when the dogs were running after him, because there was so much snarling and growling that you couldn't really hear the wild things I was doing! I could have saved myself a lot of effort.

What was your time period for composing *Altered States*?

I think it was a couple of months. But, you know, when a composer normally takes a year or two to write a piece . . .

Let's talk about your composing processes for *Altered States*.

I wrote the words "motion sonority" at the top of the *Altered States* score. And I said to myself, I am going to develop symbols that will create extreme action in the players, but will involve a single sound with simple notation that generates a lot of motion—just like a trill or a tremolo. I said, let me think of all the ways I can make a lot of motion with a single symbol, so I don't have to write out a lot of notes. And I invented the symbol of the box with two notes in it, and playing in between the boxes, as fast as possible, which, for multiple instruments, gives you a tremendous, boiling cluster of sound. And then, the box with a line up to the next box. And then, the jagged line, like two bolts of lightening, almost like the SS sign, meaning an irregular tremolo, like Morse Code, instead of two lines, meaning a sixteenth-note tremolo, or three lines, meaning a measured tremolo. So I could write a single note with a time value and a single symbol where Penderecki would write out little motives with something like forty notes.

The precompositional process for *Altered States* was two things: One, I developed my own techniques for "motion sonority"—the box techniques, the cueing techniques, the jagged-line techniques—which produced tremendous activity with single notes. The second thing was, of course, the love theme, which I wrote by the swimming pool at the Beverly Hills Hotel. It was written for the scene in the hospital corridor where he sees the schizophrenic girl who says, "Let's live together," and he finally says to her, "I'm just in another world . . . but let's give it a try," and they kiss. Well, the look on her face at that moment was my inspiration for the love theme. I wrote it for that moment and then transformed it into the passionate version at the end.

It's a beautiful, bittersweet theme—cautiously passionate and vulnerable.

Vulnerable, yes, because I felt that she was kind of helpless: She loved him but could not get through to him. He loved her but could not get through to her. And she was so tentative—I wanted the love theme to be tentative. It had to have that quality. I didn't want it to be passion so much as tentativeness and intimacy. I didn't want it to be out-and-out love music because, in a way, it never got resolved until the very last line of the story. So, as I was lying by the pool, just mulling over that scene, the first phrase [Corigliano hums the motive] came to me and I wrote it down. Later, I took it upstairs and developed it into the full thing.

That's a wonderful composer-finds-inspiration-by-the-babbling-brook story, like the sort we often hear about the old masters, but never believe really happened. This time, it happened.

It really did. You never know when the answer will come. Usually, with something that simple and direct, it will not come at the piano. It's the kind of thing that has to come out of the subconscious. It will come when you're wandering around, like at the supermarket or driving or doing something else, because that's when the mind is relaxed and free to associate, free to wander. If you sit and focus on it, you get tense and too objective.

Were you artistically satisfied with the last half hour of the film? Some critics believe that it went a bit over the top.

From the very first moment in that film, you were in acceleration. Ken Russell almost forced himself into a dramatic corner by doing the first two-thirds of the film with such rapid-fire energy. If he didn't go to the final peak, the film would have died. So he had to go someplace that was maybe ludicrous, but the only option open to him once he had gone so far. Ken needed to go that far to make the film work. That's what Ken does in all his films—goes into staggeringly high energy right from the second the opening credits are over. It's forte and allegro right from the start. There are no lentos and pianissimos in Ken Russell.

james newton HOWARD

One foot in the classical-music-inspired world of orchestral film scoring and, at various times in his life, one foot in the top-of-the-charts pop-music world (as arranger, songwriter, record producer), James Newton Howard's busy music career has been one of parallel developments. His deep passion for and involvement with all types and styles of Western music has led him down many often-intersecting musical paths—from his string arrangements for Elton John in the 1970s to his aggressive, contemporary orchestral scores for *Flatliners* (1990), his Oscar-nominated *The Fugitive* (1993), *Wyatt Earp* (1994), *Just Cause* (1995), *Outbreak* (1995), and *Waterworld* (1995).

As the result of his apparent enchantment with movies that depict the subtleties of human emotions, Howard has provided touching scores for such pictures as *Pretty Woman* (1990), *Grand Canyon* (1991), *My Girl* (1991), *Dave* (1993), *French Kiss* (1995), and *My Best Friend's Wedding* (1997). His natural gift for humor emerges in his delightfully wacky scores for *King Ralph* (1991), *Junior* (1994), and *Space Jam* (1996), while the introspective *Dying Young* (1991) and *The Saint of Fort Washington* (1993) and the apocalyptic *The Postman* (1998) reveal the mystical side of his musical personality. *Marked for Death* (1990), *Guilty by Suspicion* (1991), *Alive* (1993), *Falling Down* (1993), *Intersection* (1994), and *Primal Fear* (1996) present the composer as a master of nervous suspense, and the malevolent Faustian story of *Devil's Advocate* (1997) is echoed in Howard's icy score for massive forces.

Howard's scores often include an effective and innovative mix of acoustic instruments and electronics and often sing with lovely and emotional themes, such as those found in his evocative scores for *The Man in the Moon* (1991), his Oscar-nominated *The Prince of Tides* (1991), and *Restoration* (1996).

We met for this interview at his gold-record-lined, high-tech studio behind his suburban-Los Angeles home.

james newton HOWARD

You have the rare ability to come up with beautiful tunes in this day and age of generic, tuneless, hyper-techno-pulse scores. In *Prince of Tides*, for example, and in *Junior*, you have poignant, evocative themes. *Man in the Moon* is fairly simple, but cutting through the simplicity is something much more serious, more communicative, almost profound. Are these themes effortless or do you work very hard to come up with just the right tune?

I suppose they're effortless in that they're essentially part of an unconscious process. I truly believe that melodic writing, more than anything else, is just something that happens by a process in which I actually get out of the way. By a process of working, but not really chasing a theme. Usually, I just let the first germ of a theme appear by itself.

Beyond that, isn't there a certain amount of architectural development—nuts and bolts construction—as you alter a theme's form and make decisions about its direction?

Tune writing is relatively simple for me, but it's also a very intimidating problem. I approach most scores from the "theme is king" perspective—I try to put the thematic material in perspective before I do too much else on the score. I'm afraid that if I commit myself to too much non-thematic material early on, I might miss an opportunity down the road in the composing process that I could have plugged into those areas. So, I do try to get a theme early.

Are the more abstract, non-thematic, or action sections of your scores derived from your main themes?

Sometimes. Perhaps it's because of my upbringing and my exposure to the classic film composers. I think that if thematic material isn't being presented all the time, at least some kind of little handle that you could hum or whistle or think about should be running through the film. I never construct this in a conscious way. I just instinctively feel the theme woven throughout. I also think this can become a weakness. As I look back on some of my older stuff, it comes back too often for my taste—I just find that some of it is too melodic, too thematic, too much of the time.

Are you willing to offer an example?

Well, you know what? It's not even about using the main theme too much. It's about the recitative-like music being too thematic in nature—too melodic and melody-driven, which is a form that has become kind of boring to me. I think that I'm only lately getting away from that or becoming able to write freely. I think that it's really all about counterpoint—more counterpoint and less melody. Just dig into the texture of the music rather than the melody or the theme.

That seems to be happening more in your recent scores. In *Waterworld* and in *Outbreak*.

Yeah. I'm glad to hear you say that because I've been making a conscious effort to do it. I think that it's a by-product of having more confidence with the orchestra, knowing the orchestra a little bit better. You end up doing what you're ready to do.

Earlier in your career, you weren't necessarily typecast as a light, romantic, teen-angst, relationship-movie composer, but you did a number of movies that fall into those categories. As you moved into the 1990s, you composed a greater variety of scores—everything from action and science-fiction and black comedy to Westerns. And although your scores were written for genre-specific films, identifiable "Howardisms" emerged. Did you work hard to escape the teen-movie mold?

Yeah. I found that I *was* being typecast for a while. I was anxious to break out of the mold. I was anxious to do an action movie. First, to get me out of the rut and, second, because every composer in Hollywood knows that an action film is *the* challenge—it's difficult to do it *well*. I underscore those words ten times—"to do it well" is no mean feat. It's difficult to hide behind an action film. You can't, really. Your limitations are much more obviously displayed in an action idiom than in a romantic comedy. In a romantic comedy, people can be fooled by music that sounds like it's the right kind of thing. It can be devoid of content and yet have a style that feels fine, appropriate. With action stuff, if it's not right, it's incredibly wrong! There are a couple of guys doing action films who I truly admire to this day. I aspire to do it as well as they do.

Is there one specific film that pulled you away from the light romance and into the action genre?

It was a long, slow process. Actually, it was a terrifying experience for me because I was really green. I was a late-bloomer. Elliot Goldenthal, for instance, whose work I greatly admire and who stands on his own as a really strong force, came right out of the chute with two or three scores that sounded truly amazing. Maybe it's because Goldenthal was already secure in the concert-music world, already very comfortable with the orchestra. That wasn't the case for me. In my opinion, I wrote something like fifteen really bad scores before I started to sound half-way decent. But, was there any one film for me? There was a succession of things: *Flatliners* was a big one for me, and an unusual opportunity—a canvas were I was given license to do anything I wanted. It was the first time I'd worked with a choir, the first time I'd worked with a large orchestra, the first time I'd blended a lot of synth and percussive elements with orchestra and choir. I've done that a lot since then. Then came *Falling Down*, then *The Fugitive*. Once I did *The Fugitive*, all of a sudden, I was typecast as "the action guy." Then came *Just Cause*, *Outbreak* . . .

Were you being offered little romance films at this point?

Well, I was offered a few, but most of them were bad. I guess every A-level composer gets offered a lot of films. And you don't do a lot of them. I wasn't offered any good romantic films, which I probably would have taken.

***Flatliners*, with its brooding, Gothic chorus and orchestra, seems to represent one of the first distinctive changes in your sound. You mentioned that you had a free rein with that score. Do you experience that luxury often? Or do you often find that you're facing frustrating restrictions?**

I think that more often than not I have few restrictions. In *Waterworld*, I had no restrictions. In *Outbreak*, I had no restrictions. In a movie like *French Kiss*, sure, you've got understandable restrictions. You're in Paris, there are conventions you have to acknowledge. What "no restrictions" means to me is that I can use as large an orchestra or as small an orchestra as I want, for as many days as I want, and with any instrumentation that I want.

And no producer or director breathing down your neck, saying . . .

I didn't say that! They *will* breathe down your neck. That just comes with the turf. That's a given. But within the context of them breathing down my neck, I'm always very clear about one thing—that I'm working *for* somebody, writing music for a movie. I'm very comfortable about that. Some guys aren't. It doesn't bother me at all.

Let's back up in time to *Night and the City*. When I first saw that film, I was already a fan of the original Richard Widmark version with Franz Waxman's film-noir, jack-hammer-pounding score. Your version begins with "Wooly Bully"! So, we go from Waxman to "Wooly Bully." And there was very little score in your film. Was it a frustrating experience? Did you know the original film and wish you could have done an urban orchestral score?

You know, I'm embarrassed to admit it, but I'd never seen the original. I still haven't to this day. I just did the score I wanted to do, the way I saw it. I wanted to do a contemporary, urban, edgy, almost new-wave, guitar-oriented thing because there were extremely violent and unpredictable elements in the movie that I responded to strongly. What was frustrating for me was that a lot of my score didn't get used. A lot of songs were used instead.

It's funny you should bring up that movie. You know, I was one of about ten people who liked it. I wanted the score to feel and speak of anarchy. This guy's life had just completely gone, he was in way over his head. My score was probably a little youthful for the characters, now that I think about it. Orchestral would maybe have been a better way to go. I don't know. It was a puzzle. I learned a lot and I had a lot of fun doing it. There was some pretty good stuff in there. That's all I know. It was a very experimental score, particularly in the realm of the percussion and guitar work. Although, if I listened to it today, it would probably feel pretty tame.

Your orchestral percussion section seems to be expanding very rapidly in your last few scores. You use a lot of experimental sounds

blended with ostinati, mixed irregular meters, and all that fun rhythmic stuff.

Yeah. Actually, I kind of got stuck in 5/8 meter and had trouble getting out of it for years. I would feel like I was in four and I was really in five. You get so used to it. It starts to feel so comfortable. But when someone else hears it for the first time, it has a limping quality to it. I ended up writing 5/8 in *Wyatt Earp*, which was probably a big mistake.

In *Outbreak*, a lot of the military scenes are written in 5/8. It's like a militia that's out of step, morally askew, out of whack.

Yeah. Completely out of whack.

In the last few years, you've moved into some very interesting rhythmic grooves. Your favorite seems to be 5/8, then maybe a 3/4 and a 2/4, and then some 7/8. So, sometimes it's difficult to find the downbeat, difficult to tap our toes, which keeps the drama edgy. There is one particular cue on the *Just Cause* CD— the car chase—that's a terrific four-minute rhythmic tone poem that every orchestra in the U.S. should be playing. In the film, however, you barely hear it. Was your score for *Just Cause* dubbed too low?

Yes, it was. I lost that one. What can I say? The dub took place in New York and I was out here. My usual music editor, Jim Weidman, was not on the movie by then, I think he was finishing *Junior*. We were overlapping schedules at that point. Neither one of us could be at the dub. It doesn't bother me that much. It especially doesn't bother me if there's a CD. If there's no CD and the score's not memorialized in any way and the only thing that people have is the movie in which they can barely hear the score, then it's kind of a drag. It has been that way with several scores.

For example?

My biggest problem was on *Pretty Woman*, where I actually wrote a pretty theme that nobody ever heard. I gave a DAT of that theme to an editor named Don Zimmerman, who is a friend of mine. He was trying to get me the job on *The Prince of Tides*. So he cut the opening scene to the *Pretty Woman* love theme. The whole thing, all three and a half minutes, was a voice-over. And it was outstanding! It was so much better in that movie than in *Pretty Woman*. It had a tremendous emotional quality to it. But I try and stay fairly calm about cues disappearing under cars. What are you going to do?

Your car-chase music in *The Prince of Tides* is relentless, except for the one moment when the bridge is jumped. There you use silence, acknowledging a traditional approach to scoring. When you first view a spot like that, is it an instant given that, yes, I need to stop the music there? Or is that something you might wrestle with, saying to yourself, everybody would expect me to stop the music there, so maybe I shouldn't?

I wrestle with all of it. I don't think there are any givens. The closest thing to a given for me is a strong instinct. Generally speaking, I experiment a lot with ins and outs, starts and stops, hitting, and timing. Especially with comedy, I watch it over and over. And I guess I watch out pretty well because I'm getting offered too many comedies. It's driving me crazy.

But you have such a natural approach to comedy. In *Junior*, for example, in a scene in the lab where all the weird experiments are beginning, you create this great spooky, sci-fi atmosphere with a cute, innocent edge to it. You know the right harmony, the right pitches, the right instrumentation to give the cue a "wink of the eye" edge, even though it's actually *scary* music.

Getting there, getting there. I mean, comedy has been a tough one, too. There's been an evolution for me there as well. But *Junior* had a couple of good spots.

In the middle of *Just Cause*, in the scene where we first meet the Ed Harris character, there's tension music that shifts to Bobby in his cell. The very next scene is Sean Connery and his wife. The very next scene is something else entirely. You have completely different music for each scene, but also a thread that ties them all together. How much do you concern yourself with the Wagnerian approach of blending motives and/or thematic material? For example, Connery's material changes, adapts itself, depending on whom he meets along the way.

I tend not to assign thematic material to individual characters. I should probably do it more often than I do. In that particular case, it was the sequence of events. Thematically, I try to present a continuous thread. The music that I wrote for Ed Harris [he sings], I have to just forget about. It sounded really bad to me after a while. I don't know what happened. I went off that whole score. My feelings mirror my experience of writing the score, which was just not very much fun. The director was in New York and I was here. The original editor was fired about three weeks into it. The next editor and I had a difficult communication problem. He did strange things to my cues and tempos. He took two or three cues and played them simultaneously. I had a lot of problems with that situation. I was also trying to score *Restoration* at the same time. I had to cancel being present at the recording of *Restoration* in London because I was here, writing. *Just Cause* was tough. I really labored wildly on that score. I was just never sure.

***Alive* is your coldest score. It sets the landscape, the locale, and the situation perfectly with its icy chill. And it has more multi-voice linear counterpoint than many of your other scores. Were**

you trying to work with the complex weaving together of people's lives—of their attempts to deal with shared existential survival problems viewed from individual perspectives?

Alive has to be one of my favorite scores. It was very much a breakthrough score for me, one of the first times I felt like I had really succeeded in writing an orchestral score that worked well. With the counterpoint, I was striving to write an orchestral score that was more complex than my usual piano-oriented scores.

Let's talk about *Falling Down*, one of my favorite movies. As Michael Douglas's character gradually evolves to an extreme emotional-explosion level, your music intensifies in a long, natural flow from very soft to very loud, with brief manic outbursts along the way. Overall, the score has an extended arc that drives to the end of the film. Did you see the role of your score as a parallel or compliment to what was happening with the character?

It was very conscious. I tried to restrain and contain the score for the most part, with a couple of notable exceptions—like the heavy-metal bit when he shoots the Mexican kids. Most of the time, the score bubbles like a simmering volcano and then explodes at the end with his final outburst. I very much tried to get the feeling of a lot of confined rage. I tried to have it contained somehow to create an edgy feeling.

And I really related to the tragedy of the character—a well-intentioned individual who just had a very dysfunctional way of dealing with the whole rotten world crumbling around him and, as a result, fell into mental illness and complete isolation. That isolation is something that I personally have related to at different points in my life. I related to being on the outside the way he was on the outside. There was the cue when he called his ex-wife from the basement of the army-surplus store and said, "I've left it all behind. Now, I'm on the other side of the moon. I'm on the dark side of the moon now. And you won't know when I am coming back. You won't see me for a while." All of a sudden, pow! I really liked that imagery of being so outside and so gone that you are kind of floating free-form through the void.

When he is first armed, you unleash a brutal *Terminator*-style sequence that at once generates two responses—a cringe and a smile. Is this a little musical comic relief in the midst of overwhelming, tragic emotional decay?

I think comic relief, or some dimension of lightness, is extremely important in action scores. They can become unwieldy and really pompous if they are not somehow lightened a little. If you look at most action movies today, there's not a lot of humor in the writing. I think they have become very burdensome lately.

In the Whammyburger hostage scene, there is no music whatsoever, which made it very frightening and realistic. It is one of the few dry scenes in the entire picture. What were your thoughts behind that decision?

I can't remember. When Joel [Schumacher] and I worked together, we'd rarely spot a movie. I would just start writing and bring it over and show him. We'd usually preview the movie with a temp score and then, if there were spots missing, we would go back and get them later. So, I guess it must have been a situation where both of us felt that we didn't need any music for the scene.

When the Douglas character buys the magical snowglobe for his daughter, the score is a tender, innocent, intentionally underdeveloped music-box motive. This brief moment of tension relief actually makes the overall escalating tension of the music more powerful. Was this a difficult scene to decipher and/or manipulate?

I didn't struggle with the concept of it because it was simply dictated by the image—he is picking up this thing for his little girl.

But I *did* struggle with it technically—just laying it in there, the timing of it, and the segue into it and the segue out of it. I remember specifically working on that cue for a long time. This is very astute of you. It must have sounded too elaborate.

No, it almost sounded as if the music was coming from inside the little snowglobe itself. After buying the snowglobe, he shoves it into his bag of guns. At that moment—that great contrast of images—the little snow tune is swallowed by an angry vertical dissonance that crashes us back into reality. Was this one of those moments where, as soon as you see the rough cut of the film, it just naturally hits you, "Yes, we need something like that there"?

I don't remember how we arrived at it. That could have been a situation where Joel said, "I think we should try this here." Directors often have ideas about a scene. Sometimes they have very conventional ideas, and sometimes I miss the conventional ideas, which sometimes are fantastic. I'll tend to be a little bit esoteric and they'll suggest, "Why don't you just come in here, after he says. . ." So I'll try it. We all know that sometimes clichés are the best way to go.

You seem to be very comfortable with both the classic Golden Age, Steiner style and the more modern composing-against-the-action style. In *Outbreak*, for example, during the Cedar Creek exodus, static, frightening, atonal string-orchestra material is heard instead of the expected driving musical accompaniment. Do you find there are certain spots in each film that call for direct comment on the action and certain spots that call for commenting on a larger emotional scale?

Oh, I do. That was a moment when I wasn't particularly interested in driving the film rhythmically. If I can afford to have a choice in a situation like that, when I am not compelled to be writing in a faster tempo, then I will consider alternate approaches. Inevitably, what I do in those situations is respond to what I think is the dramatic essence of the scene. While there was a great deal of action going on in that scene, what was resonating for me was the large-scale tragedy of the situation—that there were so many people involved. It had a monolithic, slow-moving impression to it, so that is what I addressed.

How often, in any given film, do you need to step back and look at the big picture—the whole 90 minutes, 105 minutes—and think of the score as one long, through-composed dramatic piece? Conversely, how often can you just focus on one particular scene without too much regard for what precedes it or what follows it?

Most of the time I am paying attention to the score on a cue-by-cue basis. The reason I write the temp music for the preview myself is because it gives me an opportunity to watch my score with the film, to listen to it and feel where it is weak and where it is strong and where we are missing a thematic statement and where it is slow and all that stuff that you need to observe at a larger structural level.

Recently, one thing that has helped me a lot is a hard-disk system that we have in here so that, as I do a demo, I can load in all the demos and watch the previous five minutes of music coming up to the cue I am currently working on, which helps to keep me from straying too far from wherever I last left off. I think that it is very important to always remind yourself where you are in the field of a film, because you can easily get lost in it. You can spend all this time working on one scene but, in the context of the big picture, the cue you have been working on might be ridiculously wrong—it comes in in the wrong key or it's too fast or it's emotionally wrong.

Obviously, you are comfortable in the romantic style, but some of your recent scores have become much more aggressive. Do you like the early twentieth-century composers—Berg, Stravinsky, et al., and the 1960s' soundmass architects?

I really do. I spent most of my childhood immersed in the romantics and the classics, but I think my interest in more modernist music is the result of a couple of things. One is a certain degree of exposure that I have subjected myself to in preparation for certain scores. When I was preparing for *Flatliners*, I spent a lot of time with the music of Penderecki and Ligeti and various other people in sort of Cliff Notes versions—you have to write eighty minutes of music in three months, and you are just trying to get some kind of context for it. I think my interest is also a function of just the natural maturation or evolution of my own writing—I am finding unusual harmonies a lot more interesting, and I am writing more virtuosic material for the orchestra because I enjoy the sound of it. I like more notes, more counterpoint, faster and louder music. I remember, in the beginning, I would write a big, loud, dissonant piece—a short burst of fifteen or twenty seconds—and if it worked well, I was just incredibly proud because it wasn't that familiar to me, it was something that was far more experimental. But, yeah, I am a huge Ligeti fan, a big Penderecki fan. Elliott Carter's interesting. I really like Hanson.

Eastman's Howard Hanson?

Yeah, he's great. He's kind of the older stuff, neo-romantic. I am not a *huge* modernist, I am basically a tonality guy. Even my atonal material is tonality-based. I am pretty much rooted in tonality, and I probably always will be. I suppose even Corigliano and Goldenthal and guys like that are still tonality-based. I like those guys.

Your *Wyatt Earp* score is not mined from the distinctive Western-genre styles of Tiomkin, Bernstein, or Morricone, but is a much more restless, edgy, and complex sound.

I really like that score.

I know you employ assistants with your orchestrations. Hummie Mann is one . . .

And Brad Dechter. Brad's my main guy. He's been my orchestrator from the beginning, but there are a couple of other guys now.

Do you give them detailed sketches?

Well, I used to. The whole process changed on *Outbreak*, quite honestly. Until *Outbreak*, I gave fully detailed sketches on score paper to everybody, it was literally all there, note for note, and it was pretty much a spit-'n'-polish kind of thing—proofreading, putting it on score paper without the mistakes that *I* make, because I write things down kind of funny.

But *Outbreak* was a time crunch?

There was just no time for me to orchestrate. I had composed *Alive* in five weeks, then wrote out the full score in six weeks—longer than it took me to compose it. In the case of *Outbreak*, I had to write eighty-five minutes of music in five weeks. There was just no way in the world that I could have copied it out! So what I did— what I was informed is now convention for a lot of guys—was give my sequences to my copyist, who created a midi-file extraction and output my demos, which are pretty complete and extremely elaborate. Once they're printed, I get them back and add phrasing and dynamics and build it. It is a shorthand. And I have repeatedly found that if I didn't have this shorthand, I would be up the creek. And now, and I am half-ashamed to say this, I am so used to the process that it is very tempting to luxuriate in it. The idea of going back and sketching is now foreign to me. I hate it.

I liked the old method on one level because I got inside the music in a way that I don't now. I probably affected a ten- to twenty-percent compositional change on the music as a result of going through the orchestration myself. The downside was that it prevented the injection of additional personality dimensions. I like other people in my music. When you are writing six or seven or eight hours of music a year, it's crazy if it is all going to be only you all the time—

it runs the risk of getting dull. I like an orchestrator coming in who, if I say, "double this," he'll double it, but he'll also write a counterline somewhere. We'll try it, and I'll like it or I won't like it, but it is nice to have those options.

Waterworld has a swashbuckling, sail-the-seven-seas, Korngold foundation that moves in and out of a more aggressive, futuristic sound. Some people feel that a futuristic movie shouldn't have a nineteenth-century European orchestral score.

Well, the first thing that you have to remember with the *Waterworld* score is that there is an hour and fifty-seven minutes of music. Within that hour and fifty-seven minutes of music, there are probably fifty-seven minutes that are completely electronic, atmospheric, and futuristic-sounding. The movie, when I first saw it, had a very bizarre temp score that was very bleak, very distancing, and very impressionistic. But I understood the concept: Not only were we in a movie that was visually not like anything we had ever seen, we were to be in a sonic world where everything was completely different. Consequently, everything was kind of dream-like, which tended to anesthetize or mesmerize you in a way. I found myself just kind of staring or drifting away, and the movie felt incredibly long and dull.

Mark Isham was the original composer on the movie. He was hired by Kevin Reynolds. Before Mark even wrote a note, Kevin Reynolds was gone and Kevin Costner was running the show. I had worked with Kevin on *Wyatt Earp*, and he really loved my score for it. He felt that *Waterworld* needed to be futuristic and three-dimensional and atmospheric, but also it needed to be a summer popcorn movie—it was an action movie, we needed a hero, there was a bit of a love story, there was fantasy, there was fun, there was a sense of humor. Sense of humor is a big one. I don't think you can play a strong sense of humor in that nineteenth-century, tonal way. So I found myself exacting a pretty good balance of orchestral vs. electronics, trying to serve many masters: getting Mariner into a heroic dimension, getting the Smokers into a nasty but comical dimension because, let's face it, these guys are bizarre. How seriously can you take them? They're pretty funny. So I tried to play them in a kind of Gothic, tongue-in-cheek way. The most serious stuff I did had to do with Mariner's personal relationship with the ocean. To me, that is what made the film, that is really where his heart was. That was what I wanted to emphasize in the score, as the grounding of the score, and everything else could be fairly fluffy or secondary.

Believe me, when you have six weeks to write two hours of music, you don't have any time to consider if you are making a mistake. At some point during that movie, I thought, "I am making grievous errors on the most-expensive high-profile movie ever made. I am going crashing down in flames. It is going to be a complete disaster." And then, the next day you look at it and you know you're really helping the movie. I think I did help the movie in the end. The movie was a huge target. I'd really expected to be slammed for it as I have been slammed for some big things in the past, but the overriding response has been really positive.

Waterworld has a lot of rhythmic 5/8s and 7/8s that keep you on edge, but I also noticed a real attraction to those classic Hollywood minor-third progressions. The C-minor area moves to E♭ minor to F♯ minor, but take your time, stretch the modulations. It works well because of its association with endless stretches of water. Was it your conscious choice to use these classic, suspense-building progressions that you allow to take a long time to get where you're going?

Yeah, it was conscious. I resisted those kinds of chord progressions for years. I really did. I would hear them in horror movies and I would hear them in Goldsmith and in John Williams. I still hear them. But I resisted and resisted. It became self-deceiving in a way. I was in a kind of denial about it, because audiences, directors, producers—everybody watching the movie—has certain expectations. Even though you aren't necessarily expecting a progression of minor thirds, there is a sound to that sequence that, when tied to an image, particularly when tied to a spectacular, ultra-large image, is hard to resist. When I did try to write something completely new, it ended up being, well, not quite right—too complicated, too notey—so I finally abandoned it.

Actually, *Alive* is when I first started getting into a more conventional harmonic approach in some places. And doing that freed me. By giving myself over to certain harmonic progressions, I found a liberation. The act of embellishing and the act of working melodically in that context was liberating—it would lead me to other places. Anytime you give yourself over to an existing device, it is going to inevitably open up some other doors for you that you just can't anticipate. It was just a matter of consciously bringing those chord progressions into my toolbox as just another place to think and another place to go.

Your music for *ER* is a classy tune for a quality program.

Thanks. This show just seemed like it would be one of the good ones. I told the producers that I'd write the theme and the first show if they'd give the show over to my friend Marty Davich. They said okay. So, I wrote the theme and did the pilot. Then I gave the show over to Marty, who has been having a great time doing it ever since. It was a way to help my friend and yet have a good time doing it.

It has been surprising to learn what many film composers will do that for their friends. In the concert-music world it often seems quite the other way around. Composers sometimes push other composers away to keep that rare performance by such-and-such an orchestra to themselves.

I don't blame the composers in your world, by the way. If they were funded as well as we are in Hollywood, if there was as much work there as we have here, they would probably be more generous. There is so much work here, so much money to be made here, and so many great opportunities here. It sounds like a cliché, but this business has been so wonderful for me. And some of the most satisfying parts of it all have been the opportunities of sharing it with my friends.

Let's talk a bit about James Newton Howard, composer/arranger of the pop music world. You are natural and sincere and professional in both worlds—from the manic, avant-garde orchestral music of *Outbreak* to your arrangements for Elton John and Aerosmith. Do you have strong roots in pop music, or is that something that has evolved alongside your film scores?

My roots are in both. I started classical piano when I was four. I studied for a few years at the music academy near Santa Barbara, and I was a piano-performance major at USC. But I quickly moved into rock-and-roll because I just loved popular music. I would give piano recitals at little old ladies' homes in Beverly Hills and Pasadena, then go home and listen to The Beatles. I knew that I was never going to be a concert pianist. I was a good pianist, but I wasn't *that* good. I absolutely loved the classical repertoire, but I was drawn to popular music. Interestingly, it has kind of gone full-circle now— I am back to loving the classical again and wanting to do more orchestral music.

I love just about every kind of music. I was lucky that I was able to go into a rock-and-roll band and play with Elton John in the 1970s. It was the perfect place for a guy like me—perfect because he was making rock-and-roll records but had Paul Buckmeister doing orchestral arrangements. The records had a very classical, orchestral dimension to them.

If somebody had asked me my goal in life in 1974, when I first heard "Yellow Brick Road," it would have been to write string arrangements for Elton John. A year later, I was doing it, and it gave me that whole sense of a rock-and-roll track related to an orchestral track—how you sweeten one with the other. I was doing them in a co-existent fashion, concurrently, and it has been that way ever since. Ninety percent of the time these days, I am writing movies, but rock-and-roll is still something that I am very comfortable with and I still enjoy a lot. I have a great deal of regard and respect for a lot of young, contemporary bands, and I didn't feel that way until about three years ago. Now there are a bunch of bands out there I really love. I love Soundgarden, The Cranberries, Smashing Pumpkins, Pearl Jam, Jewel. There is a lot of good stuff out there that I listen to. These guys are totally plugged in and they've got it—they've got the juice.

When you get a dramatic or romantic film that is initially planned to include a big, hit-potential single, do the producers ask you to write the song or do you ask them?

Sometimes both and sometimes neither. I am doing a Michelle Pfeiffer movie, a romantic comedy called *One Fine Day*, where I submitted a song, but there are other people who submitted songs, too. I may write another one, but there are no rules. I mean, I am known first as a film composer and second as a songwriter, so I have no problems with that. Most of the time, I would rather really focus on the score and spend the other time with my kid.

Will they use the Chiffons' original "One Fine Day"?

Yeah, they will use it at the end. It's a fun movie. I am having a good time with it. I'm using Gershwin's *American in Paris* as sort of a template for it a little bit, just the sound of the hustle-bustle—urban car horns and that stuff. I'll probably get nailed for it.

Did your life change when your son arrived? Did your life change musically? Your approach to music, composing, and what this world is all about?

Absolutely. I think it has to. Everything changes, right? You look at things differently. You relive childhood innocence and all that. You just somehow re-ignite internally. Life is much richer. I'm not going to say work is less important—it is very important—but it is a little less critical now. Perspectives and priorities change around a lot. I mean, it *is* just a movie. And it's not even my movie, it's some other guy's movie and it's giving me a hard time.

I am lucky. I was a total workaholic. I was doing between eight and ten movies a year for a long time, but I was alone during those periods. Now, the timing is all worked out. Now, I look at my work more as a way to give us a good life, as opposed to something running my life. I love my work, and I'm just as dedicated and loyal, but it's all in perspective now. It sounds simplistic and maybe old-fashioned, but this is a concept that had eluded me for a long time.

mark ISHAM

Mark Isham somehow balances his incredibly busy film-music schedule with the demands of his extensive performing, recording, and teaching activities. In addition to often composing more than a few feature-film scores each year, Isham is active in jazz ensembles, and he regularly offers comprehensive film-music seminars at the Celebrity Center in Hollywood, the Musicians Institute, and UCLA. An artist of great energy, Isham's imaginative scores often reflect the interplay of his many interests.

Before turning to film music, Isham was active as a new-music performer in the Bay Area, played trumpet with the San Francisco and Oakland orchestras, and composed and performed with progressive rock and avant-garde bands. Isham's early scores for *Never Cry Wolf* (1983), *The Hitcher* (1986), and *The Beast* (1988) exploited his interest in electronics—synthesizers and electronically altered acoustic instruments. However, around 1990, his film scores turned more acoustic and orchestral: He has written alluring, effectively dramatic music for such films as *Reversal of Fortune* (1990), *Little Man Tate* (1991), *The Public Eye* (1992), *The Browning Version* (1994), *Nell* (1994), *Losing Isaiah* (1995), *Last Dance* (1996), *Afterglow* (1997), and *October Sky* (1999).

His knowledge of and experience with many eras and styles of popular music has given birth to wonderfully stylized scores for *The Moderns* (1988), *Billy Bathgate* (1991), *Quiz Show* (1994), and *Mrs. Parker and the Vicious Circle* (1994), while his command of large orchestral forces has been unleashed in *Fire in the Sky* (1993), *Timecop* (1994), and *Blade* (1998). An understanding of the demands of the thriller genre is evidenced by his scores for *The Net* (1995) and *Kiss the Girls* (1997), both of which blend orchestra and electronics. His evocative, pastoral scores for *Of Mice and Men* (1992), his Oscar-nominated *A River Runs Through It* (1992), and the touching *Fly Away Home* (1996) speak in wistful voices that sharply contrast with the aggressive, edgy jazz that propels his urban-thriller scores *Romeo Is Bleeding* (1994) and *Night Falls on Manhattan* (1997). The most outrageous fusion of his many musical lives and interests is found in the bizarre *Cool World* (1992).

We met for this interview at Isham's home, a half-hour's drive from the hustle and bustle of L.A. proper.

mark ISHAM

You're a composer who moves in many directions, but you came to your present work in film from the jazz world, and still have a strong connection to that music. It's obvious that you're comfortable in jazz of all different eras—from early jazz and related music through the futuristic jazz of _Romeo Is Bleeding_. When preparing to score _Quiz Show, Mrs. Parker and the Vicious Circle_, and _The Moderns_, did you do a lot of research or did you have those styles already internalized from your experience as a performer?

The jazz world is pretty ingrained in me. I would not put myself in the class of Wynton [Marsalis] in terms of really being a student of jazz, shall we say. I couldn't sit down and play in the style of Bix Beiderbecke or Louis [Armstrong]. I've seen Wynton do some of his seminars, and he really knows that stuff inside and out. My education is reasonably good—I think I know enough about those styles that I can, within a day or so, sort of find myself operating within them. Usually, like in the case of _Mrs. Parker_, all I have to do is just pull out some Louis Armstrong records or King Oliver records or real twenties and teens stuff just to get that flavor back in my thinking and remind me of certain orchestrations. If we use a tuba, if we use a bass, it has to be played in the way that makes each style what it is.

You try to at least remain true to the flavor of a style?

I'm sure a jazz critic could listen to *Mrs. Parker* and pull it apart for authenticity in a flat second. I mean, it's not real, it's impressionistic. I think of myself as being impressionistic when it comes to different styles of music. It's not that interesting to me to get right down with a fine-toothed comb and get it exactly right. I'd rather get the feel of it and get the music to communicate that we're in New York in 1920. As long as I'm communicating that we're in New York in 1920, I'm doing my job. And if I do it slightly off-kilter, that's actually a little more interesting to me than being just exactly right. If you want to be exactly right, you should license the music—just go get that record that was made in 1920. All those guys are dead, so I can't get their exact points of view. It's not interesting to me to take five days and train five guys in their thirties to play like that. I'd rather just put up an idea for these guys and say, "Let's react and interact within this context, but do it in your own way."

Not even *Quiz Show* was a hundred percent authentic. For my inspiration, I actually went to the Thad Jones/Mel Lewis Big Band—a seventies phenomenon. *Quiz Show* is the fifties, but the Thad Jones/Mel Lewis Big Band, to my way of thinking, was one of the last, great big bands in that tradition. A lot of great writers and all the players from that era were in it. I mean, really tremendous players who'd come up in the forties and fifties. That was a very emotional band for me. It wasn't exact to the period—it was what interested me. It was what got me off, got me excited. It was what would do the job—communicate that we're in America in the fifties and everything's swinging.

When you were growing up, what were your principal influences? Were you listening to both jazz and concert music?

I had a very fortunate upbringing. There was a lot of music in the household—a classical music household. My mother's a symphonic violinist who still works professionally. My dad is a professor of humanities and music history. My dad was also an amateur violinist, and they'd have string quartets in the house. So I grew up with a big classical background more by osmosis, by environment, than by study.

My mother stuck a violin in my hand when I was ten. But then I heard Bach trumpets, clarion trumpets. My mother would play the Christmas shows in the local symphonies, which usually included a Bach oratorio or some cantatas or something that would have the Bach trumpets. When I heard those, they got me excited about playing trumpet. And during the first couple of years that I played trumpet, I was interested in being a classical player. I used to play the Haydn Trumpet Concerto and the B Minor Mass.

There was very little popular music in our household. I didn't really know who The Beach Boys or The Beatles were—I just sort of knew they were out there, doing something. I wasn't that interested. But I would occasionally go to films, where I remember becoming aware of Henry Mancini. And that is, in a way, where I first heard the jazz influence.

Although I don't think anybody would say Mancini was a real jazzer, he certainly was one of the film composers who let jazz influence him tremendously. He wrote popular songs in a sort of Cole Porter tradition, which, of course, is very interlinked with the jazz tradition.

It wasn't until I was in high school that I heard *real* jazz. My family had moved from New York to California, and, while I was looking for radio stations, I came across a jazz station. And that was *it*. Never before had heard anything like that. What's the trumpet player doing? It was Nat Adderley, the Nat Adderley Quintet. From there, the rest is history.

Romeo Is Bleeding is a gritty, futuristic, urban film. I was struck by the fact that, within this context, you employed a number of traditional film-scoring techniques. When the characters run, for example, the music gets a little faster; when they slow down, the

music slows down—that sort of thing. In a film that is stretching the boundaries of tradition, was this a conscious effort to help the audience out a little bit? Instead of letting the score be completely "out there," along with the film, let the score work with the film in some traditional ways to give the audience a more secure footing?

Yeah. Because I've been doing this long enough, it wouldn't occur to me to just sort of blast through a film, and not pay attention to my job. I think this sort of rubs shoulders with something that I'm adamant about: I, personally, don't think that film music has anything to do with a stylistic genre in music. But I think you will find a lot of film-music purists who say that, unless you write like Miklós Rózsa and those guys, you're not writing a good score. And, if you use another genre of music in a film, it's just, sort of, "Well, he's slumming on this film."

I think that's about as ridiculous as you can get. Film music is music that *supports* a film, and that's really *all* it is. To me, it makes no difference what the musical genre is. If it's avant-garde jazz, there's no reason that it can't change tempo with the scenes. Just because it's another genre doesn't mean it has to blast through the film and not pay attention to doing its job in terms of being film music. No matter what genre I use to score a film, I'm still a film composer, and I'm still writing film music. And I'll be going back and rewriting if I don't do my job.

In *Romeo*, there are many powerful sound effects that are fused with your mechanistic, propulsive score. When you prepare to score a film, are the sound effects in it when you first look at it? Do you consciously work around the sound effects for them to become part of the percussion section of your score?

Well, I can immediately answer that question conceptually: If I have the opportunity, I love working with the sound effects. I have actually traded sample disks with sound-effects departments and made musical things out of their effects. And they use some of my musical things as sound effects.

The problem with postproduction is the time limit toward the end, which, usually, just gets worse all the time. So, a lot of the time, you won't have access to final effects. So you just try and keep them in mind. You see that there's an elevated train in a scene, so you call the director and say, "Well, how are you gonna play this? Is that train just going to take over the whole sound design here, or are you gonna abstract this out, so you won't hear the train?" And I'll sometimes force a decision. I'll say, "What should I do? Should I keep going? Should I get out of the way?" A smart director will have in mind what he wants to accomplish. If the director seems to be waffling around, I'll call the sound department and say, "What are you guys planning for this?"

In the case of *Romeo Is Bleeding*, Walter [Murch] did all the sound. He did all the postproduction, other than the music. He cut it and mixed it. And I don't remember whether I had his sound cut to work with.

In a wonderful spot in *Romeo* you've got cha-cha music that begins to mix with clusters and then a music box. It's a wonderful fusion of styles that crash into one another. Moments of this sort show up in many of your films, especially *Cool World*. I notice that you're smiling now, and I suspect that you're also smiling when you actually do this sort of thing, or conceive it.

Oh, yeah! Especially the one in *Romeo*, because that was very specifically designed. We did all our homework on the keys, the rhythm, everything, so we knew we would have a very interesting effect. Now, I can't say that things were that well planned for *Cool World*, which was a debacle in postproduction. So, if there are some good moments there, they're probably mostly happenstance.

The Hitcher **is an electronic score with a couple of acoustic elements. Was your choice to work this way due to budget restrictions or a particular aesthetic leaning or the director?**

My own insecurity. When I started off in this business, I never wanted to be a film composer. I never studied film composing, and I still have never studied film composing. I always figured, well, I do this *thing*. And then I got offered a chance to do it in a film. A number of years and a number of films had to go by before I said, "Well, I guess this is a career. Maybe I should actually start to learn a few things."

The Hitcher was an early action film, and I would have run scared with my tail between my legs to do an orchestral action film at that point. I figured that the only way I would be able to do a film like that was in that sort of Tangerine Dream, electronic world that I knew pretty well. And, really, that was it.

You know, *Never Cry Wolf* and *Mrs. Soffel*, which were before *The Hitcher*, use small chamber orchestras overdubbed on top of the electronic score. As a matter of fact, *Mrs. Soffel* turned out to be mostly acoustic, because it felt like the score needed to be acoustic. But it was mainly done by overdubbing and replacing things. I constructed the score with tape loops and piano loops in my own little weird world, and then the blanks were filled in and it was written down for an ensemble to play. Whereas now, I actually write something out for orchestra and pass it out like a *regular* guy.

When I started off, I definitely came from a whole other point of view, which was, "I do what I do and, if it works in the film, fine." *The Hitcher* was still part of that world, and the decision to have an all-electronic score was fine with the director. He just wanted my sensibility—he loved *Never Cry Wolf*. Really, it's all a matter of how you're comfortable doing it.

How did the "regular" guys react when you started doing bigger orchestral scores?

I'll never forget one time when I was doing *A River Runs Through It*, which was probably my first 100-percent acoustic score—you know, pass out the parts, play. When I was mixing it, I ran into James Horner, who was working in the next room. I said, "Oh, hi. How ya doin'?" And he said, "What are you working on?" I said, "I'm doing a score for . . ." And he said, "Are you doing that electronically?" I said "No, acoustically." And I just saw his face kind of go . . . [Isham makes an I-can't-believe-it face.]

The thing is, composers don't usually know each other. We rarely work together. It's only by happenstance that I even knew Horner enough to say hello to him: We had worked together on a song that my band was going to play in one of the *Star Trek* movies that he scored. I've only met Hans Zimmer because several people who work for me have studios in his facility. I don't think I know any other composers. Composers just don't hang with each other because they never work in the same room at the same time.

The score for *The Hitcher* seems to have two basic elements: a floating, *Hearts of Space* music and an aggressive, complex, contrapuntal music, both of which tend to follow the action, *except* toward the end, when the kid blows Rutger Hauer away. At that point, there's a lot of action, but your music—a moody, electronic landscape—plays against that action. Did you choose to do that because the kid is out there, alone, against the elements?

I occasionally do that in action films. It's instinct.

I must admit that when I first saw *The Hitcher*, I asked the director, "What the hell are you making here?" It was like a slasher movie because it really impacted you with its violence, although there is a Hitchcockian element in that very little violence is actually shown, it's all implied. But it's implied in a way that really is upsetting. The director struggled with that himself—he struggled with what he was trying to do that he could look at as having any sort of positive connotations. He said, "Look, I'm trying to, as much as possible, make this just a journey of self-discovery for the kid, who comes to realize that if you come across pure evil, you have to fight it, which isn't the most pleasant choice but, sometimes, perhaps, it's the only choice." I think that not just making the kid a hero as he finally decides to blow this guy away, but sort of playing the scene as if this is the human condition, was a very interesting choice. There is evil in the world, and the kid, who's not violent, is put in a situation where violence is his only recourse, or his best choice. For him to walk away from this evil would be a poorer choice than for him to actually confront it.

You can intellectualize about all this forever. And you can make any film in the world sound really serious and really cool. And it's just as easy to poke holes in a thing like that. I like [Robert] Harmon a lot—he's a very bright guy, and I've done a lot of work with him as a director. But sometimes you just do films because they pay the rent.

You score big-budget films and smaller-budget, independent films. I suspect that you don't do too many films just to pay the rent, but more because you really enjoy working on them.

I *have* consciously tried to make intelligent choices, to pick things that are interesting. But I did *Timecop*, so I can't say that I have done nothing but great *changing-the-shape-of-twentieth-century-art* films.

Maybe you did *Timecop* because it was a chance to do a large orchestra-synth combination.

Exactly. There are lots of reasons to take a job. One of which is because September is coming and the kids' school fees are due. And that's just as valid a reason as any other. But you put your finger on a very good point: Here's a film that will let me do something that I've never done before. It may not be the greatest action film in the world, but I've never done a really tough, ballsy action film and been given a budget of $350,000 to record an eighty-piece orchestra. Well, here's that opportunity. It's Jean-Claude Van Damme and it isn't going to change the history of cinema, but I'm gonna learn a hell of a lot. That, for me, is a completely valid reason for choosing a film.

Timecop contains a lot of classic Steiner/Korngold-style synchronization of action with musical commentary. I recall one particular fight in which the swords clash and lock onto each other and you have this huge dissonant chord suspending the tension until the swords pull apart and the music disintegrates.

When I did _Point Break_, which is probably the first real action film that I decided to do in a more traditional manner, there was a point in the project when I wasn't really getting much good response from the director. She said she just needed great, classic film music, which means that when the guys are doing this . . . the chord suspends, and when they're doing that . . .

When it came to _Timecop_, I said, "That's what _it_ needs, too." I checked with the director, and he said, "Yeah. I want you to hit _everything_. I want this to be the most mickey-mouse score in the entire world. I don't want any predictability, I don't want any grooves, I don't want the music to stay in a pattern. I want everything jagged and ragged. Hit everything." So, at points, it almost became like a sound-design job. But, once again, it was a challenge to learn how to do that.

You seem very comfortable with it. You hit all the right spots at all the right times. But there are a couple other places in this film where you have what some people might consider a more Isham sound—a soprano sax floating around, which also seems to be as perfectly in context as the action music.

In a film like that, which is futuristic and contemporary, there's always the question of what do you do for the other side—the non-fighting side. I like the idea of finding a more contemporary vocabulary than just the violins soaring out there. And, in using an instrument like the soprano sax, which is, thanks to someone who shall remain unnamed, a generic love instrument, you need to jump on that bandwagon for a little bit and just use it. You throw a soprano sax in there for the romance and it works fine for a film that's gonna play its five weeks in the theaters and then sit in the video store. Why not?

You've worked a few times with Robert Redford. Is he a musically aware/intelligent director? Can he say things other than, "I want it fast," "I'd like it loud," or "I'd like it in the background"? Can he speak musically with you?

Yeah. He's not a player. He's not like Mike Figgis, who's a composer in his own right, but Bob is very, very smart—one of the most intelligent guys I've ever worked with. He's got a solid music-appreciation education. On *Quiz Show*, he actually knew a fair amount about 1950s jazz. He was a big jazz fan in the fifties, and he used to go and see all the guys in the clubs.

On *A River Runs Through It*, he had a score that he rejected before I came on the picture. So, he'd been around the bend on this one and knew a fair amount about what worked and what didn't work. When I saw the film, I just immediately said, "I know what will work on this." And, luckily, I was right—everything that he pointed in my direction supported my take on it. He brought me a couple of pieces of music that he felt were in the right direction: the Malcolm Arnold *Scottish Dances* and a Jean-Pierre Rampal record of Celtic music, which was exactly the realization that I'd had. I said, "I need the right five beautiful Celtic melodies, almost like five folk songs, which I'll then just orchestrate in different ways. That's what will speak. That's what's gonna tell the story about this film."

The music had to have a poetic quality because the film had a poetic quality. You have this beautiful narration all the way through the film, which is a very high-aesthetic film and a very subjective film. The guy gets killed, but, other than that, everything else is sort of up in the air as to what's really happening. The film never really explores on the surface. It's like poetry. And so the music needed to operate on that same level.

I must confess that *Cool World* is one of my favorite scores—a fertile creative imagination and wit at work. And my son loves the song in which the fat cartoon character growls, "Oh, yeah."

That's great! That "Oh, yeah" was on a sampler CD of all these rap bits, so I put it in there. Usually, all these sampler CDs are licensed—you buy the CD and you get the opportunity to use it. But, just as the film was being finished, I said, "Just in case, let me just check on this and make sure." Now, nowhere on the CD did it say, "By purchasing this CD you are buying the license to use . . ." So, I called up Paramount and told them that they'd better check this out. Well, the guy at Paramount called me back, quivering, and says, "We got a quote for $25,000 for that 'Oh, yeah.' You've gotta take it out!" So, my orchestrator just did a couple of "Oh, yeah" samples, which we tuned down a bit and put in the film. And it cost us, well . . . I think I bought him a bottle of wine.

I know a lot of critics were negative about *Cool World* before it even came out. I read that, going into the film, you felt it had big problems—that it was not going to be a success. How did you work with that? Could you escape the negative publicity and go at the project with your professional musicianship, saying, "I'm gonna do the best job I can," or did you take it to the next level and say, "Maybe I can help save this film"?

Box-office is never really a consideration for me. I really figure that that has so little to do with me. Actually, at the end of the day, it has very little to do with anybody in the postproduction end. There are so much bigger forces at play in terms of whether a film does well at the box office.

Quiz Show should have done better at the box office. Now, why was that? It had nothing to do with the quality of the film. I think it had to do with a lousy release from Disney. Maybe a bad poster. Who knows? There are so many elements in play in the release of a film that I can't afford to get involved. But what I *can* do is ask, "Is this film working. When I look at this film for the fiftieth time, am I cringing or am I still enjoying it?" And I like to think that most of the films I've done, including even the more straight-ahead films, like *Timecop*, worked. At the end of the day, that's a good fight scene. It's fun.

Filmmaking is a collaborative art form. There's no doubt about it. It's a group that's making the film. Well, on *Cool World*, the group was nuts. By the end of the film, the group that was making it, as a group, was insane. It had stopped working. Nothing was happening. It was a nightmare. People were dropping like flies, quitting.

This was before you started the score?

No. This was just as I started, and all the way through. I just said, "All right," because I very quickly had a concept for the film: We have a traditional film orchestra. We have a swing band. And they collide. Some of the cues are straight swing, some of the cues are straight orchestra, but we have this whole other part of the film where it's collision between them. And then we have this third element that's just weird dance music—nasty techno stuff.

It was a tremendously ambitious score, and I got very excited by that. I thought that if I could just stay organized and get it done, I would have gotten what I need to get out of it. But there ended up being a lot less money than we expected. We ended up having to go to Germany and England to record it, so I had none of my regular players, none of my regular team. But, we still got it done. And I think it's a good score. The record is pretty impressive. But I can't watch the film. It's a disaster.

On the CD, there's a cue called "A Night Out in Cool World." In the film, it's when they're performing Wagner on this bizarre cartoon stage. It's an outrageous cue—Wagner against a big band, against this dark techno stuff, ending up with a kind of Charles Ives effect. In a cue like that, is it incredibly complicated to get all the pieces to fit, or is it somewhat effortless because you just slam them all together?

That was the easiest thing in the whole score. We literally just went out to the music shop, put our money down for a score of Wagner's Ring Cycle, and copied out the first twenty bars of the opening. Then I went out to the orchestra and said, "All right, I want you to play the first twenty bars, but just start playing whatever you want from bar 12 through bar 30. The conductor's just going to do this— he'll raise his hand, you'll crescendo, and then you'll come down to nothing." One take and it was done.

That's where a jazz background in improv helps. You don't need to go to all the trouble to write out all this stuff. You just give a few simple instructions and make sure people follow your instructions. That's why my jazz background has a tremendously larger influence on my style than just what I do in the jazz scores.

The Beast is a perfect example. Very few things were written out for it. I had maybe two themes, for which I wrote out melody and chord changes. But I chose the musicians who were willing to improvise, put them together, and set up structures. And some of the structures were to picture, although a lot of that music was not to picture. We recorded something like ten hours of music— just improvised. And then I played music editor for a week to find places for a fit. That all comes from the understanding and the trust in improvisation. You become like a director: You cast particular musicians in a role, and then you give them instructions— certain boundaries and certain limits. Then you just say, "action" and let them run.

But the players that you "cast" are all tried and true—all dependable.

You cast them very well. You can't just go down the musicians' union list and say, "Give me a bass player." You need someone who you know can deliver. And, by working this way, you get a very different type of score that I really love. That's my favorite type of music. There's a freshness to it. There's a life to it.

Are you attracted to composers from the concert world who explore with improvisation—various composers from the 1960s and the John Cage-types?

I always thought that Cage was much more influential as a writer than as a composer. I never liked what *he* actually did with his concepts. But I certainly like a lot of what other people have done with his concepts, Brian Eno being probably the first and foremost. The musicologists say that he's a rock guy. In another fifty years, this won't matter to musicologists, and they'll actually realize that he was a very influential figure in taking the work of Cage and bringing it more into the mainstream. That's a tremendous thing to have done. It's very valuable. It's really creating a future in music.

Your early influences include?

One of the most influential periods of my life was in San Francisco when I was young and still sort of playing a bit in the classical world. There was a new-music ensemble, 1750 Arch Street, that gave concerts there and had a small record label. Actually, there were several different groups like this in Berkeley in the early 1970s that were really promoting modern chamber music. And I was peripherally involved with these groups for a while. In one of them, we did Stravinsky and things like that. But another one was more of a showcase for young composers. I remember playing a lot of these pieces. And one in particular used improvisation in a way that classical musicians could use the idea. It was basically the idea of mimicry. In one player's part, something would be written out. But your part said, "Mimic what the violinist is doing," and you had to play by ear what you heard them doing. The piece had this tremendous cascade effect—this huge body of music just sort of rolling around, which is basically the same idea that [Steve] Reich used with his phase music.

That experience and observing Reich are sort of crucial little gems in my development. They showed me that a lot of ideas work across genres. Look at the Art Ensemble of Chicago or the Coltrane band when he sort of abandoned standard rhythm and you get the idea of just sort of pushing through time, that time is liquid in music. Once you start to observe these things, it doesn't matter what genre you are in—there are a lot of interesting ideas that work in any genre. It all just supports my basic philosophy that genre is unimportant.

Was Weather Report an influence on you?

A *huge* influence. I would say that listening to the second Weather Report album may have been the most significant musical experience of my life.

I'd been to a friend's house, and he had their first record. I listened to it and thought it was really great. On my way home, I went to a record store to buy it, but it wasn't in. Weather Report's brand-new, second album *was* in, so I bought it, went home, and put on the first side. I never took it off the first side for a week. I couldn't get enough. These guys were taking avant-garde jazz, melodic jazz, and classical chaos music and bringing them all together. For me, this was *it*. For me, that record still is one of the most influential records of all time. It's wonderful.

I notice that you still play with your combo, outside of film music, and make records.

Oh, yeah. We were just at the Montreal Jazz Festival. We'll be up at the Eddie Moore Jazz Festival in Berkeley in a couple weeks. We always do at least a couple shows a month here on the local Los Angeles circuit.

Has the band personnel stayed pretty regular?

The core rhythm section—bass, drums, keyboard—is the same. We've changed saxophone players; we've added a guitar. We're more of an electric band now, everything's plugged in.

And you have racks of synthesizers?

Oh, yeah. I have a little sampler with just some effects and ambient things that I'll fool around with a little bit. But I sort of stay out of the keyboard side of it. I leave the synthesizer stuff to the keyboard guys. I just concentrate on playing trumpet.

When you did your 1992 *Of Mice and Men*, did you listen to Aaron Copland's 1939 *Of Mice and Men* score?

I refused to listen to it. I did everything I could to avoid listening to it. It was unnerving enough that it even existed. And I very consciously tried to stay away from any Americana symphonic flavor. Although, there is one theme in my score that has that sort of style, but it's limited.

You have some innocent, gentle guitar bits that sound atmospherically rustic, but not . . .

I wanted to comtemporize it. Country picking, bluegrass, but in an impressionistic sense. There's more in common with Steve Reich minimalism or a Keith Jarrett/Ralph Towner duet, perhaps, than there is with authentic music of that period. Again, it's sort of an impressionistic touch, I hope.

It comes across that way. There's definitely an Americana flavor, but it's not direct, it's understated, which makes it effective. Your

musical painting of Lenny, for example, was genuine in that, whenever he would speak about the rabbits, the good life, and all that, the music was as simple and as basic as it could be.

Yeah. That was the idea—to find something that didn't get in the way. It needed to be exactly what it was.

The Net strikes me as yet another direction for you. It's one of those self-generating, propulsive scores that, I must say, is a little like what Hans Zimmer is doing these days, although there are a lot of Ishamisms in it. Is this a new direction for you or something that you've been evolving for some time?

It was a conscious choice for that film.

I'd just been let go from *Waterworld*. I was the composer on *Waterworld* until Kevin Reynolds left the picture. I really believed in Reynolds' vision of that film. And then Costner took over and told me he didn't like that vision. I said to him, "All right, I'm a flexible guy, I don't wanna get fired. Let's have a meeting and let me write three cues for you." I knew he wanted me to quit, you could tell. But I refused to quit. I said, "I can write this score for you as well as I could for Reynolds, but I have to know what you want." So, I had the meetings with him and I wrote what I thought he wanted. And he still fired me.

Then, like forty-eight hours later, *The Net* just popped into view as a film to do, which was interesting because I was already in this momentum of an electronic-based action picture. I said to myself, well, fine, I'm just gonna sort of stay in that mode. And, yeah, I was experimenting with what Zimmer sort of does: You get the rhythmic drive from a synthesizer and overlay an orchestra on top of it to give you that big Hollywood quality. I did that on *The Getaway*, too. But, at the end of the day, the music in a film like *The Net* has a very utilitarian role. It's just there—it's just churning along. You could write decent music, you could write brilliant music.

I don't really know if it would make that big a difference in a film where music is used in that way.

The Last Dance strikes me as a little bit of a nod back to some of your earlier work—little floating voices; mellow, laid-back piano . . .

Yeah, it may actually have a certain amount of similarity to *Of Mice and Men* in that regard, and, like *Of Mice and Men*, it's a tragedy. So there's a certain similar type of poignancy—that great grief of the human condition, which is, ultimately, what you're trying to express in those films. Why does life allow Lenny to be that way? What is the spiritual nature of existence that allows Lenny to be on that path?

Has anyone ever come to you and said, "I want a score like *Never Cry Wolf*. And be more experimental, ignore everybody else"?

I don't get "be more experimental." I *do* get people who really love *Never Cry Wolf*. The really off-the-wall thing about it is that it's a nature film for Disney *and* it's an electronic score. I still think a lot of people can't get it. I think that idea still frightens people. But, in terms of concept, it worked.

What are you up to these days?

I just finished an HBO film for Robert Harmon. It's the story of John Gotti.

Is it an orchestral score?

They have no money at HBO, so we did about nineteen minutes of orchestra music and fifteen minutes of bizarre little chamber-ensemble things with percussion instruments and then some accordion music.

Do you have little Sicilian or Neapolitan folk tunes in the score?

I ended up writing a "neo-Neapolitan folk song," and then basing the whole score on it. But it was mine.

What's in the future?

I'm starting a Sidney Lumet film, which should be very interesting—he's a great master. I've only met with him once so far, but he's really delightful. Also I'll be doing the next John Woo film. That's not for a while, but we're starting negotiations on that, so I can safely say that I *may* do that. Nothing's for sure in Hollywood until it's in the theater, with your name on the poster.

Representing a new generation of Hollywood film composers, Daniel Licht hit the scene less than a decade ago with an ambitious and spooky orchestral score for *Children of the Night* (1990). Armed with an academic degree, original music for student films, New York City jazz experience, a love of movies, and a sophisticated knowledge of world music, Licht rapidly proved himself a significant talent—a versatile, imaginative, and dependable film composer.

His restless, spine-tingling orchestral scores for *Severed Ties* (1991), *Children of the Corn II: The Final Sacrifice* (1993), *Children of the Corn III: Urban Harvest* (1995), *Bad Moon* (1996), *Hellraiser: Bloodline* (1996), and *Stephen King's Thinner* (1996) represent Licht at his blood-curdling best, while such recent scores of his as *The Winner* (1996), *Permanent Midnight* (1998), and *Splendor* (1999) and the television movies *Woman Undone* (1996) and *The Patron Saint of Liars* (1998) effectively explore other musical territories.

We met for this interview in his Hollywood studio, surrounded by dozens of unusual instruments and artifacts from around the world.

daniel LICHT

You are a relative newcomer to film music. *Anthropados* is your first credit.

That was the first film I scored. I started it when I was in college—Hampshire College, which some people call Hippie College because of its loose, non-regimented structure. A fellow student, Matthew Patrick, began directing the film as his senior thesis, or whatever you call it, and I scored it as he shot it. Matthew was always raising funds, and, when he'd get funds, he'd shoot more, and I'd score more. I continued working on the film after I graduated, and did the last cues in New York City. It's a Spanish-language film starring a Puerto Rican soap-opera star. He mortgaged his house to pay for it. It's really a pretty interesting little film that got some acclaim, but no commercial release. That was my first film scoring experience, and it was a good place to test the waters.

You moved to New York City after Hampshire College?

I went to New York and played jazz. I'm an eclectic kind of guy—I've always been interested in a lot of different forms of music. I studied world music when I was at Hampshire. There was a great world-music department next door at Amherst College. My parents moved to Indonesia, so I'd go there a lot, and also go to Jakarta and study Javanese music and Bali and study Balinese music. But, I finally settled in New York, where I played jazz and wrote commercials. That was the work that was to be had there. I spent maybe eight years in New York, pursuing little films here and there, finally realizing that if I really wanted to do films, I was in the wrong city. So I moved out here. I was inspired by Chris Young, a good friend of mine who I also went to school with. He was always saying, "Man, this is the place to be." So, I finally just left it all behind and came out here. And I'm very happy that I did.

This was in the late 1980s?

Well, I've been out here for almost seven years. For a while, I was going back and forth, leading a bicoastal existence. I moved here around the time that I scored *Children of the Night*, 1991 or so.

Many film composers talk about "paying their dues," getting experience working in television, documentaries, industrials, low-budget films with zero music budget, or whatever they could do on synthesizer or fund themselves. But your early films—*Children of the Night*, *Children of the Corn II*, *Children of the Corn III*, *Separate Ties*—have large orchestral scores.

I came here at a time when everyone decided that you didn't need a real orchestra anymore, but there were still a few people who you could talk into hiring an orchestra for low-budget films, *Children of the Night* being a perfect example. If they were making that film today, I doubt very much that I could convince anyone to let me hire an orchestra. The budgets have shrunk to meet the availability of cheaper synthesizer scores, and new directors budget even less money for music.

What kind of reasoning or leverage would you use to convince producers that their film needed an orchestral score?

A lot of begging and twisting. In my first scores, I used, as a kind of a bargaining tool, the idea that I would make less money myself: "I'll put the entire music budget into the costs—contractors, copyists, performers. Give me this, and I'll give you that. You'll get more than your money's worth."

In fact, I made very little money doing films for a long time. In general, I've spent a lot because I just wanted to get music out there, and I thought it would be good for my career to have it as high-quality as possible. You put three months of your life into something, you want it to be the best that it can be.

One of the reasons that I'm doing film scoring in the first place is that I love film scores, and I think that they're an important part of the entire spectrum of twentieth-century music. They're also a good way for composers to have immediate feedback about their compositions. That's a big draw for a lot of composers—you write something and get it played within two or three weeks, while the ideas are still fresh in your head. It's a great learning experience. There are a lot of frontiers to explore. But, right now, I'm beginning to feel more limitations than frontiers.

I am attracted to things that are emotional. It's the expressive quality of music that is the most attractive to me, not the technical or intellectual constructs. I want to communicate an emotion to an audience, and I find that it's much easier and much more human through live players. It doesn't necessarily need to be a full orchestra, it could be a small instrumental ensemble or solos or oddball instruments, not that synths don't have their part.

Some of your scores seem to embrace a strong gamelan influence, an Eastern approach to music and time. Others seem to have a very strong association with contemporary jazz. Others are massive orchestral horror-genre scores. Others are traditionally romantic. Is a broad stylistic range just part of the job?

My tastes have always been extremely eclectic. I don't always sit down and listen to ten different things in one day, but I've gone through periods in my life where I've studied a certain kind of music in detail. Basically, I felt like I was doing research into the essence of music.

In film scoring, you're not as defined by any particular style, as you are in, say, concert music or jazz, where people are expecting you to perform in a certain style. With film music, it's anything that dramatically creates what you need to get across at any given moment. Film music is a great opportunity for me to explore and blend different styles. I love synthesizing different styles of music in an organic way—not just saying, "I'm going to do something that's Indian raga with a back beat," which is an intellectual decision.

Doesn't it ultimately, beyond the impulse spark, become an intellectual decision?

It's more like, How can I create a mood with more than one musical element going on? There are different levels to things, always. Nothing is ever cut and dried.

Many film composers avoid intellectualizing their music, but there's got to be more to it than you're acknowledging. There must be an intellectual process at some point. You might say, "I'll fuse an Indian raga with a back beat and a tenor saxophone," as an emotional reaction to the film. But, at some point you have to intellectualize the actual procedure of fusing those things on paper. At some point, you must use your musical intellect after you use your instinct.

It's not necessarily reacting, because, as a film composer, you're not asked just to react, you're specifically told to create something that doesn't exist in the film. Absolutely, you use your intellect, but it's more like, How am I going to make a contribution to this film that is unique and takes it a step further?

My point is that if someone is presenting a concert piece, they can have the freedom to say, "Well, what would happen if I add this, reverse this, augment this?" They don't know what the outcome is going to be, and it really doesn't matter because it's the intellectual idea that they develop that is the end in itself. With a film composer, that may not work. The film composer has to figure out the direct, gut-level, emotional response of mixing raga and saxophone. Film composing comes down to all sorts of intellectual processes, but, at the end of the day, the bottom line is whether it conveys the correct emotion, which is *not* something that is perceived intellectually. The audience isn't sitting there going, "Wow, he blended raga and serialism." Many times, they're not even aware there's music.

What are some of your experiences in the area of composer vs. producer/director?

It runs the gamut. Some directors have spent a lot of time directing me. That's frustrating. I feel like saying, "I am not going to finish this score unless you give me some space and some time by myself to work these things out!" Then other directors have said, "We trust you. See you at the stage," which is scary as well.

I like working with directors who know dramatically what they want the music to do. There are always so many questions to answer when you're scoring a film. Having a director who knows what he wants can answer some of those questions, because he has laid out a groundwork that I find helpful. On the other hand, if you don't agree with the director, then that can be a big problem. And the temp score can be a real danger.

The director gets used to hearing a certain sound on the temp and says, "Give me something that's not that, but is that"?

Yeah. You start working from a negative space. You have to decide if what was temped works or doesn't work, rather than just looking at a scene and starting with a clean slate. But, it would not be honest for me to ignore the fact that sometimes temp music has given me ideas—perhaps a way of dealing with the scene that I might not have thought of myself. I think temps sometimes help all composers, although they may not admit it. I'm sure every composer has, at one time or another, seen a temp score and said, "I never would have thought of handling it this way. That's a great idea." But, overall, the effect is probably more negative and restricting than positive.

Do you feel that you've been typecast as a horror-movie composer?

The horror and splatter films used to be ghetto films. Now they're even nominated for Academy Awards—*Silence of the Lambs*, *Pulp Fiction*. The genre stuff is getting a little more respect. For me, personally, if a film is well-done, there are some interesting things that can be done about dark things. They're tragic in nature, as is most great opera. People think of music for horror films as being all about flesh-ripping and stabbing, but there's also always a tragic undertone to it. There are always places for writing very emotional music in those kinds of films.

I like working on a variety of films. I guess that, among certain people, I've been typecast, and, among other people, I haven't. The people with whom I've done horror films—the people who were heavily involved in doing genre films—definitely think of me as the guy who does that. But, for the people who don't follow those films, I've done enough other kinds of films. And I'm not that well-known that everybody's sitting around talking about what I'm doing!

You seem to enjoy mixed meters, multiple meters, irregular phrasing, and complex syncopation.

I do. But, like everything, you can't make generalizations. I find that it's easier to write for film using odd meters for fast-paced stuff. It's based on the unexpected. Things can be unexpected, but they must not seem forced.

You scored a series of *Amityville Horror* sequels in the 1990s. The Academy Award-nominated 1979 *Amityville Horror* was scored in a neo-Bartók fashion by Lalo Schifrin. Did you study the original film?

I did.

Were you inspired by Schifrin's approach? Did you make conscious choices in your score to avoid a critical comparison?

I didn't consciously respond to his score, which I like a lot. It has some beautiful moments with the frantic stuff. I've always been tempted to play it for producers who feel that you can't have anything pretty for a horror film.

I've had main titles rejected because people thought they were too pretty, *Children of the Corn II* being a perfect example. The main title is on the CD, but not in the movie. People say, "How is the audience gonna know it's a horror film?" Well, it's a sequel. They've already seen *Children of the Corn*. There won't be any confusion in their minds. There's no reason why we can't present something haunting and beautiful as the main title.

In *Amityville: A New Generation*, every time a character gazes into the mirror, you create a counterpoint of extended vocal techniques, synthesizers, and acoustic instruments. There's also angry whispering and harp fragments.

That's partially the sound-effects people. I did something with harps and two solo women. In that score, I used a synthetic scale influenced by my study of gamelan music. A lot of the score is based on one scale, to which I intentionally limited myself. I can't remember exactly what it was—some kind of a quasi-octatonic thing.

For the evil-clock scenes, did the director instruct you to use some kind of clock pulse?

My main goal in that score was to give the clock a personality. If you have an entire film that is based on an evil clock, you need to help sell the clock's personality. That's why I used the little music box.

I did use clock sounds in the score, but usually to maintain the off-stage presence of the clock in scenes where you didn't see it. Because something is obvious doesn't necessarily mean it's not a good idea.

You seem to have had a lot of fun in your score for _Severed Ties._

Yeah. I played a lot of the parts myself. I played all the harp parts, the piano, and a fair amount of the percussion. It's sort of a hand-made score. I also enjoyed working on that score because it called for synths that were unapologetically synths—they weren't trying to pretend they were something else. I loved the textures. The music had an anything-goes feel—I didn't feel that I had to worry about the music going too far at any point. But it was a lot of work because I was playing a lot of the instruments, composing, supervising, engineering, mixing, directing.

At one point, while Harry is regenerating Garrett Morris's artificial leg, the record spinning on the dusty old record player is your main title music transformed into a scratchy 1930s recorded version.

Some people find that amusing, but what I did _not_ find amusing at all was that I wasn't at the final mix in Chicago, and on the cue directly after that record, they forgot to take the equalizer off. What was to be a score piece was actually EQ'd as if it were a scratchy record. When I first heard that, I just flipped out. But, by that time, it was too late to do anything about it.

That same scene begins with old-time gospel-organ music that gradually becomes the accompaniment to your main title theme.

Suddenly, the whole thing abruptly ends when the needle is scraped off the record and there's a very pregnant silence. In *Severed Ties*, or in any your films, where and how are the decisions *not* to have music made?

It's really tough. I think one of the hardest things to do is spot a film, because there are always so many possibilities. Once you've decided where the music goes, all you have to figure out is what the music is doing: What am I trying to say with the music here? What am I trying to accomplish? When you don't even know where the music should be, you're really looking at a blank piece of paper.

Sometimes the directors have used temp music and you don't even have to be at the spotting session—they can just take notes and give them to you. Sometimes the directors have no idea and say, "Oh, you decide." I've experienced both extremes. In general, if I've got to figure out the spotting, that's a good three, four, maybe five days of work. If I'm on a short schedule, that's time I would have spent writing.

There's also nothing worse than trying to score a scene while thinking in the back of your mind, "I don't know if there even should be music here." You've got this many minutes of music to write and you're asking yourself, "Am I wasting my time here?" In general, I find that if I cannot come up with the right approach to a scene, it's usually because there shouldn't be any music there. Nine times out of ten, when I'm not able to score a scene—when I can't find anything that I think works—I'll decide that the scene should be dry. I'll call up the director and say, "Look, I don't think this scene needs music." Sometimes they'll agree with me and sometimes they'll say, "Well, let's have it anyway."

How often are a film's sound effects known or available to you when you begin writing a score? And what part do sound effects play in, let's say, adding percussion elements to your score?

Nine times out of ten, you do not have final effects, and that's too bad. On *Hellraiser IV: Bloodline*, I was fortunate enough to get a six-track mix of the temp effects, which I found to be invaluable. Sometimes, especially in an effects-heavy movie, you need to know what aural space is left to you.

I am, in general, very sensitive to the other elements of a film—the dialogue and the effects—because I want my music to have presence. I don't do so-called wallpaper scores—I don't think that music should be just lightly floating in the background. I feel music should be there with and for a definite purpose, which is not to say that it can't be soft music. If you write soft music, you play it soft. But if you write loud music, it should be played loud, and heard.

I spend a lot of time thinking about what is going to happen on the stage, and I always go to mixes. I think it's very important for a composer to go to the mix, even if it is, and it can be, a very painful experience. If, in your initial conception of the score, you start with the mindset that you are competing with other things, the chances of your music having the presence that you have in your mind are better.

Your music becomes an additional voice?

In the first place, you stay out of the way of the dialogue. And, if you know that the effects are going to have a low rumble, you don't write a cue that has a low bass pulse, because it will never be heard.

I don't always know what the effects are going to be, but I always try to guess. If there's a scene where people are driving in a car, I won't write a cue that's bass-line dependent, because the low-end engine sound of the car is probably going to be there and obliterate a lot of the musical information.

Dialogue is obviously essential. I always write around it, which is time-consuming—I could probably score a scene in half the amount of time if I wasn't spending so much time thinking, "If I start this melody one bar later, this theme will come to a rest during this line." It's all chance, but you can sometimes move things so that, eighty percent of the time, dialogue happens on the sustain at the end of a phrase. You find the biggest pauses and shape your music around the dialogue.

In general, I try to get the whole shape of the cue done before I start writing it out to a fuller orchestration. I'll do a four-line sketch or even just a piano sketch of the whole cue first, even if it's only a minute long. I try and shape the general form around the dialogue or the effects, and then I can just turn off the video and know where everything is. Maybe I won't know what's going to happen in the middle, but I'll know where I'm going. Then I can think, "Okay, so this is what I've got, now what's going to sound good musically?" I find it to be a challenge. Say I have my theme, which wants to be eight bars long, but I've only got seven bars or I need nine bars. Then I go, "Okay, I'll start with a little intro, and then the theme will start here." It's like one of those kids' puzzles where you move things around to make a picture. Film scoring is solving a lot puzzles. It's an intellectual challenge.

Your music for both *Children of the Corn II* and *Children of the Corn III* suggests a strong Stravinsky influence. Is Stravinsky one of your heroes?

Absolutely. There's no question about it. In those particular scores, the influence of Stravinsky may have been more roundabout—through Jerry Goldsmith. Pretty much from the day I got hired, all I heard was, "*The Omen, The Omen.* Give us *The Omen.*" That's all they wanted!

Did they temp it with *The Omen*?

Absolutely. It was, "We want a score like *The Omen*." Well, all right already! You and about fifty other people making films want a score like *The Omen*. But, sure, why not?

One of the things that helped was deciding to tie it into the American Indian themes. I did *not* use Latin, like *The Omen*. The film took place in America, in the Midwest. Why are we listening to Indians chanting in Latin? What does that have to do with this film? I actually used Indonesian texts and created some of my own language. There was a lot of Indonesian influence—weird Eastern vocal styles.

You constructed a synthetic language with various bits of words and sounds and effects?

Yeah. I made up some words. When you're working on a film score, unfortunately, you don't have time to write up a whole text. You can spend three or four days out of thirty days coming up with words that you want to use. I think I might have used a little Latin there as well, I can't remember. It was a mixture of Latin, Indonesian, and just vowels and consonants that I liked.

But jumping back to your Stravinsky question, yes, I love Stravinsky. And I want to say just one little thing: People are always saying, "Those damn film composers, all they do is steal from the classics." My attitude is, if you go through the classics and find something that works for a scene, that's great—you know your literature pretty well and can make intelligent, informed choices, because most classical music just does not work for film scoring.

For me, it's much easier to write something new for a scene than to find something that was written for the concert world that would work in the film. Concert music is a complete statement in itself—it doesn't need a film. So, if you add it to a film, it's probably too much information at one time.

Definitely, no question about it, all film composers are influenced by concert music. Ballet music is a little different because it is already an accompaniment to something visual. In a sense, ballet music is probably more relevant to film scoring than symphonies and concertos.

Many younger-generation concert composers are directly influenced by contemporary film composers. I've known many students who proclaim, with as much sincerity and dedication as you've expressed for Stravinsky, that guys like you or Christopher Young or Elliot Goldenthal or Danny Elfman are the ones influencing their music. I don't hear too much about Elliott Carter, Ligeti, Penderecki, Messiaen, or Lutoslawski anymore. Even Cage seems almost old-fashioned for some students. Although Christopher Young, Elliot Goldenthal, and the others would be the first to remind us of the important influences that Ligeti, Penderecki, and company had on their own music.

Right. Me, too.

There's a healthy, eclectic interaction or crossover taking place: John Zorn's Morricone tribute album, John Adams' conducting of CDs of classic Takemitsu and Rosenman film music, and Philip Glass's scores for *Koyaanisqatsi, Candyman,* and *Kundun.*

I've always thought it was interesting to listen to *North By Northwest* and then listen to Philip Glass and see that there *is* a strong connection there. It could be purely by chance. I don't know that I've ever heard Philip Glass mention Bernard Herrmann as an influence. I know he's talked a lot about LaMonte Young—they sort of fight among themselves about who invented minimalism. If you asked me, I'd say Bernard Herrmann invented minimalism—he was doing it in the forties. Maybe even Stravinsky in *The Rite of Spring*, with all that repetition. Maybe some anonymous guy in the ninth century.

I'm always surprised that the L.A. Philharmonic doesn't play film music. To me, that's the same as Vienna not playing Mahler, which of course they didn't for a long time. Mahler was there, living in Vienna, and they all stuck their noses up at him. I think there's a similar thing going on here. The L.A. Phil was very proud of the fact that they got out of doing the Hollywood Bowl contract.

Might it be the prophet-in-his-own-backyard syndrome? If you're living in Beverly Hills, writing film music, you can't possibly be as important as some mysterious, destitute Czechoslovakian composer?

I don't know. I think it's just sloppiness, I honestly do. Lately, film music hasn't been anything to get too excited about, and so it doesn't advertise itself very well. I'm just always surprised that there's not some kind of relationship between film composers and the largest orchestra in the city. I think John Mauceri [conductor of the Hollywood Bowl Orchestra] is great. Here's a guy who's saying, "Hey, we've got great music in our city, let's perform it, people want to hear it."

In *Children of the Corn III*, organ music is heard in the score long before we realize so much of the action will be taking place in the parochial school and the Catholic church. Informing the audience that something's going on while the people on the stage are clueless is a classic operatic device. Was it a conscious choice to psychologically or unconsciously prepare the audience?

Not necessarily. Really, it was more deciding what the elements of the score should be and just sticking with that. In general, a film is going to tell you where you're going: Main titles give you a general idea of some kind of a destination or lay out some of the elements. So, in a sense, yeah, it is foreshadowing but not necessarily consciously.

In addition to the orchestra and chorus in *Children of the Corn III*, there's a constant presence of malevolent electronic grumbling and bubbling. Did you enjoy fusing the orchestra and the electronics? Can electronics get in the way of a big orchestra when you eventually mix it all down? Do you ever worry that there's going to be too much musical information?

That's a complicated set of questions. One of the reasons that I prefer working with an orchestra is that an orchestra can sit behind the action better than synths can. And this seems to have a lot to do with the way an orchestra is miked. Most orchestral recordings are going to be miked in stereo. I actually read about this in some recording manual that came out in the 1930s: When you have two mics that are placed distantly, that physically puts the orchestra behind the players on the stage in the same way that you could be at a cocktail party and, let's say, I'm talking to you while all sorts of other people are also talking, and you have kind of a parallax in your ear. I can focus on you, because you're in front of me, and tune out the others. I'm always aware of them, but I block them out.

The score can work on an emotional level when it's distant and behind the players?

Yeah. And I think that you can make more interesting music, you can have more going on in the music, because it has its own space to exist in. Whereas, with the synths, it's very hard to put them back there. Their sounds are, in general, very dry. You have to add reverb, and then you never really get them back there because their sounds are usually recorded too close to the mic. So, the answer to your question is mostly yes. Synths can get in the way of the drama. I find it very difficult to work with synths and orchestra for the same reason—it's hard to put them in the same space. Usually the most successful mixtures of synths and orchestra occur when you don't put them in the same space.

Did you study electronics at Hampshire College?

I'm completely self-taught. Everything I've learned about electronics, I've learned from manuals and experimentation. Anything I've learned about mixing, I've learned from engineers who were doing it. There was an electronic music studio when I went to school, but I wasn't that interested at the time. At that time, there were Arps and Moogs, and that was about it. The first synth I ever bought was a DX7. I was fascinated with it because it was so versatile and open-ended. It didn't actually sound that great, but you could program it like doing mathematical theorems. What you did was unique, and I found that very attractive. I find a lot of today's synths less attractive because what you're getting is a prepackaged sound—there's not much of anything original that you can do with them. They are what they are. But I do like sampling, and I like to do my own sampling because then it becomes more personal.

In *Children of the Corn III*, within very short periods of time, you will develop a phrase in many traditional ways—unexpected harmonization, augmentation, diminution, inversion, retrograde, extension, mini-sequence, major/minor mode. Did your prefilm composing experiences transfer smoothly into your film work?

My composing, before I got to film, was really only what I did in college, and that was mostly whatever the teacher wanted me to do.

For me, themes and motives are always important. I can't write something without a theme. There are plenty of film composers who can score a whole scene or write a whole score without a theme. I wouldn't know what to do without a theme. For me, the theme is primary, it's what I'm going to make the cue out of. It's almost as if I'm the theme. That's my personality—I expand, I develop: How can I expand on this theme? What can I do with this theme to fit it to this scene?

When you listen to my stuff, you probably notice that there's always a hook. It might just be a simple motive, but everything is thematically related, as opposed to textural or soundmass or just expository writing. I guess you could say that it's kind of a crutch, but it's my style.

In one of the scores I just finished, *Stephen King's Thinner*, I have a very simple motive that appears in nearly every cue. It may only come in for a second, but it's always there.

Some composers tend to present a theme the same way every time. For me, a big challenge is presenting a theme in different ways: Let me just see what I can do to this theme to get where I'm going. I guess that if there is any form that appeals to me the most, it is theme and variations, and that may have a lot to do with my jazz background. That's what you're doing in jazz, you're taking a simple tune, doing all his stuff way out there, and then coming back to the original tune.

Have you come up with themes that can work in all extremes— themes that are quiet and slow and depressing and melancholy that can mutate into loud and fast and raucous and optimistic?

Well, I haven't had the opportunity to write much optimistic music! [Laughter] I can probably count on one hand the cues I've written that are optimistic.

Let's say that you've got a new film with many opportunities for big, healthy, optimistic Americana musical statements set in the middle of Iowa. Could that potential soaring Licht theme also be connected with some lugubrious, underground monster that's preparing to eat all the farmers?

I would probably write the optimistic theme first. It would be easier to make that dark as opposed to taking a dark theme and making it lighter. The practicality of scoring a scene also has something to do with it.

I try to make my themes as long as possible. If you have a very long theme, you can score a whole scene with it or use fragments that can develop in many ways. Then it's really about orchestration. Once you set the theme in motion, it creates its own momentum. I like to spend time writing themes in advance.

Before you've spotted a film? Before you've even seen a rough cut?

Sometimes before I've even seen the film, especially if I know it's going to be a short schedule. I've actually scored scenes from a script. I was really amazed that it worked; I never thought it would work, but sometimes you just have to do what you have to do. On *Zooman*, I had only two weeks with the locked picture. I wrote all the themes in advance.

Let's talk about *Zooman*. It's yet another style of Licht music—gritty, sometimes dissonant, 1960s urban jazz and acid jazz. I've heard the CD and seen the picture. The acid jazz didn't make it onto the CD.

No. The producers felt that the soundtrack audience wouldn't appreciate it, which I think was a big mistake.

Did you play on these cues? Did you conduct the little jazz group?

I was playing percussion on some of the acid jazz stuff, but I didn't play on any of the orchestral or the jazz-quintet stuff.

Was your jazz material written out as traditional jazz-improv notation? Did you use basic charts with chord changes, or were those sections more specifically orchestrated and notated?

The stand-alone jazz cues were charts, maybe five-line arrangements or something like that. But the orchestra stuff was a more detailed, larger score.

I really enjoyed that film because I finally got a chance to work with jazz and orchestra. Actually, that score has some of the stuff that I'm most proud of. Interestingly, there's trumpet on nearly every cue. Part of that has to do with the director—he just loves trumpet. I like trumpet, too, but I use different kinds of trumpets, different mutes, to try and break it up. I used muted waa-waa pedal for some of the acid jazz and the Miles Davis sound.

Woman Undone is more of a Bernard Herrmann suspense environment—a lot of string orchestra, dense contrapuntal writing, big minor shock-chords in minor-third progressions, menacing half-steps, and all that. Was that score the result of the director or producer requesting something in a thriller vein? Did the name Hitchcock come up?

No. Well, actually, Herrmann probably did come up. I can't remember. It's quite possible that Bernard Herrmann was mentioned, but you don't even have to mention Bernard Herrmann's name with me.

He's a hero?

There's no question about it. Bernard Herrmann has some kind of influence deep in there. I would definitely say Bernard Herrmann is one of my main influences.

Those classic Ray Harryhausen fantasy pictures: When you were a kid, would you watch Bernard Herrmann movies and be inspired by the music?

No. I can't say that I was focusing on film music when I was a kid, but I certainly watched all those movies and loved them. I still love to watch them on TNT now. There's something nostalgic about people, sailors, a bunch of teenagers getting chased around by skeletons or giant crabs or whatever. And a movie like *Them!*, Bronislau Kaper! I have very vivid memories of all those films, but I can't say I watched them thinking that some day I wanted to do horror-film scores. All young American composers have been influenced by the music of those films. Whether they admit it or not, they watched them all when they were kids. Just like a lot of the minimalist composers have been influenced by jazz. Most of them played in jazz bands to make money. When I read interviews with them, I was surprised to find that Philip Glass played jazz, Terry Riley played jazz, Steve Reich—they all played jazz. And it surprised me to find out how many times Coltrane was mentioned, because I was a big Coltrane fan myself. When I was thirteen or fourteen, listening to Coltrane turned my world around. His music can do something different, make you want to snap your fingers weird, or go out and find some girl to kiss.

How did *Hellraiser IV* come your way?

It was definitely Clive Barker. No question about that. As my manager loves to put it, I was "hand-picked by Clive Barker." Of course, I don't know what really went on.

How had Barker become familiar with your music?

I'd been up for a few things. I'd done two films for Miramax, so it's not like they didn't know who I was. There was sort of an inevitability to it. I was up for *Hellraiser III* as well, but I was taken out of the running on that one because I was still doing *Children of the Corn II*. My name was probably floating around for a while.

***Hellraiser IV* has some direct references to the Christopher Young's *Hellraiser II* theme.**

Right. I call it the "Pinhead Fanfare." I'm not sure what Chris calls it.

Did the decision to use that bit of existing material, that easily recognizable motive, come from the production company or was that your choice?

It was a direction from them. They wanted to use some of the original themes, and I didn't have a problem with that. I didn't actually use them very much. Some people might say, "I want to do my own thing," but you can't let your ego get in the way of doing what you're supposed to do—it's a collaborative thing.

Chris had created part of the aura of Pinhead, and I think that's great. To be able to do something musically that's part of a film means that you're not just doing wallpaper—you're helping create the persona. Pinhead himself became much more important in the whole *Hellraiser* series. In the first film, he wasn't a major character, he was auxiliary—he didn't show up until the end of the film. So, thematically, the themes from the first film were less relevant to him. I only used Chris's theme when Pinhead first appears and when he dies. I tried to approach the story of *Hellraiser IV* the same way that, say, Goldsmith might approach *Homeward Bound III*. He's not going to rewrite the Bruce Broughton score, but, occasionally, he might draw from the original material. To consciously avoid it, I think, is a mistake.

I've seen a recent *Star Trek* movie where the well-known main theme wasn't used very much. And that's a disappointment to the audience. The main theme is part of the history, part of the *Star Trek* mystique.

You maintain the dark image of the other *Hellraisers*, but you also heavily exploit the low end of the orchestra—a lot of low brass and low strings—with densely weaving contrapuntal lines. Counterpoint, of course, is writing lines against lines, characters working against characters. Did you mix your motives to support the mix of many personalities on the screen?

For *Hellraiser IV*, absolutely. It was definitely written in the Wagnerian leitmotiv style. I think it helped tell the story.

The film is about three generations of the same family. It takes place in three eras. And at a certain point, there's an erotic love scene in the present day involving a character who comes out of the past. The temp score for this scene was some bad new-age music. I used my 1800s theme, and the producer said, "Well, that's sure romantic, huh? That's an interesting approach." I said, "Yeah, I'm trying to relate this to the other part of the story."

So, I pulled back the theme from the eighteenth century. And the seventeenth-century theme came in and out of the picture, even when they're on the space station. If you just saw that one scene, you'd wonder, "What is this florid music doing here?" There's a disconnect, but it's telling the history of the whole thing. And it was fun.

Like I said before, I like working with themes, seeing what I can do with them. It was fun to present interweaving themes, to take one theme and then have a theme for another character work as an answer or a counterline. To me, that's a challenge, like that puzzle we talked about earlier. To me, getting things to relate to each other is the fun part of writing music.

Did you use a similar approach in *Thinner*?

Thinner was all about one principal theme, with no specific theme for any particular character. Sometimes a monothematic approach is more applicable.

Alex Cox's *The Winner*.

This is one score that's completely different from anything I've done. It's almost go-go music—it's style music, it's bluesy, it's a synthesis of South Indian drones with pop. It's a song-oriented score. Everything happens in song form—there are no five bars of this, no odd-metered stuff. Everything happens in eight-bar phrases, a bridge, and then eight more bars. It had its own internal rhythm, and, for some reason, it seemed to fit just right. The film was all cut in master shots—there was no intercutting, a scene was all one long setup. There were scenes that were three, four minutes long. The score had to have its own life as well.

Is it easier to work on a score like that? Do you compose set pieces, like a little pop suite?

Yeah, in certain ways it was easier, I guess. Once I had the materials, I was pretty much ready. There were all different styles of pieces that would come back in different lengths. And sometimes they would be an integration of this piece with that piece. I'd say that once I figured out the take on everything, it was easier to score than something that's always interacting with everything else and in which all the elements of all the fragments or motives or harmonies should be present in any cue at any time.

Is there any question that you wish interviewers would ask you, but they never do?

I'm always glad to hear that concert composers are interested in film music. I rarely hear anyone talking about that.

Have you read Gardner Read's book? It's basically a history of orchestration, but he makes one very interesting point that I think is relevant here. He says that a lot of orchestrational innovations in symphonic music, things that were eventually incorporated into the standard symphony orchestra, were first tried in the opera. It was through dramatic form that people were introduced to, let's say, military drumming or an extended percussion section.

I think that it is possible that film music might be having the same effect on what is called serious music. It would be great if concert-music people were influenced by film music. One thing that attracted Bernard Herrmann to film music was that you could work with odd groups of instruments that you could never pull together for a classical concert. It wouldn't be economically feasible to write a piece for eight trombones, twelve harps, sixteen horns. No one's ever going to perform a piece with twelve harps in it.

Often, we hear that the young people can get a "painless" introduction to contemporary music by going to horror or science-fiction movies. They can hear music that's similar in style to modern concert music that is usually branded as avant-garde or

experimental. In film, they have convenient visual distractions—
Pinhead, Cat Woman, or whatever. Are film composers the flag-
waving frontline of a small army that's introducing new orchestral
music to new audiences?

On a realistic level, we probably *are* the flag-waving frontline. Let's
face it, where are people going to learn much about classical music? It's been pretty much cut out of school programs.

When I was in school, I would take art classes and my teacher
would play Ravel's string quartet or whatever. I mean, that's the
first time I ever heard a lot of that stuff. I'm from Detroit. When I
was in elementary school, we went to see the Detroit Symphony. I
know that had a strong influence on me. There was just something
about hearing the live orchestra. I'd never heard anything like it in
my life. It profoundly influenced me. I remember that I just loved
the sound of the basses. If there hadn't been that school program
that took a bunch of kids to go see the orchestra, who knows?

In terms of all the budget cutting that's going on, my guess is
that kids are getting exposed to very little classical music. I think
film music is going to be a conduit for people to appreciate music
of the orchestra. In terms of twentieth-century music, it's hard to
say. I'm sure that there will be a certain amount of people who get
exposed to it through film music. One can always hope.

**How about Dan Licht on getting started in the film-music
business?**

Oh, boy. I'm going to try to think succinctly. Well, one very important bit of advice is to become familiar with the territory. That's
obvious, but a lot of people don't think of the obvious. They think,
I want to be a film composer, but they don't go out and listen to
film scores. Like anything else, like jazz, like any type of art form,
the greatest masters have always started by imitating someone. You
make your craft better by comparing yourself to someone—setting

yourself against a lofty but touchable standard and pushing yourself. And what else?

Off tape, you said, "Don't do it."

Don't do it, yeah. [Laughter] It's not a good way to make a fast buck. If you want to make a fast buck, you should get involved in selling real estate here, or get involved in the production end of filmmaking, not film scoring. Some people do think, hey, I'm a great composer with impressive music degrees from whatever famous university and I want to make a lot of money, I'll move to Hollywood. But the two do not necessarily equate. I think that anybody who's planning on coming out here to make a career in film should be prepared to either come here with enough money to totally support themselves for a couple of years or figure out some other way to earn an income, but then you don't have enough time to try to find film work. It's a stalemate.

If they insist on giving it a try?

There are two ways to approach it: go out and scrounge up every crummy little low-budget film you can find, write for free, and start from the ground up, or work for another composer as an orchestrator or arranger and come up from the inside of the business. Many orchestrators have made the transition from orchestrator to composer.

Did you ever work uncredited or as orchestrator?

I came pretty much from the outside in. I didn't go the orchestration route. I did do some work for Chris Young—synthesizers and whatever—just getting to know the field, getting to know the technology. That way, when you do get your first gig, you won't get hung up on some stupid technical problem, you can just think about the music.

The other thing that I personally stress is working with themes—learn to write themes and force yourself to write themes. I find that nine times out of ten, when people bring me tapes of what they think is film scoring, there's nothing thematic in there, it's just sound. That's why I say, listen to film scores and go, "Well, that's a great theme. Let me try to write a theme like that." It's not easy to write a good theme, not to mention transforming it. There are a lot of people who are doing vamps and grooves and loops and whatever, but I think that one of the things that's going to separate out some people from others is whether they can write a good theme.

Should young, aspiring film composers who are not from the Southern California area move here and try a few semesters at USC or UCLA? Clearly, many young film composers have connections with those schools.

If you've got the money, it's absolutely a good idea. Aside from learning your technique, it is good to have the opportunities to meet people who can get some work for you. Most people I know who've gone through the film-scoring programs here have benefited from being hooked into a network of people who get hired by other composers. If you don't have the money, then the next best thing is actually getting a job with a composer. The way things are working now, in terms of schedules, all composers need assistants. Film scoring has gone from six weeks as standard to four weeks and less. There's always a lot of work. Somebody's going to get it.

joel MCNEELY

Joel McNeely came to film music well prepared. Born into a family of musicians and writers, he attended the prestigious Interlochen Music Academy, the University of Miami, and the Eastman School of Music, where he embellished their standard composition degree programs with jazz and film-music studies. Following his move to Los Angeles and several ambitious scores for low-budget studio features and television movies, McNeely struck gold in 1993, when John Williams, who had been impressed with the young composer's early work, strongly recommended him to George Lucas for *The Young Indiana Jones Chronicles* television series. Working week by week and side by side with legendary composer Laurence Rosenthal on multiple episodes of varying dramatic styles, McNeely found all the practical training he needed and won an Emmy.

Joel McNeely considers himself a traditionalist, yet his scores for *Iron Will* (1994), *Squanto: A Warrior's Tale* (1994), and *Radioland Murders* (1994) clearly show that he is not tied to the tonal, rhythmic, and dramatic restrictions of the past. His muscular and driving orchestral scores for *Terminal Velocity* (1994), *Soldier* (1997), *The Avengers* (1998), and *Virus* (1999) show an imaginative and versatile composer in command of many modernist styles, creating scores that are vital to the success of the films.

McNeely is also extremely active, and critically acclaimed, as a conductor for a series of re-recordings of classic film scores for the Varèse Sarabande label.

We met for this interview at his home studio—an attractive, poolside building that was recently rebuilt after being leveled by a powerful California earthquake.

joel MCNEELY

Were you interested in pursuing a film-music career when you were a graduate student at Eastman?

Yeah, I came to the whole thing very backward and, as a result, I am somewhat insecure as a composer, which I guess most of us are. I came at it as a jazz saxophone player. I came up in big bands, but I was just always fascinated with classical music. My mom is a classical pianist, and I had interests going both ways. So I just decided that I didn't want to be a saxophone player for the rest of my life.

I found out about this contemporary-media writing program they had going on at Eastman. There were just four grad students in the program, and there was the chance to study with Ray Wright, a great orchestrator and composer. So I applied and I was accepted. Then I really tried to catch up on my lack of training, since I had spent all my time playing jazz saxophone, which I got pretty good at, but it doesn't teach you much counterpoint. I learned what I could learn in those two years. Ray Wright was an amazing teacher, probably the best teacher I have ever had.

Did you study with the classical composition teachers Joseph Schwantner and Christopher Rouse?

Yeah, I got to study with some of the guys in the classical program as well. Chris Rouse was a really great teacher. I got it together as much as I could in those two years—a lot of orchestration train-ing—and just came out here.

But the real beginning of my interest in film music came when I was a kid. My dad was a college professor, but he was kind of an anomaly—he sold scripts to Hollywood, but was a serious writing professor at the University of Wisconsin. He actually was pretty suc-cessful as a writer in Hollywood. It kept the family in the Midwest and gave us a good, wholesome Midwest upbringing while he com-muted back and forth to Hollywood. He created this new show when I was about twelve. For my birthday he said, "I'll fly you out, and you can go to the recording session of the music." The com-poser was Elmer Bernstein! I went to the session and I met him. I watched him conduct the orchestra, saw the movie projectors, and said that was it. Ever since that point, I was on the path and knew what I wanted to do.

Eastman was a good jumping-off place because Ray Wright had done many films and was chief orchestrator and conductor for Ra-dio City Music Hall for twenty-five years.

Did you learn a lot about the business side of the career?

Yeah. Ray Wright was very conscientious about educating us about the business—about how it all works—the process, getting jobs, the most efficient way to talk on the stand. Don't just say, "Let's do it again." Never say that. Say, "Let's try it again, *because* . . ." He taught us all the minute details he had accumulated. I was in one of his last classes of students—he passed away shortly after that. So I feel really lucky.

Does a film-music legacy survive at Eastman, or has it returned to a more traditional academic/concert music environment?

The program was taken over by Fred Sturm, a guy who was actually in graduate school with me and studied with Ray. He was head of the jazz department at Lawrence University in Wisconsin and left there to finish his grad degree. He really soaked up everything that Ray had to teach and is going to continue Ray's tradition. I stay real tight with Fred, and whenever I finish a movie, I send videotapes out to Eastman, so that they have a library of things for the kids to score.

I read about an early score of yours, something called _Franken-stein: The College Years._

Sure, I'll talk about that. At the time, the guy who directed it and I were both at really low points in our young Hollywood lives. I had done some stuff and then it all kind of slowed down. I was really depressed to take that job, and really depressed doing the job. The director was depressed about it, too. But we did it because it was work. The director went on to do _Ace Ventura: Pet Detective_, which broke Jim Carrey, and _The Nutty Professor_. He has done these big movies, but hasn't called me since _Frankenstein_!

That was right before _Young Indiana Jones_, and I was wondering what I was going to do here. Then _Young Indiana Jones_ came and turned things around.

How did your involvement with the _Young Indiana Jones_ series come about?

It came about through John Williams. George Lucas called John Williams and said, "I need two guys to do this series, and here is what it is . . ." John said that he should definitely call Laurence Rosenthal and, "I know this other young guy who is represented by my agent. You should listen to a tape of his." So they set up a meeting. George and I met and things clicked.

The _Young Indiana Jones_ years were the early 1990s. Then four CDs came out from 1991-1994. Was that series of films a huge career stepping stone for getting into feature films?

That was film-scoring boot camp. The filmmaking was at such a high level—the cinematography was gorgeous, the stories were interesting, the actors were fine. The shows were really mini-feature films of the highest caliber. I felt extremely passionate about them. I also felt that I was in way over my head, especially since Larry Rosenthal, who is just a brilliant man in every respect, and I would be sitting there, and he would be talking about stuff with all his knowledge and experience—and I am only thirty.

But you trained with Schwantner, Sidney Hodkinson, and Rouse at Eastman.

Yeah, but Larry is just amazing. I love him dearly. I have so much respect for him.

Anyway, George Lucas likes to score things with wall-to-wall music. The shows would be two-hour episodes, but broken down individually on an hourly basis. Out of forty-eight minutes of show, there were about forty-two minutes of music. Usually, we had about three weeks to write a score, and this pace went on for three years. I was writing reams of music. Finish one, start the next one. There was no time to second-guess, just get it done. When I would look back over the year, I would all of a sudden realize that I had written four or five hours of music that year. I had all kinds of different opportunities to try different ethnic styles—dabble in this, dabble in that. It was the opportunity of a lifetime. That work changed my life in so many ways.

How were the decisions made about which scenes would be McNeely-scored, which scenes would be Rosenthal-scored?

The way it worked out was really nice because we never, ever got into a conflict. Sometimes it was just scheduling: "I've got these two to do, and these two are ready, so you had better take those two." And sometimes we had strong feelings—Larry really wanted to do Indiana, so fine, be happy. I really wanted to do the Gershwin show, *The City in the Shade*, and it just worked out so beautifully. Luckily enough, we were scoring together, or we overlapped. We would be in Munich or Australia at the same time, so we managed to hang out, just sit around the dinner table and talk. It was great.

You know, they kept making *Young Indiana Jones*. It was off the air for years, then it was on the Family Channel for a bit. George had a whole chronology—a real story arc starting when the kid was eight years old and going to, I believe, when he was twenty-eight. Then the show got canceled around three quarters of the way through, but George decided, "Screw it, I am going to finish." And so they just went ahead and finished them, with no outlet that I know of. They made them, and ultimately they released them.

In *The Mystery of the Blues* episode, you have some great Gene Krupa-style big-band music. Are those your arrangements?

For the most part. I worked closely with Dave Slonaker, my orchestrator. He did a couple of them. But, for the most part, they were all mine. Some of them were just exact takedowns of jungle-band style.

That score also has some effective moments of film-noir/1940s gangster music. You seem to be really comfortable with that genre.

Like I said, I was just trying a little bit of everything. I would just throw it against the wall.

***The Phantom Train of Doom* struck me as experimenting with Korngold.**

Yeah, just trying it on for size. Admittedly, it was totally derivative.

In *Doom 1916*, you seem to be trying your take on Carl Orff, but much more mean-spirited than *Carmina Burana*.

Well, that one had an interesting bone in it. There is a scene in which Andy goes into a field hospital that is set up in a church. It's one of those striking things—incredibly maimed soldiers are lying on the floor of this incredibly beautiful church, which they shot in Prague.

Ben Burt, who is the sound designer for the *Star Wars* movies and the *Indiana Jones* movies, came up with the brilliant idea of this field hospital with the *Moonlight Sonata* under it. I said, "We should use this. This is brilliant. This works great." George Lucas said, "Oh, but I love the theme, the theme that has been developed and interwoven." He said, "Just write something like this, *only better*." Those were his exact words. And, you know, I fell off my chair and picked myself up and said okay. What came out is very reminiscent of the *Moonlight Sonata*, but it does have the theme woven in, which does unify it.

Congo 1917 has a wonderful scene with Albert Schweitzer and the music of Bach weaving in and out of your music, creating a dreamscape atmosphere.

That was a similar thing. We started in the script stages talking about pieces of music. I said that we really should do Bach's *Jesu, Joy of Man's Desiring*. The whole thing sequenced really well, put together with the natives and just a montage of going through the hospital and then ending in the cabin with Schweitzer playing.

You are refreshingly honest about your heritage with film composers and concert composers of the past. I think it is very healthy to hear a young composer say, "Yes, we all have our inspirations, and then we outgrow them." So many composers pretend that they are all on their own, that they don't have ghosts floating around. You use them, draw from them, and grow beyond them.

I think it is important to stand on broad shoulders—it's a musical food chain. I have done my growing and learning in public. I had to learn. I think that now I am starting to amass a lot of different kinds of knowledge. I'm starting to find who I am and what it is that I want to say. That is really what I am striving for now: to assimilate that kind of stuff and out of that to be really true to myself. I don't think I have gotten there yet.

How many restrictions are imposed on you that would prevent you from exploring all that more quickly? In *Squanto*, for example, the themes work perfectly with the material, especially the broad theme in the opening and the little sacred progressions with the monks. Are there directors/producers saying, "Well, Joel, in the monks' scene, you might score it with a Bach-style organ piece"?

In the case of that movie, I was really on my own. But, yes, that does happen often. And it has happened to me in a really aggressive way. In the case of *Iron Will*, I would write a particular cue and the studio would say, "No, we really like the temp. Go back, rescore."

In the case of *Squanto*, the director and I didn't see eye to eye about things, so I wrote what I wanted to write. In the course of that score, just as I started to write, sitting where we're sitting now, in this little ten-by-twenty-foot poolhouse, the earthquake happened and the whole place fell down. I wrote that score with two two-by-four-foot holes in the ceiling. I remember one time when I was sitting here at my piano, writing in this rubble, and it started to rain. The water came in on my piano, so I put trays around it. Here I sat, writing *Squanto*, hearing this ping, ping, ping, ping. I had tarps and plastic sheets on my piano, and I thought, you know, *this is as bad as it gets.*

Did Mother Nature inspire you?

I don't know. In a weird way, I guess it did. I kind of like that score, but it was really hard.

The action music in *Squanto* is terrific, but you have to listen way beyond all the sound effects.

Yeah. I am sorry that there wasn't a record on that one. I thought for a while about putting it on a promo CD, but decided that that wouldn't be fair to the musicians—they are supposed to be paid for doing that. There is just no way that I could afford to do it by myself. And it wouldn't really be worthwhile for a record company to do it for a movie that no one saw.

It seems that you are already very comfortable with Hollywood's Golden Age school of scoring. Not only in your tonal vocabulary, but in your *use* of the score—sometimes commenting on the action, sometimes composing the emotional backdrop.

Yeah, I have to admit that I really love that style of scoring. I love those guys. I think they really had something in terms of the way music works with drama. I get very frustrated by what goes on now, by what passes for dramatic music. And I worry sometimes that I have become sort of antiquated in my tastes. My tastes don't jibe with what people seem to want now—those rock-and-roll, orchestral-synth drones, and patterns that people don't seem to notice.

Directors will come to you when they want your style?

I guess, but I don't know how in vogue it seems to be right now.

There are some American Indian chants in *Squanto*—people humming, singing, chanting—are those authentic native melodies that you researched, or are they original McNeelys?

The Indian chants and whatnot were there before I came to the project. Those are real chants.

This was a movie in big trouble. I came very late to the project. Chris Young was supposed to do the movie. I don't know the circumstances of why he didn't end up doing it, but it had to do with the temp. They didn't like the temp that was done, so they fired everybody, and, *boom*, even fired the composer, who hadn't written the score yet.

Since you are so honest about very strong influences in your music, I must ask you about a particular moment in *Squanto* where I detect what seems to be a Vaughan Williams *Antarctica* reference as the ship sails away into the icy night. I smiled. Is that the kind of reaction you want from a knowledgeable audience?

Well, if I had had a huge amount of time to develop the score, it would have been different. In the case of *Squanto*, I think I had three weeks, and then my house fell over. So there I sat, looking at my scores, looking at anything and everything, just trying to prime the pump to get started. Sometimes the primer bleeds through. You are right, I was listening to that piece. So, if you get it, hopefully it doesn't take you out of the movie.

I thought it was very effective. It's just a little fragment, and it grows beautifully out of your music. Then it gives way to this icy blast as the ship sails away.

If I might jump to another of your scores, in *Iron Will*, some of the cues on the CD sound much more musical in terms of balance and editing than they do when mixed into the film. "The Devil's Slide" cue, for example, could be a terrific concert-opener for any professional orchestra. Is there a part of you that is interested in having some of your film cues discover an independent concert life?

Sure. I would be happy and honored if that happens.

I am starting to do some concerts. Not pops concerts, but concerts of film music. We did a concert in Scotland with the Scottish National Orchestra that was just tremendously successful. It was an evening of great, classic film music. We did music from *Ben Hur* and *Spartacus*, some Jerry Goldsmith, and some Herrmann

Vertigo. It was sold out in the Royal Hall, over 3,000 people attended. It made a wonderful evening of intelligent music.

If my stuff were included on a concert like that, I would be thrilled and honored. The interesting thing about such a concert is that it is about the *music*, not about people sitting at a table having white wine and eating hors d'oeuvres, listening to a suite from *My Fair Lady* or *Strike up the Band* and all this rah-rah stuff. I have no interest in doing that. So it was really encouraging to have a concert where people sat and listened like they would at any other serious concert. The music was the thing—the music came out from behind the movie. I loved it, and the audience seemed to love it. It was great.

Vertigo, obviously, is a good example of film music that can exist just as wonderful music. Tell me a little bit about your *Vertigo* project—the recording is excellent, the sound is perfect. And all those extra portions of music that otherwise weren't available on any previously released CDs are great. How did the project evolve?

It came about through Robert Townson, producer with Varèse Sarabande Records. We started this idea by going to Seattle for the *Fahrenheit 451* recording. We were going to do a whole series in Seattle, but things just didn't work out with the management there. So Patrick Doyle found the Royal Scottish Orchestra, and we went to Scotland and did *Hollywood '95*, one of those little compilation albums Varèse does every year, and *Vertigo*.

It was tough to do *Vertigo* because Herrmann didn't actually conduct the film's score. It was done in London during a musician's strike. Since he wasn't allowed to conduct it, the tempos in the score are sometimes wildly different from what ended up in the movie. And sometimes, mostly from an expressive point, there are moments in Herrmann's score indicating that it is to stretch and stretch, but in the film they really blew right through those moments. So I was determined to stick to Herrmann's performance indications throughout.

It took a lot of work. It also was very difficult to record because a lot of it was very quiet and very high, and you know how difficult it is for players to sit for long periods of time being really quiet and playing really high. It is exhausting, actually. But we worked our butts off, and I am so proud of how it came out. I love the music. I love the way the record sounds. I love the orchestra. I loved the way they played. They are wonderful people. We had a great time.

How are the choices made about what to include on the annual *Hollywood* compilations?

Bob [Townson] chooses all those. I am just the hired conductor.

Do you have any input? Do you get to say, "Bob, I'd like to put on this little bit from such and such"?

Yeah. And in other certain cases it is, "Bob, *please*, do we *really* have to do this?!"

I suggested the inclusion of the Miklós Rózsa piece on *Hollywood '95* because Rózsa had passed away that year. The 1996 recording is a whole suite of logos. We are going to end it with an original Varèse Sarabande logo that I'm writing.

Will your original Varèse Sarabande piece show any Edgard Varèse influence?

I was thinking about that yesterday. It was such a neat idea, and I thought it had to be a Sarabande. I should find a neat Varèse piece and just have a stone-cold quote from him at some point.

Maybe those police whistles from *Amériques* or something from *Ionisation*—pieces complete with belching smokestacks and factory sirens.

Yeah, *Ionisation*. I don't know. I'm not very familiar with his music yet.

The CD of your *Terminal Velocity* score acknowledges a number of orchestrators. Do you regularly deal with specific orchestrators, time after time, or do you try out different people? Have you found that perfect Korngold/Friedhofer or Goldsmith/Courage collaboration yet?

In the case of *Terminal Velocity*, those guys were more than orchestrators—they actually wrote some cues.

Here, I am going to touch on the two films that I had major disasters with in my life. They are interesting stories that tie into one another. My wife and I lost our house during the earthquake, then we found out, four days later, that we were going to have a baby. We moved into a rental house, and I began writing *Terminal Velocity* in August.

I am under a huge deadline, and the baby isn't supposed to come until the end of September. But while I am in the middle of writing this show, my wife comes to me one night and says, "I'm having the baby."

The baby was over two months premature. We go to the hospital for a long, emotional weekend. The baby had a very difficult birth—it was touch and go. The baby was very sick and in intensive care, so, of course, I am down at the hospital most of the time, for three weeks. I had this major action-movie deadline coming up, and it couldn't be moved because the release date was so tight. So I just called in the forces and said, "Guys, you have got to help me get this done!"

I would write fourteen hours a day and then go down to the hospital and spend the night there. It was a real stretch to get that movie done. In the end, it affected *my* health. I ended up in the hospital with heart problems. As a result, I was a completely wrung-out wet rag at the end of it.

Then, right after I finished *Terminal Velocity*, Disney came to me, wanting me to do *The Jungle Book*, which I really wanted to do. But I had to turn it down because of my health.

What was one of your happiest projects? *Radioland Murders?*

Yeah. *Radioland Murders* was very hard, but it was enjoyable. *Radioland* lasted a year because it had thirty-eight songs in it, and I had to do all the prerecords for all the songs and be there on the set while they shot to make sure everything was done correctly. The score wound up being relatively small in the overall context of the picture. But it was just fun doing all those production numbers. It was a good time.

Iron Will was also a good time, working with all those good people. And *Flipper* was a wonderful experience. The director and I became very good friends. It is always the coolest when you work with someone that closely, and then wind up keeping that person as a friend. It doesn't happen often. You work so hard trying to please the person, and, if the person is a jerk, it makes the experience really tough. But if the person you are trying to please is someone who you don't want to let down, then it is just fun.

Radioland Murders is such an eclectic slant on different genres. Your score shows many influences—some 1950s Glasser/Salter sci-fi, you've got a theremin, some *King Kong*isms, and that Gork business—that are manipulated into recognizable McNeelyisms. It sounds like it must have been a hell of a lot of fun to work on it.

It was a lot of fun. It was like, "If it doesn't make me laugh, I'm not going to do it." I am really glad that you *get* it. The movie had problems, so not many people saw it, which was kind of a letdown— you spend a year of your life working so hard, and the movie just kind of comes and goes.

The death on the tower scene, with that campy *Vertigo* touch, was a great moment. I just smiled. I knew you wouldn't slide that by as original; I knew there must be a story attached to the Herrmann reference, aside from the tower shot.

Absolutely. That was a joke between me and the director. He kept saying, "You know, I love *Vertigo*, I love *Vertigo*." I was like, "Hey, let me write my own score." But because he knew *Vertigo* really well, I thought, "Well, I'll get this guy at the climactic moment." So I worked in the principal motive. And the first time he heard it, he just couldn't stop laughing.

You are an extremely active conductor in the film business.

Well, it is something that I really love doing. I took two semesters of conducting with Donald Hunsberger at Eastman, and I got some great fundamentals. But conducting is something that is difficult to practice. There is no point in conducting records, so, unless you have people playing for you, you can hardly practice.

I didn't really start getting serious about conducting until I started having the opportunity to conduct my own scores out here. Then I took some lessons. Beyond the lessons, I started listening to classic classical recordings—pieces I knew very well—listening not so much to the pieces but to their interpretations. And I started collecting laser discs and watching conductors, studying their ways, studying the different responses. I love to watch Bernstein. He does some things that are just so unbelievably subtle, and yet you can hear the incredible musical response to this one little gesture he makes. It is total beauty to me.

So I have been teaching myself, and sharing music with my wife—one of the most musical people I have ever met. She is an incredible violinist, an incredible musician. She has taught me about phrasing and about the way to get a result when standing up in front of a group of a hundred people, where psychology is really important, too.

The recordings I have made have given me the opportunity to really grow. And the *Young Indy* thing, if you look at all the music I conducted for that, was an opportunity to really learn. I conducted the Munich Symphony, the Munich Philharmonic, and the Australian Symphony—all good orchestras. Each time, I just tried to get a little better.

Going to Scotland, I think, is the greatest opportunity. And some of the music we are doing, I am not particularly nuts about doing, but it gives me the opportunity to stand up in front of a group of great players and continue to learn. The payoff is to get to do things like *Vertigo*. So, every time I get really bummed out about the really awful things about this business—the awful way that people behave—I think, "Yeah, but I have this over here, which is pure music." It's all about the music. I don't have anyone breathing over my shoulder, saying, "Less trombones here." I don't like that—I don't know why, but I just don't like that.

Is there anything about the business or your composing style that you would like to talk about?

There is one thing, but I am not sure if it is right to talk about in print because it's a negative issue. I don't want to come across as being negative about this whole business, but when I listen to Alex North, I think, "Okay, those guys started off this tradition. They set the bar pretty high." Then I get very frustrated by what is happening and what people seem to want. Certain composers, you know, take on a bunch of projects simultaneously, and then field them off to their assistants, getting a factory kind of thing going.

I actually spoke with a producer at a party a couple of weeks ago who, referring to one particular composer he admired, said, "This guy is amazing! He has so many projects going, and he has this whole team of guys. When he can't do something, he hands it off." The producer was really impressed by that! I kind of choked because I thought, "Whatever happened to the value placed on individual artistry? What happened to the value of the individual voice?" When you hired one of these old guys, when you hired Bernard Herrmann, you got a distinct artist, a distinct point of view, which is something of value to me. You didn't just get somebody who can write like this guy and write like that guy and, when he's too busy, he has a whole backup system and can do fifteen films a year!

We are talking a lot about the tradition. I hope that you are right, that the tradition is something that is still valued somewhere, because it is of real value to me and the people I look up to.

Who are some your composer colleagues whom you respect for their sincerity, their integrity?

I think of Bruce Broughton. Actually, he and I talked about this last night. You know, getting work will always be a crapshoot. But the way things seem to be happening now is troublesome. A lot of people who are composing now never pick up a pencil—they sit at a keyboard and noodle around, play some things in, and then hand that off to an orchestrator who will extract a sketch from that, and they'll extract a score from that. What's happening to the tradition of putting a line or a note or an orchestration on paper and then sitting back and looking at the page and reflecting, reacting to the page? On a sequencer, you don't even see the notes—it's a sterile, cut-and-paste technology. A lot of guys sit and watch the picture and play with their sequencers: "Okay, that's the cue, now we'll put some more stuff on top of it and we'll ship it." And the music usually ends up sounding like a cut-and-paste job.

I am very heartened that orchestral scoring still seems to be valued in some studios. And I hope that, in time, it helps out the composers who are trying to do something *imaginative*, something beyond setting up an eight-bar phrase and repeating it eighteen times.

You're a pencil-and-paper man, right?

I keep my computer turned off! No, that's not completely true—I keep one computer on just for my breakdown notes, to get all my hits and timings.

I don't use any of the sequencers. I work at the piano and come up with tunes and harmonies; I improvise, I do a sketch the old-fashioned way.

I did an electronic score for *SuperCop*, a Jackie Chan movie, and I did it all here. I had a big synth-percussion setup here and another synth player at the elbow of the piano. It was the first time I had done a movie without ever picking up a pencil. I sat at the sequencer and I played it all in. And I can see how seductive it is. It's a lot easier and it takes a lot less time. I was writing five minutes of music a day and putting in easy banker's hours—I was here at nine in the morning and knocked off at five. I can see why people like this technology. My *SuperCop* score worked fine, but it is not what I was put on this Earth to do. And I wouldn't put the CD on and listen to it.

You've spoken of connecting with certain directors.

I think that probably my most interesting collaboration was with George Lucas. He is really, really musical. He would give me specific musical references and say, "I want a *Peer Gynt* kind of thing here . . . you know, the slow movement." Beyond that he would say, "Here, where his head turns, I want a clarinet and viola thing." Now that's pretty specific! It was interesting working with someone who really knows what he wants. And I felt very compelled to do exactly what he wanted. But also interesting were the times when I *didn't* do exactly what he asked, the times when I tried to extrapolate the gist of what he wanted and bring something of my own to it rather than using his road map. Many times, those were his favorite moments.

Another example is the case of *Iron Will*. Charles Haid, the director, is a very musical guy. He brought in a stack of CDs—some really great stuff, including Japanese taiko drums and some Prokofiev. And we sat down with the movie, laying the CDs out against the picture, saying, "Yep, that works . . . No, that doesn't work," deciding on the tone of the music by collaborating in that way. That was really useful to me. It gave me an idea of what he wanted and a chance to find out about his aesthetic sensibilities.

Obviously, you try hard to please your boss while maintaining your personal integrity.

It is ultimately about pleasing the sensibilities of the director. He made the film—it's his vision. He has been on the movie for a couple of years. He has controlled almost everything in the movie up to this point. And, now, at the very end, here comes the composer. So the more you get inside this guy's head, the better the film will be.

But I have worked with directors who have really awful taste in music, and there are times when you think you are right and the director says, "No, no, that's not the case at all. I want this instead." And even though you don't believe in it, you do it and sometimes realize, "Ah, it is better. It brings out this motion of . . ." So I try to make it my rule to trust the director, even when I disagree with him.

thomas NEWMAN

Film music of the highest expressive caliber is in Thomas Newman's blood and soul as the youngest son of the great Alfred Newman, nephew to both Lionel and Emil Newman, brother to David and Maria, and cousin to Randy Newman.

Now regarded as one of the most imaginative and interesting composers active today, after completing his studies at USC and Yale, Thomas Newman took a time-worn Hollywood path—rising through the ranks, cutting his film-scoring teeth on such pop-oriented pictures as *Reckless* (1984), *Revenge of the Nerds* (1984), *Girls Just Want to Have Fun* (1985), *Desperately Seeking Susan* (1985), and *Jumpin' Jack Flash* (1986). His highly distinctive, strikingly original musical voice emerged with his dramatic music for *The Lost Boys* (1987) and *Less Than Zero* (1987) and went into high gear with *The Rapture* (1991), *The Player* (1992), *Scent of a Woman* (1992), *Flesh and Bone* (1993), his Oscar-nominated *Unstrung Heroes* (1995), and *American Buffalo* (1996)—elegant scores that offer a captivating, sometimes edgy mix of traditional and unusual instruments and electronics and employ both traditional and experimental performance techniques.

Known for his preference for intelligent, sometimes offbeat films that allow him to explore his very personal sound world of vivid, transparent textures and delicate motives that blend with one another in carefully wrought micro-counterpoint, Newman is equally comfortable with more traditional movie fare. His scores for *Fried*

Green Tomatoes (1991) and *How to Make an American Quilt* (1995) establish a cautious, gentle American romanticism; his pastoral evocation of the past propels *Little Women* (1994); and his Oscar-nominated music for *The Shawshank Redemption* (1994) stirs moviegoers with a compelling psychological soundscape. Among Newman's more recent scores that engagingly embrace his varied sound worlds are *Oscar and Lucinda* (1997), *Red Corner* (1997), *Meet Joe Black* (1998), and *The Horse Whisperer* (1998).

For a composer whose music seems to seek a state of continual evolution, exploration, and experimentation, Thomas Newman is also very much a part of the great tradition of Hollywood film music—very much concerned with why a score exists in the first place.

We met for this interview at his studio, tucked away off Sunset Boulevard in Pacific Palisades.

thomas NEWMAN

I'm intrigued by a statement of yours that I came across in Fred Karlin's book *Listening to Movies*: "Even if you don't particularly like the music, you can recognize its effectiveness in the movie." Your scores rarely blast the audience with a big tune. Take *Shawshank Redemption*, for example: Your score uses evolving musical material that almost yearns to be a big tune, but which you seem to consciously hold back for the good of the film.

I guess that comes from experience. You can't force the square peg in the round whatever. As much as you may want the form, as much as you may yearn to be heard, the forward motion of the whole film experience will never allow it to be anything more than it is. By that comment, I mean that you must see the situation for what it is. Don't try to fight it; don't try to slip in under the door, through the keyhole.

Music is secondary. It's there to help, it's not there to be listened to, unfortunately. You can argue that it *is* heard and listened to, but usually that's accidental or that's because it's appropriate for a particular dramatic moment in the movie, as opposed to, "Well, gee, I really wanna be heard." Find the moments when you can speak out and the moments when it's inappropriate to speak out. I don't want to say, "Well, I'm a composer and I want to be heard" as much as, "Here's what I can do in this environment." Some environments are more avant-garde, more progressive, than others. Some are very conservative, and you kind of have to do what you have to do.

As you're trying to stick to one of these particular environments and the film is moving your musical imagination, do you find yourself saying, "Hey, this is great. I wouldn't have come up with this on my own had not I had this particular scene, this particular character"?

Sure. It's the whole issue of referencing anything against anything. You're often surprised by the direction it takes you. If you're not totally concept-oriented, it's very interesting to see where it leads you and then to try to follow it. I think that's probably one of the great attractions of film music.

Let's talk about some of the unusual sounds and timbres for which you've become well-known.

You know all the people. ·

Well, I've met Rick Cox and Chas Smith. Is it a collaborative process with these guys and the other musicians you regularly use? Do you look to them for ideas, or do you bring ideas to them and say, "How can we elaborate on this?"

I try to give them vague direction. I try to capitalize on their talents as players and sound conceptualists. I try to corner them and, at the same time, try to keep them wild, because the minute you start dealing with odd sounds and try to be specific, it just doesn't work. When you sample sounds or try to find sounds, it's best to dumb down in terms of questioning the appropriateness of a particular sound or how is it going to work. Normally, you just find sounds that are either useful or less useful.

I've gotten such a shorthand with people like Rick that often we'll improvise—we'll just mess around with colors. Both he and I will take material and sample it. We'll sometimes sample a similar phrase and, by virtue of the manner of sampling, the sounds will be different. If you take any small phrase and alter it just a bit, it becomes something almost entirely different. I tend to like where sounds lead me, so I tend to give musicians like Rick some information and then let them feed information back to me. I guess I'm kind of the great bandleader or something.

So, sometimes, the sounds become, for you, a stepping stone into the completed score in a way that perhaps a theme or melody would have functioned for your father?

I guess so. The danger of working with abstract sound is that it can be anything for any amount of time. So, sometimes, I wonder how deep down into this well I dare dive, discovering my own instrumentation, my own orchestrations, along the way. It *is* a discovery process. And that's good *and* bad. It can be very time-consuming; you can do five hours of work for ten minutes of result. Yet it's fun because a lot of the sounds that are explored are exceptionally interesting, but probably too complex for movies.

Often a complete film score needs to be delivered in four or five weeks. Can you build a little extra time into such a composing schedule to allow you to explore sounds?

If it's appropriate. It's less appropriate for some movies, period movies, which you realize aren't going to be sonically experimental, so you just step away from it. But, when it is appropriate, you've got to roll up your sleeves and do it faster, and maybe the ways in which you're trying to cull these sounds come in a more abbreviated manner. You rise to the experience and do what you can.

What's your process for scores that fuse electronics with acoustic instruments? Does one of those elements tend to come before the other?

Usually the electronics come first because, to me, they're the more interesting sounds—they're the things that give a more unique, dramatic flavor. The minute you start putting an orchestra on top, you're kind of doing that movie thing, which, in a way, is a requirement because, to a degree, people want to sit around as they did way back in the old days, watching their movie while listening to a full symphonic complement as it's going down.

I think that music for movies is so abstract that the orchestra has become a ludicrous ritual in a way, although it's very effective, and huge orchestral sounds are great in movies. Probably their best asset is how large and full-bodied they can be. With electronics, the ear often has no reference to decide if a sound is too loud or too soft because you don't know the source of the sound. Electronics are usually taken at face value. If you hear a loud trumpet, the ear has a reference for what a loud trumpet sounds like. With electronics, that doesn't happen.

Do you often find the director saying, "More orchestra"?

Yeah. It's how they see things. It's a way of bringing class to an environment, and I say that pejoratively because, obviously, good music is good music however it's created, however it's motivated. Sometimes I ask myself, "Why am I adding strings to this? Why am I taking it in that direction?" Often it's because that's where the ritual of dramatic film music takes it. To a degree, I fight the ritual. At the same time, I understand it and embrace it. That's the yin and the yang of this—you want to fight it, but there's no fighting it. It is what it is. To a degree, it's an obligation. And once you've fulfilled that obligation, then you think that it isn't really necessary.

Postproduction in movies is just not a hugely experimental time—people don't want to spend more money, and they're scared that you're going to ruin a movie if it's good and not save it if it's bad. So you face just huge philosophical and political requirements. What I've tried to do is recognize the requirements and not be stunned by them, not feel stifled by what I'm supposed to be doing.

In many of your scores, you seem completely comfortable working within the traditional expectations.

I never would have been able to survive out here otherwise. In Hollywood, you are what people *think* you are. If you're just this guy with electronics, this guy who just primarily does electronics, you're "the electronics guy."

The famous Newman film-music family—Alfred, Emil, Lionel, etc. As you get older, do you look back on that with great pride and emotion, whereas, when you were growing up, it was just dad's job?

Yeah. When I was quite young, it was just the thing he did. The family would go down and watch him record, which was very dramatic because he would almost never use a click track—there would always be free time, with double punches and the streamer and things. The stage would darken, and there was just something very *wow* about it all, kind of like when the lights go down in the theater. It was interesting and fun, but I had no interest in it whatsoever. It was just something over there that he did.

He died when I was fourteen, and I started getting interested in writing a year or two later. It all came very late to me. And then it became very daunting that he was who he was.

Emil and Lionel?

Uncle Emo was a good man. He was music director at Fox, and was basically retired by the time I started to write. He taught me to conduct a bit, and he was very interested in my music and encouraged me when I was in high school.

And then, along the way, it all became rather daunting for me in terms of what it was that I was supposed to be. You look at the job of film music, and what are you supposed to be? There's a lot of "supposed to be" written into the bylaws of film music in terms of "Well, this is an action scene; it's *supposed to be* done in this way." I never thought I'd do it very well. It was tough enough to write music, much less write it in a week and be greeted by people who were not interested in your effort, only in your result.

I struggled when I first started. I struggled a lot with "What could I do?" and "How could I be different yet be myself?" I think that's what drove me toward electronics—the idea that I could lock myself up in a room and discover what I liked about music and what I didn't like. All the book knowledge I'd had up to that point, and I'd been well-trained, was not applicable for some reason. Everything I knew in terms of aesthetics or what orchestral music was was over there, and I was over here. The early part of my career was spent trying to understand the over-here part of it, and then, bring the over-there into the over-here.

It took me quite a while to put together a sense of who I was and how I was to deal with musicians. I'd had some experience just talking to players, and I was always told, "You get on the podium and you kind of talk Italian—whatever Italian you know." I remember the first time I got on a podium to conduct, it was just *wow*! Then you realize that it's not that big a deal. A musician friend of mine once I said, "You get out on the podium and you look at all those players, and you think they're looking at you as if to say, 'Now what do you want us to do?' But no, they're asking themselves, 'When's the next break? When's lunch?'" Once you start to realize that, some of the mysticism goes away, which is a good thing. I don't want it to be mystical. When my dad was doing it, it was always mystical to me, like jazz is always magical. But when you finally learn enough about it, you realize that people turn tricks and that they do their thing.

A couple of your early scores—*Reckless* and *Desperately Seeking Susan*—were mostly electronic, if not entirely.

There were actually a couple of solo players, but never an ensemble of any kind.

In those scores, did you record the electronic parts first and then put the solo players on top?

Yeah. I remember my first *Reckless* session: I came home and said, "I don't have a clue about how to do this." I'd had some drum programs and I had tried to use a live drummer. I thought, "Well, a live drummer has got to be better that a drum machine." But I was wrong. Not that the machine was better but that, the minute you try to change course, your sense of where sound goes and how the ear perceives it suddenly changes. So the process was certainly a "from scratch" thing—mostly trial and error, with a lot of things going wrong. And then you finally realize, "Well, this sounds good now. Why? Why did this work out okay?" Then you work backward from there, and you learn another trick or two. It's all trickery, and it all adds up.

In *Desperately Seeking Susan,* there are little hints of Newmanisms-to-come—sounds that show up later in *The Player, Unstrung Heroes,* and other scores.

It's true. That was kind of the start of understanding a little more. A lot of that's Rick Cox, whom I've worked with since my very first job. It's funny how some things don't change.

***The Man With One Red Shoe* has a great opening sequence where your tiny musical events dart through the initial orchestral tuning-up section.**

The main character was the concertmaster of an orchestra, and the idea of tune-ups have always interested me. Tune-ups are interesting because the players are noodling around, doing their own thing. But what they're doing is musical—usually haphazard or unconscious, but instinctively musical. I thought, "What if I take this big orchestral tune-up over a period of twenty seconds or so and, *boom*, immediately go to someplace different?" That was the beginning of *Aha!* If you put a tune-up next to something electronic, what does that do to the ear? How does that jag the ear?

The Lost Boys seems a more traditional score in terms of orchestration and requisite mickey-mousing. For example, at the close-up of a vampire baring his teeth, there's a big, scary diminished chord. But even within that kind of classic Steiner horror-shock technique, the scenes maintain personal, modernistic edges to them.

Thanks. Those were the days when I was trying to reconcile my scores with rock tunes. I thought about how one could deal with that. And then there was the whole idea of this deep, dark, Gothic organ music. To a certain degree, you could argue it was a circumspect choice. But, again, the directions that we go in often are not solo ideas—this was a Joel Schumacher opus. How much of that had to do with him and how much of that had to do with me? To tell you the truth, I thought that I was a little lost in *The Lost Boys.*

The Rapture was one of the first Thomas Newman scores that really nailed me. It had a very strong presence of that experimental orchestral sound. Is The Rapture maybe *the* film that helped you break through, break out of teen comedies and allow the more sophisticated Thomas Newman to breathe?

I think it was. Before that, I did *Men Don't Leave*, which was not a comedy. But before that, *Desperately Seeking Susan* was probably my best credit. It was a comedy, but it was a very stylish comedy. It was certainly a movie I was proud of.

I remember wanting to do *The Rapture* because it was a fairly small-budget movie. I thought it would be fun to get together with players I knew and just mess around in an experimental environment. I worked with Rick Cox on it, and Chas [Smith] may have worked on it. George Budd did great scratch phonograph work on it. *The Rapture* was an opportunity to do some bizarre, wild things that I always felt I was capable of doing.

But you start where you start, and people don't allow you to do much. I used to have this theory that as long as I could write something that didn't offend me, I was going to be okay. If it was something that would interest my ears on some level, it would be all right. When I finally got around to *The Rapture*, I was starting to think that I was just getting better at it, too. It's funny how, after you do it for a while, you feel like you improve at it. Or you kind of get the exercise.

There are many avant-garde/contemporary elements in that score—experimental timbres, tone clusters, extreme dissonance, synthetic scales and harmonies.

Right. But in a totally dramatic context. When you're doing comedies, you can use weird sounds, but it's a lot like you do in hip-hop, not that my music is anything like hip-hop. But, if you think about a popular music using strange sounds, a lot of it is rap and some alternative music. You can get away with some of that in comedy, especially if it's contemporary comedy, because that's kind of the current popular language. To be able to finally use strange sounds in a more serious, dramatic context was new and fun.

Did you have anything to do with the Meredith Monk material in *The Rapture*?

I had nothing to do with it. I usually won't have anything to do with music that's not my own, unless I'm asked. Normally, directors hire music supervisors to do that.

Often, directors will come in with their own conceptions. I remember Michael Tolkin, the director of *The Rapture*, wanted to use some horn tune and a fragment of a Brahms symphony for the last horn calling in the apocalypse scene. I thought it was just not a good idea. But, nevertheless, it was an idea I needed to entertain because this was *his* concept—he had written the script, he had directed it and, as much as I didn't get it, I had to deal with it. You have to deal with such ideas from directors and writers somewhat delicately because there's something to be said for their having that concept or having written a scene while some kind of music was going on in their head. In the case of the Meredith Monk, I think that was Tolkin's idea. And not a bad one.

In *The Rapture*, you used a xaphoon, along with many other curious instruments. What the hell is a xaphoon?

Oh, the Maui xaphoon! That's a Rick Cox instrument. It sounds fluty when he plays it, although I bought one in Hawaii and it sounds more like a saxophone. They actually call it "the Hawaiian saxophone." But the way Rick plays it, it sounds like a deep flute.

Okay, that's an authentic instrument, but what about "door," which is listed on the CD liner notes? What's the "door"?

Ha! The door was literally this. [Newman goes to his studio door and slowly closes it. It squeaks and creaks.] I was doing some sampling while my buddy Bill Bernstein was in the bathroom. When he came into the studio, he closed *the* door, and it ended up on this one sample! You can argue that it was precious of us to name it "door," but it was just there and I kind of wanted to remember it.

Other things: there are resonators and bowed plates and things—those were Chas [Smith] instruments.

Processed hurdy-gurdy and prepared guitar? We know Cage's prepared piano, is this similar?

Yeah. That's a Rick Cox thing. Rick did that before I knew him. That was one of his calling cards: putting all kinds of small metal objects toward the fingerboard part of his guitar and sometimes bowing the strings with beveled glass and sponges. Processed hurdy-gurdy: If Rick and I mess around on hurdy-gurdy, we do odd things to it. I think the reason I wanted to call it by its acoustic name is because it was the acoustic side of the instrument that interested me. I like the idea of processing acoustic sounds. That interests me a lot.

You take all these different sound sources and pull them together into individual, unique-sounding bits.

That's right! Then no one can touch you in terms of color, and color is what I find most interesting. The sky's the limit—from bowing to blowing to knocking. I've played things on tables. Anything's possible. But I don't mean to imply that I'm this great experimentalist. I just find abstract color really interesting.

I remember playing the sound of some cicadas for someone who said, "Ah, cicadas. That's a bug sound," as opposed to saying, "Wow, here's this *sound*. Now what happens if you listen to the sound of a xaphoon next to it?" Often, I get criticized for being "ethnic." But if I play an instrument that sounds like a koto, but it's just an instrument that kinda plucks, that's all it is to me—it's an abstract sound. But, unfortunately, people often hear it as "ethnic," which, I guess, would make an interesting study in itself: Why are people drawn to such conclusions?—bells, oh, sure, it's Christmas time, right?

There's a scene in *The Player* where you have a lot of music-box sounds—multiple music boxes playing at the same time.

Do you remember the name of the piece? Was it "Six Inches of Dirty Water"? It wasn't music boxes so much as it was kids' toys that you roll like little spools.

Do people ever say, "Thomas Newman is great if you want these modern, experimental sounds, but what about traditional orchestral scores?"

[Laughter] Yeah. See, again, we go back to the notion of obligation and expectation. Most people expect the traditional orchestral score. I think you could argue that it's valid. Right? If you go see *Star Wars*, you're kinda knocked off your seat by just the sound of all that brass coming at you. That's a great thing, and it's a fun thing. In a way, it embraces the whole tradition of what movies are and what movie scores are.

But *Star Wars* definitely looks back to Korngold, Steiner, and the Golden Age. What do *The Rapture* or *The Player* or *Unstrung Heroes* look to?

No looking back! That's what's fun about it.

But with *Little Women*, you do look back.

Well, you have no choice. In the case of *Little Women*, the film didn't have a big budget and they needed to record out of the country. I had to go to London, so I wasn't going to have my regular team. And it was a period piece, so it was actually less appropriate for whackings and pluckings. You could argue that a less-traditional score could've been really interesting, but if you think about it, if you were score a movie like *Little Women* strangely, it would probably end up being self-conscious. You'd probably say, "Oh, yeah, that composer's trying to do something different just for the sake of being different." I guess that's why, finally, we can never rise above our material. If we do, we're probably pretentious, we're probably not serving whatever it is that we're scoring. And that really rankles a lot of us, because we always want to make smarter choices than we're allowed to make.

As you worked on *Little Women*, did you miss the experimental process or did you find yourself simply enjoying this "new" environment of little set dance pieces?

I really did like scoring it. The reason I like being experimental is because I find that's where I live—I think I'm most sophisticated in that environment. When I'm scoring for traditional orchestra, I find it hard not to remember all of the amazing composers who have preceded me and who have done it so exquisitely. I feel like I'm immediately more like them. And by being more like them, I bring myself up for comparison against them, and I don't enjoy that as much, because it makes me feel I'm less than myself. Yet, at the same time, my God, what power there is in a symphonic environment!

God, there have been amazing things written before any electronics or any sound processing existed! But I want to be a product of my own time. You always hear people say, "Well, if Beethoven and Mozart were alive today . . ." I hate all that. Beethoven's not alive today, and the world has gotten to where it is *because* Beethoven lived when he lived. Sometimes I think film music is an opportunity for people to justify their own basic conservative musical natures.

Do composers now, by the nature of the business, seem less creative, more derivative?

The other day, I was thinking about George Antheil. I was looking at his *Ballet mécanique* and its set design, wondering where all the thinking has gone. It seems like people used to think more about things. Now, it costs twenty million because you have to get David Hockney or Robert Wilson. Budgets are too expensive. People used to get a hundred bucks and a free meal, but, at least, it seemed like there was aesthetic foresight. Now, with movies, if it's a wheatfield scene, it's got to be the rough-hewn, rustic solo-trumpet melody. And, to a degree, we all get caught up in that. What bothers me is that it's always some kind of homage that's unique only in that it references the movie. It's certainly unoriginal in its concept and in its sense of harmony and in its own sense of how music happens.

In a particular scene in *Little Women*, the girls scamper around the house in their nightgowns and you have little bits of scurrying pizzicato strings.

Sure. That's always good for a laugh.

Absolutely. I'm smiling while I'm watching, thinking that you're smiling while you're doing it.

Sure. You have to bow to what is put in front of you when making your choices. I guess smiling would probably be seeing it in its most optimistic light. Sometimes, I'm weeping. But not in *Little Women*. *Little Women* was actually quite a fun experience for me, and the director, Gillian Armstrong, was great.

But there have been other movies that I won't even mention where I just felt like, "Oh, man, I've gotta *sell* this moment." And I felt cheapened by having to sell it. It's never interesting to me to sell the movie through the music. Although, I guess you could argue that the theme to *Gone With the Wind* sold *that* movie, and that was pretty great stuff.

In *Little Women*, there's an old, out-of-tune piano in the living room. The girls are constantly playing it. These are very innocent, wholesome moments. Did those scenes inspire your larger score in any way? Did you wish you could employ more out-of-tuneness? The out-of-tune brothel piano in Alban Berg's *Wozzeck* is such a pivotal scene in his work.

The thought did occur to me. We actually rented an old tack-piano—a beautiful Crown upright. We took it to a studio and had it untuned. Already you're into problems because you're conceptualizing, "What is an out-of-tune piano?" We did all the source music. Then, after weeks went by, the director said, "Great." So we put up that music and none of it worked! There I am, sitting with Bill Bernstein, my music editor, wondering why it didn't work. It was just one of those weird things where ideas change. We had to do it all again in London.

In *Little Women*, Jo's manuscript is burned in the fire. This extremely emotional scene is accompanied by a soft string orchestra—very traditional. Your music is often *so* subtle. *Shawshank Redemption* is the perfect example of this approach.

As I've said before, I always hate it when music takes over, leads the dance. It always embarrasses me, because music can be so abstract in film. Do you ever think, "What's the music doing there at all?" Woody Allen has joked about it. And do you remember that Count Basie thing in *Blazing Saddles*? There's truth to that! What's it doing there?

I like subtext, and I like dimensionalizing a scene as opposed to commenting on it or making sure you get it as it's going down. I have worked with directors who say, "At this point, it's a little more hopeful, so the music should change and be a little more hopeful right there . . ." I hate that, because I think it demeans the actors to a degree. It also patronizes the audience—they're not going to get it, so you'd better tell them. Often, you're instructed to do that. Sometimes, I've had people roll their eyes at choices that I've made, and I want to grab them and say, "Wait a minute!" But, there you are—the director's looking, and he has that concerned look in his eyes that we've all grown to know. "What is it?" "Well, I just feel like you ignore that moment. What can we do about that?" Then you start to backpedal. As my cousin Randy sarcastically says, "Let's all lower our standards (or was it expectations?) and move forward."

In *Little Women*, when Amy falls through the ice, and everyone's running over to her in a panic, there's no music, just icy, cold silence.

There was music. It probably didn't end up in the movie. There was a low tremolo tone. I wanted to do it that way because it strikes me that the most awful moments in life are these little moments when, literally, you're not breathing.

Part of what I like to do is decide what works—what, all by itself, without having anything to do with the music, is compelling dramatically. I think a lot of us get very caught up in the idea that we're "doing the job." There are moments when we sit here, or at the piano, and look at the movie and say, "We are expected to come up with something." And the expectation makes us less inclined to be tasteful—to exercise our good judgment and say, "This is a very compelling scene. Don't score it." But maybe we feel we should because maybe we're getting too much money and we feel we should respond to that. All of a sudden, you realize that, out of this small environment, it will go into a bigger environment with an orchestra, and that will get into a bigger environment when it's dubbed, made into a movie, and people see it. I guess that the point I'm making is that our role as composer ends up just shrinking and shrinking and shrinking. It's most important when we're having the ideas, because that's when we're crossing all the great self-loathing valleys—climbing the hills and valleys of self-loathing. Forgive me!

In those moments, we address ourselves and our sense of our musical selves, and we can really go wrong. I remember when I did *Flesh and Bone*, a movie about little ideas becoming huge ideas, there was a piece of temp music in it just before a gunshot went off. It climaxed with a crescendo to a single gunshot—*boom*! So I think, well, of course, you gotta go *boom*! Sometimes we get into these lethargic places where we think, well, that's just how it's gonna go down. But Bill Bernstein said, "This just sucks. It's just too dramatic." So in this case, we decided to subdue the crescendo, so everything dissolves and you get this deadly silence . . . and then . . . *boom*!, the gun goes off.

You went in a reverse direction from the temp.

Totally. And it was a great dramatic idea. Now you could argue that, in a movie theater, it wouldn't be effective. Less, like nuance and subtlety, is never more in the movies, it just has to go up another twenty percent.

It's like when I'm mastering a very dynamic CD: I love the idea of something being very loud, something being very soft, but, when you think about someone listening to it, you realize that they're going to turn down the loud and turn up the soft and you're going to either kill their ears or they're never going to be able to hear the nuance. It's true in the movies, too. You can't be so subtle that you screw yourself in the end.

It's wonderful when you *can* get somewhere a little bit different. That choice I made in *Flesh and Bone* was a good choice because it was confident. I wasn't selling the moment. It doesn't pander to the audience. I think audiences are much smarter than most people here think they are. But, sometimes, we're told exactly what to do—no arguments. Those are sad moments.

One last *Little Women* question. In 1933, Max Steiner's *Little Women*; in 1949, Adolf Deutsch's *Little Women*; and, in 1978, Elmer Bernstein's *Little Women*: Did you study any of these earlier scores?

I didn't even listen to any of them. Not because I thought, I don't want to get screwed up. There was just no time. It was, "All right, hit the manuscript!" Maybe I *should* have listened. I don't know.

***Shawshank Redemption* is a terrific score. You wrote powerful, moving, emotionally charged string lines, yet no big hummable tune. You wrote a quasi-tune that is constantly emerging, searching—perhaps a reflection of the characters themselves. What about the very opening of the picture, with The Ink Spots singing "If I Didn't Care"? I assume that you had that to work with.**

After I had struggled with building my score around that tune, I played the whole opening for the director. He said, "You know, I've not quite decided on that or another Ink Spots tune." I said, "If you change it, I'm just going to kill you."

You begin *your* music in the same tonal area as the end of the Ink Spots' tune. The Ink Spots' tonal center of A gradually yields to your material arriving in A, then E and E♭ on top. Outside of Wagner's *Das Rheingold*, I don't know of a longer opening pedal point.

Yeah! Did it get boring?

No, no, no. Quite the opposite, but there's always a little . . .

It's just a goddamn drone!

Everybody writes drones these days, but this drone had an extremely dramatic purpose, in the way *Das Rheingold* has its never-ending E♭ opening.

Wow. That's interesting. I like the way that you're referencing me to *Rheingold*. Why not?

The gunshot shatters everything, and then there's silence for a long time—a silence pedal. What about the scenes where you are dealing with the mini-duets of solo violin and guitar? Did these motivic fragments come to you while improvising at the piano or some other instrument or come to you mentally, while driving out to a get a cheeseburger?

Usually not when I'm driving. A lot of times, when I'm driving, if I have the radio on, I'll listen to it and ask myself what would happen if *that* piece of music were in this movie. It's like doing homework in any place you can do it. But, normally, I come here, take out certain instruments, and try to create as much of a playground environment as I can. I studied violin as a kid, so in the case of that

Shawshank violin piece, I took out a violin and started experiment-ing with open strings. I got my ideas for that music on the violin, and then I went to the piano to actually plunk them out, thinking that, basically, it was going to be a fairly rough, folksy kind of melody.

In terms of the other stuff, I just tend to go back and forth. In terms of the main piano theme in *Shawshank*, I knew I wanted it to have kind of a quintal/quartal, open, non-consonant feeling to it. I guess the tritone was the big dissonance, the one bit of dissonance between the fourth and the fifth.

When I write, I mostly just let my mind go. I try not to over-think. I try to save the over-thinking for when I have accrued a lot of ideas, and then it's like taking spices off the shelves: There's an idea! What if I try that? Then I look at it against the movie, and it works or it doesn't work. I'm not much into playing at and look-ing like and trying to be the stern composer. I just try to have ideas and see if they work, all the while trying to have as much fun as I can, and being as inspired as I can be.

Was the tragic *Shawshank* scene where James Whitmore has finally been released and then hangs himself a tough scene to deal with? He was a great character whom we'd grown to know and admire.

The hardest thing about that scene was whether I should give away the fact that something bad was going to happen. Did the audi-ence know by then that something bad was going to happen? Ulti-mately, I think I should have played the ending a little more. When I listen back, I wonder if I should've had a low, tremoloing bass drum or something that said, "All right, here's the last bit of busi-ness." But I remember wanting to remain neutral because, well, he's on that chair and you cut to his feet and you know he's going to hang himself.

That was a tough scene. It was a little long and they ultimately went back and shortened it. And they had to cut some of the music—a hymn-like tune with just tremolo strings behind it. I think that I probably try too much to get different ways of sustaining strings. There have got to be different ways to create just blank tone, other than strings doing nothing but tremolo—being there, but not being there.

Perhaps like minimalists Philip Glass, Steve Reich, and others who write a music of constant but similar activity?

Yeah, a kind of micro-counterpoint or something. It'd be interesting to take a violin and try to do some weird thing around E and record it six or seven times. Even tones are hard to come by. They're there, but you don't listen to them. They're rare.

In Shawshank, when the police come to arrest the warden at the end, you come up with an arresting cello-like sound, a string-scraping—short, abrupt, choppy fragments of solo cello against an eerie, floating string orchestra. The warden looks out his office window and realizes that the police know everything

I wonder if it was Chas Smith on pedal-steel guitar doing some weird shit. There's also some bass marimba in that score.

When you learn that there's going to be opera in a film, like the opera that's piped into the prison in Shawshank, does that affect your score? Do you say to yourself, "I wish they'd asked me"?

Sometimes. I worked on Milos Forman's *The People vs. Larry Flynt*. Forman is from the Czech Republic and ended the movie with some Dvořák. Dvořák is a Czech composer. You could argue, "Well, this is an American movie. What is that piece of music doing in the end of this movie?" I actually said that to him. The Dvořák is very dramatic on a certain level. It works—it's super dramatized or just plain melodramatic, but not in a terrible way. It's just justifiable drama to a certain degree. Dvořák, is a composer of considerable meaning for Forman—it has to do with peace and freedom. The choice is clearly personal. And you cannot argue. You can say, "This strikes me as too this and too that, but if you like it, okay." To a degree, you're disappointed that certain musical decisions have already been prescribed, because it would be interesting to score the end of the movie. At the same time, there's something very effective about it when it's not new material.

I was flying home from London and saw *Trainspotting* on the little video. There's no score in it whatsoever! It's all British pop songs. I thought it was so nice that there was nothing composed for it, because there wasn't this interpretative thing happening. That's one of the dangers about being a film composer—you run the risk of being interpretive. And being interpretive, you sometimes get into those highly ritualized things about what works.

Movie music is highly ritualized and interpretive. When you take those things away and, against the image, put up music that's been composed by a rock-and-roll group, for example, it's interesting because it's casual—it doesn't matter as much. And, when I look at the Dvořák at the end of *Larry Flynt*, it strikes me the same way. If I would have composed it, I would have had something "to say" about it by virtue of the fact that the music was there at all.

Martin Scorsese often uses source pop tunes in his films, without original scores. In *Raging Bull*, for example . . .

Raging Bull is a perfect example of that. If somebody had written original music for those scenes, chances are, the film wouldn't have been nearly as good. That's the bane of film composition in a way.

You can see why directors like Scorsese and Robert Altman don't like scores. They think it cheapens the drama. You can see why Woody Allen said that there's nothing better than music badly played by people who love it. The minute you get professionals interpreting your ideas, there's something high-minded about it, and something potentially disgusting.

A few questions about *Phenomenon*.

Don't hold it against me.

***Phenomenon* is gently following in the footsteps of your other recent scores, *Shawshank Redemption* in particular. But, I sensed that *Phenomenon* presented you with many more restrictions. It felt like you wanted to do so much more, but the director was saying, "No, don't do it here. No, don't do it there."**

Right on! I love you. He was a director who said specific things, like, "Right here, this is a little happier and the music should reflect that, the music should be a little happier." So you do it, and you try to do it as well as you can and not ever be disrespectful to the director or to the movie. But, on my own, I would never have scored the opening the way it opened: "Here's the dawn. Here's darkness turning into dawn."

An orchestrator you often work with, Thomas Pasatieri, was heading for a significant concert career in the 1970s. He was writing emotional, neo-romantic operas. The press proclaimed him "the new Puccini." How much is he involved in your scores?

I think he orchestrates appropriately to the task as, in the end, anyone does. In many cases, I'll say this is a string group, and he'll assign voicings. But often he comes in here with great ideas about using a woodwind choir or muted horns—that kind of thing. He's someone I respect quite a lot in terms of his knowledge of the orchestra. It's as if I get orchestration lessons when I hear this stuff done. I can orchestrate myself, and I wish I could do it more, but I usually don't because there's not enough time. I like Tom's input, and I like how he encourages me. He's been nice to work with.

I like to include interesting people in my work simply because, in a way, I always want to be the student and never be the master. Often, people have more to tell me than I have to tell them. I like to be open to what people have to offer. But, sometimes, that can get me in trouble. We all bring our own biases and, to a degree, we have to be careful about other people's biases because they're nothing more than that—how someone sees it—as opposed to what's necessarily appropriate.

You recently returned from Cleveland and a trip into the surreal, dangerous world of concert music.

Yeah. That *was* a surreal experience.

Was it a commission from the Cleveland Orchestra Summer Series?

It was the Cleveland Bicentennial. They had a big birthday party in Cleveland. John Williams recommended me to them. They offered me this commission for a piece that involved a letter that had come out of a hundred-year-old time capsule. It was bizarre—1896 sends greetings to 1996. "We of today reach forth our hands across the gulf of 100 years" kind of stuff. Actually, it was fairly intense and emotional, but also gentle, subtle, and lovely.

The commission was for an outdoor concert, and my piece was to come after "Take Me Out to the Ballgame." So I kept thinking to myself, "Oh, my God! What can I do here? What's the appropriate thing to do here?" I could do a lot of really interesting things with a letter that was written 100 years ago to people who were not yet born, and now *we're* born, and *they're* dead. It really just tickled my imagination. At the same time, this was to be a big outdoor event for hundreds of thousands of people. There were 400,000 people at the concert.

We go to Cleveland for the performance. We're on bleachers on a bridge; the orchestra is across the river. They were so far away that if I had put up my hand, I would have blocked out our view of the entire orchestra! It was raining, but here I was with my son on my shoulders. It was surreal in a kind of stepping-outside-of-myself way.

They had done *Rhapsody in Blue,* and I turned to one of the managers of the orchestra and said, "Ah, familiar music that you can barely hear. What happens when it's unfamiliar and you can't hear it?" And, sure enough, the quiet sections of my piece just disappeared. Debra Winger did the narration, and you could hear her voice bouncing off of the high-rises across the river. But, it was surreal to think that strains of my music were traveling across this river up to Cleveland in this Bicentennial Celebration. On that level, it was just gloriously great. I wish I had recorded it. And to have my son on my shoulders, asking, "When are we gonna see the fireworks?"

This was my big chance, but it was not what I'd expected. All these cars driving by. When they said an outdoor venue, I assumed something like the Hollywood Bowl. I assumed people would be quiet and that you would be able to hear a quiet moment. I was wrong. Dead wrong.

Do you think this experience, musically and aesthetically, will inspire your future film work? Cars zooming through your music? The rain?

It was more like a film score than I ever would have guessed. Turn up the tire screeches! But it was an experience I was very glad to have had. I'd never been commissioned before, and I was flattered. I would hope that, in the future, there might be more ideal circumstances, but I was very pleased and flattered with the circumstances that were there.

marc SHAIMAN

If you look up "kid in a candy store" in your dictionary of slang phrases, you should find a picture of Marc Shaiman. Rarely does a composer seem to have so much fun and reap so much enjoyment from working in Hollywood. Born in New Jersey, precocious young Shaiman was quick to learn his trade through playing, arranging, and music-directing community theater and off-Broadway shows, accompanying Bette Midler, and arranging for NBC's *Saturday Night Live*. At *SNL*, he befriended Billy Crystal, who drew Shaiman into his first feature-film job, music director for *When Harry Met Sally* (1989). After that, Shaiman's association with Crystal flourished, begetting wild, rousing scores for *City Slickers* (1991) and *City Slickers II* (1994), as well as tender, reflective scores for *Mr. Saturday Night* (1992), *Forget Paris* (1995), and *My Giant* (1998).

Shaiman's long association with director Rob Reiner began with the composer's dark and disturbing orchestral score for *Misery* (1990) and has gone on to yield striking, dramatically understated scores for *A Few Good Men* (1992), his Oscar-nominated *An American President* (1995), and *Ghosts of Mississippi* (1996).

Never one to linger in any one musical style, Shaiman's wildly original and fertile imagination has provided moviegoers with clever, mischievous, and brilliantly bustling scores and arrangements for *The Addams Family* (1991), *Sister Act* (1992), *Addams Family Values* (1993), *Sister Act 2: Back in the Habit* (1993), *North* (1994), *That's Entertainment III* (1994), his Oscar-nominated *The First*

Wives Club (1996), *George of the Jungle* (1997), and his outrageous, parodic *South Park: Bigger, Longer & Uncut* (1999). His more intimate musical thoughts have found homes in the mystical *Hearts and Souls* (1993) and the heartwarming *Mother* (1996), *Simon Birch* (1998), and *Patch Adams* (1998).

We met for this interview at his studio, nestled in the foliage behind his Laurel Canyon home, perched in the hills above Hollywood.

marc SHAIMAN

Your scores often demonstrate a fascination with and a fondness for theater—Broadway, community, backstreet—and pop music. However, I notice Stravinsky's *The Rake's Progress* and Berg's *Lyric Suite* scores on your bookshelf. There's a quite an eclectic guy at work here.

Definitely! I like that about myself. Maybe I should be more focused, maybe not. I just like everything. My teenage attraction to Bette Midler was obviously due to the eclectic nature of her records. I often leave the radio on scan, which plays just ten seconds of something. You're supposed to hit the button if you hear something you like, but I just enjoy letting it go. I even enjoy letting something that I like pass by—"Oh, I like that, but let's see what's next." It's exciting to me that I'm not sticking with it. People always ask me what kind of music I like the most. But I really just like it all. People always ask me who my favorite film composers are. But I don't ever make any distinction about that. I just hear what everyone is doing and appreciate it.

Hearing about your radio-listening style helps explain many of your wildly eclectic scores. *City Slickers* is a good example. It has rapid-fire changes and unpredictable extremes—instant changes of mood, tempo, instrumentation, texture, and dynamics.

The animated opening of *City Slickers* called for that style. That was only the second movie I'd scored, and I had to write that opening in a day and a half while I was mixing the rest of the score. We set up a midi piano in an isolation booth at the recording studio, and I sat in there and wrote until they would call me in to hear a mix. After hearing a mix, I'd go back and write some more. That was the first time I'd done that, so the tempos are very bizarre. To me, it seemed like the elephant was waltzing, or he was lumbering a little; the cowboy was at a certain tempo for a moment, but then was faster. So I just kept changing tempos. It was just insane. It was a nightmare to record. We ended up recording it in about twelve little snippets, instead of doing the whole thing from beginning to end.

With your use of harmonica in *City Slickers*, were you referencing the classic Western scores of Tiomkin, Morricone, and Bernstein?

Absolutely, but you make it sound like I'm such a historian. It's a Western, so there's a harmonica. It was as simple as that. There's even a scene where Billy [Crystal] actually "plays" harmonica. We had to call in a harmonica player to do what Billy had pretended to do. That really spurred me on, because the guy we called in, Tommy Morgan, is brilliant.

***City Slickers II* seems even more frantic and instrumentally eclectic, with saxophones and extra percussion and your references to Steiner's *The Treasure of the Sierra Madre* score.**

We got the rights to *The Treasure of the Sierra Madre*. They kept referring to it, and then they put it into the temp score. But even before they put it into the temp score, we agreed that it would be great if I could use it. I wrote my theme to be a kind of kissing-cousin to it, because that was what the whole movie was about—this conglomeration of characters and memories from old Westerns, old looking-for-gold movies. It just made sense to me.

The cartoonish elements of your score continue even when the animation stops. You blend a 1950s Broadway-overture style . . .

Wherever I can get away with it, I do it. That's just who I am, for better or for worse. And, hopefully, usually, it's for better.

Do you turn down some projects because they might not allow you the Broadway style?

No, just the opposite.

Do you embrace some films, such as *Ghosts of Mississippi*, for the compositional variety they offer you?

Well, basically, I turn down nothing. So it's a moot point. Ironically, I almost turned down *George of the Jungle*. I had just received my third Academy Award nomination, and here's my agent calling to say that they wanted me to do *George of the Jungle*. I said, "Hello? What is wrong with this picture?" But I got over myself really quickly when I saw the movie. I thought it was so silly, but also so sweet. I enjoyed it.

But there was a point when they wanted me to score the movie in England. And that was just the worst thing that could have happened as far as how I work and the amount of time and the style of score it required. So the fighting between me and the filmmakers and Disney got really ugly about them springing that England business on me. And I really *quit*! When I came back, they didn't want me, because I had been so obstinate. But I held on to the movie because I knew it would afford me the opportunity to be outrageously wild—I could throw anything up against the wall. And I was really glad I stayed with it because I hadn't had a movie like that, which allowed me to be so theatrical and funny and get it all out of my system, in a really long time. There's actually this ending. [Shaiman sings, "da-da-da-daaaaa!"] I couldn't believe I did it, but there was nowhere else to go. I had used every cliché possible—it seemed only proper to have it end that way.

Is a great deal of your composing done by instinct?

For better or for worse, I write what I hear. I didn't get to exercise the composing muscle like it always had been exercised up until modern times. Obviously, these brilliant people who wrote great classical works heard every little texture and every different member of the orchestra who's playing at once in their head. I don't know how I would be in that situation. When I started getting the chance to compose music, I had all this stuff. [Shaiman gestures toward his piano and electronic gear.] So I could kind of play around with something and hear it come back at me—do a string line against a certain thing and I think about whether it's what I want. If I just had a score pad, I would have just written that string line. I'm set in my ways, this is just how I work.

The idea of setting all this up in England or anywhere else, even in another room? No! I've been working here for over a decade, and everything is sort of tweaked. Why do you want to get me at less than my capacity? Also, the style of the music I needed for *George of the Jungle* was going to be so Warner Bros. cartoonish—almost like Carl Stalling. It was the kind of music Hollywood orchestras would play so perfectly right away. I just didn't know that an English orchestra would nail it or get it.

All this generated the uncomfortable confrontation with the studio?

The situation did get kind of ugly with the phone calls and the negotiations and that stuff. I cursed my agent, gave in, and thought, "All right, I'm going to get through this because I actually do want to score this movie. It will be fun. But can I possibly still have fun with the bad feelings between everyone?" Luckily, I got past that and was able to write.

The first time they came over and heard the music, they were ecstatic. Then they passed a little tape of my music around at Disney, because that's a very Disney thing to do. When the president of Disney heard it, he called me personally and just said, "This is fantastic." I said, "If I may be so bold as to say so, if you liked this music, you won't get what it deserves if we go to England. I'll still be in the middle of writing, and they won't play it as well. It just doesn't make sense." And the next day, everything was back in Los Angeles. The good thing was that the music, not my demands, ultimately steered it back to what I thought was the best way to do it. That was the greatest way for that whole chapter to have ended. It was a very good feeling. It doesn't happen very often.

Stuart Saves His Family has a lot of 1920s through 1940s period music, but not much score.

I loved that movie! And I love Harold Ramis, the director. But I was writing theme after theme and Harold was just like, "Yeah, I like it but . . ." I don't know who will be reading this, but I would even tell Harold that I really feel the movie would have had a better score if he had stuck with some of the earlier themes I presented. But he was scared that the studio was scared that it was getting too artsy. I had written stuff that was a little, for lack of any other way to put it, Felliniesque. Harold kept asking, "How can we make it less of an art film?" because the studio was so frightened of how it was going to market it. Of course, the movie ended up making less than my salary.

But, I still adore that movie. And I did get to write "Sweet Song," the song that's in the end credits, which was the theme used throughout the movie. I'm very fond of that song. The lyrics just popped out of me because I rarely write a musical theme where there isn't a lyric somewhere in my brain.

Your music for the opening hospital birthing sequence in Addams Family Values is fantastic—five minutes of throwing in and piling up every possible tune that will happen later. It's like a manic

Broadway overture, but with a short-circuited, machine-gun approach. You're mickey-mousing like crazy, following each little event—following the baby, the kids, Gomez. How do you compose an action-saturated scene like that?

The same way I write anything. It's right in front of me on the TV set, and I look at it and start to figure it out.

It was a sequel, so I already had some melodies. But you're completely right—so many things that I've done have the feel of overture up front. I always love that if that can happen.

Then, suddenly, you find the tempo and realize that that door's going to open on the end of three. How do I deal with that? How do I not only hit the end of three, but also make the line seem like it was supposed to end on the end of three? I love that puzzle, when things happen on an odd spot in the music. How do you make it sound like it was meant to be there? Often, I come up with a little rhythmic hook that I'll end up using a lot.

All of the Addams characters are presented, and your music eventually evolves into a portion of Vic Mizzy's original *Addams Family* television theme, only meaner, darker, more aggressive. But, because of the pipe organ, you achieve a campy horror effect at the same time.

Right. I only used the beginning of the original tune. But it was fun to put that great old *Addams Family* tune in that more majestic, grown-up, overblown cinematic bed. For *George of the Jungle*, I ended up using the original TV theme more extensively, much more than on the *Addams Family* movies.

Was that a direction given to you?

No, we all agreed. But I think I went even further than they ever would have imagined. I would just throw a bit of it in at the end of a cue. But they were loving it! I also wrote a heroic theme for

George that worked as a nice counterpoint. I've done that in a few movies. *Sleepless in Seattle* had the same thing: I wrote my main theme for the Meg Ryan character as a counterpoint to the song "An Affair to Remember" from the movie *An Affair to Remember*, the movie that she keeps talking about. When she is running to the Empire State Building, we're hearing the theme that we've been associating with Meg Ryan, her main theme, *and* "An Affair to Remember"—the themes from her movie *and* her life—playing together.

You use that technique in *First Wives Club*, too. At the very end, when the ladies are singing "You Don't Own Me," your original themes for each of them are blended in.

Yeah, yeah, you noticed! That was great. I love doing that.

Cynthia's gone, but she's still alive in the hearts of her friends.

Exactly! I just got a little chilly about how you got it. That's absolutely it—she's still alive—that's exactly what that was supposed to be.

It's a versatile theme that travels through numerous transformations and mutations. Especially effective was the rich, chromatic version that harmonically dissolves into ice-cold open fifths as she's getting ready to take the suicide plunge. And her theme never disappears completely, because she's alive in her friends' hearts and minds throughout the movie. Which version of that theme came to you first?

The scene where they all read the letters that she'd sent was where I first wrote the theme, and then I traveled backward in the movie. I went back to the front and figured out how to make the theme minor, darker, and more extended.

Is this a typical approach for you?

You pick scenes to write themes for, and that just seemed like a perfect spot. It was obviously a scene that was going to be all music and needed a melody—it wasn't just going to be about chords and harmony. And I realized that that melody should be Cynthia's melody. Although she's not really even in the movie, her spirit should have a theme.

When the girls commence Operation Hell's Fury, you combine Cynthia's tune with the other girls' tunes and another theme. You give us really terrific multiple-voice counterpoint.

Yeah. "Hell hath no fury like a woman scorned." I made a melody from that line. I write lyrics to everything, and I write melodies to everything. In my mind, that lyric fit. That expression just came to mind and I wrote a melody to it, which just goes to show you, it's ridiculous that I'm not writing musicals. It's what I should be doing. Meanwhile, I'm writing movie scores that sound like musicals. However, Broadway doesn't seem to want the kind of score I would want to write, which is like a traditional Ethel Merman score. Even though people say that they wish people were writing that, no producer seems to really want to produce that kind of musical.

Your other *First Wives Club* themes also reflect their respective characters perfectly. Diane Keaton's theme, like her character, is a cute, old-fashioned, wholesome little tune. Goldie Hawn's theme is a sexy little number with solo saxophone. Do these things often just hit you instinctively?

Instinct. That Goldie scene where she's walking down the street with the big lips? I thought, Here's my chance to do that *How to Marry a Millionaire*, 1950s-Hollywood-score melody that has that kind of Gershwin-meets-Marilyn Monroe thing in it. But, how do I apply that to other spots in the movie? Bette doesn't actually get a theme. Because her son's listening to the headphones, I just couldn't figure out how to do it. It was so wall-to-wall music. But I knew, when I finally saw the movie again, I should have figured it out: Couldn't he be listening to something other than music? Much later, when Bette comes in with her coat and puts her stuff down, she gets a little plaintive melody, which only comes up one or two other times.

At the funeral, when gangster Uncle Carmine greets her with, "It would be my honor to take him out for you," you let loose some fun _Godfather_/Mafia music.

That was just an obvious one for me. But that was perhaps a moment where I stepped out too far as the composer. I was paraphrasing the _Godfather_ melody. Maybe that was too much for me to do, because people are then probably laughing at a musical joke instead of just being in the movie. That may have taken people out of the movie. I wondered about that, but Scott Rudin, who was the producer, just got a kick out of it. And it was Scott who I really collaborated with, a relationship that you usually have with the director.

First Wives Club is a good example of your approach to traditional scoring—avoiding the trendy synth-groove/drone in favor of counterpoint, development, and thematic alteration.

Yeah, I'm conscious of that. And, hopefully, it just happens naturally, because it's just what should be happening. It's just me in this room. I try everything, and then I realize, "Oh, that's working the best." Or the producer or the director will say, "That works the best," and the decision is made like that.

The music for Maggie Smith's character is sinister, but also very proper, as is her house.

That's the revised version. I loved the original cue. I was broken-hearted when I got a call from the dub stage, and they said that they felt it was just too wall-to-wall with music and that it was time to just take a break from score. Much to my chagrin, they had me redo it. So, I figured out a way to have her theme sound like source—when we cut to the house's interior and this big portrait of her, we hear that melody, but we hear it in a kind of string-quartet style. Then that music comes way down under the scene. And at the moment when she brings out the designer's business card and we know she's up to a scheme, the source becomes score. But in the first version, it was just total score. I had so much fun playing it, and it was a really good cue. It really broke everyone's heart, because everyone loved the cue, but they just thought it was too much score, especially since the very next scene was wall-to-wall music.

The next scene in the apartment was nonstop, rambunctious silent-movie music.

I know! It was wall-to-wall music! That's why I have these black rings under my eyes and fifty extra pounds around my gut.

Speaking of wall-to-wall, not to mention off-the-wall, allow me to jump back to *Addams Family Values* for a few moments. The bizarre children's summer-camp Thanksgiving musical is hilarious. I crack up imagining Marc Shaiman battling the community-theater folk, à la *Waiting for Guffman*. The bungling of lines, the bumbling directors, the bizarre egos, the bad sets, the problems with child actors, the miscasting—and that song "Eat Me"!

Thanks. It was a lot of fun. Actually, I'm on piano in that scene. I usually don't play on the scores. My chops are pretty nonexistent now, but on something like that—especially that eager oompah-oompah beat—or something fun, I'll be there.

Multiple Shaiman musical personalities—including great suspense

music for the nocturnal chase scene, with a lot of mickey-mousing, even pizzicati for the people sneaking around. Then, when the bad kids end up in the detentional Harmony Hut, your suspense music segues into the rehabilitating "Kumbayah"—a 180-degree turn. Perfect! Why?

"Kumbayah" was a part of the filming—it was already in the movie. I knew all along that I was heading for that. And I knew the arrival at "Kumbayah" had to be a big kick.

You wrote a very tender young-love theme for Wednesday and her shy little boyfriend. It's a beautiful, simple theme that goes through a few unexpected harmonic transformations. Do you improvise with harmonic progressions or key changes at the piano, just to see where they take you?

Absolutely. Especially in movies that really afford me those great harmonic changes. As you know, I'm an arranger. I came into the business as an arranger, so that's why I should bring up interesting harmonies, and, often, that's what film music is so much about. The love theme with Uncle Fester also had some great changes in the harmonies. I love that kind of stuff, and I don't get those opportunities that often. The *Addams Family* movies allowed me to do that more than most movies.

Wednesday's little love-interest theme was a hard spot. In the temp score, they had put in a very short Cousin Itt cue, a silly little melody from the first movie, against all the Wednesday-and-her-little-love-interest business in the camp. I think that was the first time that I found my own music in the temp score. And it was hard to beat. I couldn't come up with something. The Itt theme worked so well in the temp score for those scenes, I almost wanted to give up and say, "Let's just use that Cousin Itt theme. No one's going to remember. At least it's part of the fabric of the *Addams Family* movies."

Often, your score is the reason a given comedic scene succeeds. How do you avoid taking over a scene?

Usually, the director says, "Calm the fuck down!" Again, *George of the Jungle* was a great opportunity because they let me go as far as I wanted. And I've been getting a few phone calls saying that I was really an important part of why that movie worked. Despite what my ego may seem like, I have trouble taking a compliment. But there are a few cases where I can—*Sister Act* was one. I could take a compliment on it because I knew that my work was integral to the success of the movie. I put what the screenwriter had written—the idea of girl-group songs as hymns and hymns as girl-group songs—on screen. I did it. I found the songs and I arranged them. And I know that that movie was a big success, in large part, due to those moments.

Your *George of the Jungle* music is often blown away with sound effects.

Yeah, I wasn't happy with the way they dubbed the music with the sound effects. They obliterated a lot of music. But that's every composer's complaint. It's a broken record. Still, I can't believe some of the choices they made. I'm not just saying this because it's my music, but because it was so helpful to the tone of the movie, and they were so enjoying it. It's not like they buried it because they didn't like it. When I record things, I try to give them as much separation as I can, so that if they want to tweak the drums or bring up an over-dubbed soprano sax, they can. Maybe I learned my lesson. Maybe it's time to stop giving them that.

But isn't that part of the game?

Yeah. You do it because you don't want them to call you from the dub stage and say, "We're dropping this whole three-minute cue because that triangle note interferes with the bird-chirp sound effect that you didn't know was going to be put in there."

In the opening scene of *In and Out*, they added this little bird chirp that was like a quarter-step off from the note the oboe was playing! When I first heard it, I thought, "That oboe's out of tune!"

The same thing happened in *George of the Jungle*—a monkey laughs at the same time a flute plays. So I asked them if they could please just move the effect, and they were very nice about it. I've learned, I guess just because I'm more ballsy now, that you can call up the editor and say, "If you gave me another frame at the end of this scene, it would really be great for the tempo." You can call the sound effects guy and do the same thing. Everyone wants to collaborate. So do I—I love to accommodate anyone.

Speaking of collaboration, you've done a great deal of work with director Rob Reiner. Have you and Reiner maintained a solid, healthy working relationship?

Oh yeah. He enjoys working with me. I collaborate with him really well. But I never want him to feel like he has to use me. I want him to use me just because I can do the job for him, because I understand him. I'm sure there are times when he must wonder what it would be like to have James Horner or Danny Elfman score something for him.

Two Reiner/Shaiman Americana pictures—*A Few Good Men* and *An American President*. They are similar in their musical approach—both are proud and patriotic, but also cautious and reserved. Is your understated, minimal score for *A Few Good Men* an atmosphere or an underscore for the emotions that are presented in the dialogue?

Some of both. Rob wants music to be as simple as possible—both literally and emotionally. He feels that if it's not happening through the actors and the screenplay, it doesn't belong in the movie. We've talked about this at length. Rob talks about anything at length!

Rob is very fearful of music becoming too present or primary. He loved the *American President* theme, and it just worked out that the theme got to be a little bolder at the end. We get this lovely statement of the main theme early in the movie, and then it really isn't repeated until the end, when he makes the speech at the press conference, during the montage of great presidents. At that point, Rob said, loudly, "That's the moment he's becoming a great president!"

In answer to your question, I don't write the densest music, but I'm very capable with simplicity. Maybe that's why I'm a good match for Rob's musical preferences.

Misery, your first score, is quite complicated.

I saw *Misery* a few months ago. Can you imagine that that was the first time I ever wrote anything? I don't know if I would write *Misery* again the way I wrote it then. And I mean that in a bad way. Would I be simpler now? I would really like to get more movies that have multiple textures. I've been really conscious of that lately.

During the opening credits for *An American President*, your patriotic tune modulates and arrives at a surprising new tonic key at the very moment your name appears on the screen, a trick that reaches back to the films of Korngold, Steiner, Waxman, and numerous others. Occasionally, a composer will even synchronize silence with his credit, creating an attention-grabbing time-freeze. Do you intentionally synchronize your musical autograph?

City Slickers was the one where I really out-and-out hit my credit with a big deal. It just cracked everyone up! And then I did it again on *City Slickers II*. But I don't think I've done it on many others. If the movie can handle it, I'm obviously not above anything. It was particularly fun with *City Slickers*. The theme just flowed along in the right place at the right time—I had just come to the end of a phrase and, suddenly, there was my name and it was time to go, "da-da-da-*da*!"

North offered you an opportunity to write an original score and extensive arrangements in a variety of international styles and genres. What comes to mind—historically or personally—when you think back about that unusual picture?

All those different styles from all the different countries were exactly what made that movie fun to work on. And the main title is something I'm very proud of. All these years later, I think it's safe to say that it was clear to everyone working on it, Rob included, that something just hadn't quite jelled. But, working on it, cue by cue, you kind of forget what the problems might be, and it's just fun to watch.

Yet this unique movie must have started as an interesting and exciting project for all concerned.

If you could have sold tickets to watch Rob first describing the movie to me, it would have been a smash! I really, really thought I was about to work on the *Wizard of Oz* of our generation!

Is he that enthusiastic about all of his projects?

About everything and anything he applies himself to. It's enthusiasm bordering on the maniacal.

Rob Reiner's *Ghosts of Mississippi* is very serious moviemaking. Aside from the expected traditional gospel examples, there's an aggressively atonal Marc Shaiman at work in many scenes. We hear non-functional tritones everywhere.

That sound just makes you feel undecided. It's music that sounds musically undecided. It also helped with the wavering of the characters and the undecidedness of the case. You know, I'm now discussing it with you more than I ever thought about it when I was writing it. At the time, that interval just seemed to suit the fact that everything in the movie is unresolved. I was after that kind of Copland Americana sound, but with a Southern drawl and more dissonance.

I saw a movie on TV the other night that had this great Delta guitar stuff. I only did a little of that in *Ghosts of Mississippi*. Sometimes, I wish I had done more of it. I write on the piano, and sometimes only a guy who plays a guitar can write a really good cue that really uses the guitar in the perfect way.

Your score for the opening scene is layer upon layer of transparent yet tense forward motion to the gunshot climax.

I remember watching the opening scene on television and just being so intimidated. How can I possibly score this scene? Someone's getting murdered. How can I not write trivial music for such a powerful moment?

I liked what I ended up doing with the harmonies and all, but it's nowhere near the musically density that other composers are capable of, and probably I am capable of. But I also had Rob sitting on my shoulder, and even when he wasn't there, I knew I couldn't get too dense.

The music comes right back in after the guy is shot, but, as you said, that whole first section is just building and building. It's the tension of the inevitable.

I may have embarrassed myself in front of the orchestra on that, because I know that everything should just be in the music, or with an Italian word above the music. But I said, "Okay, everyone, that melody is like the pureness of this man and what he was trying to do. And, no matter what that rising line is, the lower harmonies, just moving back and forth, are the inevitableness of this evil guy who's now about to shoot this other guy!" Whether they rolled their eyes not, I don't know. But then I realize I'm not embarrassed because, if I were, I would be so embarrassed by things that I do all the time. And I realize that if I were playing and someone said that to me, I would take that in. I would play something a certain way if someone said, "This is a mother saying goodbye to her child" or "This is someone hitting someone." I would apply that to the way I played it, so, yeah, go ahead and say it. Why not?

For the bomb threat at Alec Baldwin's house, you create great musical hammer strokes as the clock keeps ticking away in almost a silent-movie suspense-building fashion. Is the elaborate orchestration yours or in collaboration with your orchestrators?

Well, no more or less than any other composer. I make it rather clear in my scores, but I will certainly say to the orchestrator, "What don't I have a sound for here?" "What is something else we can do to really pound that big moment?"

I was uncomfortable with that bomb-threat cue because there's nothing else like it in the movie. I felt that just about anything I was writing for that cue was sticking out like a sore thumb—like this dumb, get-out-of-the-house suspense cue. But there is no bomb. It's a false alarm, a red herring. It needed the suspense, but the bigger the music, the bigger the letdown that nothing happens.

Toward the end of the film, as Mrs. Evers' testimony gets deeper and deeper into the tragic story, your musical accompaniment follows right with her—it's intensifying, becoming more and more harmonically complicated. There and throughout the picture, you capitalize on the classic "teardrop" suspension—in this case, F♯ down to E. When the "not guilty" verdict is finally rendered, there's a huge, explosive, patriotic version of that little motive. Is this a through-composed reference to the very beginning of the film? Did you blueprint it this way?

In her testimony, I do use the music from the opening—both the pre- and post-gunshot music. But that all happened naturally.

I don't think it's pompous of me to say that I know I have the gift of instinct—an instinct for how to use music as a communicative language. Some people who are good musicians may not have that instinct, but I do. I have said that to other interviewers, and they've said, "Oh, are you like a child prodigy or something?" Well, I play piano really well. I have good instincts, but a prodigy to me is someone who wins the Van Cliburn competition. Maybe if I'd practiced classical piano, I could have been what they would think of as a prodigy. But maybe I was a show-business prodigy. I just get it. I understand it. You either get it or you don't. No one can teach you that. I fine-tuned it with movies and theater cast albums. And I got it.

Growing up in northern New Jersey, did you take advantage of New York City theater?

I went to New York a lot when I was a teenager.

Community theater is very active in New Jersey.

Community theater! When I discovered community theater—or when it discovered me—that was it! I probably did ten thousand shows in the space of three years.

As a performer, a music director?

As musical director and as piano player/musical director. I was this thirteen-year-old kid with big braces on my teeth, teaching adults the music and harmonies of *Fiddler on the Roof*. And these adults would never question the fact that there was this pimply faced twerp telling them what to do. But even then I just knew, definitely, I just had it. I was just full of it, meaning full of music and show business and theater and energy.

When you were that thirteen-year-old, pimply faced twerp in New Jersey, would you listen to Broadway records and imagine other versions of the songs, other arrangements, additional counterlines?

Well, most of the time, it was all there. But when playing the boring stuff, yes, I would imagine all that stuff on top of it, underneath it.

In both *Sister Act* and *Mr. Saturday Night*, you again get opportunities to wear that Broadway hat. How many song choices were yours?

With *Mr. Saturday Night*, it was a hodgepodge of me and Billy [Crystal] and the music editor, the poor, unsung hero of the movie-scoring business, because the music-editor gets involved in every aspect of the music and so many decisions. For *Mr. Saturday Night*, his name was Scott Stambler. He's been music editor on a lot of the films I've worked on. I sometimes get paid an additional fee as music supervisor, and he gets his music-editor fee, yet he's making as many of the choices as I am or as the director is. In one movie, I tried to rectify that a little, so I gave him my percentage off the record.

Another good guy is Nick Meyers. He was the music editor on *Sleepless in Seattle*, which was chock-full of song choices. Now, I stand proudly for many of the things that I did bring to that movie. But, as for song choices and the artists singing them, Nick, along with some input from me and director Nora Ephron, made those choices. I had two credits: Music Composed by Marc Shaiman and Music Supervised by Marc Shaiman. So, I proudly, pompously, martyr-like called them and told them to please put Nick in the title credits, because he did more than half the work. And if someone else had done the music-supervisor job, their credit would've been there.

Sister Act was all me, and I'm very proud of myself on that movie. But, on that movie, we had to contend with this hideous thing, the "*Rear Window* clause," as we call it.

What is the "*Rear Window* clause"?

When the movie *Rear Window* was re-released on video, the legal heirs of the man who had written the original book it was based on, much to the shock of Hollywood, successfully sued the movie company, saying that their uncle, Cornell Woolrich, never gave up his rights for video-cassette release. Well, this was a huge decision. Suddenly, if the studios didn't have every heir and family member's name on a contract for a certain amount of time, they'd hold the production.

So, there I was with *Sister Act*, all about Motown girl groups, sixties music. First of all, they couldn't clear any of the choices that the screenwriter had already written into the script, which were kind of obvious choices, like "Chapel of Love," but they would have been wonderful. Every last one of them was unclearable. Sometimes, especially with Disney, it's also just so cost-prohibitive. They refuse to pay certain fees, especially to guys who have some of those classic rock-and-roll songs. A Phil Specter song? Forget it.

Impossible to get?

Almost, until some director finally pulls enough of a hissy fit. You will hear those songs now and then in the movies, but I was told I couldn't use any song written after October 1962. Well, the whole era was only beginning in '62, '63, '64, '65, '66—Diana Ross and the Supremes, great stuff.

But, all's well that ends well. I took that little year's worth of explosion of girl groups, and within that short list there was "My Guy," which I just jokingly recorded with some session singers one night as a demo to prove that this could work—this musical idea of Motown girl-group songs becoming hymns and hymns becoming girl-group songs. I'm just a little Jewish boy from New Jersey, so I told one of the casting directors that I needed to learn hymns. I had heard her talking about church, so I said, "You're a church-going Christian. Get me a hymnal!" She brought me two hymnals! I sat there at the casting sessions, and I found one that was perfect for a girl group. I'm already putting this funky little rhythm to it that isn't there on the page. "Oh, Maria" just stuck out like a bolt out of the blue.

The reverse of "My Guy" becoming "My God"?

Which was really just kind of a bad joke on my part. But everyone laughed and loved it, so we recorded it and it became a huge moment in the movie. "I Will Follow Him" was also on that short list, but now it was Him with a capital H. And the original lyrics to that song, from beginning to end, applied to Jesus as well as to a love interest. And there was this big musical montage of other hymns done in Diana Ross fashion that they ended up not using because there was no more space in the movie for it. Too bad.

What about *Sister Act II*?

Unfortunately, none of the songs applied to *Sister Act II*, which I refer to as *Sister Act II*-soon! That was just a bad collaborative experience for all involved parties.

All different people or were some carried over from the first movie?

I think I was literally the only person who worked on the first movie who they involved in the second movie, which is very bizarre. Unfortunately, the director of the first movie, Emile Ardolino, had died. And Scott Rudin had disassociated himself from it because he thought what they were trying to do was wrong. They had a script that already existed, into which they tried to cram Whoopi Goldberg and the nuns. It was a true story about a teacher in South Central L.A. who got the kids to create a gospel group. But when I went to a production meeting, I found out that they didn't want the nuns to sing. "You don't want the singing nuns in the movie? Huh?

What?" I finally said, "I feel like I'm working on *Superman II* and you just told me you don't want Superman to have his suit on or fly or bend steel in his bare hands. Am I in the Twilight Zone here?" It was a very bizarre movie because everyone had a different agenda about what they wanted the movie to be.

How did you survive such a confusing letdown after the blast of the original movie?

Even after my success in *Sister Act*, having proven myself knowledgeable about a lot of music, Disney was still not convinced I could pull off the authentic gospel thing. Believe me, I can. But there you are, finding yourself saying things like, "but some of my best friends are black." I mean, what the hell am I saying? Black music, gospel music is my most cherished, favorite music.

But one really good thing came out of all of this. A guy named Mervyn Warren, a brilliant arranger who helped create the vocal group Take Six, was brought on board. I said, "If it's Mervyn Warren, bring him in," because I thought Take Six was just about the greatest thing ever. We had a great friendship during and after that movie. He's a joy to work with.

The arranger of the rhythm-and-blues/gospel Handel's *Messiah* recording?

Yeah. It's terrific. And, for the end of *Sister Act II*, he did a great arrangement of Beethoven's "Ode to Joy," done in a kind of gospel hip-hop, a lot like what he'd done on that brilliant *Messiah* record.

I read an interview with you from about a year or two ago in which you talked about Skitch Henderson and Oscar Levant. The interviewer, who I think was young, had never heard of these people. It seemed to be bothering you that this person wasn't responding. Is there something critical you want to say about a Skitch Henderson influence?

Well, I must admit I was just playing into that whole thing. I'm used to all that now. You can bring up people like Gary Grant, Fred Astaire, Gene Kelly, and Oscar Levant, and the people who're interviewing you don't know them. Well, *seriously*, they're supposed to be fans of movies and movie music, so they ought to know that stuff. I wouldn't be upset if the guy on the street doesn't know Skitch Henderson or Oscar Levant. Am I the oldest man on Earth? Am I just like the clichéd old, crusty guy who's saying, "Well, when I was a kid . . ."?

Is it simply a generation gap?

My theory is it's the remote control and cable. When I was a kid, we only had nine channels. You had to get up and walk over to the TV to change the channel. So, eventually, you'd just leave it on whatever channel was on. Eventually, you'd see *King Kong* or some old black-and-white gangster movie or a Fred Astaire and Ginger Rogers movie or whatever, because it was all that was on, and you'd just learn who these people were. I did not grow up in the era of Oscar Levant, but I learned who he was. Not that I'm saying that knowledge of old movies is such a grand thing, and, believe me, I don't know all the great writers or artists that I should really know.

I've heard they're making a picture about Oscar Levant.

Pass them my phone number! I'd love to be involved with that.

howard SHORE

After studying at the Berklee School of Music, touring extensively
with the rock group Lighthouse, and composing music for CBC
radio and television broadcasts, Canadian-born Howard Shore
settled in New York City in 1975 as the newly appointed music director for NBC's *Saturday Night Live*. However, within a few years,
his musical focus was to shift when he found himself in the thick of
significant film-scoring projects for director David Cronenberg. The
ensuing twenty-year Cronenberg/Shore collaboration has created
a significant body of deeply disturbing—yet artistically compelling
and extraordinarily original—films: *The Brood* (1979), *Scanners*
(1981), *The Fly* (1986), *Dead Ringers* (1988), *M. Butterfly* (1993),
Crash (1997), and *eXistenZ* (1999), all of which boast unusual, influential scores that speak in a variety of contemporary musical styles,
and the hallucinatory *Naked Lunch* (1991), which inspired Shore
to compose a most eerie juxtaposition of avant-garde jazz and orchestra that featured the inimitable Ornette Coleman with the London Philharmonic.

Although Shore tends to select unique projects that allow him
full use of his musical and dramatic talents, the types of films he
has scored are quite varied: His compassionate and dignified score
for *Philadelphia* (1993) contrasts with his cynical, hypnotic electronic soundscape for *Videodrome* (1983). His breezy and bittersweet scores for *Big* (1988), *Mrs. Doubtfire* (1993), and *Nobody's
Fool* (1994) stand in stark contrast with his chaotic orchestral

madness for *She-Devil* (1989). As a master of suspense, intensely disarming music of real danger, psychotic behavior, and personal terror abound in the Shore catalogue, which includes his relentlessly menacing orchestral scores, often enhanced with electronics, for *The Silence of the Lambs* (1991), *A Kiss Before Dying* (1991), *Sliver* (1993), *Guilty as Sin* (1993), *The Client* (1994), *Seven* (1995), *Cop Land* (1997), and *The Game* (1997). In a genre of its own is Shore's simultaneously nostalgic, campy, and sensitive score for *Ed Wood* (1994).

During a weekend of recording sessions for his aggressive orchestral score to Ron Howard's *Ransom*, a score that was later rejected for reasons unknown, Howard Shore graciously accommodated my endless questions by arranging for a series mini-interviews at the Sony Recording Studios in New York City and over lunch, dinner, and breakfast at three midtown-Manhattan restaurants.

howard SHORE

I first noticed you when you appeared in hospital drag as the director of the *Saturday Night Live* Howard Shore's All Nurse Band. Tell me about your path from Toronto to Berklee School of Music to *Saturday Night Live* to David Cronenberg to Ornette Coleman to today?

They all sort of go together. When I first became interested in music, as a kid in Toronto, a group of friends and I would put on little shows with lots of music. I would write original music for these shows. I loved music—performing, writing, arranging—but I was also interested in acting and directing. That's why these little shows were so great: I was doing some of each.

By high school, I was mostly active in music—playing jazz. I became interested in jazz when I was about fifteen or sixteen. I was interested in Art Blakey, Bobby Timmons, Horace Silver, Cannonball Adderley, Charles Lloyd, Miles, and all that.

When I went to Berklee School of Music in Boston, I studied composition and began to take music much more seriously. I had studied music as a kid, but at Berklee everything started making a lot of sense—suddenly everything gelled. I was this guy sitting in the back of the class going, "Oh, now I see!" I was so fascinated that I just couldn't get enough information. They were explaining everything that was already going on in my head. It was all becoming clear and making sense. They were not only showing me where and how to find answers, they were also making music chronologically clear to me. They were basically putting two and two together for me, musically. We studied scores—how things are constructed and developed—and it all just made incredible sense to me.

What were your compositional experiences at Berklee?

We would write for whoever was in the class. They didn't have a lot of string players at Berklee, so I wrote for woodwind ensembles, piano and saxophone, brass trios, percussion, mixed quartets, all that kind of stuff. I was always writing. Even when I left Berklee, I was constantly writing and getting my scores played wherever I could. I'd go to high schools to get them performed; I'd go to amateur ensembles.

Berklee is best known for its jazz-studies programs.

Berklee was a school that wasn't very academic in the traditional sense. Musicians would come off the road and go through the Berklee system for a couple of years—stay a couple of semesters, get their chops together, learn a little more about this and that—and then go back out on the road. Berklee was constantly pushing you out onto the road. So, as soon as I had the inkling of a job, I left and went out on the road. I was on the road for four years as a saxophone player in the band Lighthouse, based in Toronto. Lighthouse was a kind of late-1960s Blood, Sweat and Tears rock/fusion band. We did eight records and four years of touring. I probably did over a thousand one-nighters by the time I was twenty-two.

Did the band limit your creative instincts?

When I would come off the road, I would get together and work with my old friends—the guys I used to do those kid shows with. A lot of them were now working for the Canadian Broadcasting Company, which was opening its doors to anybody who could create any type of interesting programming. I had already written charts for radio shows that had a band. Plus, I'd been on the road throughout the states and Canada. Our band would open for The Grateful Dead and Jefferson Airplane. I played the Fillmore when I was nineteen—I was part of that whole psychedelic era. When I came off the road, I settled in Toronto for a while, doing nature films.

Your wrote the musical scores for these films?

Yes. I composed scores for little nature films, Canada parks films—little six-minute movies about birds or beavers or nature parks. Visitors to Canada's parks would go to an orientation center before actually going into a park. There they would watch an orientation video with my music on it. I got together with friends and recorded little four- or five-piece classical chamber-ensemble scores. At the same time, I was also playing a lot of jazz—a lot of free stuff.

Like the Ornette Coleman-style free or action jazz of *Naked Lunch*?

Yeah, very free, improvised stuff. But I also kept doing television and CBC stuff whenever I could, just to help make ends meet. I also had my own little fusion band, which was an offshoot of the rock style. I wrote and played all my own material and I sang. It wasn't too successful, but it's what I was also interested in doing at the time.

How did *Saturday Night Live* come along?

From some of my CBC variety-show friends. Lorne Michaels, the producer of one of those shows, asked, "Do you want to do my new show in New York?" I said, "I don't know. I'm sort of happy here in Toronto." I had a nice existence with my musical friends and everything—I didn't really want to move, and I didn't want to live in New York. But Lorne said, "Well, why don't you come down and try it?" I thought this show would probably only last one year—

so why not? Of course, *Saturday Night Live* became tremendously successful, and I just stuck with it.

What were your responsibilities as music director for *SNL*?

Because of my experiences, I basically knew how to do everything, but I was also very Canadian and really naive. In the show's early years, I wrote all the charts—I mean everything. I didn't know that you could use arrangers, so I basically wrote and copied out everything. I was a good copyist. When I was at Berklee, I couldn't legally work in the states, because I was Canadian. So, to make ends meet, I copied theses and dissertations for student composers—guys from Boston University and the New England Conservatory. I did it for rock-bottom prices because I needed the work. It was the only way I could get a few extra bucks. But it was also a great opportunity to get to know these big orchestra scores intimately. Eventually, I went from copying to performing to orchestrating to arranging to composing. It all fit together for eventually doing a show like *SNL*.

How did you move from *SNL* to feature-film scoring?

Film scoring has a lot in common with live TV shows and live music—you have to work with pacing and timing and moving from one cue to another in a way that makes sense and keeps the story moving. I thought about film music as an outlet for my concert music—pieces that I was continually writing that had nothing to do with *SNL*. Remember when I talked about writing pieces for my Berklee classes? Well, once I got to *SNL*, I no longer had the outlet or the time to do them. So I thought of film music as a way to get my concert music performed.

Many film composers have frightening first-movie stories, but you jumped right in to work with David Cronenberg.

I knew Cronenberg because we had some mutual friends in Canada. He knew that I wanted to do movie scores. I had actually done one film score before *The Brood*, yet I always think of *The Brood* as my first score because David was so supportive. He gave me the chance and the freedom to be very creative. We started a director/composer relationship that has now gone on for nearly twenty years.

Your scores for both Cronenberg's *Scanners* and *Dead Ringers*, although they are nearly a decade apart, identify you as a composer with very strong attachments to the avant-garde, to improvisation, to action-jazz, to Penderecki and Ligeti, to soundmasses and clusters, to experimental techniques and atonality. Is the Cronenberg style of filmmaking a natural outlet for the kind of music you like to compose?

Absolutely. He's a great artist. He's always way ahead of you. He's always pushing it, and he wants you to push it as much as you can, too. As a film composer, you're lucky to find someone to work with like David Cronenberg—he's fantastic. You treasure it.

Does he constantly explore that thin line between the conscious and the unconscious?

Absolutely. What a great thing to work with! Can you imagine how great it is to work with that kind of psychological nuance? We've tried so many different things; we've done eight movies together. The first three were done very low-budget and in a very cut-and-paste method. *The Brood* was written for twenty-one strings and recorded in only seven hours. It was, "Here's the cue. Here's the rehearsal. Here's the take. Okay?" *Scanners* and *Videodrome* were more electronic—we started getting into tape recorders.

When I was doing *SNL*, I would record my movie scores during the summer. It was like *SNL* became my day job.

With *SNL*, once you had created the basic show, a group of people would sit down and say, "Okay, what's it gonna be here?

What can you do?" "I can tap dance. I can do an impression of Jesse Jackson. I can play the saxophone. I can arrange music." We ended up creating the show through discussion. It was a format, but the form was so slippery. Actually, there was no form—we *created* the form and the music and the timelines. But once it was basically done, it wasn't so interesting to keep going back into it and rewriting it. Suddenly, they would have a new actor or a new star, but it was always the same movie. It was like a movie that you had scored, but they keep calling you to ask, "Could you fly out to Baltimore to change that one scene?"

Did your work with Cronenberg come from a need to do something else?

Yeah. It was a totally different musical experience.

You know, I loved Takemitsu's music, especially all his mixing of electronics with acoustic instruments. *Scanners* was created electronically, and I played all the electronics myself on whatever instruments I had available from *SNL*. Sometimes, I would order a new electronic instrument for some guest performer or for the *SNL* band knowing that I'd be experimenting with it myself, late at night, for my own movie scores.

I'd experiment with the instruments and record hours and hours of stuff on cassette. Then I'd select certain parts and cut out the rest of it. I created loops and sequences, printed them on a 24-track machine, and then wrote orchestra parts to it.

Videodrome was the first score where I actually used a computer. I did it very academically, note by note. It was an early version of what we're doing now, and it's still the same computer, the Synclavier. I think I had one of the first ones ever made. The inventor, [Sydney] Alonso, created it as a student project at Dartmouth. It didn't occur to him that any musician would ever really use it. But once I managed to get hold of one, I started composing with it. Alonso would come down from New Hampshire to work with me. He couldn't believe that somebody was actually using the thing.

What was your aesthetic reason for choosing the Bach-style organ chorale sound for *Videodrome*?

It wasn't so much an aesthetic choice, the Synclavier just didn't have that many tone colors back then! It came with only a few set sounds, and I didn't know how to program anything into it. There was this dark, sort of cello/organ sound that I liked and did a lot with for *Videodrome*.

Serendipity. It works perfectly in the film. That organ/cello material begins as a long pedal point and increases in texture and contrapuntal complexity as the film becomes more complicated.

Yeah.

In the *Videodrome* convention scene, various styles of music occur simultaneously. These include authentic-sounding Renaissance dance music with early keyboard instruments, period percussion, lutes, crumhorns, and sackbuts. Is this original music?

It's all original. Doing *SNL*, I learned to do everything: We would do a calypso one week and a Beethoven send-up the next. It was great experience, and it wasn't that tough because of what I had done at Berklee.

Berklee is a great system. It's very realistic—it teaches you, as a musician, to be ready for anything. It prepares you for feeling totally comfortable with all kinds of musical performances—playing with the Boston Symphony or playing with an improv jazz ensemble or playing a wedding, and everything in between. You know how a Bach double fugue works, but you also know how to play "Stardust" and bar mitzvah music.

Did your heavy emphasis on strings in the early Cronenberg scores fulfill a need for experimentation with strings after so much brass, winds, and percussion writing for *SNL*?

Exactly. The whole reason for doing film music was access to great musicians, especially string players. It was a totally different creative outlet.

***The Fly* was one of the first scores that attracted me to certain contemporary film scores as a new-music alternative, much to the disappointment of my university colleagues. In American universities, film music doesn't seem to be such a good bedfellow for Schubert or Brahms.**

That's too bad, because the piano accompaniments of Schubert song cycles basically do what we do for film. But that's been going on for a long time.

In *The Fly*, the harmonization of the principal motive is atonal, but moves in parallel thirds and by root-third relationships.

In different scores, I try different techniques. In that score, I was experimenting with inverting thirds and superimposing triads over other triads—kind of a polytonality. I used films scores as opportunities for experimenting. I'd get into a tonal thing and add extra pitches until it was spooky enough.

Videodrome has an austere quality too—lots of sevenths. I experimented with sevenths for the entire score. I experiment more on David's movies because he allows me that freedom and his movies are suited to those kinds of sounds. Other movies call for more traditional approaches. In David's movies, we don't talk about the emotional thing at all. It's more an emotional canvas; it's an intuitive process.

The echo effect has become a recognizable Shoreism. It's not synthesized, it's performed orchestrally. I've heard it in all the

Cronenberg films, and I hear it in the music you're recording to-day. It's an effective dramatic device—the musical action freezes and moves simultaneously.

Right. It's not just repetition, it's like electronically processing the orchestra. My notation is very precise about this, and I work with creating spaces of varying lengths for the delays.

In *The Fly*, when the fly shows up as a graphic on Jeff Goldblum's computer screen and Goldblum has the frightening realization that he and the fly have actually fused, your music is canonic, is fusing two motives . . .

I love doing that. I love canons. I've been writing them for years and years—tonal canons, atonal canons, canons based on imitation at the tritone, seconds and ninths, you name it. And I love finding ways in which they can work in a movie. It's a great compositional technique for movies—a lot of movie scenes are canonic, a lot of dialogue is canonic. Canons can add dynamics and harmonic density to underscore a movie's character or plot development. There are a lot of canons in *The Fly* because the characters' lives are so intertwined.

Did you study specific post-Bach examples of canon and fugue, such as Stravinsky, Hindemith, Bartók, and Berg?

I love Hindemith. *Ludus Tonalis*. You have me nailed. The things that you're talking about—upper partials, imitation at dissonant intervals—I love that stuff. And I love Bartók.

So, when your Berklee professor first played a recording of Bartók's *Music for Strings, Percussion and Celesta*, your eyes opened wide?

You've got me, man. *Strings, Percussion and Celesta* was a major, major, huge thing in my life—a score that I've studied ever since.

Hindemith's *Mathis der Maler* was another huge thing, a big rev-elation. When I heard that at eighteen or nineteen, it was like, "Oh, man! No way!"

Many composers cite Stravinsky's *Sacre du printemps* as a major early influence.

The Rite of Spring scared the shit out of me. It was so brilliant. It was like looking at something that you could maybe never hope to get to in your life. It was this pinnacle. You thought [Laughing], Oh, my God! Well, we'll just put that up there on that pedestal.

Years later, when I came across a double-piano reduction of *The Rite of Spring*, I looked at it and thought, Oh, wow, look at these notes! Geez! Forget about the incredible orchestrations, look at these notes! It taught me a lot about different note relationships, and that's how I work. And I thought, this will help me get along really well with Ornette, because he thinks of music the same way. Seeing the condensed, two-piano version of *The Rite of Spring* brought it all into reality for me.

I enjoyed your *She-Devil* score—it's energetic, kind of nasty, and tongue-in-cheek.

I like it, too. It was a lot of fun, but it was really a bastard to write. It's a huge score. It was in 2—so it's like two scores. When you're writing that much music, and you're writing under a deadline, you have to be conscious of how many measures and how much music you're creating from the completely practical standpoint of the re-cording.

She-Devil, because of the kind of music it was, really wasn't in 4. You couldn't write it in 4 because everything was going, "ba-dum, ba-dum, ba-dum, ba-dum." It was the first big score I'd written in 2. When I was about halfway through it, I realized, "Oh, shit, it's in 2—I have to write two scores here." It became monumental—a massive score, this huge amount of paper everywhere.

The opening sequence of *She-Devil* is fantastic. It begins with an innocuous, Rock Hudson/Doris Day style of music that gradually descends into evil she-devil music, which dissolves into a funky Latin groove, and finally ends up at the hairdresser's salon. But it's all the same tune, morphing through various styles. A classic film-music technique—the versatility of a tune—and it's done so well.

Thanks. That's cool that you realize that, because the tune *is* the same, but it changes so much for each style.

"Strangers in the Night" runs throughout the picture, often in a slightly formal but also harmonically rich string-quartet arrangement.

I love to use thick harmonies. I think that an audience usually doesn't differentiate between source music and original music—they just went to see the movie, and there's music, you know? I like to integrate source music into the score. It's there anyway, before I get on it, so why not make it a part of the score? I try to do that whenever I can, especially in subtle ways, because I think it just makes a better movie—it's all integrated.

I think that one of the reasons that *Philadelphia* was successful was because I had the Springsteen song at the beginning and the Neil Young song at the end, and I had to write everything in between. I tried to honor their songs, in a way, if only by similar tonalities or fragments of melody.

In *She-Devil*, when Ed Begley Jr. first leaves his house, there's no dialogue, but there is nonstop action music for six minutes. It's a wild ride, an orchestral tone poem.

I love that scene. I think there's some really cool stuff in there.

Another Shoreism that I detected in *She-Devil*, and which I've heard in your scores many times since, is parallel mode shifts. For

example, F major shifting to F minor with no preparation or harmonic pivot. Similar to the effect of your orchestral echoes, it keeps things the same, but moves them at the same time.

Think of it as anticipation. It's great for moving a picture forward while keeping the juggling balls in the air. You're not sure where the tonality's going and you're not sure where the movie's going. *Ed Wood* has quite a bit of that, too.

Compared with your large-tapestry Cronenberg scores, *She-Devil* is packed with classic mickey-mousing cues. As vixen Meryl Streep begins to go down on the adulterous Ed Begley Jr., the picture instantly cuts to frustrated wife Roseanne hacking a huge cucumber with a butcher knife. On cue, your musical chord is both blood-curdling and hilarious.

[Laughter] Right. Well, you write them the way you see them. A lot of it's in how the movie's been edited. In *Looking for Richard*, the Shakespeare movie with Pacino, there are a million edits because it was filmed over three years. The music doesn't try to follow the action that carefully—it's complex, but it can't keep up with the edits. *She-Devil* was just the kind of movie that wanted traditional scoring. *Ed Wood* has some of that, but it's not scored so tightly to the picture, it's more mood setting or commenting on the relationship of Eddie and Bela or Eddie and the actors. If Danny [Elfman] had done the movie, his score probably would have been much more synchronized to the action. That's his style. I was trying to focus more on the period of the film and the relationships.

***A Kiss Before Dying* has a few hotel-room scenes where the television is on during the action. In one, the girl is murdered by an intruder as she is watching *Abbott and Costello Meet Frankenstein*. The total musical wash is Howard Shore plus Frank Skinner plus sound effects. Did you have the TV scene information when you were writing, and, if so, how did you blend your score with Skinner?**

I just love to work with that kind of thing. There's a scene in *Big* where they're dancing to some kind of Glenn Miller tune. I re-recorded it and blended it right into my score. I do that in a lot of my movies. *Prelude to a Kiss* does that. I match the keys so they blend or just keep the source playing and layer my music over the top and have them bleed together.

Yesterday, you spoke about perhaps backing away from film to pursue other musical projects.

I won't stop doing movies, but I will probably be more selective so that I can have the time to write other music. I feel like I've pretty much accomplished what I set out to do with movie scores. I feel like it's time to move on to another or an additional phase of music and composition. The medium most available, even thought it's not necessarily the best, is recordings. That's basically our top medium for hearing music. When people think of music, they think of records. I make soundtrack records all the time, but I'm not making real records—soundtracks are just representations of movie scores, music for a particular movie and not necessarily complete musical developments in themselves. When I'm doing movie scores, I'm not thinking about what's going to make a good record—just doing the movie is a massive enough job. But, by making solo records, I can concentrate on just the music, and how it will work on a record.

The *Naked Lunch* CD sounds more like a jazz recording than a movie soundtrack.

The *Naked Lunch* CD is, I think, personally, one of the best of my soundtracks as just a record to listen to. It's not just the cues assembled in chronological order—the decisions on order were based more on how the whole record flowed. But then I think I could just do a record; I don't need a movie.

You can get your own little slot at Tower Records. But would it be in the jazz or the classical section?

[Laughter] Well, I don't know. I try to ignore all those distinctions in music. I'm not so interested in that—it's all just marketing. There are too many different slots, and the executives often don't have a clue about who fits where. When I was growing up, record stores had jazz and rock and classical, that was it. Now, there's something like fifteen delineations of each one of those groups. Everyone's trying to be so precise about where they fit in—acoustic jazz and fusion jazz and acid jazz and classical jazz and jazz rock and this kind of rock and that kind of rock and alternate rock and rap and hip-hop and alternative rap . . . I don't understand it. It's all corporate marketing.

The distinction between film music and concert music, or whatever you want to call it these days, is such a stale separation, but it has been going on for over fifty years. It's interesting how some people try to cross over, back and forth, film into contemporary concert music or vice versa. How does it work when Elliot Goldenthal does *Batman* and also does his big Vietnam oratorio? Can people's brains really adjust to these two together? The oratorio is a very good piece, but there's some *Batman* in it, which is okay—it's not wrong, it's just very interesting. Hollywood film music came from the European concert world—Korngold, Rózsa.

There's a lot of money to be made in film music. There's also now a lot of contemporary musicians—pop artists and that kind of thing—wanting to do film scores, probably for the same reason: It'll pay for them to go do their other stuff.

But isn't good film scoring based on a composer's dramatic instinct and theatrical flair, beyond the respectable compositional craft? Some great concert composers could never work well in film, and some great film composers could never succeed as concert composers.

Exactly. It's not a language that you can learn, it has to be almost second nature, an instinct. That's why crossover guys like Goldenthal are so interesting. He's very successful in both worlds. Some classical composers probably would have been terrific for film—Strauss, Wagner, some of the great opera composers, Puccini and Verdi—they understood the dramatic line.

Did you know Ornette Coleman before working with him on *Naked Lunch*?

Well, I wasn't close to him, but I knew a lot about his music from the 1960s, which is incredible stuff. When I did *SNL*, I was allowed to book the musical act once every month or so. So, I put Ornette on network television! He did *SNL*, and people loved it. He liked the *SNL* band and wanted to actually produce us. I was young, I didn't really understand what it all meant or how it was all going to work, so I never really followed through on it. I had looked up to him so much as a kid, and in those *SNL* days, I couldn't imagine that he really wanted to produce us. But as I got older, he seemed less daunting.

When *Naked Lunch* came up, I kept on thinking jazz and Moroccan music and I remembered an Ornette recording, "Midnight Sunrise," from his *Dancing in Your Head* album that I heard in 1975. It's a fantastic album. I played it for David [Cronenberg] and he said, "That's great! It's like the Kurd national anthem." Ornette was just jamming with all these Moroccan guys, and that was the track we used, newly recorded by Robert Palmer. Researching the period, I sampled and looped the Moroccan ethnic stuff with improvised, harmonic, slow Spanish tango music. That was my *Naked Lunch* vibe—a very slow accompaniment with Charlie Parker playing very fast on top.

Was Charlie Parker a big influence on Ornette Coleman?

Parker was what got Ornette interested in jazz. As a kid, growing up in Texas, Parker was who he heard. When Ornette's mother got him a saxophone at a pawn shop, he tried to play like Parker. For *Naked Lunch*, I played him all the Parker stuff I wanted, and Ornette said, "I know all this stuff perfectly," and he did. All those heads, all those solos—he knew them all. He played the whole thing perfectly.

I asked how he felt about recording some of this stuff for the movie. He thought about it for a few days and said, "You know, this stuff is so great . . . I don't know." I said, "I do, man, and it's even going to be better." I'd written some bebop-like pieces to go with the Parker stuff, and that's what we recorded. That's what's on the *Naked Lunch* record—Ornette and a trio playing Parker/Shore bebop tunes, but playing *as* Ornette.

Did you write any improvisational charts for him?

One piece was all samples of different instruments that I had recorded on location—Indian instruments and other ethnic instruments. I overdubbed on the original tracks and used that underneath. Besides the jazz materials and a little bit of electronics, the rest of the score was orchestral, performed by the London Philharmonic. And it included some improvisation. Ornette studied the orchestral score and made a lot of weird charts of his own design—little drawings and astrological figures—and then he came in and improvised with the orchestra. I tried to edit it, but it never really worked. I just decided to go with it.

Did the Howard Shore/Ornette Coleman collaboration continue after *Naked Lunch*?

We're good friends now. I talk to him all the time. We want to do some concerts together—maybe Paris, maybe New York. We'd like to do some *Naked Lunch* concerts with orchestra and Ornette and his group.

Thelonious Monk's "Misterioso" is in the score, but the arrangement includes unusual bass harmonies.

That's actually Ornette's version of "Misterioso." The contract piano player came to the studio to play the piece, and Ornette had him play all those fifths in the bass as flat fives. He was an English piano player, one of their top jazz guys, and he knew the tune. But when he played it the original way, Ornette listened to it and then came to me and whispered, "God, it sounds like 'Tea for Two'!" but it was exactly "Misterioso." So, Ornette just changed all the fifths to flat fives, and the piano player went nuts. The guy did it, but he was so reluctant, so offended. I added another track—a processed vibraphone—and that made it even more bizarre. There are other great stories about that movie, like working with Ornette's son, Denardo.

As I said earlier, I wrote some really slow pieces for the orchestra, but I wanted that really fast bebop stuff on top. When Ornette first heard the slow orchestral score, he thought he would be playing slow too—"Oh, I see, it's kind of a blues, and real slow, so I'll play slow along with it." But jazz musicians don't play with an orchestra, right? They play with a rhythm section—they play with a beat; they need a drummer, right? So I put Denardo in a soundproof booth in the studio and had him play double-time, triple-time, completely crazy. The orchestra's going real slow, "*bum*-da-di-da-di-da-di-da . . ." and Denardo's on top going "dibidibidibidibidibidibdibi"—just wailing away all over the drum set. So, I fed *just* Denardo to Ornette, through his headphones, and he took off on Denardo's "dibidibidibidibidibidibidibi." Meanwhile, the orchestra's plodding along "*bum*-da-di-da-di-da-di-da . . ."

Were you a fan of other free-form or experimental, avant-garde, "action jazz" musicians?

Yeah. I love that stuff.

There's a terrific recording from 1971—Don Cherry and The New Eternal Rhythm Orchestra, conducted by Krzysztof Penderecki.

The disc includes two pieces: Cherry's *Humus* and Penderecki's *Actions for Free Jazz Orchestra*, a piece where fixed notation disintegrates into improvisations.

It sounds great. Penderecki and action jazz have a lot in common. I love Penderecki. I've studied a lot of his scores. That's the kind of stuff I was always interested in. I was also always interested in Takemitsu, who just died. I finally met him when they gave him a Lifetime Achievement Award at the Society for the Preservation of Film Music dinner. They knew that I liked Takemitsu. I had given a seminar for film music students, and I urged the students to be interested in all kinds of film music—not just American film music, but also Japanese, French, Italian. Global differences and international sensibilities are so interesting. It's interesting to see how Morricone scores a scene. It's so unique. You can learn a lot by looking at other types of cinema. Americans, generally, are pretty much closed in—they don't really see enough of what's outside. I'm Canadian, so I'm a little more detached from American traditions and expectations. I live in New York, but I'm extremely interested in world cinema.

I do see a strong stylistic and/or aesthetic connection between your Cronenberg scores and such Takemitsu scores as *Ran* and *Black Rain*.

It's just great stuff. They're not just mickey-mouse shoot-'em-up scores, even though there are a million samurai warriors running around, ravaging the countryside!

Guilty As Sin. Sidney Lumet hires so many different types of composers—they seem to be hand-picked for each project.

I'm not sure why, but he just called me up and asked me to do the movie. I said, "Yes, of course." I was so flattered to have the opportunity to work with him. A year later, I said [Laughing], "Wait

a minute! I did a Don Johnson movie? What the hell am I doing ?"
And then my wife said, "But, Howard, it's Sidney Lumet!" And I
said, "but they're gonna remember Don Johnson!"

Not quite *12 Angry Men, Dog Day Afternoon,* or *Fail-Safe.*

But, at first, I was pretty full of myself—I was telling Cronenberg
[in a faux-superiority tone] "Hey, I'm doing a Sidney Lumet film."
And he was really excited. Then the clouds wore on and I suddenly
ended up with just a Don Johnson movie.

**After Don Johnson torches Moe's office and throws Rebecca off
the balcony, your music is *not* the typical, expected, action style,
it's a soundmass of chimes, glockenspiels, bells, and other ringing
things.**

[Laughter] I love doing that stuff. Fear in movies is a great musical
inspiration. And personal fear is another great inspiration: "Will it
get done?" "Will it be good?" "Will the producers like it?" This
kind of fear is crippling for some composers. It's inspirational for
me. People who don't write music don't really understand anything
about what we do. But, for people who do what we do, there's this
inherent universal nervousness in the beginning: "Where do I start?"
"What's the first theme?" "What key?" For me, a lot of film music
is intuitive, but for the other parts, to break though the fear, I analyze my own music. Once you start to analyze, you're feeding into
the fear and breaking it down. Once you've conquered your fears,
you like the music better—you enjoy it, you're friendlier with it,
you're on much better terms with the material.

Did you experience a similar fear breakthrough with *Ransom*?

Not as much. After ten or fifteen years of doing this, you become a
better musician. You learn more practical applications but still try
to maintain that musical personality that keeps you attracted to the

composition. When I did *The Fly*, I was a nervous wreck—I was consumed with fear and apprehension; I couldn't make any decisions at first; I couldn't decide what clothes to put on in the morning. But after doing a lot of movies, you learn tricks. Well, they're not really tricks, because each movie is so different, but you develop an approach, a technique. You learn how to take the most advantage of your days, because you don't have that many days to finish the score. But back to the chimes and bells in *Guilty As Sin*: I'm more fearless now, so I try things like that, things that are more unexpected, more unpredictable.

You're less apprehensive about trying unusual sounds and effects now?

Yeah. With a lot of my early movie scores, I had the ideas, but I didn't do them because of fear. And now I wished I had. It was always, "Howard, use caution! Be careful about all those cool things you're thinking about! Is it really D♯ against the E? No, better not do that. Better just go with two Es. It's safe. Yep, it's definitely better with two Es."

Now I'm much more conscious of the process. When I look back at my older scores, like *The Fly*, I think, "God, I wish I had done that." Now, I do it.

As you get older, you tend to throw caution to the wind and try more stuff. You're excited about what you can accomplish with new sounds. You're more willing to go with your intuition, plus you've matured compositionally, so you know how to handle those things with more success.

Some composers, such as Prokofiev and James Horner, seem to *begin* their careers by throwing caution to the wind—only to become more relaxed and conservative as they get older. Maybe this stems from an "ignorance is bliss" stance, maybe from youthful rebellion.

With me, it's been the opposite direction. But it depends on the movie. I do bizarre comedies, jazz scores, more experimental movies. I try to avoid movies that would lock me into a very conventional or conservative approach.

Do you turn down many movie offers?

All the time. I turn down many more movies than I accept.

Are these primarily artistic/aesthetic rejections or timing/scheduling problems?

All those things. You can only do so much, and you want to be your best on each movie. Some people churn 'em out and do three or four movies in the time I might take to do one or two, but they often have a team of people working on a score. If you look at the number of movies being made in Hollywood, compared to the number of composers who are scoring them, not that many guys are doing them—it's the same guys over and over again.

Were the opera excerpts in *Philadelphia* your choices or the director's?

The writer, Ron Nyswaner, was a big opera fan. Jonathan Demme wasn't so familiar or knowledgeable about opera. He went with Ron on that one.

Did you work your score around those excerpts?

Not this time. I thought they were so strong, so dramatically rich, that I left them alone as set pieces. I love opera. I love that style of music, and a lot of times my music tends to sound that way. I go to the opera regularly. I've had a box seat at the Met for almost ten years. I see seven or eight operas a year. I love the stories; I love seeing how the music works with the libretto. I love watching the conductors. I think opera *is* film music.

In relation to what I do in film music, there are so many comparisons to opera. If you noticed, in the *Ransom* recording sessions, I have my orchestra set up like an opera orchestra. I think of film music as the pit orchestra, I usually visualize the music in a movie as coming up from the pit.

Which of your other scores use that compositional approach?

I wrote *The Fly* as an opera. I thought of it that way. In *M. Butterfly*, I combined and blended together Italian and Chinese opera with my own score, which uses dramatic and operatic elements of its own. I'm so interested in how the music relates to the drama—that's what I listen for.

If the Met or City Opera or Houston Grand Opera or any legit opera company came to you with a commission proposal . . . ?

I've thought about it a lot, but I'm not sure that I'd be comfortable with such a large form, frankly.

Is that perhaps a fear of the massive proportions of traditional grand opera or music drama—Wagner, Verdi, Mozart? But opera has gone in so many unusual, eclectic directions with Philip Glass, John Adams' *Nixon in China*, Michael Daugherty's *Jackie O* . . .

I know. The closest I've been is the *Looking for Richard* score—a fifty-piece orchestra, a twenty-eight-voice choir, and a lot of dramatic implications in the music. I wrote it like an opera. I used a Latin text, an original text that was created for the movie. If I had a big libretto? I don't know. I love using voices and music, but I'm not sure that I have the "big picture" sensibilities you need to work in long, three-hour stretches of time. The music, the characters, the plot—it's a little scary. I don't know. I do know that I *would* like to write a concert piece for orchestra and chorus, and make a recording of it. That would be interesting.

Do you do your own orchestrations?

In the early scores, I wrote everything, I orchestrated everything. Around 1986, I had a guy helping with some orchestrations, but I've gone back to doing everything myself: *Philadelphia*, *Mrs. Doubtfire*, *The Fly*, *Nobody's Fool*. I just felt that I needed and wanted more control over my own scores, over the entire process, to get exactly what I wanted, to get the right sounds.

The *Ed Wood* orchestra was created specifically for the sound I wanted—not too big. Those 1950s horror movies always used little thirty-piece studio orchestras with a few strings, six or seven trumpets, and a few woodwinds, percussion—and a Novachord! I tried to get a Novachord, but I couldn't find one. They had one in a museum in The Hague, but that was about it. So I used a bunch of vintage 1950s organs that I found in London. I found Lydia [Kavina], in Moscow, to play the theremin. When we were getting ready to record the score in England, they asked if there was anything special that I needed. I said, "Yeah, there's this player in Moscow." And they were very tenacious about getting her. They had to get her a visa, make all these arrangements, and even then, it was still hard to get someone out of Russia to record in England.

Wasn't there an American or British player who could have handled the theremin part?

Nobody I knew, nobody who could actually read and play with an orchestra. Lydia plays it like a real instrument, she's really a theremin soloist. She's not just messing around with the weird sounds the way a lot of people do. By the way, when she plays, the sounds are beautiful, they're not weird anymore.

Her playing contributed to the bittersweet tone of the film.

Absolutely. It wasn't just mimicking the 1950s sound. It wasn't corny. It became part of the sadness.

Do you know of the film *Theremin*?

Absolutely, that's how I found Lydia. I knew Steven Martin, the creator of *Theremin*. I met him through Hal Willner, a record producer who does Altman's pictures, like *Kansas City*. Steve and I had many conversations, including where I could get a good theremin player. He put me in touch with Lydia and helped me with the process. At maybe thirty years old, she's now probably the top theremin player in the world. I think she's Léon Theremin's great niece, and studied with "papa" for ten years.

Unfortunately, we usually only think of the theremin in a nostalgic sense—a sound associated with the Golden Age of low-budget, 1950s sci-fi/horror movies.

Right, but it's a fantastic instrument. There's so much more you can do with it besides [he sings] "woooooOOOOoooo." When it's played by a real musician, not a technician, but a musician with strong musical instincts who really knows the instrument, it's an amazing sound. Most guys have to punch in every note, or they miscalculate its range.

White Man's Burden **makes use of many source cues—pop songs— but not much original score. Were you compositionally frustrated, or was it *your* decision to keep the score thin?**

Well, I was not real happy about that picture. I didn't have much control. It was an interesting project, but it just fell out of my control.

Many ultra-violent scenes in *White Man's Burden* are accompanied by soft, slow, painful music. Does this show your Takemitsu influence, composing against the action?

Yeah. I use an electric string quartet, an amplified string quartet. It's processed a little bit.

Like George Crumb's *Black Angels*?

Yeah. Great stuff. I used a lot of electronically processed, small instrumental groups on that movie—string quartet, percussion. There was no orchestral score, it's all processed.

Processed marimba or steel drums for the little boy?

[Laughter] Yeah, I remember that! This little, innocent calypso thing. But, you know, the whole project just had this cloud over it for me. I didn't ever feel like I had enough input.

The recording sessions for *Ransom* seem quite the opposite. There seems to be a very strong and agreeable camaraderie among you, Ron Howard, the editor, and the producer.

Yeah! This is the way you would like to make movies, everything feels smooth. And the director is experienced, decisive.

Ron Howard seems very flexible about the music—he'll offer intelligent opinions, but he's still quite agreeable to considering your interpretation and asking for your advice.

Yeah, we actually discuss things. He sees what you're doing, and he likes it, but then he might want to give you his ideas too. He wants both things—he likes the traditional and he enjoys the more experimental approaches, too. A lot of the *Ransom* score pays attention to the genre and the kinds of things you'd expect, but I'm also trying to keep it edgy and contemporary—paying respect to the genre, but not locked into predictability or cliché. On *Seven*, the director didn't want me to pay any attention to the drama, he was just interested in sounds. Occasionally, I would slip something in, like a little mickey-mousing or an operatic thing or a little genre referencing, and he would go, "Oh, really? Well, okay." But he didn't want me to do too much of that. Ron Howard wants more of a balance, more respect for the drama of the picture. That's just the kind of director he is.

Ransom seems like a very comfortable situation for all of you—I sense a lot of sincerity and honesty floating around the studio.

Yeah, exactly. It's totally cool. We're all working for the same goal, and nobody's trying to rush anything, or be "king" of the studio.

• • •

[Author's note: Less than two weeks after this interview (which took place during the final recording sessions of Shore's extensive *Ransom* score), director Ron Howard rejected Shore's original music and replaced it with a quickly scribed James Horner score. I contacted Howard Shore by phone a week later and sympathetically asked a few questions regarding the *Ransom* situation.]

What happened? It was a great score and Ron Howard seemed to be so happy with it.

Well, these things happen—all the time. It's frustrating because you spend so much time and so much energy. I aged about ten years in those two weeks!

Will sections of the score transfer to some future movie or composition project?

Probably not a movie, it's too specific to *Ransom*. A lot of guys do that, but I can't. I'd like to make a record, maybe. I like the score and, I think, with some revisions and some rewriting, it could make an interesting record. But I'm not really in the mood to think about that yet.

Were you told why this happened?

Not really. All I can figure out is that he came into the picture wearing a black leather jacket and left wearing a white sport coat. I think he got nervous—the music was probably too contemporary or too experimental in the long run.

• • •

The Client contains fragments of classic Southern gospel music. Did you study that music for the picture, or had you already had enough experience with gospel and blues?

The blues, yeah. I love that music—the early blues. I love The Band, the Allman Brothers. It's easy for me to do. I grew up with that stuff in the sixties.

How about the Hammond B-3 gospel/blues/jazz organists—such as Jimmy Smith and Shirley Scott?

Absolutely. I love that Hammond organ sound. I've found ways to use it in a lot of my scores, not to mention *SNL*.

Silence of the Lambs is a powerful, important score that moved you onto the "A" list.

Silence of the Lambs came out of my Cronenberg collaborations—*The Fly, Dead Ringers, The Brood, Naked Lunch*. I was developing more orchestral technique from working with those pictures, and I was becoming more connected to what was happening on the screen. For me, *Dead Ringers* was a breakthrough for working around the dialogue in a very intimate way. I applied the Cronenberg techniques to *Silence*, which is more like an opera. It's not really scored like a horror movie or a thriller—the music is operatic, dark, but very beautiful. Like *Dead Ringers*, it's actually not a very dissonant score, it's more of a dread tonality.

What harmonic structures did you use to create tonal dread? We usually think of major/minor tonality as safe and optimistic and atonality as more suspenseful and aggressive.

Working in fourths, fifths, a lot of ninths and sevenths, a lot of seconds—but not necessarily in a functional way, more in a way of overlapping and playing them against each other—as opposed to triads. It's unsteady—the tonality is insecure, but I'm not creating a great deal of dissonance. Many intimate scenes between Jodie Foster and Anthony Hopkins are scored dark. It's operatic. It's dramatic. But I'm not trying to push any buttons in that movie.

You mean emotional buttons?

Yeah, never. Never trying to say, "This is going to be really scary, folks."

To clarify, when you speak of "operatic," you're not referring to Pavarotti or sopranos with iron breastplates and horned helmets!

Right. It's more of an aesthetic feeling—it's operatic music *as* film music, like music from Richard Strauss' *Rosenkavalier*, in the context of film. Even in Puccini's *Tosca*, there are instrumental pieces, like at the beginning of the last act, that are so emotionally devastating and yet so incredibly beautiful. They're not dissonant pieces—they're not using so-called contemporary techniques, they were written at the turn of the century—but they've got such feelings of dread and decay, like the dungeon scene. It's not thriller music, it's about feelings.

Your dark music comes from the darkness inside the characters—from their deep, dark, inner emotions—not from the overt dramatic suspense of who's going to kill who next?

Exactly. I think that Sidney Lumet paid me the biggest compliment about *Silence of the Lambs*. In his book, *Making Movies*, he said that he considered it a great score because he felt it, he didn't hear it. There's probably about an hour of music in the movie, but I doubt anybody would actually realize that. Maybe the purest form of film music is music that supports the film, but also works on all the sub-jects—not just commenting on what you're seeing on the screen, but operating on another level that you or they are feeling emo-tionally. That, again, is opera. Why do we *feel* the way we do when we hear the last act of *Tosca*? It's a kind of conditioning that we've all passed through over the last 500 years.

As Wagner said, "My music speaks the unspeakable."

Exactly.

Do you create private, personal subplots as you score—subplots that don't exist in the screenplay or the director's vision?

Absolutely. For me, that's the goal. That's why I especially like psy-chological movies, like *Silence* and *Seven*, movies of the psychological dark side, the unconscious demons. Of the two, *Silence of the Lambs* is the more interesting mind-game—it's simply the story of two people trying to outwit each other, but it's not simple at all. *Seven* is more the FBI just searching for a serial killer—it's more about victims and police action. *Silence* is more about women being vic-timized and male vs. female power struggles. There's a lot of subtext in a story like that. It's fantastic to write music to these psychologi-cal problems.

Your constant references to opera make great sense. You've got multiple characters, interactions, secrets, dreams, leitmotifs, and musical materials that are a counterpoint to the characters.

Yeah [Laughter], or you could hear that cue and say, "What the hell does that have to do with that scene?" And taken on its own, it might not have anything to do with that scene. But seen in the context of the film, it could be completely chilling. There's a scene at the end of *Silence* when the killer comes up from the basement and Jodie's in his cluttered kitchen and a little moth flutters down, out of this ray of light, and lands on a spool of thread. It's at that moment that she realizes that she's now in the lion's den—this is *the* guy. There are many ways to score a scene like that—the casual to the frantic realization—escalating to the intense emotional-awareness climax of the moth and what it signifies. If you listened to the music for that scene out of context or without the movie, it probably wouldn't make much sense. But watch the scene: The music doesn't relate carefully to the action, but it creates tension and emotion—it's the third element in the room—it drives you into the basement.

How do you make musical decisions about such an important dramatic moment?

I watch it, then I know it. I don't need to look at it a lot. Many times I almost dream or imagine the music. I can close my eyes and imagine what should be there. It's a very intuitive and almost subconscious process. The rest of the process is getting it down on paper and working out the timings and all that stuff.

When you close your eyes and "hear" music, do you usually go with your first instincts?

Many times. Then, later, I open my eyes and analyze and figure it out. But that process comes much later. It's not a matter of just closing my eyes and quickly reopening them, it's keeping them closed for a long time and really working things out in my mind and then opening my eyes. I've come to really trust my instincts and intuition. In some of my earlier scores, and I think we talked about this in a different context earlier, I rejected my original instincts in favor of a more traditional method or safe approach, only to look back later and wish I had gone with my gut feelings.

You still have to make the practical application of the dream music.

Yeah, but you can do that later. Then it's like, "Now, let's see, he's going to jump into the pool and drown, so I'll need to stretch this idea a little here because it's taking him a little longer." But when I'm writing, I'm never thinking about "he's going to jump into the pool," I'm thinking it's a four-minute piece that needs to embrace the emotions and inner feelings of the character. Sometimes, depending on the film, I don't take that eyes-open step and synchronize or structure it into the film, I just go with the musical atmosphere. Some directors say they like that approach, but some directors say, "Maybe you'd better make sure he jumps into the pool there." Directors like David [Cronenberg] won't even bring it up. Cronenberg's so much into the peripheral. As long as you're getting the right feeling, he's fine.

It must be difficult to change and adjust to different directors' expectations.

Not really. There are so many ways to use music in a film. The expectation of it is really all based on our own assumptions—how we, as people, go to see movies. We think, "But shouldn't the music go like that?" And I say, "Yeah, it could go like that, but it doesn't have to go like that. We've seen *that* so many times before, wouldn't it be cool if it went like *this* this time?" Sometimes the directors say, "That's cool," and other times they say, "No, I don't want it like that." It just depends on what a director's expectations are, how good he is at making movies, and how imaginative or experimental he is.

Although we don't witness it too often, film music does have the capability of being very sophisticated and intelligent.

Absolutely. The great directors use film music in very sophisticated ways. It's fascinating. I'm always interested in *how* the director wants to use film music, like all those classic Hitchcock/Herrmann stories. That's why I'm so interested in Takemitsu and other cultures—

how *they* use music is often quite unusual by Hollywood standards. Takemitsu will use tribal logs and wooden sticks, all percussion—no tonality, certainly no big tune—for a complete movie.

In that culture, such scores feel as natural and expected as a soaring, heroic military theme feels for us in a patriotic American picture.

Exactly, and they can watch it and feel that it's perfect. We watch it and feel that it's great art, because we don't really get it. Somehow, I don't think Kurosawa watches too many Hollywood movies and reacts with, "Wow, that's great art!"

When I use quotations and musical references, I sometimes wonder if the subtle humor is worth it when only seven people in an audience of 2,000 get it. How about you?

It's okay with me, but I don't do it that much. I actually consciously try not to do it. I don't want things to stand out from the score. But it depends on the movie. In comedies, it's different. We haven't talked about my comedies—that's a whole other life for me in film music, aside from *Silence of the Lambs* and *Dead Ringers* and the Cronenberg madness.

I appreciate the emotional quality of your scores for such films as *Mrs. Doubtfire* and *Nobody's Fool,* but I'm personally very attracted to your dramatic scores for their uniqueness and experimental temperament. *Ed Wood* has a strong element of comedy. At first, I was disappointed with the bongo-heavy dance music for the opening credits. I had expected 1950s sci-fi/horror music à la Bert I. Gordon productions. Later, I realized that the bongo music provided the perfect homebase security with which to contrast your variety of musical choices for moments of humor, tragedy, nostalgia, and poignancy.

That was the idea. Beatnik dance music—a conga player and a bongo player. At the time I recorded the score, there were no studios available in Los Angeles. I wanted to record at the Fox studios because they had this huge pipe organ, but the organ had been damaged in the earthquake and the studio was closed. We ended up going to England—I recorded the score with the London Philharmonic—and it was very fortunate that we did. The British percussionists were so square, but it was the perfect sound! The bongo player was English! He was a good player and a good musician, just a little square, a little straight. In Los Angeles, they probably would have been too hip. As soon as I heard this English guy, I thought, oh, we're so lucky to have this guy play this bongo track.

Did you consider using the classic, 1950s sci-fi, Albert Glasser small-orchestra sound?

I pay a little homage to that—the very opening is like that, as is the scene where they all go to steal the octopus. Big chains of ascending diminished chords, big minor chords with added tones. But I didn't do a lot of it, I didn't want to take the obvious route. I struggled with the opening—the animation and the credits. My first instinct was to do the 1950s Glasser things, but then I quickly realized that a bizarre zombie dance would work much better. And I could always return to that music, from any scene. I went for the rhythmic, jazz-zombie approach because the other approach would have ended up being a parody of a parody, plus the opening sequence is so long that it would have been a little boring. The opening credits for *Ed Wood* are much longer than the typical two- or three-minute 1950s movie openings, which got to it much faster. Also, the *Ed Wood* opening doesn't move in a way that would have allowed the sci-fi stuff to be very interesting—it moves very smoothly, slowly, and fluidly. The old movies were much more frantic in their beginnings.

Your choice of zombie bongo dance music might be taken as a direct reference to such Ed Wood movies as *Orgy of the Dead*.

Yeah, that's all zombie stripper music, with bongos. [Laughter]

The Lugosi music is fantastic. It operates on many levels, but primarily focuses on the inner torment of this dejected, drug-addicted has-been. Martin Landau is terrific as Lugosi, but it's also from your heartbreaking score that we become so deeply emotionally involved. And your miniature references to Tchaikovsky's *Swan Lake*—the music in the original Lugosi *Dracula* films—doesn't make me laugh, it makes me cry.

Thanks. That's what it was meant to do. It's the dying-swan idea, and it pays off at his funeral. I knew that he had to be a tragic character—there was no camp aspect to him at all, it was pure tragedy. I'd always loved the Ed Wood pictures, but I wanted to embrace a lot of different emotions.

I felt comfortable doing *Ed Wood*. I was ready and I had the training—*Naked Lunch* and *Dead Ringers* dealt with drug addiction, *Naked Lunch* was also 1950s jazz. *The Fly* was a remake of a 1950s sci-fi classic. And I also loved all those Henry Mancini scores, both his early Universal horror stuff and his jazz scores.

I didn't expect to be so dramatically sucked into *Ed Wood*. I thought I would be simply an observer. A very unexpected, tender moment occurs as Ed walks through the carnival with his new girlfriend, talking about his past, and we don't hear any carnival music—the music is gently romantic, bittersweet, chromatic.

But very fifties. Just like when he tells her he likes to wear women's clothes and the music stops when she says it's okay, then it starts up again. It's also a very fifties type of theme. It's nostalgic. I wanted to make it nostalgic for him and for us looking at him.

Ed Wood also has some very effective mickey-mousing moments—when they steal the octopus, when Ed meets Orson Welles and is inspired to "hang in there."

Sometimes you just have to do that. But I was very careful not to abuse the technique. I tried to keep the movie on other emotional levels and not just play the straight comedy or be cartoonish.

The music during their shooting of *Plan 9 from Outer Space* sounds like a documentary, the accompaniment to a 1950s Movietone newsreel. We're watching them make the movie!

That was the idea. [Laughter] You got it. All that proud, marching-on Americana.

The end credits brought tears to my eyes. It was charming and pathetic at the same time. Tchaikovsky couldn't have done it any better.

Exactly. You got it all. Ascending chromaticism, winding upward. You feel sorry for them.

For a musical cue of such complicated chromatic development, do you figure it all out on paper, do you write it at the keyboard?

I can hear most of it—you know, that eyes-closed business—but something like that I have to work out on paper. There's a lot of contrary motion and parallelism in that cue. I hear the basic lines, then I just check it all on paper or at the piano to make sure the harmonic movement is right. I'm not afraid of passing tones, I let a lot of intentional dissonances go by that most people never really notice. But I work with these big orchestras all the time and they're always checking on things like, "Are you sure this is supposed to be an F♯ here?" And I'm like, "Yeah!" That's a stubborn streak in me. I'll do unresolved cadences or I'll have some parts of the orchestra resolve and others not, so they're always questioning me. I'm stubborn in that I don't give in to things doing what they're "supposed" to be doing. It's almost become a subconscious thing now, it's all part of my style. *Dead Ringers* has a lot of stuff like that. You take this beautiful thing, and it's resolving nicely, but it never gets there—it resolves into this giant *cluster*! You just never get the resolution, and you're just going insane!

The intense chromatic extremes of your scores prompt me to ask, are you a Wagner and Mahler fan?

Yes. It's terrific stuff. It's so emotional.

The final scene of *Ed Wood* is not unlike the mood of "Liebestod" from Wagner's *Tristan und Isolde* in its tense chromatic winding, unexpected arrival points, and unresolved cadences.

Sometimes I'll play with the material that way. I'll write the lines, then I'll overlap them, use fragments with other fragments, move to unexpected keys, so it's never really predictable at all. I did that with the *Swan Lake* bits, too, working them around my score. I'm always doing that.

Also, I'll know, for example, I have four minutes, so I'll just write a four-minute piece. I'll make some minor adjustments to make sure it fits the picture, but I always like to think of the cues in a broad sense, as little pieces. And I can see the shape—of course, a lot of the final version has to do with how it's directed, how it's shot, how it's acted, how it's edited.

I used to use calculators, and then computers, to figure out exact timings. Computers made it a lot easier, but they locked you in. So I found ways to get the computer to free me. Once I was freed up, I just got freer and freer and freer and stopped worrying about timings and precision. I'd love to record scores without the movies. Having the film on the scoring stage sometimes slows me down. I don't always like the synchronization; sometimes it's inhibiting. I know it has to be there, but sometimes I just want to do the music. For me, a lot of music in film is purely for emotional value, not for commentary.

In the studio, as I watched you conduct the *Ransom* orchestra to picture, I noticed that your head was down.

I'm looking at the score, and peripherally looking at the screen. The first time we play, I watch the screen much more carefully. After that, I just check to make sure I'm in the right spot. It's a bit of an encumbrance—you want to go faster but the picture slows you down. We used to do movie scores without the video. There was a time when synchronization of music to picture was not as precise or as effortless as it is now. You couldn't lock things up as fast. I did *The Brood* in seven hours without the movie, with nothing running, just playing the music.

For film music of the future, will synthesizers win out over orchestras?

No. You'll never be able to synthesize the subtleties of an orchestra. There's just nothing like an orchestra. It's also part of what we think of as movies, it's part of what people like about movies. If they stop making movies, they'll stop recording orchestras. But as long as there are movies, they'll record film music with orchestras.

Is the concert orchestra, as Leonard Bernstein once said, a museum and the conductor its curator?

It has become museum. Especially here, in the United States, where most conductors avoid contemporary music like the plague.

Why do people flock to see the newest Schwarzenegger movie, the newest Andrew Lloyd Webber musical, the newest NBC sitcom, or to read the newest Marlon Brando biography, but avoid contemporary concert music?

I don't get it. Maybe it has something to do with reference points.

Some critics and some younger composers insist that such experimentalists and avant-gardists as Penderecki, Ligeti, Cage, Babbitt, and Elliott Carter ruined the concert audience for future generations and that the audience has a bad reference for "new music."

But that kind of music is in film scores all the time—the same movies people are flocking to see, and that's a lot of flocking.

But the same people who love your music for *Silence of the Lambs* refuse to listen to the similar music in the concert hall.

Yeah, but in the concert hall they're wearing their tuxedos and their mink coats—that's for their beloved Beethoven and Mozart. There's no serial killer to go with it.

The name Shirley Walker may not be well-known in most households, but her music surely is. Hollywood's best-kept secret musical weapon for many years running, she has co-composed, orchestrated, and conducted for many highly visible composers, including Hans Zimmer, Danny Elfman, Cliff Eidelman, Jurgen Knieper, Richard Band, and Brad Fiedel. Within the film-music industry, she is celebrated as a great master-of-all-trades and a savior of lost scores.

Walker's earliest feature-film work was in collaboration with composer Carmine Coppola for the classic *The Black Stallion* (1979). Among the many other movies to which her considerable contributions were vital are *Ghoulies* (1985), *The Dungeonmaster* (1985), *Paint It Black* (1989), *Nightbreed* (1990), and *White Fang* (1991). As conductor for many of the now-classic Danny Elfman scores, including *Beetlejuice* (1988), *Batman* (1989), *Darkman* (1990), and *Edward Scissorhands* (1990), Walker's artistic command and in-depth practical understanding of the orchestra is highly evident.

As her career continues to evolve, her own film scores are taking a front seat, and Shirley Walker is now on her way to long-deserved critical recognition. Her music for *Escape from L.A.* (1996), co-composed with John Carpenter, is disturbing and bold, and her complex orchestral scores for *Asteroid* (1997) and *Turbulence* (1998) are full of fury and emotional extremes. Musical mystery, magic, and mayhem abound in her scores for *Memoirs of an Invisible*

Man (1992) and the animated film *Batman: Mask of the Phantasm* (1993), and her sophisticated work for the 1990s television programs *Space: Above and Beyond* and *The Adventures of Captain Zoom in Outer Space* features wide-ranging, dynamic scores of the type usually associated with big-budget pictures.

I interviewed this most sincere and delightful composer in her San Fernando Valley studio, surrounded by keyboards, electronic gear, sheets and sheets of orchestral manuscript paper, and a giant stuffed gorilla.

shirley WALKER

Tell me a little something about your past, and your path into the business.

I'm a native Californian. I've always composed music. As a child, I sat at the piano and played music to stories I made up in my head.

I had the good fortune to have two very good high-school teachers. One was right out of college and just on fire about classical music and orchestra music. I was in his orchestra program. He was in the military reserves, and was called off to the Vietnam War. I got to conduct and teach his orchestra class while he was away for a year. That was a very moving experience for me. The other teacher was a jazz aficionado who had created a jazz-band program. I had never heard of jazz until high school, but he had me transcribe Neal Hefti and Quincy Jones arrangements off of Count Basie records. And he had me learning to play jazz.

We also had a drama teacher at the school who did major productions. I don't know how many musicals we did, but I was involved in all of them. And I was the pianist for his modern-dance class. I wrote a musical with him, which, when he left the high school and went to teach at a university in Illinois, was performed at that university. When I was in high school, there was just a very rich, creative environment in that community—East Contra Costa County, in the San Francisco Bay area. It was remarkable.

At this same time, I had a very demanding classical teacher who was quite upset that I was studying jazz. His students were concert pianists, but he had a few unique, musically gifted beings like myself. He was interested in helping us develop our technique and path and so forth. Under his tutelage, while I was still in high school, I did recitals in the Berkeley area and competed in a concerto competition, which I won, and played with the San Francisco Symphony. At that time, my high-school orchestra teacher was a violist with the Oakland Symphony. Later, he became their personnel director and hired some of his more talented students, so I became the orchestra pianist for the Oakland Symphony at a time when they were a new-music orchestra. Gerhard Samuel was the conductor.

I also did local musical theater, accompanied ballet classes, played in clubs, played in piano bars . . . blah, blah, blah.

I tried going to San Francisco State College, as it was called at the time. They had a real good music program there, but I did not have the political skills to do well in college. I was very, very shy and just couldn't deal with academia. I came in as a freshman, took their tests to determine who this kid is and what she can do, and scored off the thing at the graduate level. But the head of the department said, "Well, this just must be a mistake. She should take beginning this and beginning that." And I had no idea about saying, "Hey, I'm paying you money. I'm gonna take this and this and this." So . . .

Did you formally study composition?

I actually did, with Dr. Roger Nixon. I can hardly remember it—it's sort of a blur. I remember that I brought things in and showed them to him. I don't remember that it was anything that I could really connect with. I was going through what anybody does at that age—I was living away from home for the first time and dealing with all of that sort of thing. So, college really didn't work for me.

Then, I got the opportunity to start doing industrial film scores. Al Giddings, who is an underwater photographer, was making his own movies. Al heard me play in the house band at a little jazz club in the Haight-Ashbury. He would come and listen to us two or three times a week. And then we got to talking. He said, "Would you do the music for my movie?" And, you know, that was it.

Could you fill me in a little bit about going from there to your feature-film and television work?

Yes. There's an interesting gap there. I got married and quit music because, for the first time, I didn't have to do music. For my generation, it was socially acceptable for women to just drop what they were doing when they got married. Back then, in the late sixties, I didn't have the pressures of the liberated-woman concept. And it wasn't until I'd had both of my kids that I woke up one morning and was terrified that I couldn't play the piano anymore. There was about a seven-year gap there. And then my husband, Don, who's always been a big fan of mine—my playing, especially—was in the industrial film market, public television, and there was always some engineer who was a bass player, playing at some club. So Don would get me to sit in with them. I kind of wended my way back, and I did ski movies and stuff like that.

You played keyboards on *Apocalypse Now*, among other things, and worked on *Black Stallion*. Did those two experiences hook you?

They absolutely did. But, more than that, I met Dan Carlin, Jr., who is second-generation industry here. At that time, he was a music editor, as was his father, and the two of them had a company in Los Angeles. One day, he said to me, "Shirley, there's a whole community down in Los Angeles that does this all the time. People with your talent are working there and getting paid. They're not being exploited like you are up here in San Francisco." So, he mentored me into the business. He and his dad got me my first agent. They got me started. They got me some *Lou Grant* episodes to score. So, stepping away from Zoetrope and ghost-writing and that stuff,

I came down here and started working in television as a composer and as an orchestrator for features.

Was the animated *Batman* movie the film that moved you away from ghost-writing and into commanding your own credits?

Actually, I had to say no, stop doing things. And a little, terribly frightening, dry period was the result. This town likes to just eat people up. When you have specific abilities and the studios get used to being able to turn to you for specific things, they don't want you to change your role. They want you to just always be there for "Shirley, the score's in trouble. Could you help us out here?" I said no for two years. So I had about an eighteen-month dry period.

You've saved a number of scores. I suspect we've heard a lot of your music that doesn't necessarily have your name attached.

Oh, definitely.

Maybe that's something you don't want to talk about, but . . .

I came into the business at a time when the nature of ghost-writing was that you were paid big money to not talk about the fact that you were doing it and to support the illusion or delusion, whichever you prefer, that composer X was actually doing the work that they were being paid for. I'm very old school in that sense. And there are certain things that I will admit to and certain things that I won't.

Even though ghost-writing was keeping you in the business, and getting you some nice paychecks, was it an artistically or an aesthetically frustrating exercise? Or was it okay because you were "paying your dues" to get on to what hopefully would be a project that would have your name attached?

Both. When I was starting, I wasn't starting as a youngster—I was already in my thirties. But I had that incredible enthusiasm that you have when you discover a whole new world that you didn't even know existed. And you're just sort of blinded by the enticement of the money. You're just staring into those headlights, not realizing that there's a car coming at you from behind those headlights. I was quite happy to be standing out on the highway there for a while. But then, ultimately, the impact happened—I realized that I had had too much of making other people look as great as I was making them look. So, at that point, I said, "Boy, I just don't have the tolerance to continue doing this much longer." And I found that I could step into the role of being strictly an orchestrator and a conductor for composers. Hans Zimmer was the first major-star composer I worked for in that capacity, where I wasn't ghost-writing.

Were you a teacher for him?

I think, in a sense, yes. Although neither one of us would describe it that way, necessarily.

Tell me about life as a Hollywood orchestrator.

As an orchestrator, I've noticed something funny that goes on with a lot of composers: As soon as they learn what an oboe is, they think they're orchestrators, which is quite amusing. A lot of them think, "I'm doing all my own orchestrations because I talked to this orchestrator and said that I wanted the oboe to play here." We all contribute to it—it takes two to tango, always. And, as orchestrators, we have our secrets that we don't ever want the composers to learn, because, if they did learn them, then they really *could* be orchestrators. But composers don't have the time to do it. They're too busy getting the next job.

It strikes me that there are very few musicians, in either the film world or the concert world, who seem so comfortable and

amazingly capable with so many different aspects of music—with conducting, with arranging, with orchestrating, with composing, with performing. You're one of the rare ones, *and* you're a woman. Maybe it's not, as James Brown sang, "a man's world!"

"There ain't nothin' like the real thing, baby."

What brought you to conducting, and do you want to stay involved in the conducting side of things?

When I first came here, I was terrified to conduct. I saw that podium and the mechanics of conducting to film and knew that I didn't know a thing about it. My first composing, my first *Lou Grant* episodes, for example, were conducted by Dan Carlin, the music editor who brought me into the business. After about a year in the business, I realized that people would think I couldn't conduct if I didn't start doing it. So I became determined to do it.

At that time, the early eighties, we hadn't yet been hit with the wave of people who can sit and play to the picture with the toys that we now have—with midi and with sequencers—you know, people who might be dramatists but who aren't necessarily musically literate. Right now, we have an awful lot of recreating the wheel going on. It's very expensive for the industry, but the industry seems to love it because they feel like they're getting a more artistic vision at this point. But, if you're going to fly some guy in from London to conduct your film score, it better be great, because it's expensive.

Conducting film scores is like being a traffic cop. I understand that the musicians sitting out there are capable of giving an incredible performance if the time that we spend together can be structured in a way that gives them the space to perform. I think that's the best thing I did as a film-score conductor—I ran the sessions in a way where the musicians knew that their questions would get answered, would not be ignored. The recording engineer knew that there would be time allowed for him to get his sound and do the things he needed to do to get it sounding great. The music contractors knew that there would be an attention to the responsibility of the union requirements—the musicians need to have a break so that they can go to the bathroom, eat, get on the phone.

You let everyone know that the score's in very good hands and that there's a commitment, both emotionally and musically, to the product?

Absolutely. Even when the composers and I didn't get along great, for whatever reasons, once I had committed myself to doing that job, I was there for them and for their music. Unfortunately, a lot of them couldn't get beyond using the orchestra as a tool to write their score. So, frequently, they really hadn't finished the writing. They needed that pressure, that deadline collision, to finally get it all out of them, to get it done. And in that environment, there isn't room for that. It's just a mad scramble to get something on tape that everybody in that control room is happy with. You've got a director and a producer and a composer in there. But I just enjoy that kind of chaos.

Your personality seems to have come out unscathed.

Oh, yeah. But I had one incident where I was in tears on the podium, and I was very embarrassed about that. But God bless the orchestra: They covered for me. They could see that I was so humiliated and upset. I guess I still haven't gotten over it—I'm getting teary-eyed right now, just thinking about it.

Something was directed at you, something that was out of your control?

It was out of my control, and it was done by a composer with a colossal ego who was in a transition period. He did something that was incredibly offensive to me and hurt my feelings. I think enough of him that I believe he would not have done it if he had realized what he was creating. At the time, he was just involved in himself and not thinking. Well, that stuff happens, this business is like that. You get bumped around. And, that's okay. Whatever personality conflicts I've had with some of the guys I've worked with, they don't take away from the fact that I was part of these guys' teams at a time when they were doing some very exciting things. And I'm proud of that. I'm proud that I got to participate with some of these characters at a time when they were doing very exciting things.

It seems as if you've taken all your experiences along the way, the negative and the positive, and turned them around into healthy visions of where to go tomorrow.

If you can't do that, you've got to get out of the business.

I'm curious about your work with Richard Band, a composer whose work I greatly admire. I see some co-composing credits.

Rick is a treasure. I'm trying to think of how many zillion film scores he'd already composed at the time I met him. He was principally servicing his brother's and father's productions, but he also did other film scores as well. I'm not real knowledgeable about his credits. I think he came and saw me conducting for Charles Bernstein, on *Cujo*. And Rick had a big score, *Metalstorm*, which he was about to record. I conducted *Metalstorm*. That was the first time we worked together. I think music supervisor Don Perry kind of brought us together. After that, Rick asked me to do some orchestrating on some other things. And when it was clear that he liked to share the compositional tasks, I asked him for credit, and he was willing to give it. We did *Ghoulies* and *Dungeonmaster* and other things. The projects that we worked on were fun. Rick is always respectful of the musical talent he has around him. He's a real appreciator of the profession and other people's work. I liked that about him. I liked the fact that even though he clearly had ambition, he still could step away from that and go, "Oh, wow, that guy's doing that over there, and that's cool!"

You've been involved in extensive collaborations with Danny Elfman—orchestrating, writing additional music, conducting. Is that collaboration still ongoing or has there been a parting of the ways?

Danny and I have parted ways. But I was thrilled to be part of his team at the time, part of the first *Batman* score in particular. I was very disappointed that that score didn't get an Oscar nomination. I thought it was absolutely the most wonderful score of that year. It was ground-breaking because it was a shift in the way super-heroes were portrayed with music. Danny created a whole new sound. Just like John Williams put the orchestra in space, Danny put this dark, kind of Gothic thing to the comic heroes. But one of the misfortunes for Danny is that every wag who's out there is taking pot shots at people who are succeeding at the level he succeeds at. They're always trying to create stuff that isn't really true, which sort of tears away at the fabric of his work and is very hard on his team. So, the constant perception that I was writing his music was ultimately detrimental to our relationship. I was glad when I finally said to myself, "I need to stop working with this man because, number one, I have my own aspirations."

***Black Stallion* is a beautiful score. How deeply were you involved in it? Was there co-composing involved?**

That was an amazing project. But I was politically so, so stupid at the time. I had absolutely no political skills whatsoever. But I was totally committed to that score and to working with Carmine Coppola. Carmine and I, at the start of the *Black Stallion*, had a wonderful relationship that came out of *Apocalypse Now*. I had a lot of emotion about working with him. He was a father-like guy.

He was older than old enough to be my father, and I realized that I was sort of like a music nurse for his work. He could write great music, but writing to picture wasn't exactly the best thing that he did. And that's where I finessed a little bit. You know, Carmine was not Carroll Ballard's choice as the composer. Carroll had hired a composer who was in academia.

Before Carmine Coppola?

Yes, before Carmine.

I'm curious to know who this composer was.

This man had his own notation system. I looked at it and thought, he isn't going to put this in front of a studio orchestra in Los Angeles and have it come out the way he thinks it's going to come out. He had this whole smoke-and-mirrors number because he was having trouble interfacing with the commercial work. And, in fact, the music of his that Carroll Ballard had heard and loved, when I heard it, I realized was stuff that a harmonica player had improvised. Maybe we shouldn't remember this guy's name. So, he was out. Who was next? Oh, God, I wish I could remember the names. I'm so sorry that I can't. There was another composer who then came into the picture.

Composer number two still wasn't Carmine Coppola?

Right. But, ultimately, Carmine got the job. Carroll had struck out twice. Carroll arranged to have me work in the studio with Nyle Steiner, the creator of the Electronic Valve Instrument, improvising to picture under Carroll's direction. We would improvise stuff, refine it a little bit, record it to picture in Richard Beggs' studio, and then give it to Carmine to write into his film score. I was so stupid—I didn't get it that there was absolutely no way that Carmine was going to like any of it or use any of it in what he wrote for the film score. We're talking territory here. That was sort of the beginning of a strain in my relationship with Carmine.

And then there were the big orchestral things. I used Carmine's themes and wrote those. It was a requirement that I use his themes, which I was more than happy to do because I thought they were wonderful. I loved them. I loved them for the horse. They were just bang-on. So I had no hesitation about that. But we were stuck in the quandary about who was going to tell Carmine. Our faces were white about this.

They were going to let him just hear the score?

Nobody was going to tell him. I wasn't going to be a patsy and call him up and say, "Oh, Carmine, I'm throwing out everything you did for the island." So, we had to go to Carroll and say, "Look, somebody's got to tell him." And Carroll went to Francis [Coppola], who was the producer, and said, "Somebody's got to tell your father." And Francis said, "Okay, he's my dad, I'll take care of it." Well, the dynamics in that family were such that it never did get taken care of. And, to my horror and *deep* regret, Carmine found out from an old friend, a flute player who'd been hired to do the session, that we were re-recording pivotal moments of the score with a huge orchestra. Of course, Carmine was explosively furious and called up all of us. He was gonna blow up cars; he was gonna break legs.

You can't blame him!

You cannot blame him! He was quite gentle with me—he didn't threaten to break any legs or blow up any cars. But, clearly, he was upset. And, that was it. It was over. He felt that I had stabbed him in the back. And I can understand how he felt that way. Again, I didn't have great personal skills. I wasn't up to the task of pursuing a resolution of that with him. And we did not speak again. He insisted that he be there when we recorded a lot of the small things.

And he was in the control room just screaming and yelling and making the recorders crazy. It was dreadful.

When it was time to create the licensing document, Dan worked with me, and then he worked with Carmine. Then Dan said to me, "Look, Shirley, you and Carmine have to settle this because he says that his name should be on stuff that you say he didn't write. I'm not a composer. You guys are gonna have to talk to each other and work this out." We did that, and it was horrible. I felt like shit. I believe Carmine may have had a health-related attack of some kind as a result of all this. To this day, I just have very bad feelings about it. And then, to see him win the Golden Globe Award for that score, and to have them play a piece of music that I wrote, all on television, that was devastating for both of us. And yet, we had not repaired our relationship to the point where we could share the discomfort of what that was doing to both of us. I never did speak with him again, and then he died. That type of story is the movie business right there. It's a classic example of the kind of thing that can happen in the profession.

Let's talk about *Batman: The Animated Movie*—the first big-budget, superstar theatrical release with a full score by a woman. Is that true?

Just about, not quite. In fairness to the women who got to do that before me, you have to qualify it a little more than that. There were several women songwriters who had credits before me. Aretha Franklin and, I think, Carol King had one before I did.

How about orchestral composers?

Suzanne Ciani, out of New York, did the *Incredible Shrinking Woman* score for Lily Tomlin and Jane Wagner. But, again, it wasn't like the traditional process out here. So, we can sort of qualify that. Angela Morley, *Watership Down*. Okay, we disqualify her because she's a gender-bender—she was a man. We have to go through all those steps before we can reach the plateau where we can barely say that I was the first one. And Bebe Barren is still upset with me because she feels that the score that she and her husband did for *Forbidden Planet* qualifies her as the first woman to have done a feature-film score.

The animated *Batman* is a full-length movie with a big orchestral score. Could you give us a little bit of background about the musical demands made on you? Were there restrictions on the kind of music that you wanted to do or on what was expected from you?

By the time we did the animated feature, we had already done sixty-five half hours of the animated series. From the beginning, the producers on that show—Bruce Timm, Alan Burnett, and Eric Radomski—did not want a Danny Elfman sound for the Batman character. They had seen my work on the *Flash* television series and liked my work from there. They wanted me to do the theme. They were very, very dismayed when Danny insisted that he was the only human being on the planet who could write for Batman, and that it should be his theme for their show. I didn't get to have the theme until after that had sort of subsided. Then we created the theme we wanted for the show. As I said, they were not interested in it sounding like Danny Elfman, but I think that I was influenced by Danny's work for the first *Batman* movie because it was a great sound for the Batman character. Personally, I knew I didn't want to go away from that Gothic, overdone, overstated method of treatment for the Batman character. On a purely musical level, I went in places Danny wouldn't necessarily go as a composer. I'm real happy with the sort of evolution that I took it on over those sixty-five half hours, so that, by the time we got to the movie, I felt like I had complete musical freedom, especially in a chromatic way. And not just in harmonic changes, I mean the real chromaticism that's in some of those cues. I have to say that they didn't put restrictions on me about the style. I felt like I was getting to do what I wanted with the character.

Did you have a team of orchestrators on *Batman*? Did you make very clear sketches and basically have the orchestrators help copy out the score for time constraints?

Well, I do complete sketches. Let me take a second and just pull that out so we can see it. [Walker pulls out the score.] I like to work with composers as my orchestrators because they have the ability to look at that complete sketch and find my mental errors. They can look at my source material and say, "Oh, when she transposed for this cue, a couple accidentals are missing." They will bring things to my attention. They will say, "It looks like you forgot here that you were going up to this key, and you probably meant this, but just take a look at it." They're note police, in the extreme. They really help me stay on track in terms of that meticulous detail that allows the orchestra to really perform well.

Looking at your score here, I see a big chunk called brass and a big chunk called woodwinds, and exactly which woodwinds are playing is clearly denoted. And the dynamics and the phrasing are all clear. Are orchestral film scores usually in C or are they transposed scores?

We tend to use C scores out here. When you're just starting, and you want to save money, you can do a transposed score, because the orchestrators don't get paid for that, but the copyists do. So that's a way to save money in the beginning. But when you're past that phase, it's about getting the job done in the time that's available. The C score is the most flexible, because the film changes are such that we're just scrambling to keep up. There's stuff coming onto the scoring stage at the last minute, and sometimes you just have to dictate from the podium.

In the animated *Batman*, I sense a real commitment to good old-fashioned Hollywood film scoring. There are times when your music comments, both directly and indirectly. There are a few times

where you compose against the action, which I found very intriguing. And there are the almost necessary moments, such as when he's in the graveyard, the big minor chords and the organ. All those wonderful moments—every time he sees the family name on the crypt and the love themes—seem to involve tipping your hat to the past, the traditions of film scoring. But, also, new Shirley Walkerisms emerge in your score. Would you talk a little bit about the way you approached that film?

Well, first of all, thank you. I love to think that I did all those things. And many of them I was trying to do, many of them were on purpose. The nod to the past is a big one for me. I love old movies. I grew up with old movies. I was a kid when they were *new* movies. I have a deep affection for *Victory at Sea* and stuff like that. That's meaty stuff. In this business, we sort of go in cycles. And, fortunately, I'm in the business at a point when that stuff has come back again. I think I'm in a wave of appreciation for that approach, and, definitely, an orchestral sound. In every score I've done, even *Escape from L.A.*, which has some very modern things that people didn't even know Shirley Walker could do, there's still that kind of classic approach. I think there are always going to be echoes of that in everything I do. And the whole thing about commenting is that it's delightful when you can get away with it.

A director or a producer may say, "Don't do that"?

Oh, yeah. A lot of people are so involved with their work that they don't have the distance to appreciate that music can do that. They'd prefer you to just stay literal. Personally, I always try to do it whether they think they want it or not. I just can't help myself. It's there, and then they get rid of it if it's wrong for their vision. But I always start out with a little bit of that in there. And that over-the-top thing—we certainly had that in the animated *Batman*. You almost couldn't overdo it for that character, and the fact that it was animated. I think you mentioned the big organ and choir on the grave, the thing in the storm. That was one moment where Bruce Timm looked at me and said, "Gee, Shirley, maybe that's a little bit over the top." And we softened it.

Then a little choir, almost a church wedding in the future sound, and then, of course, the bats come out and all hell breaks loose. Those are your ideas, which you throw in, and the producers and directors say, "Okay, they're enhancing."

That, to me, is the interpretive storytelling part of writing for film. I don't think there are a lot of composers working in the business who do that.

Do you feel that there aren't many composers working that way because it's *old-fashioned*?

That would be the most gracious thing to say. I think that many of them aren't because they don't know how. They don't have the talent or the craft to do so. Well, a lot of people may have the talent, but they don't have the craft.

I noticed that your *Batman* score seemed to allow the sound effects to be part of an extended percussion section of the orchestra. Do you use the sound effects as part of your musical atmosphere?

Oh, absolutely. I'm a real believer in that. I think that goes back to having started in the business with Walter Murch and Richard Beggs on *Apocalypse Now*. I was so stunned by the work that they were doing, and Richard Beggs was particularly outspoken about the fact that music and sound share the soundtrack, and that they each have a contribution to make. Sometimes it's literal and sometimes it's interpretive. And it's everywhere in between those extremes. I just treasure looking at a picture and guessing, "Okay, the sound's going to be doing this here." I love writing around sound. My music is capable of having a transparency even though the architecture of the composition might be dense, as it is in *Mask of the Phantasm*. There's a transparency there that allows you to hear sound through the music, so that the music isn't just this big wad that's taking up this much of the frequency range of the soundtrack. Why should music be doing the same thing that the effects are doing? Let's get out of the way. Let's let them have that. I'm not going to have a timpani going as the car rolls up, because that's what the sound of the motor's going to do. It's already going to be there.

Would you talk a bit about your work with Brad Fiedel?

Brad and I actually came into the business at about the same time, in the early eighties. He came in from New York, principally getting to do television. And, at that time, I was conducting a little and orchestrating a little for him. I think Brad and I have had and continue to have a personal relationship that is wonderful. In fact, we're still friends. This project that I'm just starting, *Turbulence*, is one that he was actually up for. I wasn't sure how we'd deal with that. But he was just great. He called to congratulate me when it was clear that I was being chosen to do the job. That was *such* a classy thing to do. Brad is a class act all the way. It's been wonderful to be a part of his career, and assist his career in the way I've been able to. He has a relentless curiosity about the orchestra and learning how to orchestrate. He's one of the guys who has really, really been educating himself about the esoterica, not just the "Well, I'm a composer, and I don't need to do any more than that."

How about Hans Zimmer?

And Hans is such a dynamic personality. I had the great pleasure of working with him when he was first getting established in America. Right after his Oscar nomination for *Rain Man*, the next big film for him was *Black Rain*. And I was his orchestrator and conductor on that. I had a wonderful time with him as he was just beginning Media Ventures and getting all that stuff going for himself. I really enjoyed working with him.

Have there been any particular musical struggles involving your scores? Struggles that may have ended in disaster or, hopefully, great success?

I haven't yet hit the point where I'm doing a score that involves a big struggle over what the music's going to be. I don't know whether that's good fortune or the result of the dynamics of my process, and how I include the film people in it. I haven't been put under that test of fire yet, where you're worlds apart from the people who've hired you and you have to find some commonality or some way to get the thing to work so that you aren't fired or your score isn't tossed, which is even worse. My feet haven't been held to that fire yet. I'm sure they will be at some time. Most of the time, as I'm working with people, I enjoy the collaborative nature of the medium because it forces me to do stuff that I wouldn't do if I were just doing what I wanted to do and had only my own tastes to consider.

Do you compose much without the video monitor on top of your piano? Do you find that you need the imagery?

I'm at a phase now where the demand for me to be writing for hire is keeping up with my need to express music, which also is a very big concern of mine. My sons are pretty upset with me about that. That I'm not writing real music on the side. So, I know that I'll get back to that at some point. But, right now, I'm having way too much fun with what I'm doing.

I may actually restart my playing. I recently had the experience of doing some free jazz with some New York friends, Anthony Jackson and Roland Vasquez. And the idea is brewing of maybe doing a recording and going to Germany, where there's a big wave of that going on right now. So, I'm sort of teasing myself with the idea that I could play again. We've recorded some of the sessions that we've done out here, and it has reminded me that I am a player. And some musicians have been pushing at me to conduct in the concert world. They feel that I would do well at that. I say, "Maybe, at some future time." I was contacted by an organization in Spain last summer to come over there and conduct some of my film music, but the nature of their offer was such that it wasn't something I could take advantage of at the time. There wasn't enough lead time. So that's another maybe that the future might bring to pass. It's enticing. I like the idea of it. It's just the hard work to get there that's keeping it a bay for the moment.

Do you go to many concert-music concerts? The Los Angeles Philharmonic, the Monday Evening Concerts?

You bet I do. In fact, this year, for the first time in my life, I had the wonderful experience of being at a symphony concert and falling asleep. I just sat there, realizing that my head was going down, and went with it. I woke up when the people were clapping, and I thought, now I understand why people love to do this. It's kinda dark, it's relatively comfortable seating, and with these beautiful waves of sound coming at you, it's kinda great.

I also went to hear a premiere of a Carlos Rodriquez piece that the L.A. Phil had commissioned. Carlos worked on the animated *Batman* series, which, of course, will not show up in his concert résumé. He wouldn't want to jeopardize his career by admitting that he actually has dabbled in the commercial world.

Is it still that severe a break between the two worlds? Elliot Goldenthal seems to bridge it fairly regularly.

Yes. You can cross over in one way. And Elliot has, thankfully, done that well. I hope he continues to do so. If you're in the concert world, you can go to the top end of the film world, and that's relatively okay. No way Elliot was going to do a TV series. A sitcom? Oh, my God, get outta here! That's not going to happen. For people working as film composers, if they want to get into the concert world, it's the same thing. You've got to be a giant, like John Williams or Jerry Goldsmith—somebody who's that enormous a success in their area. Somebody else, somebody who's principally in television? "What's that? Get outta here." It's all little territories. We're not selling ground, property, and mineral rights anymore, now we've moved up. We're selling columns of air, hot air—the hot air coming off of the film composer and the hot air coming off of the concert world. It's real territorial now, and it's defined by media and by attorneys and by managers. There are so many people who have so much at stake, and there's a lot of palm rubbing that takes place around that.

While you're saying all these things that might be very depressing and very frustrating to a lot of people, you're smiling. You're saying "Hey, it's okay."

Yeah. I believe that it is. And I think that comes from the fact that I'm an environmentalist. As I see it, I'm just a little cog in this wheel here, this big thing, the total environment—musicians and people who perform, people who create, people who manage people. Even the lawyers are a part of this. So I enjoy bringing a sense of harmony to the whole endeavor. That's what's fun for me. And whatever comes out of that that has my name on it as a composition will have whatever life it has. I can't predetermine that. None of us can predetermine that, although a lot of people spend a lot of money trying to predetermine it. But that too shall pass. I guess that I'm just a relatively optimistic person.

You instantly come across that way.

It's that smile instead of the scowl?

I've already had a little bit of the latter.

Oh, it's wonderful, isn't it? The levels of pretension are just so fantastic.

christopher YOUNG

Christopher Young is the Bela Lugosi of film music (as the composer more than once has dubbed himself); the grand master of the macabre; the purveyor of panic, suspense, terror, and hysteria; the musical messenger of menace and all things frightening, demented, deadly, and psychotic. All this to describe a hard-working, compassionate father of two, a sympathetic soul who often goes out of his way to help others? Perhaps Young is very, *very* much like Bela Lugosi (or perhaps Vincent Price), a gentle and caring man who became the personification of horror through his chilling film work.

From *The Dorm That Dripped Blood* (1982) through *Def-Con 4* (1985), *Nightmare on Elm Street, Part 2* (1985), *Invaders from Mars* (1986), *Torment* (1986), *Haunted Summer* (1988), *Hider in the House* (1989), *The Fly II* (1989), *The Vagrant* (1992), and *The Dark Half* (1992), Young's shockingly original scores catapulted him to the position of preeminent composer for the horror genre. His ability to juxtapose striking, haunting themes with brutal and vicious orchestral bombast has allowed him many opportunities to develop his unique compositional style during the past twenty years. His creepy *Tales from the Hood* (1995) and his massive, powerful orchestral/choral scores for *Hellraiser* (1987), *Hellbound: Hellraiser II* (1988), *Species* (1995), and *Urban Legend* (1998) complement his tense, restless—but always alluring—music for *Jennifer 8* (1992), *Murder in the First* (1994), *Copycat* (1995), *Murder at 1600* (1997), *Hard Rain* (1998), *Hush* (1998), and *Entrapment* (1999).

However, Young's music is by no means only about blood and guts, psychopaths and pinheads: His *Pink Panther*ish, jazz-influenced music for *The Man Who Knew Too Little* (1997), his lounge-jazz for *Rounders* (1998), his introspective music for *Dream Lover* (1994), and his intimately delicate scores for *Max and Helen* (1990) and *Norma Jean and Marilyn* (1996) are but a few examples of his successful escapes from genre hell.

We first met at Chris's unusually decorated Venice, California, studio—where his large collection of magical snowglobes mixes with dozens of Halloween masks, jack-o'-lanterns, and skeletons; shelves overflowing with scores, books, records, and CDs; and a large desk covered with handwritten scores—an environment that identifies the extremes of the man and his music.

christopher YOUNG

Two of the scores that first attracted me to contemporary film music were *Hellbound: Hellraiser II* and *The Vagrant.* I played *The Vagrant* for a couple of composer friends—fans of minimalism— and they loved it, too. They thought it was much more fun than the majority of music by the popular minimalists.

Oh, really? You know, I've always wondered what the concert guys would think of it.

A lot of them think it's very hip.

That's very exciting to hear. I have tremendous respect for the guys who are working in concert music. To me, they are the true heroes.

Maybe you're one of the new-music heroes. Even though the director says, "Do this . . . do this . . . do this," you find ingenious ways to inject integrity and personality into your scores.

I try. If something tragic was to happen, like I was hit by a truck on my way across the street to buy another pack of cigarettes, I would know in the back of my mind that I've always tried my best.

There are two sides to my personality. Half of me lusts to dive head-first into a very strange and insane sonic world, a world that has no commercial potential whatsoever. The other half of me is dying to write that great all-American theme. I'm sure there's something inside you that's boring a hole in the back of your head, saying you've got to write a theme that everyone will whistle. Isn't there? Wouldn't it be great to walk out of your apartment or your office and go down the street and hear someone walk up behind you whistling your tune?

As you know, film music is a strange creature, it's in limbo. It's neither embraced by the people who purchase concert music and go to concerts of orchestral music, nor are the pop buyers really interested. I bring this up because, if you take someone like Max Steiner, a guy who worked on something like 300 pictures, out of all those hundreds of hours of music, what is he remembered for? He is remembered for about four minutes of music—the theme from *Gone With the Wind*.

When you were a young, impressionable composer, did you find yourself attracted to a broad variety of music?

Yes, definitely. But I was a late-comer to writing. I was originally a drummer, a jazz player, and thought I was going to go that route. I studied with Alan Dawson, the drummer who used to play with Dave Brubeck. And that's all I had in my head, all day long, that rat-a-tat-tatting stuff—the jazz stuff. But when you're a composer, *bam!*—all of a sudden you start thinking pitches. It was like being given an electrical shock.

Did you come from a musical family?

When I was a kid, there was no music in the house. That's a part of my upbringing that I regret. The only music that came into our house was from my older brother, who would buy pop records. I barely even knew that orchestral music existed until very late. I was jazzing away when one day one of my professors said, "Chris, come here. I want you to hear this." And he put on a record of Penderecki's *Threnody for the Victims of Hiroshima*. That blew my mind! It was as if I had finally found something that had been sub-consciously there all along. I totally connected with it. I was a late-comer in discovering the Polish school and the whole avant-garde aspect of orchestral or concert music, but immediately I began self-taught crash courses in Stockhausen and Penderecki and the whole avant-garde scene.

Did the fact that you were older—more musically and emotionally mature—help you to intellectually access that music?

Definitely. I think so much of succeeding in film music has to do with having accrued a certain amount of life experience. Although I can't claim to have lived a really diversified and exciting life, I have been able to live life a little bit. I've noticed that there are some younger guys who have gotten into film scoring and made names for themselves while they're in their twenties. One half of me wishes that that had happened to me—that I had been able to establish myself at an earlier age. But the other half of me is glad that it didn't happen so quickly. By the time I started, I was already musically mature.

You have a lot of high-tech equipment in your studio. But you also have an old upright piano with dozens of sheets of handwritten music. What are your compositional techniques?

It varies film by film.

In *Copycat*, for example, the principal thematic material wanders through a lot of distantly related chromatic areas. Do you check such complex harmonic movements at the keyboard or do you trust your ear?

I definitely check it out on the keyboard. As the saying goes, there are those composers who write at the piano and those composers who *admit* they write at the piano.

Stravinsky said that he checked every note at the piano, including his infamous *Rite of Spring* E♭/F♭ chord.

But the piano can only get you so far. It allows you to check what you imagine. If you don't have it in your head, you're in trouble. At the piano, I'm a hacker. It's embarrassing. My coordination is in my wrists, not in my fingers, so when I do demonstrations for directors or producers, it always amazes me that I'm able to get through to them.

So you do sometimes create basic or initial sketches at the keyboard?

That's right.

Which of your films have allowed you the most experimentation?

The Vagrant is one. The remake of *Invaders From Mars*, directed by Tobe Hooper, was another. It was a situation, as I recall, where Tobe Hooper was in a three-picture deal. And this picture was the center of the three. He and I didn't get to work together on it. We spotted the film and then he had to leave to start shooting the next film. His only words to me were, "Chris, I want it to be different. I want you to feel free to be as experimental as you like." I decided Chris is going to be really experimental. My electronic background had been more in the analog domain, but the whole sampling thing fascinated me. I decided that I was going to have a session in which I brought in a bunch of different instruments, primarily percussion instruments, recorded them, and then manipulated them via electronics. The sampling scene at that time was pretty limited—I think the maximum amount of time you could sample was about three seconds—so I sort of stuck to manipulating acoustic tapes. I put together this thing that was really out of this world. And it was thrown out. I learned an incredible lesson through all that.

In politics?

Politics, yes. I was dumbfounded, totally dumbfounded. It was the first score I'd ever had thrown out.

I don't see *Pranks* listed anywhere in your filmography, but there was a Citadel release of that score.

Wow, you've really done your homework. I appreciate it very much.

I came across the record at a garage sale. Twenty-five cents.

No comment.

It's an engagingly bizarre pre-*Vagrant*-style score in which you used many unusual instrumental colors, including bass harmonica.

Thanks. The bass harmonica, yeah! The interesting thing about *Pranks* is that the record was released before the film came out in the theaters. And by the time it came out in the theaters, the distributor had changed the title to *The Dorm That Dripped Blood*. *Pranks*, the film, never existed by that title. It actually went through three titles. *Pranks* was the title that the director and producer used to sell it after they completed it. When they found a theatrical distributor, I think they initially went with *Death's Door* as the title. But by the time they released it on home video, they had changed it to *The Dorm That Dripped Blood*.

I have to tell you something: At the time, I was thrilled to death that some record label wanted to release that bizarre score, but in retrospect, I wish that that score could just be forgotten. It was not my greatest noble effort. No one should be held accountable for their first effort in film unless they're Orson Welles or Bernard Herrmann or Franz Waxman.

You have high personal standards. But there's a lot of unusual music in *Pranks* that's now recognizable as "early Chris Young."

This is perhaps true. We had a tremendously limited budget. I think we had a group of maybe sixteen people. That was back in the days when people would double-track a violin or a cello to try to beef it up. What I remember most about that score is that the director and the producer were happy enough with it that they hired me for their next picture, *The Power*, a low-budget supernatural thriller.

That first picture is so critical because you're busting out the gate, and you either trip or you stay upright. For me, it succeeded in convincing them that they had hired the right guy and that they wanted to bring me back for more. Getting your first picture is tough. What's even tougher is getting your second.

***Torment*—film-noir suspense. Your score follows the action.**

That's true. As I recall, that score can be divided into two halves— the half that tries to be tonal and the half that lets tonality go out the window. For the tonal portion, I got this idea of primarily using flutes, which, mind you, is not an original idea by any stretch of the imagination. Bernard Herrmann tried this on his score for *Torn Curtain*, the only score, I believe, that he had thrown out.

Elmer Bernstein recorded Herrmann's *Torn Curtain* and released it through his Film Music Collection series. The sound of it completely fascinated me. So, I decided that I was going to use the same kind of orchestra. But, of course, we had a shoestring budget. And at the recording session, I discovered that the person playing the bass flute had just rented the instrument, and had never really played it before. I discovered that if you're going to write for a group of flutes, by God, they better all be in tune, especially once you get into alto and bass flutes. What a problem! I think it was a noble idea that kind of misfired. I can't listen to *Torment* without focusing on all the intonation problems.

Were the experimental portions of that score rewarding?

The second half of the score, written almost entirely for experimental percussion, was a lot more fun. At that time, I was working with a great percussionist, John Fitzgerald. Together we decided to build some wild, crazy percussion instruments that were based on different resonating springs. We attached springs to cans, springs to this, springs to that. And we attached wires to this, wires to that. I think my score had a few strings in it, too—I think we had four cellos— but it's pretty psychotic stuff. A small suite from it was released on an Intrada CD. I haven't listened to it in a while, but as I recall, the mistake I made in readdressing the material was that I washed it out with too much reverb and threw in too many gear effects to make it even spacier. If I would go back and redo it, I think I would get the sponge out and suck off the excess wetness. But, yeah, that was an exciting film. It was exciting for me to experiment with stuff that I hadn't done before. I can't think of anyone doing anything quite like that. Cage's three *Constructions* were sort of sitting in the back of my mind at the time.

***Nightmare on Elm Street 2* is a terrific, frightening score. Why weren't you rehired for *Nightmare on Elm Street 3*?**

I thought *Nightmare on Elm Street 2* was going to be my major breakthrough film. I thought it was the opportunity I'd been waiting for. I was honored to be asked to do it. But I was nervous, extremely nervous.

The first *Nightmare* picture had been scored extraordinarily well by Charles Bernstein. I was shocked that they didn't ask him to return for *Nightmare 2*. But when *Nightmare 3* came around, I was soon to discover that each successive director wanted nothing to do with the preceding ensemble of people. I was called back, finally, on one of them, *Nightmare 4*. And I must say that I perhaps made a mistake not doing it. But, at the time, I was thoroughly burned out on horror films—I had just finished one, I had worked on two others back-to-back. I desperately felt the need to get away from that genre.

A decade ago, horror-film scores often carried a lot of musical clout and professional respect.

Right. In the 1980s it seemed every week there was another low-budget horror film released. Everyone was cashing in on the commercial success of horror—the *Nightmare* films, the *Friday the 13th* series, the *Halloween* series, *Swamp Thing*, and dozens of solo efforts. A lot of younger directors felt they could get attention by working on a low-budget feature, which would be their "in" to the system. That's how *The Dorm That Dripped Blood* came about.

Tell me a bit about your work on *Nightmare 2*.

The first film had an electronic score, but the director and the head of the production company wanted an orchestral score for *Nightmare 2*. They thought that an orchestral score would lift the film's production values. I already had the reputation of being a guy who would give them a big bang for their buck, bringing a level of production value to the film that otherwise might have been lacking. As I remember the recording session, when producer Bob Shaye came into the studio, the first thing he did was look through the glass window and count the number of players! I had promised them that I could get them an orchestra.

When I look back on that score, the mistake that I made was that I tried too hard with too little money. Meaning, I think I was too obsessed with getting a large quantity of people in the room to impress everybody. And, as a consequence, we didn't have much time to do it. That's another score that I don't listen to at all. I've tried to forget it. Again, I was developing, still trying to come to terms with that contemporary vocabulary. I guess it was a necessary stepping stone along the way.

In the U.S. release of *Godzilla 1985*, scored by Reijiro Koroku, you have an "additional music by Christopher Young" credit. Parts of this score, especially the opening title, sound very *Hellraiser*-ish. A similar situation occurred with the 1963 U.S. release of *King Kong vs. Godzilla*, which had most of the original Japanese score replaced with Mancini's music from *Creature from the Black Lagoon*.

I didn't actually write anything new for *Godzilla 1985*. It was a New World film, and the person responsible for postproduction supervision was Tony Randel, who had directed *Hellraiser II*. He dropped in a couple of my cues from *Hellraiser* and *Def-Con 4*. Tony was critical in my career development.

Did you struggle with the use of electronics in *Bat 21*, concerned about avoiding monotonous synth drones? The score strikes a nice balance between the solo flute, when Gene Hackman is alone, and electronic counterpoint fused with the sound effects of the film itself—the propellers, the bombs, the people screaming.

I haven't seen the film in a while. Can you hear the score in the film?

It's tough. It's buried. There's so much explosive war noise.

Oh, God, I remember. When we were dubbing that film, I thought that the only way it was going to play for more than a week was if the theater owners handed out free painkillers to the audience. It's a really, really noisy film. It was my first drone score. I was always trying to stay away from that, trying to fight that. But that was what the director was looking for. There must have been some moment when I was working on that film when I finally threw my hands up in the air and said, "Okay, I've got to do it now; it's what they want." By that time, the sampling thing had arrived, the technology had advanced enough whereby I could depend on it a lot more.

That's my first score in which I get into synth-based ostinatos. And the percussion was all prerecorded. It's one of my first scores in which

I prerecorded the synths and then dropped the orchestra in on top of them. A lot of the action cues are, as you probably know, loops of vamps with drones. I was trying desperately to disguise the drones as best as I could. When I say disguise them, I mean cover them so that your attention won't be focused on those damned drones.

In *Bat 21*, you seem to use some of the film's sound effects as part of your percussion battery—swirling helicopter blades, radar bleeps.

I've done that in some instances. I've actually taken sounds from the production track, sampled them, and used them in the score. But when we get these films, they're pretty much bone dry. We don't know what the effects are going to be until we're on the stage. I'll get a cassette that might have a temp dub that will give me an indication, and I'm sure that if I worked around the sound effects in that film, I must have had some indication in advance.

Sometimes it amazes me when I go back and look at these things. Some of the stuff must be subconscious. I write so much music that it's very easy to forget the particulars of any given moment. I could tell you about the cue that I'm working on right now, and the angst I'm going through right now. But the minute this film is finished, it'll fade from my memory. Those intensely agonizing questions that I had to deal with when I was working on this cue at this moment will fade and I'll move on to some other agonizing problem.

You seem so intense about your musical decisions.

I love the challenge. But, to get back to your earlier question: I try to do my best to acknowledge what's going to be happening in the completed production. But I'm sure every composer you talk with will tell you that when directors are working with their composers, they're seeing a naked film. The directors are generally panicked if it's an action film. It's hard for them to get into their minds that sooner or later this film is going to be maxed out with sound effects, which will bring to the film that element that they're missing. So, I meet with these directors and we talk about the music. They say, "Chris, we want it big here. We need something big, really big. Don't worry about the sound effects, just make it really big. Overkill." So, I give it to them really big and, lo and behold, when they get on the dub stage for the final dub, forty minutes out of every hour goes to last-minute fixes on the sound effects, fifteen minutes goes to last-minute fixes on the dialogue, and then the cue gets brought in too late in the game for them to say, "Oh, my God, look what the cue's doing! Let's reconsider what we've done with the sound effects." That's one of the main reasons why so many scores get lost.

Another thing that I find very distracting is the whole surround-sound thing. Maybe other composers will disagree with me on this, but as far as I'm concerned, a great mix is something that can work through a speaker about the size of my fist. Surround sound is very effective in theaters and rich people's living rooms, but it can cause you to lose sight of the reality that the majority of the life of a picture is in a home-viewing situation, with all the sound played through tiny television speakers. Sure, there's that initial period when the film's released in the theater, and if it becomes a classic, it will be re-released in the theater someday. But, for the most part, its life is in the home-video venue. And how many people have laser discs or DVDs? Not many. I don't. Most people still go out and rent video cassettes and play them through the little speaker in their TV. In the theater, the music's a lot more present than it is when you rent a video. With video they have to fold everything into two channels, and if you've got a mono TV, the music gets lost. That gets very disheartening.

You have strong opinions.

Well, I want to keep things exciting here. I frequently teach at USC, and sometimes I get off-track. I look out at the audience and the minute I see someone rolling his or her eyes, I know it's time to shift the subject.

I'm not rolling my eyes, so where do you want to take it?

When I play examples of my stuff at USC, examples for a group of people who don't know anything about me, it's interesting. I walk into the room and they don't know who I am. They may ask, didn't you do such and such? Oh, you did *Hellraiser*. They may know that. But, it's tough to pick which cues you're going to play for them. It's show-and-tell time! How does your music describe you? Gut-reaction stuff. What's the first foot that you want to put forward?

First impressions are so critical. I noticed that in the class I did last week, they listened closely to the first cue that I played—the main title from *Murder in the First*. I had the score out for them, and a couple of the students came up to look at it. I didn't know if this was a class that was into tradition, tune guys. Do they want to hear a big tune or do they want to hear some experimental, psychotic stuff? Okay, they're interested, but maybe they've heard it before. You know, there's nothing tremendously novel about *Murder in the First*. So I put on the main title from *Hellbound*, and a few more students came up to look at the score. The third cue I put up was the main title from *The Vagrant*. The entire class came up! No matter what people's tastes are in music, that *Vagrant* main title seems to grab them, something happens. I think from now on I'm going to start each seminar with *The Vagrant*.

When I teach History of Film Music at the university, the main title of *The Vagrant* is the very first thing students hear as they walk into the classroom on the first day of the seminar.

You're fucking kidding!

No, I swear, I am not kidding. So, let's talk about *The Vagrant*, its rhythmic, minimalistic main title. Strings, percussion, breathing, harmonica, typewriter—how much is sampled? Is it a live typewriter? Are the breathers sampled?

That's me breathing, my sampled breathing. The strings, a quintet—two violins, viola, cello, and bass—are live. The piano is live. The melodica is live. The accordion is live. The marimbas are live. Timpani are live. The typewriter is prerecorded. In other words, all the non-pitched percussion is prerecorded.

Toward the end of the main title there's a very strong mixed-meter statement of the "Dies Irae" motive in the timpani.

That truly was totally subconscious.

The main title has a spooky, nervous humor—you don't know whether to smile or to be frightened, or maybe both.

Well, that was the tricky thing with this film. It's a horror comedy. When you go to video stores, sometimes you'll find it lodged in the horror section and sometimes in the comedy section and sometimes in the where-the-hell-do-we-put-this section. It's neither fish nor foul. Black comedies are a bitch to pull off. Really a bitch.

When the vagrant, whom I love because he's a grizzly, disenchanted university professor, is pulling his little personal-belongings cart, your music-box lullaby theme is almost like a kid's bicycle with something attached to it or the neighborhood ice-cream truck. The innocence of the music box makes the vagrant's presence more evil, but also serves as a warning.

And there is one cue much later on in the film where I do interpolate that tune into the score. Two guys and I whistled it. It appears in the score when Bill Paxton has truly lost his spine. But, for the most part, I intentionally decided to keep it separate. Even though sometimes we don't see him or the cart, we'll hear the reminder, "he's just around the corner, boys and girls."

There's the scene when Krakowski is opening the valentine candy box. The vagrant shows up, and the score is a busy blend of the music-box theme, the vagrant music, and the horror motifs. Then, at the very end, the vagrant sticks out his tongue and gives a big sloppy raspberry. That's the end of the musical cue, a snotty percussive zonk.

You can't compete with something like that. You have to work up to such a climax! That's the most poignant exclamation point we could have. Things like that are definitely intentional.

You've come up with many outrageous titles for your cues on your film-score CDs: for *Hellraiser*, "Rat Slice Quartet"; for *Species*, "A Vibrant Slime" and "Species Feces"; and for *Fly II*, "Bartók Barbaro" and "Musica Domestica Metastasis."

It's not supposed to be "Musica," by the way. It's actually supposed to be "Musca." "Musca domestica" is the genus name for a fly. But Varèse Sarabande decided that I'd made a mistake, and decided to "correct" my "mistake." They thought, oh, "musca," he must mean "musica." So they made the change. I was really pissed, privately pissed—I didn't get on the phone and bitch about it. Maybe I did, a little. I don't know.

I'm very precise about titles. Most composers aren't interested in that, but I take a private fascination in coming up with fun titles. Why should it be that film composers always come up with these generic, descriptive titles for cues, like "Helicopter Chase," "Bubble-Bath Love Scene," whatever? When they're writing a cue, they come up with a generic title and put it on top of the score and it sticks. The titles I come up with on my original scores are the same kind of not-very-exciting descriptions. For my own clarification, they're non-exciting descriptions of the scenes for which they are being written. I'll just write, "The Fly Dies," or something like that. When the cue sheets are submitted to BMI, that's the title everyone goes by. Generally, composers decide to retain the same title for their CDs. But I almost always re-title my cues if I get a chance. I take a certain amount of pleasure in coming up with bizarre titles, like some of the titles on *The Vagrant*—"A Giblet Too Tastey," "Squish-O-Rama," "Jumbo Children Splat Fat." As a matter of fact, one of my habits is including the name of a film composer whose work I really admire. So, in every CD, I've buried the name of a film composer in my cue titles. In *The Vagrant*, I have one cue called "Rag Skin Blues," for David Raksin, with whom I studied, who wrote a score for a film called *Too Late Blues*. But sometimes they're more subtly buried.

Do you have the time or the desire or the opportunity to write music outside of the film world—scores that are pure "concert music"?

This is a very significant question. It's probably the most significant question you may ask me.

Well, how about, What did you have for breakfast?

Coffee and two cigarettes. But, seriously, it's not going to be easy to answer that concert-music question. Indeed, this gets down to should I feel good about the fact that I may devote my entire career to writing music for films, and what does that mean? It's too early to say at this moment. History thus far has given us the impression that the majority of film music is totally disposable. What is remembered? Only that music which is melodic in nature and attached to a title that means something to the general public at large. I am thrilled that you're excited about *The Vagrant*. But, let's face it, even if I could do a concert arrangement of *The Vagrant* as it stands now, it could never be performed live. But, say I was somehow to rework it into a state that could be performed on a stage. It will still never get performed on a stage—nobody in the concert world would be interested in it because it's connected to a Hollywood film, and nobody who's doing a film-music pops concert would be interested in doing it because of the title and because the pops-concert audience wouldn't like it anyhow. Also, it's virtually an unknown film. More film music concerts are happening now than ever before, but, for the most part, what you'll see on the programs are scores to commercially successful or classic movies. I mentioned Max Steiner earlier. Here's a guy who's written more minutes of music for films than probably anyone else, bar Ennio Morricone. And yet, maybe twenty minutes of his output is performed, has been performed, and in all probability will continue to get performed in concert.

The concert world isn't that much different. Of Stravinsky's total compositional output, probably ninety percent of his performances are of the three early Russian ballets, and mostly *The Firebird.*

And wouldn't he love to think that maybe something else is done once in a while? Now you can bet that Max Steiner is lying in his grave, as we speak, thinking that if only the film *She,* for instance, had had more commercial success . . . Max might be saying, "That's my favorite score. That's the score I want preserved. That's the one I want to have performed on the stage." I don't know, I can't speak for him. It's the Titanic Principle. If the film sinks, everyone goes down with the ship, no matter how good your work may be. If the film bites the dust, it takes everybody with it.

I'm getting a little off the subject now. But *Species* is a textbook example of what a successful film can do for your career. Now, mind you, it may or may not be the best film I've ever worked on; I definitely don't think it's the best score I've ever written, but the bottom line is that it did incredibly well at the box office. I used to hear, "Chris, your career is inching by ever so slowly. It's not an indication of your talent, it's an indication of the fact that you just haven't worked on the right film yet." Well, all of a sudden, when *Species* came out, everyone took me very seriously. I could be suggested as a possible composer on a big-budget project and no one would laugh. And I liked that.

It's interesting to look over my credits—even though I'm perceived as a horror guy, horror is only a small percentage of my output. Even from the beginning, I was doing dramas and action films and even some comedies. But they all did so poorly that no one took them seriously. *Highpoint*, a Richard Harris action-comedy, was one of my first pictures. And there was *Avenging Angel*, albeit not the greatest picture. There were always these examples where I was not, in the majority of instances, working on horror films. But the only ones that did any kind of box-office business were the horror films. So, that's what I became identified with.

Now, back to the question: Will I be satisfied at the end of my life having committed my entire creative efforts to film music?

Well, that's your spin on the question. Mine was a little less dramatic.

Actually, this is something that gnaws at me on a weekly basis. There's no confusion in my mind now, but it took me quite some time to come to this point in my evaluation of myself: God gave me something that it would be foolish of me to deny—that particular facility or talent that not every composer has that allows him to understand what it means to act as support to the picture, that sense that allows him to understand the dynamics of working in movies as opposed to the concert stage. As you know, there have been a lot of wonderful concert composers who have tried their hands at scoring films and have not really succeeded very well. It's not because they're not brilliant composers; they are. It's just that there is something else that is required to work in the idiom. And what it is, I can't actually verbalize. No one can verbalize it. But I'm convinced that it requires a certain talent that many people are not given, no matter how great they may be. God definitely put that talent into the pot when he created my musical personality. To turn my back on it would be foolish. I can say that I'm extremely satisfied that I've been able to be a part of this. As a matter fact, when I moved out here fifteen years ago, this was all I wanted in life. And, God, it's really happening.

The downside of being a film composer is that we all, I think, get addicted to the prospect of having musical ideas stimulated by something visual. What happens when you're sitting at the piano or the blank score page and you don't have something visual to stimulate your musical ideas? That's a horrible feeling of emptiness. I think that's one of the reasons why film composers have had a problem retaining careers as concert guys. That outside stimulus becomes a way of life. Back in the old days, when composers were on staff, Miklós Rózsa could state in his contract that every summer he was going to go to Italy and set that time aside for doing nothing but writing his concert music, which he did fairly regularly for a period of time. And if you look at his concert output, you'll notice that when he was working on films, his output of concert music diminished. Same thing with Korngold—you know, wunderkind moves to Hollywood, still working occasionally with concert music. But he had a very short film career—sixteen pictures or seventeen years or something like that—and then he closed the door on Hollywood and his concert career resumed.

It's not surprising whatsoever. You get into films and it is so draining, so draining. Every day of the week you have to be in here writing, knowing that by the end of the day you have to, come hell or high water, produce a certain number of minutes of music. Who gives a fuck if you get run over by a car when you're walking across the street? You better get out of the hospital real quick because you gotta get your three minutes done today. It's extremely exhausting. There's no time, no creative leeway for you to dabble in the maybes of what you might want to do for any particular picture. You gotta get the job done. And you gotta get it delivered by such and such a date or you're in big-time trouble. I find it a miracle that so much good film music has been written under these conditions. Indeed, when I'm not working on films, though my mind and my gut are gnawing at me, saying, "get back to those projects that have been have passing through your mind over these years," the other half of me is trying to turn the machine off and just rejuvenate.

And there's the competitive thing—anyone who gets into this wants desperately to be at the top. So, even when you're not working, it's a full-time job trying to figure how to advance your career. It truly is. The grass is always greener. There are very few composers working in this industry who, I think, are really, truly content with their lot. I would suspect that even Jerry Goldsmith is probably envious of John Williams' career and John Williams is probably envious of Stravinsky and Stravinsky was probably envious of God. You know what I'm saying? It's all this big chain that's neverending. And anyone who's not on the A team of the ten or twelve guys who seem to soak up most of the work, unless they're lying to you, probably wants to get on that A team. I remember one of my agents said to me, "Chris, when you finally get onto the A team, your career is going to move forward despite yourself." Meaning, once you get attached to a handful of pictures that do good business, you're gonna be in demand. And no matter what you deliver, really, because of the success of those pictures, the interest is always going to be there and your career will move forward despite you. The demand will be there. The calls will come. You'll continue to work on successful films.

Unless you really screw up?

Unless you screw up in a major way, you'll sort of always be up there at the top of the heap. I think we're all trying to get up there. And, as you can see, there are about twelve guys at any given time who are sort of the A team. I would not consider myself a member of that very prestigious, closed ensemble, but on the verge of getting there. I've always thought that my calling card is that I always try my best to do good work. A lot of the directors I've worked with are first-time directors who, unfortunately, don't get a second film. Or if they do, sometimes they move into television. I've not connected with that *one* director who has wowed Hollywood and moved up the ladder and insisted on taking me with him. Most composers get onto that A team in that manner—through a director. Look at the teams from Herrmann and Hitchcock up to John Williams and Spielberg, Howard Shore and David Cronenberg, Danny Elfman and Tim Burton, Marc Shaiman and Rob Reiner.

I have worked with a whole slew of new directors who are very promising, who have made pictures that are successful, and who, hopefully, will continue using me. But you really never know. At least I've not confused a director to the point where he's said to me, "I can't ever imagine working on another picture with you!" That sometimes happens. Generally, when that happens, it's a bad sign.

But to go back to the big question, there are many, many, many things that I have in my mind that I am desperately wanting to pursue that do not fall into the film-music world. I would not be so pretentious as to describe those things that I want to pursue as being legitimate concert music. Concert music is a full-time thing. And the rewards that concert composers receive are so minimal. It's not a monetary thing. What is it? Film composers are paid well for what we do. We're the highest-paid composers who write for orchestra. I have to tip my hat to those people like you who've committed themselves, their lives, to pursuing this higher goal, and who do not ask that the rewards come immediately.

And, why are the leaders of concert music leaders? Simply because they devote their entire creative energies to bettering this vocabulary that exists outside of the commercial world of music. We have committed, as film composers, the majority of our creative efforts to writing the best film music we can. It doesn't leave the kind of time that we would like to have to pursue our other ideas.

There are a whole slew of things that I want to do that are not connected to film music. I've implied this in some of my film scores. *The Vagrant* is indicative of a road that I'd love to travel. The greatest disadvantage with film music is that it's in and out in two-and-a-half minutes or three minutes or five minutes at most. We can't develop anything. We can't develop our ideas in an organic manner. We're too restricted. There's this vessel, a vase, that's already shaped, and somehow you have to figure out a way to work yourself into this thing. And in so doing, dress the vase. The nature of the music, the essence of the vocabulary you are going to utilize, is described by the content of the movie at the onset.

I have had an opportunity in some instances to expand on film-music-related ideas that I've stretched out into longer pieces. On the CD of the score I did for a cable movie called *Max and Helen*, which was issued by the Bay Cities label, we didn't have enough score to fill up the CD, because there were only twenty-three minutes of score. So, I took the time and developed this electronic piece, this tape piece, to fill up the CD. It's all tape stuff. I'm fascinated with the manipulation of sound. Maybe that's what my calling is. I'm not sure what my real personality is outside of films. I try to figure out what my personality is *in* films. Usually, musical personalities are dictated by the films you work on. For all I know, such and such a composer, who works on comedies, is a guy who, at night, listens to Stockhausen and Boulez. But, his personality as a composer has been shaped by that language required by those kinds of pictures.

You're a natural in the horror genre, but the introspective *Murder in the First* and the jazzy *Man Who Knew Too Little* scores seem natural for you, too.

I enjoy them, too. It goes back to what I said earlier—I want to write that fucking sixteen-bar theme that everyone remembers. I am not sure that I'm going to be a happy camper at the end of my life if all I've done is give my entire composing time to the movies. That's one thing that haunts me. Jerry Goldsmith, for instance, is a guy who is thoroughly content. At least, I get the feeling that he is thoroughly content in contributing or focusing his entire creative energies to films. And all power to him. That's wonderful. He obviously is not haunted by it; he has come to terms with that. There is this stuff that I want to do that's floating around in my head, but will just never successfully find its way into movies.

You seem much more passionate and concerned about this than most of the other composers I've interviewed. If an orchestra commissioned a piece from you, would you be tempted to go ahead and take that detour, take yourself out of Hollywood circulation, and forget film offers X and Y for a few months?

That's an interesting question, because that involves making a living and this whole competitive thing.

The minute you stop and take yourself out of contention for a few months, there might be a dozen other Hollywood composers who'll pass you by and get a crack at that big-budget movie that you might have had?

Oh, my God! That's the horror. The panic of it all. We operate in a state of panic. Who's going to pass me by? Of course, the team that you surround yourself with would fight such a move. I love my agents. They do a brilliant job for me. I'm thoroughly thrilled with them. But you can be sure that they're not going to be on the phone with me saying, "Great idea, Chris! Take a year off from films and write some concert music. Congratulations. We're all for it." Fuck, no. And even my wife would get a little worried: "What's going on here? Is daddy flipping out? Is he losing it?" We all operate on fear, I think, to a certain degree. Because of the somebody's-passing-you-by problem, a lot of film composers have a tendency to work on four, five, six films a year if they can get the opportunities. Like Goldsmith. But my impression is that the reason why Goldsmith has done as many films as he has is because it has become a way of life for him. I don't think he can imagine getting up in the morning and not having to write some music to some scene. Another day, another scene. That's what he does.

I used to ask myself, if all I did were horror films, would I be content at the end of my life being the Bela Lugosi of film music? Would I be happy with that? Would I feel complete in my life if I had committed my entire career energies to working on horror films, and that's how I would be remembered, as a horror composer? I didn't like that idea at all. And neither did Bela Lugosi. He was tormented throughout his life. He considered himself a serious dramatic actor who had been passed over by Hollywood because of typecasting. It hasn't hurt his legacy, though. His contribution is very significant. And part of me says, Chris, if all you're gonna do are horror films the rest of your life—and that won't happen, fortunately—that's not something to be that ashamed of.

Your work in the horror genre has allowed you a certain musical latitude that other genres might not offer you.

Working in horror, or being thought of primarily as a horror composer, has been a double-edged sword. The horror genre allows the composer to do a lot more experimental things than romantic comedies, for instance. And I would have to say that some of my more memorable experiences, in terms of being given opportunities that I otherwise wouldn't have been given, are in the horror domain. Specific pictures? Well, *The Vagrant* is definitely one of them. It's a bizarre black comedy. In that instance, I knew that they were struggling to get a handle on what direction the music should go. As you know, the way directors try to get a handle on the music is they temp the film with existing music. On *The Vagrant*, they tried the minimalist, synth-drone-based score, and that wasn't working. It seemed to suck the life out of the film. And the orchestral—the traditional suspense orchestral—didn't seem to work. Finally, they said, listen, we don't know what to do here—we're at a loss. But, we want something different. I've found that the films that have generated my most original work have been those where they don't really know what they want.

Let's talk about more recent scores.

On *Jennifer 8*, I knew that they wanted me to get as close as possible to whatever the director's ideas were. In that instance, he definitely wanted a piano playing a theme. What I recall most about that theme was the situation in which it was born. I was hired on the project and immediately sent off to do a demo of the theme or the material I might be using for the film. I did a piano demo. And they did a temp dubbing of the movie, so I went to the temp dub, where they played my demo. I didn't know they were going to do that while I was there. They played it in front of everybody on the dub stage. There was dead silence. I knew immediately that I had not hit a home run, that this was the wrong theme for the movie.

What were your own gut instincts about the original *Jennifer 8* theme?

Well, I wasn't convinced that it was the right one, but it was the first one that had come to my mind. They were kind to me, but I could sense that there was this feeling of "Oh, God, do we have the right guy?" So I get in my car, and while I'm driving back, and I'm at the intersection of Santa Monica Boulevard and Wilshire, right in Beverly Hills, I turn around and I look at the fountain. Right then, the theme for *Jennifer 8* just popped into my head. I knew this was it.

Fortunately, I always carry my little cassette machine. God only knows what it was like in the time before they had little portable cassette machines! What did you do? Did you pull your horse and buggy over to the side of the road and jot it down on paper, because otherwise you'd forget? And it's nearly impossible not to forget—someone's passing by with the whole subwoofer rap thing blasting and it's gone. In the old days, there weren't so many distractions, you could carry an idea around in your head for days and not worry about it getting invaded by some external source.

Your story is another variation of the old "Beethoven wandering by the babbling brook for inspiration."

But where *I* was, the *people* were babbling. Anyway, back to the theme: All I remember is that I got on my hands and knees when I got back to my office, and I said, "Thank you, God, thank you, thank you, thank you." After that, the score came into shape very rapidly. It's amazing how things work out.

Alex North said the worst part of any project is that first period when you're trying to decide on the vocabulary. And I agree with him, totally. My wife can't stand being around me when I'm in that period. All I can think about is, "When is that idea going to come? When is this all going to happen? God, I'm running out of time! I've got five weeks and I've just wasted two weeks thinking, and I still haven't come up with any material." As a composer, when you see a film, the tune may not come, but the nature of the music will come—you will get an idea, a concept. I've always said it's like a long tunnel, and at the very far end you see this cloudy haze—these white things, like ghosts, like sonic amoebas—where it's all there, waiting to be found. The whole process of working on the score is trying to bring that image closer to you, focusing in on it, and then allowing yourself to step back and have some sense of perspective.

Finding that balance between the specifics and the broad strokes?

Right. As you know, when we're writing, it's like looking through a microscope—we tend to get obsessed with particulars that ultimately don't mean too much in the whole. I find that, when I'm writing, sometimes I like to just sit in front of the speakers, with the sound off, and just pretend that I'm hearing the score, the reality of the music, coming through the speakers—imagine the way it may sit in the context of the film. Then, all of a sudden, I realize

I don't need to do this, I don't need to do that, but I do need to do this.

Do you also imagine the orchestra up on the stage?

Yeah, I imagine that, too. But the tragedy of film music is that once it's performed with the orchestra, it's frozen. It's so weird to listen to scores for pictures from the 1940s. It's like they are bizarre ghost stories—the composers are dead, the orchestra musicians are dead, the actors are dead. Do you know what I mean? The scores get performed once, and that's *the* performance, it's frozen in time, stuck in a picture. And there it is forever. The same long note will always be there forever and ever and ever.

Did you have input in the source music in *Jennifer 8*? They use the humming chorus from Puccini's *Madama Butterfly*.

I don't know why this is, but whenever there's an opportunity for a classical source, directors immediately use opera. That way the audience believes they're cultured artists? I've never quite understood that. I remember the director asked me about this source, and I said I didn't think Sigourney Weaver would be listening to an opera. I wasn't quite sure what she would be listening to, but, at the time, I came up with a bunch of suggestions that didn't include Italian opera. The Italian opera thing is so often used. It's a director thing more than a composer thing. In *Copycat*, it's Rossini.

So, you make suggestions, but they . . .

Yeah, but both directors were really sold on this. And they wanted me to confirm their opinions. Since I was just establishing my relationship with them, and there's always a little tension at the beginning, I'd say, "Oh, yeah, that's a great idea." Then, once I'd gotten to know them a little better, I'd say, "You know, I've got another idea here." The opera thing works better in *Jennifer 8* than it does in *Copycat.*

In *Jennifer 8*, there's a great scene where the men are cleaning their guns and we hear "Silent Night." What a great emotional contrast!

Yeah, that stuff is really fun to do. They hired me for *Murder in the First* based on the director's response to the theme I had written for *Jennifer 8.* To a certain degree, they were taking a shot with an unknown. Even though I had the credits, I'd never done a picture quite like *Murder in the First.* They hired me early, during preproduction, so there was extra time for me to explore material in a way that normally isn't possible.

***Murder in the First* is primarily a sensitive string-orchestra score.**

That's right. And to divide the orchestra into a large string group fronted by an octet and a string quartet was inspired by Vaughan Williams. I did do some Americana, too. It's not earth-shattering stuff, but there's that "News on the March" theme [Young hums], which is very Sousa inspired. Why do I do this? Why do I take such an interest in this stuff? It's part musicology and part orchestration. I love to try to figure out what makes things work. And there's no better way to figure out how Sousa works than to try to do it yourself. And what better an opportunity than "News on the March"! You rarely get those kinds of opportunities in anything other than film music. Is it bad that we do this? That so much of the tradition of film music has been so often imitative? I don't know. I don't think so. But for "News on the March," it would have been foolish to write experimental music. It's a period clip. I took that as a challenge. I love Sousa! I love that music! Wouldn't you say it's probably the most American music we have given birth to?

Maybe, along with jazz and blues. When you do have a few free moments to just relax and listen to music, what do you listen to? Do you check out your film-music competition?

You want to see what I listen to? We can step around the corner, where I have a large film-music collection. I became obsessed. I became a record collector, a vinyl collector.

Before you started your own career?

No, at about the same time. I realized my best teacher would be listening to what others had done. If you wanted to study a score in the pre-videocassette era, you had to have the record. The actual printed scores, of course, were never available.

How did you become familiar with older movie scores?

If you wanted to study a classic score, you had to wait for those late, late, late, late movies. I would set up my little reel-to-reel tape recorder and record the audio track. I listened to the dialogue and studied how the music played under and around the dialogue, how the music set us up for the dramatic implications. That's how I learned. It was pretty much listen and watch and understand. I took only one course on film music, David Raksin's class at UCLA. And I studied privately with Albert Harris for a short period of time, but that was about the extent of it.

When I do have spare time, I listen to a lot of film music—I try to keep up with what's going on. But the CD thing is so expensive—there's so much available, but I can't buy it all. When I'm not listening to film music, I also have a gigantic collection of avant-garde scores and contemporary concert music.

Do you keep up with jazz?

No, not really, not at all. And I'm out of touch with what's going on in popular music. The pop music that I like is the stuff I listened to when I was in high school and college. It's not left my mind. It stuck and it never left.

Did you have particular favorites?

There were the three Bs: The Beatles, The Beach Boys, and The Byrds—my three favorite pop groups. And when I'm writing a tune, that's all definitely leaking its way through a little bit. As far as the jazz thing is concerned, everything culminated in my interest in big-band music. My first experiments with composing were for big band. I went to North Texas State University and had a number of original charts played there. I went through a major Stan Kenton period. I just loved the brass players, and everyone swinging. But after I got into film, I sort of closed the door on all that. I concentrate on listening to contemporary orchestral music. I favor the stuff after 1945.

I've got a lot of Stockhausen, lots of Berio, Penderecki, Lutoslawski, and lots of different unusual stuff, too. There are a few record stores in L.A. that sell those CRI and Louisville Orchestra recordings cheap, two bucks. I have maybe three or four hundred records back there that I've yet to listen to. Well, maybe I'm exaggerating, maybe I've got about two hundred.

Do you do your own orchestrations?

Ah, the orchestration thing. It's a complicated situation. When I started off, my heroes, my role models, were Bernard Herrmann and Jerry Goldsmith. Bernard Herrmann, as we know from his interviews, thought that any composer who did not orchestrate his work himself was a hack. So this thing was hanging over my head—to orchestrate yourself is to be a true man, to prove your creative manliness. It's the red badge of courage among the composers, along with how much music you wrote in how short a period of time.

Do you mean it's a competition over who wrote what faster than the next guy?

It's so strange. They'll exaggerate—they'll chop off two weeks from the actual time it took to write the score. You have to take it all with a grain of salt.

Anyway, Bernard Herrmann is my hero. And, for a long time, I did all my orchestrations myself. Until *The Fly II*, the first score where I did not orchestrate everything. And why did I do that? First of all, I'd just gotten married. My wife is wonderful—she's extremely tolerant, as I assume all composers' wives must be. One day, after I hadn't been home for two days, she came over here to the studio and found me like this [Young slumps over] on the desk. She was really worried, she thought that I was just going to fizzle up and burn myself out.

Was that a physical wake-up call?

Oh, yeah. That week, for the first time, I brought in someone else— Jeff Atmajian, a young guy who went through the USC film-music program. He was introduced to me by my friend Bruce Broughton. What have I discovered by having an orchestrator? Does it save time? Not really. Things haven't changed. But I look back at the days before I had someone and wonder how the hell I pulled it off. The greatest advantage of having a second man, at least from my perspective, is that your score's going through a second filter, a guy who can say, "Chris, I think this is gonna work."

Everything in your business seems so frantic now.

Wouldn't it be wonderful if we had the advantages they had in the old days? You've written a cue. How's it going to work? So you go up to Alfred Newman and say, "Hey, Al, at the end of your session could you put up this cue and just run through it once, so I could hear it?" We don't have anything like that anymore. The first time you hear your music is when you're on stage, recording. It's very tense. I'm nervous. I hope it's going to work.

Now that you don't orchestrate every moment yourself . . .

It's not like, from that moment on, I haven't orchestrated. I have never lost my desire to have control of all the colors that are so integral to the music. I'm still very detailed in all my sketches. And the synth things, or synth and chamber group things—things that are not full orchestra—I completely orchestrate myself. There is no way you can communicate these desired sounds to an orchestrator. For instance, there is absolutely no way anyone but me could have orchestrated *The Vagrant*. Absolutely no way.

How do you learn how to orchestrate? It's something that's there or it's not. You can learn in books about the registers of the instruments, you can study scores, but the bottom line is, when you're left alone, either the colors are in your head or they're not. Fortunately, they are there for me—I've always been very interested in color.

Color is so important in film music. It was Herrmann who really opened up that door. He'd say something like, "Wait a second, guys. This stuff is probably never going to get performed again. So why do we have to restrict ourselves to the standard romantic orchestra?" If he wanted eighteen horns, he'd get them, and not worry about whether it would be attractive on the concert stage. He was the first guy to try many unusual combinations of instruments. I got into that very much.

I do have an orchestrator now, Pete Anthony, who I've been working with for a few years. And I'm not going to minimize his involvement. He certainly polishes the rough edges and offers some good suggestions. But my sketches are very detailed—I've not given up or turned my back or lessened my obsession with the colors to any degree. You're probably going to hear the same thing from every composer, so you can believe me or not. It's your choice.

I'm so into color that whenever I get the chance to enhance a standard orchestra with something unusual, I will go for it. That chance doesn't happen all that often, but it happens a lot in the boogieman films and the suspense thrillers. It's interesting that the scores that you've brought up so far are more in what I call the "mindfuck" domain—the horror films and the oddball films that allow you to do a lot more experimenting. Much more experimenting than in this new kind of film I've moved into, the romantic thriller—*Copycat, Jennifer 8, Judicial Consent.* A lot of the music for these films has to fall into a standard convention that doesn't allow you to get as psychotic as you can with the mindfuck films.

Your interest in color generates very interesting musical textures.

In one student film, I did a Renaissance sound with Renaissance instruments—crumhorns, sackbuts, those big, deep tin-can things. Wonderful timbres.

Have you had occasion to use crumhorn or sackbut since?

No. I'd love to. Crumhorns, wow! Serpents, man! I'd love to use a serpent.

Have you been consciously working on moving away from your horror label?

Not really. The pictures I do now are getting better, but I don't want to lose touch with that bizarre experimental side of me, the *Vagrant* side of me. I would say that, as far as orchestration, *The Vagrant* is probably the most experimental of my film scores. That's why I'm so happy with it. I took the ideas and the philosophies Bernard Herrmann offered to Hollywood but moved them somewhere else.

I'm always asked, "What's your favorite film, Chris?" Well, that's a tough question to answer, but, in many ways, I think *The Vagrant* is my favorite film. I listen to it and can't hear direct musical influences as noticeably as I can in my other works. And that gets back to the questions of life.

And those are tough questions.

Well, the thing that kicked my career along and yet at the same time I feel held me back was, when I started my career, I was obsessed with Bernard Herrmann and Jerry Goldsmith. And it happened that the directors with whom I worked also loved those two composers and strongly encouraged me to pursue those avenues and those styles. Early on, I didn't have enough confidence in myself to believe I could go off and forge my own style.

But *Def-Con 4*, one of your earliest works, sounds very original.

Actually, the main title to *Def-Con 4* was indicative of what I thought I had to offer to the profession—something that was a little bit different. Who knows what keeps composers going in this business? For me, it's that I know I've got something to bring to films that no one else is trying. The main title to *Def-Con 4* was indicative of the direction I wanted to go. The whole thing eventually came around to *Invaders from Mars.* That was it! That was the big moment when I was going to release all this strange stuff that no one had really tried to bring to Hollywood. Well, the *Invaders* score got thrown out, and that event changed my outlook, which is too bad. It pulled me down to a certain degree, realizing that these guys were frightened of something new.

But you have many unusual post-*Invaders* scores in your catalog.

There are still moments that come up. *Hellbound: Hellraiser II* sure has some wacky stuff. *The Vagrant* was post-*Invaders from Mars.* But *Invaders from Mars* changed my rebellious outlook—my obsession with trying to infiltrate the conservative film-music world with this avant-garde approach.

As you become more respected and more in-demand, do you think you will be given a freer hand, be able to continue your musical experiments?

If my career continues to improve, I will probably be working less and less on these mindfuck films, these oddball movies.

And letting that experimental part of you dissolve into film-music history would be okay with you?

Well, that gets back to the question of life, and to my lot in life. Half of me wants to be on that exclusive A team, doing all those big-budget pictures. I have to say, *Murder in the First* was the first score I could give to my parents without having to preface it with some sort of an apology. It's basically healthy, traditional, all-American movie stuff. My two brothers said, "Chris, that's your first really good score." I never heard any response from my family about *The Vagrant*.

Tales from the Hood, musically, is like a cinema symphony—four stories, four movements, but with a few common links between them.

Of the four stories, my favorite is the first. But I have to see the film again, I think the music gets lost in it.

It does, especially in the fourth episode.

And in the fourth episode, part of the score is this strange rock/jazz material, which is part electronics and part full orchestra, with a twentieth-century Eastern-European Mass feel. It's the only time where there are three totally different types of music within one episode.

And you've got rap music with strains of Orff's Carmina Burana, which is a great fusion. I'm curious about your notation for this score.

That's right. That's another example. But my favorite underscore portion was, as I said, the grim urban jazz for that first episode. I'm a horror guy—I've done a lot of horror films—but this movie is a very different kind of horror film. First of all, it has all black actors, black situations, black locations. And there's a social message in every episode. Structurally it's very much like *Tales From the Crypt* or the old *Twilight Zone* series, or even the *Twilight Zone* movie for that matter, which certainly was looming over my head. The *Twilight Zone* movie was produced on a limited budget, but it had full orchestra blasting through every episode. The Goldsmith score is daring, not quite like anything we've heard before.

I revisited the *Tales for the Hood* score when I was doing some promo CDs, and I thought, "This weird jazz stuff is pretty cool. It's all right." Now, what kind of notation did I use? I'd have to pull the scores out, but certainly everything is accounted for in one way, shape, or form. Let's see, I recall piano, bass, guitar . . .

A few strings, some glissandi . . .

Yeah, and solo viola and lots of percussion—timpani and metals, and we used mixing bowls, gongs, cymbals. Another interesting instrument that I used was a bass shakuhachi, which was built for that episode. I had used shakuhachi way back on *Bat 21*. And, oh yeah, there's a bass melodica, which goes back to the bass harmonica thing in *The Dorm That Dripped Blood*. I had a choir of melodica players. Well, you might not want to say a choir, it was about four guys, bass up to soprano.

And the notation gives clear directions?

Oh yeah. In some instances it's quasi-indeterminate, spatial/proportional notation.

In the second episode, one of the most attractive sounds is the sinister little music-box figure. The music box's innocence suggests

a more frightening evil. **You have used a similar approach in other films—*Hellraiser*, *The Vagrant*, to name a few. Is this becoming a Youngism?**

Yeah, I think you're probably right. This goes back again to the subconscious. The eight-bar tune is very conscious, but the instinct for the music box is from inside. Wouldn't it be great to walk into a music-box specialty store where all the boxes are playing at the same time? I love music boxes. My God, you can see I've got music boxes all around this room. The first film I worked on for which I needed to provide a music-box source was *Flowers in the Attic*. I wrote that theme first, and suddenly realized I that could utilize it as the principle theme for the entire score. In *Tales from the Hood*, there's no actual music box in the movie—the kid doesn't play with a music box—but the flavor and imagery of it is there. It's one of those great orchestrational colors.

Isn't there something really fascinating about these little boxes? The particular unusual timbre you get out of them is unlike anything you can replicate anywhere else. I've also been really interested in band organs, the instruments that were built for carnival carousels. In *Dream Lover*, there was a carnival scene, and there were bizarre dream sequences in the carnival, for which they wanted me to provide the carnival atmosphere. I went to the carousel museum in San Francisco where there were cassettes and CDs for sale with nothing but band organ music. I also studied the one they use down here at the Santa Monica Pier. And in New Jersey, I actually got the opportunity to be taken inside one of the carousels so I could get up close. I learned quite a bit about the instrument and then set out to try to emulate its sound and its flavor. These days, you can really accomplish this with synth samples. Sure, I would have loved to have been able to construct an organ roll of my material and have the actual machine play it, but that was practically impossible. So, instead, through samples, I put together this piece that was used as source in *Dream Lover*. I tried my damnedest to simulate that sound, that orchestration.

In the third episode of *Tales*, you use this scratchy, voodoo solo-violin figure. It's such a disturbing presence. You've mentioned your . . .

Go ahead, say it.

. . . your Goldsmith connection. Was this directly inspired by "Nightmare at 20,000 Feet"—the gremlin-on-the-wing episode from the *Twilight Zone* movie?

Yeah, you're right. Unfortunately, that's my least favorite of all the *Hood* episodes.

Musically?

Musically. Because of the time pressure, I wasn't able to come up with what I would consider an original approach to that episode.

But it carries its own distinct personality. And aren't we all derivative in one sense or another? I think you're being too hard on yourself. Sure, you borrowed the inspiration, the idea, but you moved it into a different place.

I guess so. I must say that when I put it together, I was not cloning Goldsmith, either from the *Twilight Zone* movie or the *TZ* episode he did. But those were my models, and I would be lying if I didn't acknowledge them.

As I've said before, the greatest thing that ever happened to me was listening to all those records of all that film music. That taught me what to do and what not to do and how to do it. In a situation where I wasn't sure how to get through a scene, Goldsmith and Herrmann were my teachers. The disadvantage of this is that it's been difficult to rid myself of their direct influence. The best decision I've made recently is not to listen to any Jerry Goldsmith. I have all his CDs, but I don't put them on. I don't listen to

Herrmann much either. I'm trying to be more comfortable with who I am and what I have to offer. I'm constantly trying to find a way to come up with something that's uniquely me.

Actually, the third *Tales* episode might first call Stravinsky to mind.

And certainly Goldsmith would be the first to admit that the idea of using the solo violin in a story of evil and magic was not his own doing. We all know Stravinsky's *L' histoire du soldat.*

In the fourth *Tales* episode, you have rap, jazz, Penderecki-like atonality, and Orff-like choral music fused together. Was that a difficult coordination problem?

Absolutely. That was very difficult. For me, what made that episode distinguishable from the other three was that it was the only one that had black source music in it. In a more recent film, *Set It Off,* I had the same problem: How do you acknowledge that material and interpolate its essence into your own music so that the underscore doesn't seem like it's coming out of a totally different universe than the source? Even though *Tales from the Hood* is an all-black-cast film, my job was to utilize the same type of material I would use if it were an all-white-cast film. An exclusion to that was the jazz in the first episode, which definitely needed acknowledgment as a black element.

And the third episode uses African percussion?

For the voodoo dolls, I used kalimbas. There's a certain definite African element that was very constant—talking drums, African rhythms, two black altos singing "ooh-ah ooh-ah," a subtle ritualistic chanting. As you said, the fourth episode is the one with some rap that I had to contend with. The samples used were more from the rap-techno world—a lot of the metallic sounds you hear in some of the rap stuff. As for the *Carmina Burana* stuff, I remember the director said he wanted this and he'd sing . . . [Young sings "O Fortuna"] I thought, this is very strange—this is a black film and he wants music that is very white. Is this going to work? But he insisted on going that route, and I think he was right, it does work. At the end of the film, that material—that big, demonic *Carmina Burana* choral thing, fused with a rap-techno sound—recurs when Clarence Williams has revealed himself as Satan and they're all burning in hell. And I recall one cue where the rap starts up and dissolves into the orchestra. We had the rap stuff on tape, and I wrote my cue around it, knowing that I had to be locked into the same time. I remember the complications we had in building a clip that acknowledged the fluctuations in tempo. It was a tricky puzzle that had to be solved. I'd have to see it again, but it seemed at the time that the fusion between the two worlds was pretty seamless.

Who arranges for the recordings of your orchestral scores?

A few American orchestras record film scores, but only those without restrictive union costs and problems—Utah, Seattle. A lot of recording is done overseas. I've worked with the London Symphony and a few orchestras in eastern Europe. *Species* was done here in town, and any score that's done here in Los Angeles is performed by studio musicians.

Drawn from various sources?

Yeah. Different orchestra contractors have their different performers, people who gig all over the city doing all kinds of stuff. There's a core group that my contractor likes to bring in. It's different than it was in the old days—these guys aren't on salary, they just show up on the lot for whatever score they have to do. But you can go to Europe if you want to use regularly performing orchestras.

What blocked the commercial release of a *Species* recording? Was it a financial situation?

It was all financial. It's unfortunate that it didn't happen. I don't think anyone at the time knew the film was going to take off to the degree that it did. As you know, there is a problem with orchestra re-use fees. It was a big orchestra, and it cost a lot of money. A *Species* release probably would have happened if the MGM music department had taken more of an interest in doing something with it. At the time, it was a very green, very new music department, and this was not something they were comfortable doing yet. It wasn't a priority, and barely even a consideration.

I understand that your score for *Jennifer 8* led to your score for *Species*. What's the story behind getting the *Jennifer 8* gig?

Jennifer 8's director asked his music editor to help him find music to temp the film. Dan [Garde] went down to the CD store and just bought a lot of different stuff. At one point, he was playing *The Fly II*, and the director, who was editing down the hall, heard the cue, came running in, and asked him, "What the hell is that?" Dan knew a little bit about me, so he expounded on my virtues. The director said, "This is the guy we've got to get!" Long after I was hired, the director mentioned to me that, if he had gone out to buy CDs, not in a million years would he have picked one from a film called *The Fly II*. As a consequence to getting the *Jennifer 8* job, I got *Species*. The editor on *Jennifer 8* went on to work on *Species*, and he, in turn, introduced my music to director Roger Donaldson, who temped it with *Jennifer 8*! The temping thing plays an important part in how one gets jobs. And, unfortunately, as they say, it's not what you know, it's who you know. Sometimes it's true.

I've read in interviews with you that you are concerned about music criticism.

I'm concerned about the responsibility of the critic.

Who generally views the majority of film music as disposable. How do you change public perception and critical opinion?

Get better composers! No, seriously, I didn't know I was that outspoken on this subject.

Very few film composers seemed to be concerned about it. I sense that maybe you believe you deserve a little more positive criticism or critical acknowledgment because the quality and the integrity are there in your music. Beethoven made us want his symphonies, Stravinsky made us want *The Rite of Spring*, Christopher Young made us want *The Vagrant*. You are a composer first, writing for films is your creative outlet.

Right. Well, as you know, there are not many publications that review film scores. And newspaper film reviews rarely even acknowledge that the music exists. So, there is not much written material available that strictly focuses on film music, just a few books and magazine articles. But my hesitation on the subject of film-music criticism is that the majority of the writers who contribute to these magazines write like they haven't seen the films before they comment on the material. Also, they don't know music, so they write abstractly, which doesn't make sense. One half of me is thrilled that there is this contingent of die-hard film-music consumers out there who love or are attracted to film music enough that they feel it can be listened to out of the context of the film and evaluated on its own terms. But it is almost always impossible to evaluate the success or failure of a score unless you understand the context in which it was written, meaning the film itself.

Many critics also seem to ignore the demands, the restrictions, and the specific expectations placed on the film composer.

Would I, in a million years, have gone the route that I went in *Bat 21* if the director had not been constantly pushing the drone concept?

Would I have gone the route that I ended up going in *The Vagrant* if the director had pushed for a more conventional orchestral score? These things all have to be taken into account when viewing the product. We are never left alone to do whatever we want at any given moment in time. We are tightly bound not only by the nature of the film we're working with and the music budget that we have, but also the politics and the desires of the employer. Unless you're inside the business, it's really hard to embrace all these different parameters. As a consequence, those who usually contribute to the film-music magazines, the fans and record collectors, don't have any understanding of what really goes on, not that gut reactions aren't valid.

And the academic critic comes from the opposite side.

The academic comes from an entirely different perspective. Professional concert musicians, like the soundtrack fans, are not really in touch with what goes on in the business. Their remarks are much more musically perceptive, musically valid, but they're based mostly on musical language—"He used this progression here, that suspension there"—because they don't know the business.

How might a music critic describe Chris Young?

I've got my own musical personality fairly well defined when I leave the tonal world, when I'm not dealing with triads and traditional harmonic functions. I don't think there's a normal triad in the *Vagrant* score, except for the music-box stuff. If there is, it was an accident. But the minute I move into the tonal world, it's clear that I still feel a certain amount of the ghosts of . . . what?

All the other composers floating around you?

Right. And this is what I want to resolve, especially since I'm now moving into films that are more mainstream. After all the suspense and horror pictures that I've worked on, I must say that the one formula that Herrmann gave us, and that no one else has achieved, is if you're trying to communicate a sense of mystery and heightened suspense to your audience, what better way to do it than with a simple little ascending progression of minor triads.

You like that. I hear it in *Copycat.*

Now, I do it all over the place. On one hand, it does the job it needs to do, almost immediately, and I identify with that. Why do I identify with it? I don't know. That's what I'm trying to figure out. When I do, I'll be able to come up with a language of my own that communicates the same essence in a tonal manner, a vocabulary that communicates something instantaneously. A lot of composers have tried doing other stuff, but it's not as immediate. I remember David Raksin saying in one of my classes, "I've never seen a successfully handled true love scene that's not tonal." I think he's got a good point there. But, who knows, maybe fifty years from now Webern or Steve Reich may express that which seems to personify the great tear-jerking moment in all these romance films.

Maybe it's up to you to break that ground.

I'd love to try it. Wouldn't that be great?

Although you acknowledge the direct influence of the ascending minor-triad sequences of Herrmann, I feel that you might be too hard on yourself. The dominant-seventh chord still goes to the tonic, as it has for hundreds of years, but you find original ways to express it.

I may be a little bit too hard on myself. And there would be nothing that could make me more professionally happy at the end of my life than to have something that's distinctively recognized as my own. But there's the Hollywood film-music mentality: They have to wait until new material gets assimilated in the public awareness.

Directors and producers, who usually have not experienced much contemporary concert music, are exposed to the general sound world mostly through film.

That's right.

And it whips right back. They can pick up experimental concert music that doesn't strike their ears as strange because that stuff's been bombarding them on the screen for the last two decades.

Yet people would pour out of the concert hall if such and such a modern score from such and such a picture were presented to them out of the context of the film. But in the film, it's fine. The same music they detest on the concert stage, they embrace in the context of the picture. Does film music ruin concert music? I don't know. Does it cheapen it? I don't know. Is it a bastardization of it? Is it nothing but a collection of cheap, imitative rip-offs of the contemporary classics? I don't know.

But we, as film composers, have to crystallize and focus in on those aspects of the literature that are the most effective for immediately communicating something to the audience. One of the main criticisms that's been thrown at the whole avant-garde movement is that none of the composers knew when to stop, when to pull the curtain, close the show, stop the tape. You get this ambiance thing going, and it goes on for hours and hours, like Morton Feldman. But film composers know we always have a certain finite period of time. We have to draw the best out of all this material and place it into a context that makes its point immediately. We just don't have the opportunity to develop ideas over long periods of time.

Not unlike Korngold and company taking Strauss and Mahler and boiling them down to a concentrated five-minute Errol Flynn cue.

Concert composers love to criticize that we can't develop anything. I've never presented my music to these guys who are my heroes outside of the film world. Half of me would be thrilled to hear what they have to say, the other half would be frightened. What composer wouldn't want to give up an evening with Steve Reich or John Adams or George Crumb or John Cage before he died? Maybe they'd get a kick out of my stuff. *Would* they get a kick out of it? How would they respond?

Would it matter to you?

It really would.

It would hurt if George Crumb reacted negatively?

Oh, geeze, I'm so damned sensitive. If the mailman went to hear some of my stuff and said something negative, I would be crushed. I heard that Goldsmith had said something positive about my stuff. That was a real ego boost. When I studied with David Raksin, all I wanted was his approval. I finally got my security back, but getting the approval of the real guys out there really held me back for a while.

The best film composers, like you, seem to move within their restrictions and come up with work that is original and distinctive.

In the concert world, you have certain controlling parameters, too. There are some things that need controlling parameters. I'm rarely told, "Do whatever you want," like you are. But, at the same time, *you* can't have eighteen horns or six marimbas like I can!

about the AUTHOR

Michael Schelle is a composer whose works have been performed worldwide, including U.S. commissions and performances by the Minnesota Orchestra, the Detroit Symphony, the Buffalo Philharmonic, the St. Paul Chamber Orchestra, the major orchestras of Chicago (Grant Park), Milwaukee, Cincinnati, Kansas City, Cleveland, Louisville, Indianapolis, and Birmingham, and professional chamber ensembles from New York City to Los Angeles to Honolulu. Recent international performances of his works have included Kammerorchester Basel (Switzerland), the Czestochowa Philharmonic (Poland), Orquesta Sinfonica Nacional (Costa Rica), and the Koenig Ensemble of London. His orchestral music has been performed under the batons of such conductors as Sir Neville Marriner, Keith Lockhart, William McGlaughlin, Maxiamo Valdes, John Jeter, Neal Gittleman, Tsung Yeh, and Jesus-Lopez Cobos.

He has received composition grants and awards from the National Endowment for the Arts, the Rockefeller Foundation, the Welsh Arts Council (Cardiff, U.K.), the International Percussive Arts Society, the Barlow Foundation, the American Pianists Association, the New England Foundation for the Arts, Spoleto USA, Wolf Trap, BMI, and ASCAP, and has twice been a Pulitzer Prize nominee. In 1989 he was named Distinguished Composer of the Year by the Music Teachers National Association. He is Composer in Residence and Professor of Music at Butler University's School of Music (Indianapolis) and a frequent guest composer at universities and new-music festivals across the country.